CHRISTIAN SPIRITUALITY

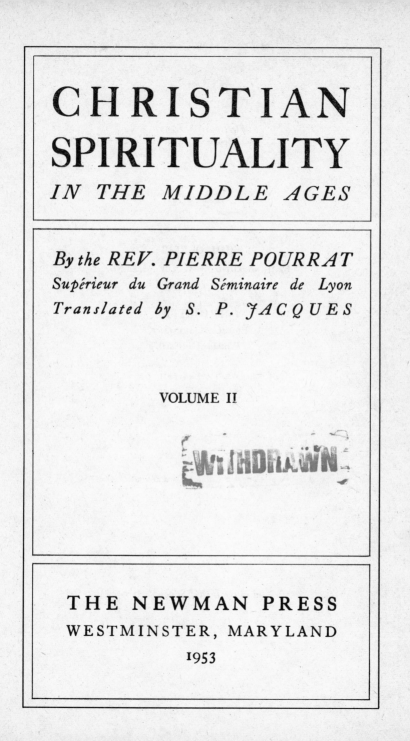

CHRISTIAN SPIRITUALITY

IN THE MIDDLE AGES

By the REV. PIERRE POURRAT
Supérieur du Grand Séminaire de Lyon
Translated by S. P. JACQUES

VOLUME II

THE NEWMAN PRESS
WESTMINSTER, MARYLAND
1953

First published 1927
Reprinted 1953

NIHIL OBSTAT:

Fr. Innocentius Apap, O.P., S.Th.M.,
Censor Deputatus.

IMPRIMATUR:

Edm. Can. Surmont,
Vicarius Generalis.

Westmonasterii,
die 28ᵃ *Julii,* 1927.

Printed in the United States of America

PREFACE

THE Middle Ages, both ascetic and mystical, lie before us like a vast forest, full of life but exceedingly dense. It is, therefore, of first importance to cut out a path which will enable us to pass through without too great labour and will serve as a landmark in exploring its depths. It is this which I have endeavoured to achieve.

The spirituality of the Middle Ages is to be found in the great religious families, which form so many schools—not to be confused with the theological schools—in which asceticism and mysticism became developed in accordance with the spirit proper to each foundation. Four religious Orders above all— I say above all, because I do not disregard the merits of the others—have left their mark strongly impressed on spirituality : the Benedictine Order, the Canons Regular of St Augustine, the Franciscans and the Dominicans. The spirituality in each one of these, whilst being fundamentally and substantially the same, nevertheless differs in the point of view from which it is regarded and in the way in which it is taught. These great Orders thus form schools, clearly distinct and characteristic, each one having its particular conception of spiritual science.

Now, these schools of the Middle Ages shared with one another a threefold conception of this science : practical and affective spirituality, which touches the heart rather than the reason; speculative spirituality, which builds up theories and concerns itself less with practice; finally, a spirituality at the same time speculative and affective, which includes both sentiment and reason. The influence of Platonism, found principally in the writings of Dionysius the Areopagite, and that of Aristotelianism with which St Thomas Aquinas was imbued in his theology, contributed to the formation of these different conceptions of spirituality.

At the beginning of the Middle Ages the Benedictine school reigned supreme. It received from St Bernard an incomparable brilliancy which irradiated all the other schools. It was characterized by marked, almost exclusive preference for affective and practical piety. The Abbot of Clairvaux disdained theories, and the result of his action on his school was such that it passed through the Middle Ages without feeling the influence of scholastic theology or of the works of Dionysius the Areopagite. It produced flowers of exquisite piety, such as the wonderful St Gertrude, the fragrance of

v

whose writings has imbued so many souls with the love of
Christ.

But the intellect claims its rights in spirituality as in other
branches of ecclesiastical science. Thus in the twelfth century, as opposed to the school of St Bernard, the Abbey of
the Canons Regular of St Victor of Paris inaugurated speculative mysticism, at first timidly and almost with regret. In
order to discover spiritual truth and contemplate it, we must
use intuition. The symbolism of Plato, so ably employed by
St Augustine and Dionysius the Areopagite, must be the
foundation of this spirituality. Thus a teaching, both affective and speculative, would be drawn up which should satisfy
the heart as well as the mind. With ideas such as these,
Hugh and Richard of St Victor constructed a wonderful
theory of contemplation, which has since inspired all mystical
writers.

It may be said that the Dominican school is identified with
the speculative spirituality of the Middle Ages. It had the
matchless glory of producing St Thomas Aquinas, who
handled the Aristotelian dialectics with such skill. The
example of this most famous master was everywhere followed, first of all by the Dominican Order itself. The
scholastic theories served to explain asceticism and to render
mystical facts understood. This systematization of spirituality was even occasionally pushed rather far, above all by
the German mystics of the fourteenth century; so far, indeed,
that it fell somewhat into disfavour.

In its beginning, the Franciscan family resisted the movement which involved piety in speculation. St. Francis of
Assisi had little love for theoretical science. But his Order
found it impossible to oppose the general trend towards
scholastic studies. St Bonaventure, inspired by the method
of the school of St Victor, ended by uniting the speculation
of the mind with the motions of the heart. He transformed
scholastic theology into affective knowledge, and so established the distinctive note of Franciscan spirituality.

Nevertheless, towards the end of the fourteenth century,
speculative spirituality ended by becoming worn out, and, as
a reaction, an empirical spiritual teaching became the vogue,
reduced to its practice and propounded in the form of sentences, detached one from the other. This mystical movement first saw light in the Low Countries; it is the *New
Devotion* of the *Brethren of the Common Life*. It produced
an extraordinary enthusiasm for the *Imitation of Christ*, the
simple and practical nature of which responded so well to the
aspirations of Flemish life. Jean Gerson and the Carthusians, who disregarded scholastic theories rather less than
did the creators of the New Devotion, gave the preference,
however, to affective piety.

Other causes, apart from those which sprang from philosophical movements, also influenced mysticism in the Middle Ages.

The centuries which are comprised in this period are remarkable for their faith and for their religious life. But there was also much that was distressing. Heresies spread by stealth. The morals of the clergy left much to be desired. The shepherds of the Church did not always possess that disinterestedness which the sacredness of their office demanded. Relaxation had found its way into many monasteries. Finally, the consciences of men were deeply troubled by the Great Schism of the West. The ecclesiastical hierarchy, itself overtaken by these evils, seemed incapable of bringing about the much needed reforms, either within itself or in those around it. God, in order to aid it, raised up a kind of extra-hierarchical prophetic mysticism, resembling the ancient prophetical order, if such a comparison may be permitted. St Hildegarde in the twelfth century, St Bridget and St Catherine of Siena at the beginning of the Great Schism, exerted this mystical prophecy and feared not to reprimand priests, bishops and even Popes.

A complete history of the religious Orders of the Middle Ages must not be looked for here. At this period they were spread far and wide; here, therefore, I cannot do them justice; I am restricted to speaking of those religious families which have exerted an influence on spiritual doctrine.

I have devoted greater space to the references in this second volume than in the first. Students of the patristic period, in fact, find in Migne's Greek and Latin Patrologies a sufficiently complete collection of texts with which most are satisfied. Bibliographical references are consequently simplified. It is not the same with the Middle Ages. Works of this period have not been thus brought together; they must needs be sought out, and occasionally, in the case of some which have not been republished, the finding of them is not an easy task. I thus feel myself under the obligation of pointing out, at least in the case of writers of some importance, the best editions of their works. I have also indicated French translations when they exist, in order to put the reader in touch with the original writings, which nothing can really supersede. With regard to those specialists who require a complete list of works which have been written on the ascetic and mystical writers of the Middle Ages, I would refer them to the *Repertoire des sources historiques du moyen âge,* by M. U. Chevalier.

CONTENTS

ix

CHAPTER IV

SPECULATIVE SPIRITUALITY AND PLATONISM OF THE TWELFTH CENTURY

CHAPTER V

SPECULATIVE SPIRITUALITY AND ARISTOTELIANISM

CHAPTER VI

ST FRANCIS OF ASSISI AND THE FRANCISCAN SCHOOL

Contents

xi
PAGE

II.—Franciscan Writers of the Thirteenth and Fourteenth Centuries—The Biographers of St Francis and St Bonaventure - - 173

III.—Meditations on the Life of Christ of the Pseudo-Bonaventure—The Franciscan Preachers of the Fourteenth and Fifteenth Centuries - 184

IV.—Bl. Angela of Foligno and St Catherine of Bologna - - - - - 191

CHAPTER VII

ST DOMINIC AND THE DOMINICAN SCHOOL

II.—Dominican Preaching: St Vincent Ferrer, Jerome Savonarola — Hagiography: Vincent of Beauvais and James de Voragine - - 200

III.—Dominican Mysticism in Italy: Fra Angelico of Fiesole, St Catherine of Siena - - 202

IV.—The German Mystics of the Dominican Order: Albert the Great in the Thirteenth Century; John Tauler, Henry Suso in the Fourteenth - 210

CHAPTER VIII

THE TEACHING OF THE GERMAN MYSTICS OF THE FOURTEENTH CENTURY

I.—The Renunciation of Self - - 229

II.—The German Theory of the Nakedness of the Intelligence - - - - - 234

III.—Mystical Union according to the German Writers - - - - - 239
    1. Union in the Essence of the Soul - 242
    2. Union without Mediation - 243
    3. Union without Difference - 245

CHAPTER IX

PRACTICAL MYSTICISM AT THE END OF THE FOURTEENTH AND IN THE FIFTEENTH CENTURIES IN THE LOW COUNTRIES

Introductory - - - - - - 252

I.—The " Brethren of the Common Life " and the Canons Regular of Windesheim - - 253

Contents

CHAPTER I
THE BENEDICTINE SCHOOL AND AFFECTIVE PIETY IN THE MIDDLE AGES

ORIGIN OF THIS SCHOOL : CLUNY, CÎTEAUX AND CLAIRVAUX — ST BERNARD—THE ABBEY OF BEC AND ST ANSELM.

THE school of spirituality which we meet with in history on the threshold of the Middle Ages is that of the Benedictines.

It is characterized first of all by its affective and practical piety. Benedictine writers are the exponents of affective spirituality, the importance of which, in the Middle Ages, was at least as great as that of speculative spirituality. They resolutely discarded high theories, subtle arguments and lofty abstractions, in order to adhere to that which speaks to the heart and unites with God. They were affected neither by the influence of scholastic theology nor by the writings of Dionysius the Areopagite. Their ascetic and mystical reflections had for their immediate object the cultivation of the love of God and not discussion of the nature of that love; they led to mystical union without seeking to explain it. A comparison of the *Sermons* of St Bernard or the *Exercises* of St Gertrude (1303) with the *Sermons* of the Dominican Tauler (1361) shows the extent to which Benedictine writers differ from those of the speculative school.

Benedictine piety, we may well think, drew its nourishment from the celebration of the Divine Office. In the monasteries of St Benedict the singing of the Office almost completely absorbed the religious life of the monk. During the chanting of the sacred words, the soul became united to God and contemplated the object of the feast that was being kept. Almost every word of the Office, or of the Mass, provided St Gertrude with an occasion for mystical uplifting. Her *Exercises* are a wonderful paraphrase of the ceremonies of baptism, of the prayers for the Consecration of Virgins from the Roman Pontifical, of the verses of the hymns. All for her expressed divine love. Benedictine piety was thus built on the liturgy. It therefore remained practical. In what way would philosophical speculations have been of use to it?

This liturgical spirituality focussed the Benedictine soul

on meditation on the mysteries of the earthly life of the
Saviour. The different feasts of the year at the beginning of
the Middle Ages had for their object the principal events in
the life of Christ—his Nativity, his Passion, his Resurrection
and Ascension. The *Sermons* of St Bernard for the liturgical
year make this clear to us. The custom of meditating on the
scenes of the Gospel in which the drama of our redemption
unrolls itself, brought about that devotion to the humanity
of Christ which is one of the most remarkable characteristics
of Benedictine spirituality. Here, as we shall see, the weighty
influence of the Abbot of Clairvaux was felt. It is he who
taught his religious to be moved to pity at the crib of the
divine infant and to mourn at the cross. St. Francis of
Assisi, who so made the world to weep over the passion of
Christ, is beholden to him. This devotion to the humanity
of Jesus afterwards descended to particulars and was directed
to certain parts of this humanity. In the monastery of Benedictine nuns at Helfta, in Saxony, St Gertrude and her companions paid a special devotion to the Five Wounds of Christ
crucified. The wound in the side was a door which enabled
them to enter into the heart of the Saviour. Towards the
end of the thirteenth century, St Gertrude introduced the
devotion to the Heart of Jesus.[1]

Father Faber declares that " the spirit of liberty " was
" the special prerogative of the Benedictine ascetics of the
old school."[2] St Gertrude is, according to him, a " beautiful
example." This liberty of spirit was not, in the opinion of
this famous writer, due to negligence, nor to indolence nor
caprice. It must be understood as opposed to " prescribed
piety " which is circumscribed with " spiritual regulations."
It is indisputable that in Benedictine monasteries no other
religious exercise was laid down than the Office. In this way
piety was not regulated in the sense that, at times other than
that devoted to the canonical hours, the soul was raised to
God freely and without restraint. But at that period this
was not peculiar to the Benedictines. Regulated spiritual
exercises, varied and reduced to method, date from the
beginning of modern times; from that epoch when religious,
in accordance with the ideals of St Ignatius Loyola, went out
from the cloister in order to carry on their apostolate in the
world. This change in the religious life rendered necessary
a less spontaneous and more ordered piety. Did not the
maintenance of the interior life of those who were no longer
protected by the walls of the convent demand that rules
affecting piety should take the place of those of the cloister?

[1] Devotion to the blessed Virgin is also a distinctive note of Cistercian
piety. The *Sermons* of St Bernard and the writings of St Gertrude
bear this out. Cistercian churches were generally dedicated to the
Mother of God.   [2] *All for Jesus.*

I—THE ORIGIN OF MEDIEVAL BENEDICTINISM—
CLUNY

THIS origin must be sought in the federation of Benedictine monasteries which took place after the tenth century. Instead of remaining, as before, totally independent, the Benedictines became grouped, at the beginning of the Middle Ages, into congregations or monastic Orders. The two most important congregations were those of Cluny and of Cîteaux.

The houses of which they were composed were attached to the mother abbey, either by the bond of foundation, or that of reform, or else occasionally, as among the Cluniacs, by that of authority. A common spirit always reigned in all the monasteries of the same congregation, which spirit was fostered by the traditions left by the founder and maintained by exclusiveness as regards what was done in other congregations, almost as much as by the discipline of those in authority. Occasionally, also, there was the very just desire, which again tended to strengthen the family spirit, to avoid certain abuses which were known to exist elsewhere, to live more perfectly up to the Rule of St Benedict, and to lead a stricter and more austere life. It was due to motives of this kind that there arose that most regrettable dispute between Peter the Venerable, ninth abbot of Cluny, who defended the customs of his Order, and St Bernard, who censured the magnificence of the Cluniacs.

Each monastic congregation, then, had its own conception of the life of the cloister, and consequently of that asceticism which is the basis of it. Each thus became a school of spirituality with its own particular spirit, its own type, which characterized it and distinguished it from all others.

The congregation of Cluny did not produce any noteworthy spiritual writer. It exercised, however, an enormous influence on the restoration of monastic life in Europe.

Towards the end of the tenth century, the system of lay abbots had almost completely destroyed the reformation of Benedictine monasteries brought about by St Benedict of Aniane in 817. These abbots, wholly lacking in the religious spirit, were only interested in their monasteries from the point of view of despoiling them of their possessions. The monks were for the most part left to themselves, without government or supervision. Thence all sorts of abuses crept in, which were further aggravated by the uncivilized standard of morality which marked this sad period.

In 910, William the Good, Count of Gothland and Duke of Aquitaine, founded the Abbey of Cluny, at the head of which was placed the Abbot Berno (927). A succession of abbots,[1] remarkable for their holiness and their love of discipline, made Cluny famous and placed it at the head of a reform which spread rapidly. A great number of monasteries—of which there were, in the twelfth century, two thousand[2]— became affiliated to the Abbey of Cluny, or were founded from there, and formed a powerful congregation of fervent monks.

The Cluniac congregation, in order to protect itself from the greed of lay abbots, found no better means than that of appealing for exemption from episcopal control in order to become directly subject to Rome.[3] The support of the Holy See rendered it strong enough to free itself from the domination of feudalism. It always showed itself grateful for the protection which it received from the Popes, by helping them, especially Gregory VII,[4] in their efforts to reform the clergy. Cluny was like a second Rome.

At this epoch the internal organization of monasteries became modified. The monks, instead of being almost all laymen as heretofore, became henceforth about equally divided between laymen known as *lay brothers,* and priests called *fathers.* This change in the character of the monasteries became general at the beginning of the Middle Ages, when so many priests entered the monastic orders.

With a view to maintaining the same spirit in all the different houses of the congregation, and to insure a good choice of abbots, the Cluniacs were induced to strengthen the authority of the Abbot-general as much as possible. In fact, the Abbot of Cluny wielded a direct and personal authority over all his houses. These were to be found in almost every country in Europe. This system, excellent as it was so long as the congregation was limited, afterwards became a hindrance to its well-being, for as soon as the

[1] Among others, St Odo (942), St Mayeul (994), St Odilo (1048), who, inspired by the monastic custom inaugurated by St Isidore of Seville (*Isidori Regula,* xxiii), instituted the commemoration of All Souls on November 2 in the Cluniac monasteries. This custom afterwards spread throughout the whole Church. St Hugh (1109), who built the famous Church of Cluny, Peter the Venerable (1156), the most celebrated Abbot of Cluny for learning. Their *Lives* and deeds are to be found in Migne, *P.L.,* CXXXIII, CXLII, CLIX, CLXXXIX. *Cf.* Dom Marrier, *Bibliotheca Cluniacensis,* Paris 1614.

[2] Monks were very numerous in the Middle Ages. "The whole world is full of them," said St Peter Damian, *Epist.* vi, 15 (*P.L.,* CXLIV, 397). As during the patristic period, men became monks in order to renounce the world, to secure salvation and to seek, by this renunciation and sacrifice, spiritual consolation and mystical joys. A desire to be protected from the vexations of feudal lords was also occasionally a motive for entering the cloister.

[3] Peter the Venerable, *Epist.* lib. I, *ep.* xxviii (*P.L.,* CLXXIX, 115).

[4] Gregory VII had been formerly a monk and Prior of Cluny.

houses of the congregation were multiplied, it was not possible for the Abbot of Cluny to supervise them all properly.

Abbot Berno, the founder of Cluny, composed no special Rule, but obliged his monks to follow as strictly as possible that of St Benedict. His disciple and successor, St Odo, also adhered to the scrupulous observance of the Benedictine Rule. But when the Cluniac congregation grew, circumstances forced the abbots to modify certain points in the discipline. Thus arose the *Customs of the Monastery of Cluny (Consuetudines Cluniacensis monasterii)*.

These modifications consisted in certain mitigations as regards the clothing and food of the monks, rendered necessary by the rigour of climate. The Cluniacs, contrary to the Rule of St Benedict, relinquished manual work in order to give themselves more to study;[1] their rich dowries provided for their maintenance and allowed them to devote themselves to intellectual work. In this they but imitated St Maurus (584), the disciple of St Benedict, in whose monastery scarcely any manual labour was performed.

Finally, feeling themselves authorized by what is laid down in the Rule respecting the celebration of the Divine Office, they surrounded with magnificence all that affected worship. They built beautiful churches, real masterpieces of Romanesque architecture, superbly decorated. The sacred ornaments which were used by them in the liturgical services were extremely rich. The furniture of their churches was luxurious. They felt that they could not better employ their abundant resources than by using them for the adornment of Christian churches, even at the risk of scandalizing the monks belonging to other congregations where the Rule of St Benedict was strictly interpreted.[2]

At Cluny, therefore, the desire was to follow the spirit rather than the letter of the Benedictine Rule. Among Rules, said Peter the Venerable,[3] there are some which cannot be changed—the divine rules—and there are others which may vary according to time and place. Among the latter are monastic rules.

This most wise principle nevertheless needs careful application, especially as Cluny was subjected to the trial, always fraught with danger, of a superabundance of possessions. Under the plea of legitimate modifications of the Rule, certain abuses were introduced, which did not fail to enhance the Cistercians—whose austere régime was a kind of protest against the Cluniac interpretation of Benedictine discipline. On the Third Sunday in Lent, 1132, Peter the Venerable

---

[1] *Cf.* Peter the Venerable, *Epist.*, lib. I, *ep.* xxviii (Migne, col. 120-130).

[2] St Bernard severely criticized the magnificence of the Cluniac churches.   [3] *Epist.*, lib. III, *ep.* xxviii (col. 148).

called together the chief representatives of his congregation in order to bring about a reform.[1] The outcome of this assembly was the *Statuta Congregationis cluniacensis,*[2] drawn up by Peter the Venerable. These statutes give exact expression to the way the life of a Benedictine monk was understood at Cluny.

II—THE CISTERCIAN ORDER: ITS STRICT INTERPRETATION OF THE RULE OF ST BENEDICT[3]

THE Monastery of Cîteaux, like that of Cluny, owes its origin to an endeavour to restore the spirit of the Benedictine Rule.

Its founder, St Robert, Abbot of Molesmes, in the diocese of Langres, sought in vain, among the convents of Champagne and Burgundy, that monastic perfection for which he yearned. He began to put his dream of reform into operation at Molesmes, when a revolt of the monks, obdurate in their laxity, caused him to leave. He withdrew with the more fervent brethren of Molesmes to Cîteaux, *Cistercium,* twenty-two kilometres from Beaune, in Burgundy, where they settled on March 21, 1098.

St Robert was obliged by the Archbishop of Lyons, Legate of the Holy See, to return to Molesmes. Alberic,[4] his successor at Cîteaux, continued his traditions. The first regulations respecting food and clothing were drawn up. In order to distinguish his monks from all other religious of the Benedictine family, whose life was less austere, Alberic gave them a white habit. There were thus from this time the black monks, *nigri,* or ordinary Benedictines, and the white or grey monks, *grisei,* or Cistercians.

As a matter of fact, so literal and so strict was their interpretation of the Rule of St Benedict, that the Cistercians really formed a new Order. This interpretation is found in the *Consuetudines* or customs of Cîteaux. They were in great part the work of the third abbot, St Stephen Harding.[5]

The clothing of the Cistercians was as simple as possible : a narrow dress or tunic of serge which covered the body to below the knee, and the cowl or flowing cloak of wool, with wide sleeves and hood; hose protected the legs and sandals

[1] Orderic Vital., *Historia ecclesiastica,* lib. XIII, cap. iv (*P.L.,* CLXXXVIII, 935). [2] *P.L.,* CLXXXIX, 1025-1048.
[3] Principal sources : *Life of St Robert, Abbot of Molesmes* (*Acta Sanctorum,* April 29, vol. iii *mensis aprilis*); Guignard, *Les monuments primitifs de la Règle cistercienne,* Dijon 1878; *Exordium Magnum Ordinis Cisterciensis* (*P.L.,* CLXXXV, 995-1198); Méglinger, *Iter cisterciense* (*P.L.,* CLXXXV, 1569-1622); St Stephen Harding, third Abbot of Cîteaux, *Carta charitatis; Exordium coenobii et ordinis cisterciensis; Consuetudines seu Usus antiquiores ordinis cisterciensis* (*P.L.,* CLXVI, 1361-1510).
[4] *Alberici Vita* (*Acta Sanctorum,* January 29).
[5] See *Acta Sanctorum,* April 17, vol. ii *mensis aprilis.*

the feet. The Cistercians slept fully dressed on a straw mattress placed on a plank and covered with a blanket; the pillow was also of straw. Their food consisted entirely of dried or green vegetables, seasoned with oil and salt. The fasts were strictly the same as those laid down by St Benedict. Wine, which was allowed in very small quantity by the Benedictine Rule, was forbidden at Cîteaux. Baths, as prescribed by the same Rule, were only granted to those that were sick. Manual labour was again given the place of honour.[1]

The spirit of poverty in the appearance and fittings of the monastery was very pronounced; unlike the Cluniacs, there were no monuments nor architectural ornaments. The chapel was furnished with the greatest simplicity, with a cross of wood and the candlesticks and candelabra of iron. The sacred vestments and ornaments were to be neither of silk nor embroidered with gold.

The reaction against the customs of Cluny extended to the Cistercian system of government. The Abbot of Cîteaux did not, like him of Cluny, rule over all the convents of his congregation. The abbot of each monastery concerned himself with the houses that he had founded, as if they were his daughters. A simple bond of fraternal charity united him with the others.

Cîteaux did not, like Cluny, petition for exemption from episcopal authority; each of the abbeys was subject to the ordinary of the place in which it was situated.[2]

The beginnings of the Cistercian Order were hard. Their austerity was fearful. But when St Bernard and his companions had entered in 1112, four new foundations were very quickly made—La Ferté in 1113, Pontigny in 1114, Clairvaux and Morimond in 1115. The holiness and reputation of St Bernard spread such a lustre on the nascent order, that at the end of the twelfth century it possessed more than five hundred houses.

The Cistercian family has produced a certain number of spiritual writers. The most noteworthy is, undoubtedly, St Bernard, Abbot of Clairvaux. It is he who rendered his Order a school of mysticism, the influence of which was felt throughout the Middle Ages. It is necessary here, on account of the place which he occupies in the history of spirituality, to say something about his life and his ideas of the religious life, reserving until later the account of his spirituality. We shall thus better understand the Cistercian Order, of which St Bernard may be considered the second founder.

[1] All this will be found in the *Consuetudines.*
[2] See, for an account of this, the *Carta charitatis* of St Stephen Harding.

III—ST BERNARD, ABBOT OF CLAIRVAUX—HIS IDEAS ON MONASTIC LIFE[1]

St Bernard was born at Fontaines-lez-Dijon in 1090; his parents belonged to an eminent family. It was noticed that even in childhood he evinced a special devotion to the Nativity of our Saviour, concerning which he was to speak so eloquently later; and also a tenderly filial love for the blessed Virgin Mary, whose faithful servant he was to be.

At the age of twenty, his brilliant gifts brought him to the notice of the world. Frivolous friendships and companionships tended to ensnare his virtue. Fearful of the danger which human wickedness and his own inexperience made him run, the young man, inspired with the holy desire of avoiding evil, conceived the project of leaving all in order to become a monk. He entered Cîteaux about 1112, with thirty-two companions, whom he had persuaded to join him in the monastic life. Among them were several of his own brothers.[2]

During his year of probation, the young novice constantly asked himself this question: " Bernard, Bernard, why hast thou come here?" (*Bernarde, Bernarde, ad quid venisti?*)[3] The answer which he gave himself in the secrecy of his soul, he expressed later on at Clairvaux, to the numerous novices who came to submit themselves to his direction. " On entering here," he said to them, " you must leave outside that body which you bring from the world; the spirit only enters here, there is no use for the body."[4]

Bernard indeed laboured to strip himself of the lusts of the flesh by most severe and constant mortification. The rigours of the Cistercian Rule satisfied his desire for austerity. He declared later, not without exaggeration, that he was so carnal and inclined to sin and that he suffered so great a languidness of soul, that a somewhat strong measure of renunciation and suffering was necessary.[5]

To the mortifications laid down by the Rule, St. Bernard

[1] Principal sources: *Vita Bernardi*, especially the *Vita prima* (*P.L.*, 225-466) and the *Vita secunda* (469-524). See also the criticism of these documents in the *Vie de S Bernard, abbé de Clairvaux*, by E. Vacandard, Paris 1897, Introduction; *Acta Sanctorum*, August 20, vol. iv *mensis augusti;* other more or less legendary *Vitae Bernardi* in *P.L.*, CLXXXV; *St Bernardi epistolae* (*P.L.*, CLXXXII, 67-662); *Liber de praecepto et dispensatione* (859-894).

[2] *Vita prima*, lib. I, cap. ii-iv.

[3] *Vita prima*, lib. I, cap. iv, 19: *Hoc semper in corde, semper etiam in ore habebat: Bernarde, Bernarde, ad quid venisti?* Among the apocryphal writings of St Bernard there is an instruction to novices which is a commentary on *ad quid venisti?* (*P.L.*, CLXXXIV, 1189-1198). See *De imitatione Christi*, lib. I, cap. xxv, 1.

[4] *Vita prima*, lib. I, cap. iv, 20.

[5] *Apologia*, cap. iv, 7.

added the strict custody of the senses, which act as such feeders of the passions. He carried custody of the eyes to the extent of never raising them to the ceiling of his cell, nor of fixing them on the windows of the chapel in order to find out their number. All the activity of his soul was directed inward, absorbed in God and in the contemplation of divine things.[1] He mortified his palate with special harshness, and his biographers tell us that it was a matter of distress for him to go to table : *sic accedit ad sumendum cibum quasi ad tormentum.*[2]

St Bernard's piety was not less than his austerity. It was chiefly nourished by the study of holy Scripture and the singing of the Psalms. The young novice made the sacred books so much his own that his mind was moulded by them. He afterwards made use of the very expressions of Scripture, above all of the Psalms, for the development of his ideas in his sermons and writings. If he knew the Psalms so well it was because, as he said, he had " ruminated " on them by dint of singing them.[3]

From his noviceship onwards we find in St Bernard this union of unsparing austerity with spiritual sweetness of contemplation and union with God.[4] Gifted with an exquisite sensitiveness, wholly directed and wrapped up in God, he already tasted the charms of divine love, of that love that he was to proclaim so well later on. The Cistercian Order, the most severe that then existed, was to become, in the following of St Bernard, a school of mysticism in which the sweetness of extraordinary and supernatural union of the soul with God was to be experienced. The body, indeed, must suffer pain, but the soul from time to time was to enjoy a foretaste of celestial happiness.

In 1115, Bernard became Abbot of Clairvaux, situated in the diocese of Langres. Austere towards himself, he was inclined, at least in the beginning, to be so also towards others.

First of all, he would not hear of hesitation in leaving the world to come to the cloister at the call of God. In order to force from their families hesitating youths, who in those times would have been lost, he was able to find words even harder than the castigations addressed formerly by St Jerome to Heliodorus.[5]

---

[1] *Vita prima,* lib. I, cap. iv, 20.   [2] *ibid.,* 22.
[3] Cf. *Vita prima,* lib. I, cap. iv, 24; *In festo SS Petri et Pauli, sermo* II, 2.   [4] *Vita prima, id.,* 23, 24.
[5] St Bernard here quotes the letter of St Jerome to Heliodorus, with a variation which is not in the ordinary text : *Per calcatum transi patrem, per calcatam perge matrem. . . . (Bernardi epist.,* cccxxii, 2). Cf. *De conversione, ad clericos,* cap. xxi, 37 : *Fugite de medio Babylonis, convolate ad urbes refugii.*

" Conquered by the love of thy mother," he wrote to one of them, " thou hast not yet been able to crush that which thou hast learnt how to despise. And what must I answer thee? To abandon thy mother? but that seems inhuman. To remain with her? It is not to her own advantage to be the cause of the loss of her son. To serve both Christ and the world at the same time? But no one can serve two masters. Thy mother desires a thing contrary to thy salvation, and consequently to her own. Choose one of two things : Thou must either fall in with thy mother's wishes or give heed to her salvation and thine own. If thou really love thy mother, leave her ; it is to her interest ; and do not, by abandoning Christ in order to remain with her, run the risk of making her perish eternally because of thee. Moreover, hearken to this *faithful saying and worthy of all acceptation* (1 Tim. i, 15) : if it be an impiety to despise one's mother, it is nevertheless a great piety to despise her for Christ. For he who said *honour thy father and thy mother,* has himself also said *he that loveth father or mother more than me is not worthy of me* " (Matt. x, 37).[1]

We are still far from the gentle and tender strength of St Francis de Sales ; St Bernard has as yet the harshness of the fathers of the desert. Moreover, the manners of the twelfth century lacked that deference and consideration which we are now accustomed to employ in our dealings with others. When certain *Letters* of the Abbot of Clairvaux or certain of his polemical treatises are read, it is a matter for surprise to find invectives addressed to those who did not share his point of view. This may be also true of his *Sermons.* The violence of his temperament is there made manifest. But this harshness of language is inspired by so great a love of the glory of God, of the honour of the Church and of the salvation of souls, that we are not tempted to be shocked at it.

In St Bernard's time, there were still to be found certain hermit monks who lived in the woods.[2] But this form of monastic life was only suitable for a very few. The Abbot of Clairvaux, in agreement with St Basil and St Benedict, was decidedly against it.[3] The isolation of the hermit, in fact, is often a cause of formidable temptations. It is in monasteries that the religious life must henceforth be developed.

St Bernard required of his monks a strictly faithful observance of the Cistercian Rule. By it he trained them in the mortification of the body and the mind. He could not suffer in his religious any tendency to follow their own will, nor

---

[1] *Epist.* civ, 3. Cf. *Epist.* cxi, 2 ; *Epist.* cv ; *Epist.* cxii, ccccxii.
[2] *De illustri genere Sancti Bernardi,* cxix, cxx (*P.L.,* CLXXXV, 1461, 1473) ; *Bernardi Epist.,* ccliii, ccxxxiii ; *Bernardi Vita,* lib. VII, cap. ii, 3.   *Epist.* cxv.

any attachment to their own opinion. " These," he said, " are two leprosies which devour the hearts of monks."[1]

" Self-will is that which does not agree with the will of God nor with that of men, but which is strictly our own. It is made manifest when that which we will does not tend to the glory of God, nor to the benefit of the brethren, but solely to our own. That which we seek is not to please God, nor to help the brethren, but to satisfy our personal caprice. . . . What is it that God detests and punishes if it be not self-will? If there were no more self-will there would be no more hell! *Cesset voluntas propria et infernus non erit. . . .*"[2]

" The leprosy of private judgement is the more fatal in that it is hidden. . . . It is found in those who *have a zeal for God but not according to knowledge* (Rom. x, 2); they follow their errors with so much obstinacy that they will listen to no advice. They are firebrands of discord, enemies of peace, deprived of charity, puffed up with pride, full of themselves and great in their own eyes, ignorant of the justice of God and desirous of substituting their own for it."[3]

The only remedy which could cure these two maladies of the soul was obedience. St Bernard exacts it with the same rigour as did the fathers of the desert. On this point we have an insight into his mind in his treatise *De praecepto et dispensatione*,[4] addressed to the monks of St Peter of Chartres, who had consulted him as to the nature of the obligation of the Rule of St Benedict.

The evil mind, this curse of communities, is one of the consequences of adherence to self-will and private judgement. It shows itself by cliques, the dominant feature of which is criticism. The malcontents group themselves together and make asides which divide the community. The Abbot of Clairvaux is pitiless in their regard.

" Watch them withdraw apart," he says; " they gather together and let loose their evil tongues in detestable conversations. One bit of tattle follows another without leaving time for breath, so great is the desire to criticize or to hear complaints. They make collusions in order to malign the others, and conspire to promote discord. They form with one another most unfriendly or aggressive friendships (*ineunt inter se inimicissimas amicitias*), and their odious meetings are passed in taking pleasure in a common malignity."[5]

---

[1] *In tempore paschali, sermo* III, 3.
[2] *ibid.*, cf. *Epist.* cxlii, cccxxii (*P.L.*, CLXXXII, 297, 527).
[3] *In tempore paschali, sermo* III, 4.
[4] Especially chapters i, ix, x, xii. According to St Bernard, the prescriptions of the Rule are so much the more easy as they are the more numerous, like the feathers of the bird, which lift it into the air with greater ease when they are thicker. *Epist.* ccclxxxv, 3.
[5] *In Cantica, sermo* XXIV.

But this refers only to a very small number; that of the lax and lukewarm. The great part of the monks, faithful observers of their rule, found in their intercourse with God delightful compensations for the sacrifices imposed. We shall see how the Abbot of Clairvaux showed them how to taste the joys of the religious life.

Austerity and, as we shall show, tender and affective piety are the characteristics of St Bernard and the whole Cistercian Order.

IV—OTHER CENTRES OF THE BENEDICTINE SCHOOL—THE ABBEY OF BEC—ST ANSELM

St Romuald[1] (1027), St John Gualbert[2] (1073), and St Peter Damian[3] (1072) are among the famous restorers of Benedictine discipline in Italy on the same lines as the Cluniacs in France. They cannot be looked upon as writers on spirituality, as they strove rather to revive the fervour of the cloister than to discourse concerning it. St Peter Damian, nevertheless, has, in several of his *opuscula*,[4] dealt with the chief questions concerning monastic life. He is a great advocate of corporal chastisements. Those laid down by the Rule do not seem to him sufficient; he calls for an increase.[5]

But the great mystic of the eleventh century, who may be looked upon as the head of a school, is St Anselm, Abbot of Bec, in Normandy, and afterwards Archbishop of Canterbury. He is usually looked upon as a philosopher and theologian. The position which he occupies in the history of theology and philosophy is, moreover, greater than in spirituality. Nevertheless, his *Meditations* and *Prayers* edified all generations of the Middle Ages, and have inspired the greater part of spiritual writers since the end of the twelfth century.

---

[1] St Romuald, of the family of the Onesti of Ravenna, reformed his Abbey of St Apollinaris de Classe by causing the Rule of St Benedict to be strictly observed there. He afterwards retired into solitude at Camaldoli, near Arezzo, in the Apennines, where he founded the Order of the *Camaldoli,* which consisted of hermit and cenobitic houses.

[2] St John Gualbert, born at Florence, founded the Benedictine Congregation of Vallombrosa about 1038.

[3] St Peter Damian, born at Ravenna in 988, entered the Monastery of Monte Avellana, in the Diocese of Gubbio, in Umbria. About 1068 he was appointed Cardinal Bishop of Ostia by the Pope. He was one of the most powerful helpers of the Papacy in its endeavours to reform the clergy. St Stephen of Muret, in Limousin (1124), should also be mentioned. He founded the Benedictines of Grandmont.

[4] *Opuscula,* XII-XV (*P.L.,* CXLV).

[5] Cf. *Epistolarum,* lib. V, *Epist.* viii, xxiv, xxvii. St Peter Damian also wrote the *Lives* of St Odilo, St Maurus, Bishop of Cesena, of St Romuald, of St Rudolph and of St Dominic Loricatus (*P.L.,* CXLIV, 504-1024).

The mysticism of the Middle Ages could not well be understood without a preliminary study of St Anselm.

Anselm was born in the city of Aosta, in Piedmont, in 1033.[1] In his youth he allowed himself to be led away somewhat by the attractions of the world, and, according to the account of his biography, " as soon as his mother died, the barque of his heart, as though it had lost its anchor, became almost completely the plaything of the waves of that time."[2] He wept bitterly on account of his faults;[3] it is possible to recognize and admire, in several of his *Meditations,*[4] an echo of the cry of pain revived by the thought of his past life.

His conversion was brought about at the Abbey of Bec, under the famous Lanfranc, the future Archbishop of Canterbury. He became a monk there at the age of twenty-seven years.[5] Eighteen years later, in August, 1078, he was elected Abbot of Bec;[6] and in 1093 he succeeded Lanfranc in the Archiepiscopal See of Canterbury. He died on April 21, 1109.[7]

The piety of Anselm is extraordinarily affective. Souls that are speculative are not, as a rule, affective. It would seem that aptitude for speculation, when it reaches a certain point, absorbs the activity of the soul and renders the heart dry. On the other hand, the affective seldom feel themselves drawn towards abstract researches which please the mind of the thinker. The history of spirituality, however, tells of some writers so gifted that they have united intellectual speculation with the most touching affective outbursts and heartfelt prayer. St Anselm is one of the number.

The *Meditations* and the *Prayers*[8] which have caused Anselm to be known as a spiritual writer are holy upliftings based on dogma. At the same time that the intelligence of the famous theologian soared to the highest regions of the Christian mysteries, his heart became inflamed with love, and made itself heard in a song of thanksgiving or a suppliant prayer; the song of the Christian soul thanking God for the light

---

[1] Eadmer, *Vita Anselmi, Acta Sanctorum,* 21 *aprilis.* This *Vita* is reproduced by Migne (*P.L.,* CLVIII, 49-120). See also by this same Eadmer the *Historia novorum* (*P.L.,* CLIX, 347-524).

[2] *Vita Anselmi,* lib. I, cap. i, 4.   [3] *id.,* lib. I, cap. i, 11.

[4] *Meditationes,* II-IV (*P.L.,* CLVIII, 722-733).

[5] *Vita Anselmi,* lib. I, cap. i, 7; cap. ii, 11.

[6] *id.,* lib. I, cap. v.   [7] *id.,* lib. II, cap. i, 7.

[8] The *Meditations* (*P.L.,* CLVIII, 109-820) and the Prayers (*Orationes*) (855-1016) are almost the only works on spirituality by St Anselm, fairly well authenticated. The *Meditation* IX (748-761) is not St Anselm's. *Cf.* J. Bainvel, *Dict. de Théol. cath.,* art. *Saint Anselme,* vol. i, 1334. The *Meditations* and the *Prayers* had an enormous success in the Middle Ages, and on that account were open to alterations. An English edition of the authentic text of St Anselm's prayers is being prepared.

received, or the prayer imploring him to grant it participation in those marvels seen afar off.

" Grant, I beseech thee, O Lord," he exclaims in his beautiful Meditation XI *On the Redemption,* " grant that I may taste by love that which I taste by knowledge; that I may feel in the heart that which I touch with the mind. I owe thee more than myself, but I can give thee nothing more than myself, and even by my own strength I am not able to give myself wholly to thee. Carry me away by thy love, carry me entirely away ! All that I am as a creature belongs to thee; grant that all may be thine by the gift of my love. Here, O Lord, is my heart before thee, it strives to give itself to thee, but of itself it cannot; do thou bring about that which it cannot achieve of itself.

" Make me to enter within the sanctuary of thy love. I implore this grace, I seek this favour, I knock at the door of this sanctuary that thou mayst open it to me. Thou who makest me to ask this grace, grant also that I may receive it. Thou who makest me to seek, grant that I may find. Thou who teachest me to knock, do thou open unto me. To whom wilt thou give if not to him who asks? Who will find if not he who seeks? To whom shall it be opened if not to him who knocks? What wilt thou give to him who does not pray if thou refusest thy love to him who prays? It is thou who makest me to desire, it is thou also who wilt hearken to my desire. O my soul ! attach thyself to God, obstinately attach thyself to him ! O good Lord Jesus, do not repulse my soul ! It hungers for thy love, comfort it ! Grant that it may be sated with thy charity, enriched by thy affection, filled by thy love, and that this love may wholly seize me and entirely possess me because thou art, with the Father and the Holy Ghost, one only God, blessed for ever and ever. Amen."[1]

St Anselm is, without doubt, a great affective writer. For all that, his intelligence is also in the highest degree speculative. It moves in the highest spheres of metaphysics without becoming dazed. His love for speculation and rational research was expressed in his writings by principles that would have terrified St Bernard had he known them.

Anselm, in fact, was firmly convinced that no better use could be made of the reason than to apply it to the study of the truths of faith, in order to understand all that can be understood here below, and to explain them in so far as they may be explained. We must not rely on faith alone; first we must believe and afterwards endeavour to understand what we believe.

" I do not claim, O Lord," he exclaims at the beginning

---

[1] *Meditatio XI de redemptione humana (P.L., CLVIII, 769).* Similar prayers alternate with dogmatic speculations in Anselm's treatise, *Proslogion seu alloquium de existentia Dei,* cap. i, 16 *(P.L., CLVIII, 225-235).*

of the *Proslogion*,[1] " to penetrate the depths of thy divine
being, for I in no way feel my intelligence equal to the task;
but I desire to understand something of thy truth, which my
heart believes and loves. I do not seek indeed to understand
in order to believe, but I believe in order to understand (*credo
ut intelligam*). For I am certain that unless I first believe
I shall not understand."

" The Christian," he says elsewhere,[2] " has not the right
to doubt what the Catholic Church believes with the heart
and confesses with the mouth, but he should always, whilst
firmly holding to this faith, loving it and living in conformity with it, seek what it is by his reason, as far as he
is capable of doing so. If he can understand, let him render
thanks to God; if he cannot, let him be guarded from rising
against it, but with head bowed down, let him adore."

This method, which consists in applying the reason, with
all data, to the study of the faith, proceeding by reason and
not by authority, has been called the scholastic method. St
Anselm, as is his right, is held to be the father of it. We
can see how this method is opposed to that of affective
mysticism.[3]

One of the mysteries of the faith which St Anselm particularly examined is that of the redemption. He made a
very careful study of it in his treatise *Cur Deus homo*,[4] in
which he drew up what has been called the Anselmian theory
of satisfaction. Sin, he says, does an infinite injury to God;
it demands, therefore, an infinite satisfaction, which could
only be effected by God made man. The soul of Anselm was
imbued with this doctrine concerning sin and its malice, the
satisfaction that it requires, the contrition that we should
have on account of it, the goodness and mercy of God who
pardons it. It was also full of sorrowing love for Christ who
paid our debt to God by suffering and dying for us. These
ideas which filled the mind of Anselm filled his heart also.
They became transformed into ardent upliftings to God, and
gave to Anselmian spirituality its characteristic note. They

---

[1] *Proslogion*, cap. i. St Anselm had first called this work *Fides
quaerens intellectum*, Faith seeking to understand (*Proslogion proe-
mium*, *P.L.*, CLVIII, 225, 227). In this treatise Anselm proves the
existence of God by the ontological argument, sometimes called after his
name : God is conceived as an infinitely perfect being. Therefore he
exists, for existence is a perfection.

[2] *De fide Trinitatis*, cap. ii (col. 263).

[3] That, again, which distinguishes St Anselm from the mystics of the
twelfth century is that he does not much care for symbolism. In his
Letter to Walram, Bishop of Naumburg, he disapproves of those who
leave the chalice uncovered during Mass, under the pretext that the
symbolism requires it, Christ having suffered his Passion in the open
air (*P.L.*, CLVIII, 554).

[4] *P.L.*, CLVIII, 359 432.

are the most frequent theme of the *Meditations* and the *Prayers*.

"O Christian soul," he exclaims in one of his *Meditations*, "O soul, raised from a dreadful death, O soul, redeemed and delivered from a miserable slavery by the blood of God, awaken and call to mind thy resurrection, ponder on thy redemption and on thy deliverance! Ask thyself again wherein lies the value of thy salvation and what its price is; meditate thereon at length, contemplate it with joy; shake off thy torpor, do violence to thy heart, give it thine attention, taste the goodness of thy Redeemer, burn with love for thy Saviour! . . .

"If indeed to sin is to outrage God—a thing which man must not do, even though all that exists outside of God should perish—unchangeable truth and true wisdom require that the sinner should give back to God, on account of the injury he has done him, greater honour than that which he deprived him of by sinning. But human nature by itself is incapable of making reparation for this injury done to God, yet, nevertheless, it cannot be forgiven without providing the needful satisfaction. In order that the justice of God should not leave unexpiated sin in his kingdom, the divine goodness has intervened. The Son of God took human nature into the unity of his person, so that in this one person there was a God-Man who was able to pay the debt that sinners owed. . . .

"There, O Christian soul, there is the price of thy salvation, there the cause of thy deliverance, there the cost of thy redemption. Thou wast a captive, but thou hast been delivered. Thou wast a slave, and hast been set free. Thus, exiled, thou hast been brought back; lost, thou hast been found; dead, thou hast been raised again."[1]

Then come outpourings of love to the divine Redeemer:

"And now, Lord Jesus, my Redeemer, I adore thee as true God, I believe in thee, hope in thee, aspire to thee, as far as I am able, with all the ardour of my desire. Help my weakness; I bow myself deeply before the wonders of thy passion, by which thou hast wrought my salvation. . . ."[2]

"What hast thou done, O most sweet Jesus, thus to be judged? What hast thou done, O Friend most dear, to be treated thus? What is thy crime, what thy misdeed, what is the cause of thy death, what of thy condemnation? I am the blow which pained thee, I the author of thy death. It is I that murdered thee in thy passion, I that laboured to torture thee. It is I that earned for thee this death and committed the crime revenged on thee. Oh, how wonderful are the terms of the judgement of God, how ineffable the dispositions of the divine mystery. It is the fool that sins,

---

[1] *Meditatio XI, de redemptione humana (P.L., CLVIII, 762-763, 765, 766, 767).*   [2] *Meditatio IX, de humanitate Christi (758).*

and yet the just is punished; the guilty commits the fault, and the innocent is smitten; the impious offends God, and the pious is condemned; that which the wicked deserves is suffered by the good; that which the slave contracts, the master pays; for that which man commits, God is charged. How far, O Son of God, how far has thy humility descended! How far has thine ardent charity brought thee! How far has thy goodness gone! How far thy kindness! How far has reached thy love! How far has thy compassion extended! For it is I who have sinned; it is thou who art punished. . . ."[1]

Emotions flood the heart of Anselm, just as much as thoughts crowd his mind. In his inability to give expression to all that he feels, to strengthen his language he multiplies synonyms like the waves of a rising tide.[2]

Let us listen once more to those cries of pain, ever " like a rising tide " in the same Anselmian strain, of the sinful soul imploring pardon :

" O my soul, my unhappy soul, miserable soul, I say, of a man not less miserable, shake off thy torpor; inquire into thy sin and stir up thy mind. Recall to thy heart thy monstrous sin and force from it doleful moaning. See, O unhappy one, and behold thy horrible crime, and stir up within thee fear and sorrow. Thou, I say, that wast formerly washed in the heavenly bath and gift of the Holy Spirit, thou that hast taken the oath of the Christian profession, thou as a virgin once espoused to Christ, O what memories! Of whom have I just spoken? I think no longer of the blessed Spouse of my virginity, but of the terrible Judge of my impurity! O bitter remembrance of my lost happiness! . . .

" Remember, O just God, remember that thou art merciful, that thou art my Creator and Restorer. Forget thy just wrath against the sinner; be mindful only of thy mercy towards thy creature; be not angry with the blameworthy, but have pity on an unfortunate. . . ."[3]

Pardon is granted because of the death of Christ, who is our whole reason for hope. This trust in the passion of Jesus is powerfully taught in the famous *Exhortation to the Dying,* which is at least a faithful echo of St Anselm's ideas on the redemption, even though the words themselves are not his.

Anselm, in order to console a dying man, terrified at the thought of his sins, would have him thus exhorted :

" Dost thou rejoice, my brother, to die in the Christian faith?—I do rejoice.—Art thou happy to die in the habit of

---

[1] *Oratio* II (*P.L.*, CLVIII, 861). It is the prayer *Quid commisisti, dulcissime puer, ut sic iudicaris?* . . . often quoted in books of devotion. Reproduced in the *Meditations,* VII, attributed to St Augustine (*P.L.*, XL, 906). [2] J. Bainvel, *op. cit.*, 1333.
[3] *Meditatio* III, *Deploratio male amissae virginitatis* (725-726).

a monk?[1]—Yes, I am happy.—Dost thou acknowledge that thou hast led an evil life and that thou deservest eternal punishment?—I acknowledge it.—Dost thou repent of it?—I do repent.—Hast thou a firm purpose of amendment if thou hast the time?—I have.—Dost thou believe that the Lord Jesus Christ died for thee?—I believe it.—Dost thou return him thanks for it?—I do.—Dost thou believe that thou canst be saved only through his death?—I believe it.

" Do so as long as thy soul remains with thee; put all thy trust in his death once for all; have no confidence in anything else; do thou confide wholly in that death; cover thyself wholly in it alone, wrap thyself wholly up in that death. And if the Lord wills to judge thee, say to him : Lord, I interpose the death of our Lord Jesus Christ between myself and thy judgement, else I refuse to be judged. And if he say to thee : But thou art a sinner, reply : Lord, I put the death of our Lord Jesus Christ between thee and my sins. If he say to thee that thou deservest to be damned, reply : Lord, I place the death of our Lord Jesus Christ between thee and my demerits, and I offer thee his merits instead of those that I should have had but have not. If he tell thee that he is angry with thee, say : Lord, I interpose the death of our Lord Jesus Christ between thee, thine anger, and myself.

" Afterwards let the sick man say three times : *Into thy hands, Lord, I commend my spirit. Thou hast redeemed us, O Lord, thou God of truth.*"[2]

St Anselm has also composed certain prayers in honour of the blessed Virgin,[3] which entitle him to the reputation of being a great client of Mary. Thus, later on, a considerable number of prayers and hymns addressed to the Mother of God were attributed to him.[4]

The fame of the Archbishop of Canterbury was such that a number of treatises on spirituality were placed to his credit of which he was not the author. His name, like that of St Augustine, and, later, those of St Bernard and of Hugh of St Victor, had the honour of clothing with his fame many anonymous spiritual works.[5]

---

[1] If the dying man be a layman, this question is modified.

[2] *Admonitio morienti et de peccatis suis nimium formidanti (P.L., CLVIII, 685-687).

[3] Particularly *Orationes* XLIX, L, LI (946-952), of which the authenticity seems to be established.

[4] Thus, *Hymni et psalterium de sancta Virgine Maria* (1035-1050). This work is not by St Anselm.

[5] These are the chief : *Sermo de Passione Domini* (P.L., CLVIII, 675-676); *Exhortatio ad contemptum temporalium et desiderium aeternorum* (677-686); *Carmen de contemptu mundi* (687-706); *Meditatio super Miserere* (821-854); *Tractatus asceticus.* (1021-1035); *Dialogus beatae Mariae et Anselmi de Passione Domini* (P.L., CLIX, 271-290); *De mensuratione crucis* (289-302); the writings *De conceptione B. Mariae Virginis* (301-326); *cf.* J. Bainvel, *op. cit.*, 1334.

CHAPTER II
THE SPIRITUAL TEACHING OF ST BERNARD

THE spirituality of St Bernard is not remarkable for any particularly new ideas. The Abbot of Clairvaux, as opposed to St Anselm, did not care for speculation; practical knowledge, which taught how to know and serve God, which gives to man knowledge of himself and the love of virtue, alone found favour in his sight. Learned mystical theories, therefore, such as are to be found, for example, in the writings of Hugh and Richard of St Victor, are not to be sought for in his. His ideas were those commonly received. They were drawn from holy Writ, of which he had a profound knowledge, always interpreting it in an allegorical and mystical sense. The Latin Fathers, St Ambrose, a little perhaps of St Gregory, and, above all, St Augustine, provided him, as they did all spiritual writers of this period, with the traditional ascetical and mystical instruction. As regards the Greek writers, he hardly knew any but the *Lives of the Fathers of the Desert,* which the Latin translation of Rufinus had rendered popular.

Whence came then the enormous influence of St Bernard's spirituality throughout the Middle Ages?

The eminent holiness of the Abbot of Clairvaux was doubtless not unconnected with the extraordinary spread of his spirituality. The reputation for lofty piety which a writer enjoys always draws attention to that which flows from his pen.

Bernard was also a strong man of action. He often left his cloister in order to counsel kings and popes, to encounter heresy, and to stir up the masses with a view to the accomplishment of some great work. No important event took place in his epoch in which he was not to be 'found in the front rank. He appears, as has been written of him, " to have absorbed all the knowledge of his time." It may be said of him as it was of Moses (Acts vii, 22), *that he was mighty in his words and in his deeds.* The immense renown which the Abbot of Clairvaux enjoyed could not but accredit his teaching in the Church. But these are only secondary causes. The true reason that accounts for the influence of St Bernard's writings is that they were specially adapted to render Christian piety affective.

Born at Fontaines-lez-Dijon, in that part of Burgundy which was to produce Bossuet and Lacordaire, Bernard possessed an oratorical temperament of a high order. He felt keenly, and his fine sensitiveness is reproduced in his writings, above all in his sermons. At the death of his brother Gerard, he gave vent before his monks to his sorrow, which moves us in the deepest recesses of the soul.[1] He could produce the same pathos when he described the crucifixion of Christ or the sorrows of Mary at the foot of the cross. St Francis of Assisi was not the first to pour forth lamentations before the crucifix, nor to weep with pity while contemplating the infant God in the manger. Before him, St Bernard had let his grief burst forth while meditating on the passion of Christ, and was moved to tears when speaking of Christmas night. This monk of grim austerity, who gave to his Abbey of Clairvaux a Rule of a severity far beyond that laid down by St Benedict, well knew how to appeal to the heart and to the feelings. He excelled in bringing into relief the touching aspects of the lives of the Saviour and of the blessed Virgin; and he was moved to tenderness by the charm of divine love. He brought out all that was sweet and gentle, moving and consoling, in the Christian mysteries, and thus he contributed more than anyone to the giving of an affective character to the piety of the Middle Ages.

The spirituality of the Greek monks, as we know, did not linger on what touches the heart and moves the feelings; it confined itself by preference to the austere aspects of piety, capable of inspiring fear. St Augustine, by way of reaction, showed more particularly the part which belongs to the heart in the pursuit of perfection. In this respect, the Abbot of Clairvaux keeps to the Augustinian tradition.

His style helps wonderfully to this end. Not that from a literary point of view it is beyond reproach;[2] the Abbot of Clairvaux attached but small importance to culture and form. That which captivates and moves and draws to God in his spiritual exhortations is the attractiveness of a keen sense of feeling and a great spiritual ardour of piety. The writings of the Abbot of Clairvaux, says M. Vacandard, " breathe life, the love of God and of souls. Their characteristic is impressiveness, that is to say, an indescribable sweetness, strong and at the same time tender, with which his style is saturated, rendering it sweet and making it penetrate to the very depths of the soul like divine grace. Bernard possesses this wonderful secret in the highest degree, whence the title of *Doctor mellifluus*, which was commonly bestowed on him in the fifteenth century, and remains attached to his name."[3]

[1] *In Cantica, sermo* XXVI, 3-12.
[2] *Cf.* Vacandard, *Vie de S. Bernard*, vol. i, 472-473, Paris 1897.
[3] *Dict. de Théol. cath.*, vol. ii, 783. St Gertrude particularly relished St Bernard because " of the gift of eloquence which he possessed, persuasive and penetrating like honey " (*Revelationes Gertrudianae*, lib. IV, cap. li).

It is, in fact, because they distilled the honey of tender devotion that the writings of Bernard attracted so many souls and began a form of piety which soon became general. They are a stage in the history of spirituality, and, from this point of view, the Abbot of Clairvaux may be compared to St Francis de Sales.

St Bernard gives great importance to humility, which, according to him, is the beginning of Christian life and perfection, ensures its development and makes it reach its goal. Bernard, so sparse in comparisons and images drawn from nature, comes out of his habitual reserve when he speaks of this virtue. He sees in it a dawn which dispels the darkness of sin and proclaims the light of justice.[1] It has drawn God down to earth, as the nard of the bride in the *Canticle of Canticles* drew the heavenly Spouse by its perfume.[2]

The hyssop and the dove are pleasing symbols of it.[3] Bernard is never sated with speaking or writing on humility; he sees the power of it in every act of the spiritual life; no virtue can make progress or even exist without it. In the mystery of the Incarnation, that which touches and moves him in the highest degree is the abasement of the Word made flesh.[4] This predilection for humility is one of the characteristic marks of Bernardine spirituality.

Devotion to the mysteries of the mortal life of the Saviour and those who were connected with it, like the blessed Virgin and St Joseph, appears in the sermons of St Bernard much more than in the homilies of the Fathers of the Church. In the twelfth century, the cycle of the liturgical year was completely formed. The Abbot of Clairvaux preached to his monks on the subject of every feast from Advent to Pentecost. He had occasion, again and again, with never-failing tenderness of heart, to preach on the principal acts in the great drama of man's redemption. We shall see what an influence he thus exerted on the whole of the Middle Ages.

Finally, St Bernard was a great mystic. He has not left a synthesis of that part of his spirituality which was concerned with extraordinary states, any more than he has left a theory concerning his asceticism, but the elements of a copious mystical theology are to be found in his writings.

The spirituality of St Bernard may be summed up under these heads : (1) *Christian perfection and the preponderant role which humility plays therein.* (2) *The doctrine of the*

---

[1] *Sermo XCI de diversis,* 3.
[2] *In Assumpt. B.V.M., sermo* IV, 7; *In Cantica, sermo* XLII, 6.
[3] *In Cantica, sermo* XLV, 2, 4.
[4] Cf. *In Epiphania Domini, sermo* I, 2 : *Quanto enim minorem se fecit in humanitate, tanto majorem exhibuit in bonitate; et quanto pro me vilior, tanto mihi carior.*

love of God. (3) *The means of sanctification.* (4) *Devotion to the mysteries of the life of Christ.* (5) *Devotion to Mary.* (6) *Devotion to the guardian angels.* (7) *St Bernard and St Joseph.* (8) *His mystical theology.* (9) *On the excellence of the sacerdotal ministry and the qualities which it demands.*[1]

I—CHRISTIAN PERFECTION—THE ROLE OF HUMILITY

PERFECTION, according to St Bernard, consists in corresponding so completely with grace that our will not only avoids all evil, but also performs good, to the extent that, and as fully as, we are invited to do by grace.[2]

This definition calls to mind that which we have already met with,[3] according to which ideal perfection excludes every fault, no matter how small.

Nevertheless, we may note two points which are proper to the idea as expressed by the Abbot of Clairvaux.

It is by the correspondence of the will with the action of grace that perfection is obtained. Bernard, in his treatise *On grace and the freedom of choice,*[4] has given great attention to the relation between grace and free will. Grace enables us to avoid evil and practise good on condition that the will adheres to its impulse. If this adhesion be full and entire, if it be constant, perfection will be attained; for grace always tends towards goodness. It even disposes us in all things to choose that which is most perfect. He who yields fully to grace will not only avoid all evil, but will be unceasingly inclined towards that which is most perfect. Always to choose the most perfect—such is the second characteristic of perfection, according to St Bernard.

The Abbot of Clairvaux is the first to acknowledge that such a perfection belongs to heaven and not to earth. Here below, no matter what degree of holiness is attained, we are not capable of conforming ourselves so entirely to the divine

---

[1] Principal sources : *S. Bernardi abbatis Claraevallensis Epistolae; De consideratione; De moribus et officio episcoporum; Sermo de conversione, ad clericos; Tractatus de gradibus humilitatis et superbiae; Liber de diligendo Deo (P.L., CLXXXII)*; *Sermones de tempore; Sermones de sanctis; Sermones de diversis; Sententiae; Sermones in Cantica Canticorum (P.L., CLXXXIII)*; *Acta Sanctorum, S. Bernardi vitae, Augusti,* vol. iv *(P.L., CLXXXV). Cf.* E. Vacandard, *Vie de S. Bernard,* 2 vols., Paris 1897. The whole of St Bernard was translated into French by the monk Ant. de S. Gabriel, Paris 1678, 13 vols. Other more modern translations have been made.

[2] *In festo S. Michaelis, sermo* II, 4 *(P.L.,* CLXXXIII, 454) : *Cujus enim voluntas ex affectione et cum desiderio gratiae cohaeret, ut nec concupiscat mala agere, nec bona minora, nec minus bene quam gratia suggerit, hic plane perfectus est vir.*

[3] *Christian Spirituality,* vol. i.   [4] *P.L.,* CLXXXII.

inspirations, and are unable, as St Augustine so clearly taught, to avoid every little fault. Should we not say, without ceasing, to God : *Forgive us our trespasses?* (Matt. vi, 12).[1]

Even though we are not able to reach to this summit of perfection, we must at least strive without ceasing to approach it as closely as possible. According to St Bernard, as to St Augustine, Christian perfection consists, in reality, in a continued effort towards the best. " No one," he says, can be perfect unless he yearns to be more perfect, and we show ourselves to be the more perfect as we aspire to a still higher perfection."[2]

Thus unlimited progress in goodness is the law of perfection; for to cease to make progress is, in fact, to fall away.

" An untiring effort to make progress and a constant striving towards that which is more perfect, such is perfection. If to labour for perfection is to be perfect, not to wish to make progress is without doubt to fail (*perfecto nolle proficere deficere est*). Where, then, do they stand who are in the habit of saying : It is enough for us, we do not wish to be better than our fathers? O monk, dost thou not wish to make progress?—No.—Dost thou then wish to fall back?—Not at all.—What, then, dost thou wish?—I wish to live in such a way, thou sayest, that I may remain at that point which I have reached, without letting myself fall back, but without the desire to go higher.—What thou wishest is impossible, for nothing in this world remains in the same state. . . .[3] Jacob saw in his dream angels ascending and descending the celestial ladder (Gen. xxviii, 12); not one of them stopped or took rest. Neither should we ourselves stop on the slope of our frail ladder, for there is nothing in the movement of this mortal life that can remain stationary. . . . We must of necessity mount or descend; if we try to stop, inevitably we fall. He who refuses to be better, is assuredly no longer good, and, in that he does not expect to become better, he thereby ceases to be good."[4] We must, then, always go forward : *semper extendamur ad anteriora.*[5]

This teaching is a sort of *leitmotiv* in the spirituality of St Bernard; it constantly recurs.[6]

1 *In Vigilia Nativitatis Domini, sermo* VI, 10.
2 *Epistola* xxxiv, *ad Draconem monach.,* 1 (*P.L.,* CLXXXII, 440) : *Nemo quippe perfectus qui perfectior esse non appetit; et in eo quisque perfectiorem se probat quo ad majorem tendit perfectionem.*
3 *Epist.* ccliv, *ad abbatem Guarinum,* 3-4 (cols. 460-461).
4 *Epist.* xci, *ad abb. Suessione congreg.,* 3 (col. 224) : *Minime pro certo est bonus qui melior esse non vult; et ubi incipis nolle fieri melior ibi etiam desinis esse bonus.*
5 *In Purificatione B.V.M., sermo* II, 3; *In psalm. Qui habitat, sermo* IV, 3.
6 Cf. *Epist.* ccclxxxv; *De consideratione,* lib. II, cap. vii; *Serm. de diversis, sermo* XXV, 4.

Christian perfection, that uninterrupted effort towards that which is best, requires, as an indispenable condition, the knowledge of our wretchedness. It is because he is conscious of his imperfection that the true believer yearns to become better. To know himself such as he is, with all his sins, all his imperfections, is the first knowledge that the Christian who desires to sanctify himself must acquire. This knowledge of ourselves, which is the result of looking ourselves in the face, of the honest scrutiny of ourselves as we are, is calculated, in the highest degree, to inspire humility. [1] For, according to the views of St Bernard, who reproduces those of St Augustine, humility is truth; it is the result of the sincere and truthful knowledge of ourselves, of what we are, and of the smallness of our worth.

The virtue of humility is thus found to be the genesis of perfection; St Bernard, like St Augustine, places it at the base of the spiritual edifice. It is the foundation without which there is no solidity in the Christian life : *nisi super humilitatis fundamentum, spirituale aedificium stare minime potest.* [2] For man deprived of humility is ignorant of himself and does not know God; he is not capable of self-sanctification and of tending towards perfection. Knowledge of oneself, humility, and perfection are realities which, in the eyes of the Abbot of Clairvaux, call for and produce one another. It is this that he expounds to his monks in his commentaries on the Rule of St Benedict; it is also the teaching set forth in his *Treatise on the Degrees of Humility,* [3] addressed to Godfrey, Abbot of Fontenay.

The definition of humility which St Bernard gives us deserves notice.

Humility is opposed to pride, which, according to St Augustine (*De Gen. ad litt.,* lib. xi, 18), is the inordinate love of our own excellence. St Bernard hence concluded that humility consists in the contempt of our own excellence : *Humilitas est contemptus propriae excellentiae.* [4] This con-

---

[1] *In Cantica, sermo* XXXVI, 5 : *Ad humiliandum nihil anima invenire vivacius seu accomodatius potest quam si se in veritate invenerit. . . . Statuat se ante faciem suam, nec se a se avertere abducatur.*

[2] *ibid.*

[3] In this treatise Bernard purposes to comment on the twelve degrees of humility enumerated in the Rule of St Benedict. Changing his intention, he describes the twelve degrees of pride (cap. x-xxi), which are : Curiosity, frivolity of mind, foolish joy, boasting, singularity, obstinacy, arrogance, presumption, hypocrisy, revolt, licentiousness and habits of sin. Bernard draws from life portraits of monks having these diverse forms of pride.

[4] *Tractatus de moribus et officio episcoporum,* cap. v, 19; *Tract. de grad. humilit.,* cap. iv, 14. .Bernard sets against the expression *appetitus propriae excellentiae* that of *contemptus propriae excellentiae. Contemptus opponitur appetitui,* he says. We shall see that the term *contemptus* is excessive as a definition of humility in general.

tempt is derived from a true and sincere knowledge of ourselves. Is it possible to know ourselves as we are, with our wretchedness and our faults, without forming a detrimental opinion of ourselves? Does not the truth concerning ourselves force us to disparage ourselves in our own eyes? St Bernard connects the virtue of justice with humility, of which it is the complement.[1]

"The soul which sees itself in the clear light of truth," he says, "discovers itself to be unsightly, and sighing in its wretchedness which it can no longer hide, does it not, with the prophet, cry out to the Lord: *In thy truth thou hast humbled me?* (Ps. cxviii, 75). For how could it not be wholly humbled by this sincere knowledge of itself when it sees itself laden with sin, weighed down by the burden of this mortal body, plunged in the cares of this world, stained by the vileness of carnal passion, blind, deformed, weak, struggling against a thousand errors, exposed to a thousand dangers, a prey to a thousand fears . . . inclined to vice and incapable of itself of being virtuous? How could it be able to lift up its eyes in boasting or its head with pride?"[2]

Hence humility is produced by two considerations, that of our own wretchedness and that of the divine power which heals us of our infirmities.[3]

The Abbot of Clairvaux is thus led to formulate his famous definition of humility. It is the *virtue by which man, knowing himself most intimately, is despicable in his own sight.*[4]

The humility thus defined—Bernard himself states it—is that of those who are advancing, of those "who rise from virtue to virtue."[5] Indeed, in order to have a sufficiently complete idea of our wretchedness to the point of despising ourselves, we must already possess a high ideal of sanctity to which we may be compared. It is therefore the definition of an eminent degree of humility rather than of humility itself that the Abbot of Clairvaux proclaims. If, in order to be humble, even in the lowest degree, it be necessary to have contempt for ourselves, "to be despicable in our own sight," very few would be so.

Humility, in its ordinary sense, is a virtue which represses the excess of our self-esteem and restrains the immoderate desire to raise ourselves above others. It is inspired by as near an appreciation as possible of what we are. If it finds satisfaction at the sight of our failings and in a sense of what

---

[1] *In psalm. Qui habitat, sermo* XIV, 10; *In Cantica, sermo* XXXIV, 2-4.
[2] *In Cantica, sermo* XXXVI, 5.   [3] *Epist.* cccxciii, 3.
[4] *De gradibus humilit.*, cap. i, 2; *Humilitas est virtus qua homo verissima sui cognitione sibi ipsi vilescit.*
[5] *De grad. humil., ibid.*

we lack, it ought not to close its eyes wholly to our good qualities, for it is truth. "Humility," says Lacordaire,[1] "does not consist in hiding our talents and virtues, in thinking ourselves worse and more ordinary than we are, but in possessing a clear knowledge of all that is lacking in us and in not exalting ourselves for that which we have, seeing that God has freely given it to us, and that even with all his gifts, we are still of infinitely little importance."

The Abbot of Clairvaux, on the contrary, recommends those who wish to be humble to turn their regard away from their qualities in order to think only of their own abjectness. This aspect of his religious psychology may be explained by the need which he felt of lowering himself in his own eyes when everything around him tended to exalt him. This famous monk, whose words had resounded throughout the West, who was consulted everywhere by all men, who roused the masses by his eloquence, found in an exaggeration of the sense of his wretchedness a necessary counterpoise to these inducements to pride.[2] Lacordaire, too, on the days when he had been applauded at Notre-Dame de Paris, on returning to his convent in the evening, needed to submit himself to extraordinary humiliations in order to suppress the pride which assailed him.[3]

If the theoretical definition of humility proclaimed by St Bernard call for certain reserves, it nevertheless expresses a very true practical rule, and one that should be followed by those who wish to become humble. The tendency to exalt ourselves is so strong and so tyrannical, that we can only restrict ourselves to proper bounds by constantly lowering ourselves in our own eyes. It is what all the saints have done, especially St Bernard, who, as his historian tells us, looked upon himself as the last of all when the whole world placed him in the front rank.[4] He recommends us to look at and admire the virtues of others and to acknowledge that we are deprived of them ourselves,[5] to hide with the greatest care the special graces which God has vouchsafed to us, so that, in accordance with the saying that the humble man dreads the eyes of the fields and the ears of the forest,[6] we may never speak of ourselves and may love to remain unknown : *Ama nesciri, laudet te os alienum, sileat tuum.*[7]

[1] *Lettres à des jeunes gens,* xxviii, *On humility,* Paris 1878, pp. 164-165.

[2] *S. Bernardi vita prima,* lib. II, cap. iv, 25 ; Migne, *P.L.,* CLXXXV, 282.

[3] *Cf.* Chocarne, *Le Père Lacordaire, sa vie intime et religieuse,* chaps. xiv-xv, Paris 1880. (Eng. trans., *The Inner Life of Père Lacordaire.*)

[4] *S. Bernardi, vita prima, ibid.*

[5] *In Cantica, sermo* XXXVII, 7.

[6] *In festo S. Martini, sermo* VIII, 13; *Tract. de moribus et offic. episc.,* cap. vi, n. 21.

[7] *In Nativ. Domini, sermo* III, 2. The *Imitation of Christ* reproduced the phrase *ama nesciri* (lib. I, cap. ii).

This humility, the nature of which Bernard loved to examine, plays a preponderant role in the Christian life. Every conversion necessarily begins by an act of abjection. When the sinner comes to know his state, when he sees what he is as contrasted with what he should be, does he not feel contempt for himself? The sight of his faults inspires him with fear of the chastisements he has deserved. And in his distress, he lifts up tearful eyes to God to beg for pardon. Humility thus makes us taste the consolations of mercy after having been dismayed by the rigours of justice.

" Those whom the truth, that is to say, humility, has made to know themselves, and to render themselves thus despicable in their own eyes, necessarily feel that that which they were accustomed to love has become bitter. For, seeing themselves face to face, they are forced to see themselves as they are, and this sight causes them to blush with shame. Whilst they are discontented with their condition they sigh after a better state which they know they cannot reach by their own strength. In their lively sorrow, like severe judges who, for the love of truth, hunger and thirst after justice, they have no other consolation than to require of themselves, on account of the past, a most rigorous satisfaction, extending as far as contempt of themselves, and, as regards the future, a firm resolve to do better. But they realize that they are unable to succeed in this by their own power. . . . Thus they turn from the divine justice in order to beseech the divine mercy."[1]

Humility, which causes spiritual life to be produced within us, also assures its accomplishment. It is the labourer who digs the foundations of the spiritual edifice, who builds it and completes it.

Christian virtue in fact would not be able to subsist without it; when it fails there is nothing but ruin and moral desolation in the soul.[2] It is truly the mother of the other virtues. It receives them at their birth in the heart of the Christian, it guards them and makes them grow, and it leads them onwards to their end. Does not St Paul himself say that it is through infirmity, that is to say, humility, that virtue reaches its perfection?[3]

[1] *De grad. humil.*, cap. v, 18. Cf. *In Cantica, sermo* xxxvi, 4-7; *In Quadragesima, sermo* II.

[2] *De consideratione*, lib. V, cap. xiv, 32 : *Virtutum siquidem bonum quodam ac stabile fundamentum, humilitas. Nempe si nutet illa virtutum aggregatio nonnisi ruina est.* Cf. *In Nativitate Domini, sermo* i, 1.

[3] *Tract. de moribus et officio espiscoporum*, cap. v, 20 : *Humilitas ergo virtutes alias accipit. Servat acceptas, quia non requiescit Spiritus Domini, nisi super quietum et humilem* (Isa. lxvi, 2). *Servatas consummat, nam virtus in infirmitate, hoc est in humilitate, perficitur* (2 Cor. xii, 9). St Bernard makes use of the words of St Paul in a different sense; they should be translated thus : *The power of God is made perfect in infirmity.*

If humility be so powerful it is because, as we are taught in holy Writ, *God resisteth the proud, but to the humble he giveth grace* (1 Pet. v, 5). The heart is a vessel destined to receive grace; in order that it may hold it abundantly it must be emptied of self-love and vainglory.[1] When humility makes therein a great space to be filled, grace pervades it, for there is a close affinity between grace and humility: *semper solet esse gratiae divinae familiaris virtus humilitas.*[2] There is nothing, then, more helpful than this virtue in order to merit grace, to keep it with us or to recover it if lost.[3]

Humility is thus the inseparable companion, the devoted friend, of all Christian virtues, more especially of such as chastity,[4] gentleness and charity, which are most refined.[5] Humility it is which renders us compassionate for the wretchedness of others; the sense of our own infirmities, of our weakness and our poverty, inclines us to be indulgent towards the failings of those around us. This compassion, which makes us feel for the evils which afflict our neighbour, is, according to St Bernard, the second degree of humility.[6] But we must not attach too much importance to this classification of the degrees of humility. We must not forget that the Abbot of Clairvaux is an orator, and not a theorist bound down by a hard and fast logic.

Finally, humility, by bringing the other virtues to perfection, raises the soul to the heights of mystical contemplation. God admits the humble to his intimacy and treats them with a special familiarity: *Familiarius semper humilitati propinquare solet divinitas.*[7]

"O the great virtue of humility," exclaims St Bernard, "towards which the divine Majesty inclines so easily! It knows how quickly to change respect into friendship, and bring it about that God, who was far from us, may soon be near."[8]

Humility is the spikenard of the bride in the *Canticle of Canticles* which spreads its perfume and draws the heavenly Spouse (Cant. i, 11).

"What, indeed, does the expression *My spikenard sends forth its odour* mean if not this? My humility has pleased thee. It is not my wisdom, saith the bride, nor my nobleness, nor my beauty, in which gifts I am lacking, which have

---

[1] *In Annuntiatione B.V.M.*, sermo III, 9. Cf. *Epist.* cccxciii, 2-3.
[2] *Super Missus est, Homilia* IV, 9. Cf. *In Cantica*, sermo XXXIV.
[3] *In Cantica*, sermo LIV, 9. Cf. *Epist.* ccclxxii; *Sermo* XLVI, de diversis.
[4] *Tract. de mor. et off. episc.*, cap. v, 17; *Super Missus est, Homil.* I, 5.
[5] *In Dominica infra octav. Assumpt. B.V.M.*, sermo XII; *In Nativitate Domini*, sermo II, 6.   [6] *De grad. humilit.*, cap. v.
[7] *Tractatus de moribus et officio episc.*, cap. vi, 24.
[8] *In Cantica*, sermo XLIII, 1. Cf. *Sermones de diversis*, LXII, LXIII.

exhaled their odour, but it is humility, my only treasure. Humility has the gift of pleasing God, and the Lord is wont to look upon that which is humble. Furthermore, whilst the divine King was on his throne in the highest heaven the odour of my humility went up to him."[1]

Bernard appears to attribute the wonders of the mystical union of the soul with God to humility. They are, however, the act of divine love, as the Abbot of Clairvaux well knows. Moreover, in order to abide by the traditional teaching without belittling the role of his most precious virtue he distinguishes two kinds of humility—that which a knowledge of ourselves gives us (*humilitas quam veritas parit*), and that which charity brings forth (*humilitas quam charitas format*).[2] The first purifies the soul and enables it to fix its sight on heavenly and divine truths in order to contemplate them.

For there are three hindrances which prevent us from reaching mystical contemplation—ignorance of ourselves, our moral weakness, and our affection for sin. Humility, by making us know what we are, fills us with regret for our faults and heals us of our wretchedness.[3] There is, then, no longer any hindrance to the vision of heavenly beauty. But for the soul to be united to God with that burning union which is known to mystics, charity must step in to enkindle humility, and impart to it divine ardour.[4] Thus do we see the role of charity in the sanctification of the soul and in its being uplifted to these extraordinary states.

"And I also, O Lord," cries St Bernard, "I shall willingly glory in my infirmity as far as I can . . . so that thy virtue, that is to say humility, may be perfected in me. For thy grace is sufficient for me when my virtue fails. I resolutely adhere to the footsteps of thy grace, and thus, in spite of my progress being rendered difficult through weakness, I shall mount the ladder of humility without fear, until, wholly clinging to the truth, I reach the vast domain of charity. Then shall I sing with gratitude, and say : *Thou hast set my feet in a spacious place* (Ps. xxx, 9). Thus I go forward with greater assurance in thy narrow way, I ascend the steep ladder, though slowly, yet with greater calmness ; thus in a wonderful way do I reach the truth in spite of my sloth and halting footsteps. But *woe is me, that my sojourning is prolonged!* (Ps. cxix, 5). *Who will give me wings like a dove* (Ps. liv, 7) in order to fly more quickly towards truth and find rest in charity? In that I have them not, lead me thyself, Lord, in thy way, and I shall enter into thy truth and thy truth shall make me free."[5]

---

[1] *In Cantica, sermo* XLII, 9.   [2] *ibid.,* 6.
[3] *De gradibus humilitatis,* cap. vi ; *In Cantica, ibid.*
[4] *In Cantica, sermo* XLII, 5.
[5] *De gradibus humilitatis,* cap. ix, 26.

II—ST BERNARD ON THE LOVE OF GOD

BUT charity does not only lend its aid to humility in order to raise the soul to contemplation; it ought also to accompany it on its journey towards sanctity. If Bernard be unstinted in his enthusiastic praise of humility, he also extols divine love. His emotional temperament, moreover, prompted him to it. If his spirituality may not be summed up wholly in charity like that of St Augustine, this highest of virtues occupies a predominant place therein.[1] It treats of the *sources* of divine love, of its *motives,* of the *measure* of it, and of its *degrees,* and extols in rapturous terms the mystical love which unites the heavenly Bridegroom in the Canticles with the Christian soul.

The Abbot of Clairvaux has his own theory as to the birth of love in the human heart.

Love, he says, is one of the four passions of man—the others are fear, joy and sorrow. It is therefore natural and instinctive : its object is man himself who loves himself for his own sake. The first love is called by Bernard a carnal love (*amor carnalis*) by which man loves himself before all things. This love becomes social, when it extends to those of his own kind who are in need.[2]

This love of himself has as yet nothing that is spiritual or divine; it is entirely natural. How does it become transformed into the love of God? Under the stress of trial and tribulation. When man suffers he ends by turning himself towards the Lord, his necessary refuge and his only true support. Assisted by grace he begins to believe in God and to love him because of the benefits that he receives. Thus divine love is born in the soul.

" Because we are carnal and born of concupiscence and of the flesh," says St Bernard, " our love must needs come from the flesh. If this love be well guided, it will gradually become, under the influence of grace, a spiritual love, for *that was not first which is spiritual, but that which is natural; afterwards that which is spiritual* (1 Cor. xv, 46). . . . Man then loves, first of all, himself for his own sake, for he is flesh, and is not able to enjoy anything but himself. Then, realizing his insufficiency, he begins to seek God by faith and to love him as his needful help. In this second degree of love he still loves God, not for God's sake, but for his own."[3]

[1] St Bernard has dealt specially with the love of God in a letter addressed to Guigo, Abbot of Grande-Chartreuse (*Epist.* xi), and above all in his treatise *De diligendo Deo,* dedicated to Cardinal Haimeric, Chancellor of the Roman Church. But he touches on it very often in his *Sermons,* especially in those on the *Canticle of Canticles.*

[2] *De diligendo Deo,* cap. viii.

[3] *De diligendo Deo,* cap. xv. Cf. *Epist.* xi, *ad Guigonem,* 8. The same conception of the source of the love of God is found in the *Epistola ad patres de monte Dei,* lib. I, cap. xiv, 42 (*P.L.,* CLXXXIV, 297).

This conception of the source of divine love is admissible. Bernard makes grace instrumental in transforming that natural and instinctive affection which man has for himself and rendering it supernatural. It is therefore not human love which produces of itself the love of God.

But exception may with reason be taken to the Abbot of Clairvaux for stating, in a treatise on the Love of God, that this natural, *carnal* love which man has for himself is the first step of love. Such a form of expression may produce regrettable confusion and tend to veil the distinction between love engendered by nature and that produced by grace.

How eloquently, on the contrary, does he explain the motives which inspire us to love God !

" Who, even among the infidels, does not know that all bodily necessities, food to live, light to see, air to breathe, are only received from none other than him who *giveth food to all flesh* (Ps. cxxxv, 25), *who maketh his sun to rise upon the good and bad, and raineth upon the just and the unjust* (Matt. v, 45)? Who could think, however impious he be, that this human dignity which shines within his soul has any other author than him who said in Genesis, *Let us make man to our image and likeness* (Gen. i, 26)? . . . God, then, deserves to be loved for himself even by the infidel who, though he knows not Christ, knows himself and the gifts that he has received."[1]

The Christian will love God still more perfectly. Gratitude towards Jesus his Saviour and benefactor forces him to do so in a special way : " Christ has given us his merits, he keeps himself for our reward; he gives himself as food for holy souls, sacrifices himself in order to redeem souls in captivity.[2] . . . In the creation, his first work, he gave me to myself; in the second, he gives himself to me."[3] The perfections of the Saviour, his beauty and his loveliness, render this duty of love still more easy.[4]

Bernard cannot call to mind these motives for loving God without his heart being inflamed :

" *I will love thee, O Lord, my strength: the Lord is my firmament, my refuge and my deliverer* (Ps. xvii, 1-3). Thou art for me all that is lovable and can be desired. My God, my help, I will love thee because of thy mercy as much as I am able, not as much as I should, but at least as much as is in my power. I shall be able to love thee more when thou

[1] *De diligendo Deo*, cap. ii, 6.
[2] *De diligendo Deo*, cap. vii, 22 : *Se dedit in meritum, se servat in praemium, se apponit in refectione animarum sanctarum, se in redemptione distrahit captivarum.* St Thomas Aquinas was inspired by this passage in composing the fourth verse of the hymn to the blessed Sacrament, *Verbum supernum prodiens.*
[3] *id.*, cap. v, 15.   [4] *id.*, cap. iii-v.

hast increased my love, but I shall never love thee as much as thou deservest."[1]

We cannot indeed love God of our own strength; it is necessary that God should create in us the love with which we may love him. The Lord, says St Bernard, is at the same time the efficient cause which puts love in us and the final cause towards which this love tends.[2]

As to the measure of our love, it will be as limitless as God himself.[3] St Bernard comments thus on the happy phrase. " the measure of loving God is to love him without measure," written by Severus, Bishop of Milevis, to St Augustine :

" Understand with what measure, or rather how without measure, God deserves to be loved. He who is so great was the first freely and completely to love us who are so small and contemptible ! . . . Since our love concerns God, it is concerned with immensity, with infinity—God, indeed, is infinite and without limitation : what then, I ask you, should be the limit and measure of our love ?"[4]

The love of God ought, then, to be developed in us unceasingly, indefinitely, since its measure is infinity itself. St Bernard notices four phases in this development, which may be considered as the four degrees of divine love. They correspond with the divers stages of advancement in the spiritual life.

The first consists in the natural love which man has for himself. In the second degree, man loves God only because of the benefits he receives from him. He reaches it through the sense of his impotence and of the need which he has of divine assistance, when he finds himself distressed. This love is interested; the beneficence alone of God is the object of it.

But, little by little, reflection, prayer and obedience to the divine commandments bring man to the knowledge of the goodness of God. When the human heart, transformed by grace, has *tasted and seen that the Lord is sweet* (Ps. xxxiii, 9), he begins by loving God for God's sake, and thus passes to the third degree of love. Here it is the intrinsic goodness of God which is the motive of loving, without, however, excluding his bounty towards us.

It belongs to the fourth degree of love to love God solely for himself, without any thought of self-interest. It is pure love.[5] But this state of pure love, in which man constantly forgets himself for God, appears to St Bernard to be impossible.

" We remain long in the third degree," he says, " and I do not know if any man in this life has perfectly arrived at the

---

[1] *id.*, cap. vi, 16.   [2] *id.*, cap. vii, 22.   *Cf.* cap. i, 1.
[3] *id.*, cap. i, 1 : *Causa diligendi Deum, Deus est: modus, sine modo diligere.*
[4] *De diligendo Deo*, cap. vi, 16.   [5] *id.*, cap. viii-x.

fourth, in which he no longer loves himself except for God's sake. If there be anyone who has experienced it, let him say so; for my part, I admit that it seems to me impossible. That will doubtless be brought about when the good and faithful servant shall have entered into the joy of his Lord and shall have been inebriated with the abundance of the house of God."[1]

It is useful to notice here a doctrine peculiar to St Bernard which occupies an important place with regard to divine love.

The object of this love may be either the humanity of Christ, with the mysteries of his mortal life, or God himself. In the first case, the love, according to St Bernard, is sensible (*amor carnalis*); in the second, it is spiritual.[2]

"Notice," he says, "that the love of our heart may be sensible when it has as its object the humanity of Christ; that which Christ did or taught when he was here below specially touches our human heart. The faithful soul, filled with this love, is easily impressed with sorrow by all that reminds him of Christ. He listens to nothing more willingly, he reads nothing with greater attention, he thinks of nothing more often, he meditates on nothing more sweetly than the life of Christ. . . . To the Christian who prays the image presents itself of the God-Man being born, fed with milk, or teaching, dying, rising from the dead or ascending to heaven. Reminders such as these necessarily attract the soul to virtue or purify it from vice, free it from sensuality and calm its passions. For my part, I think that the chief reason which prompted the invisible God to become visible in the flesh and to hold converse with man was to lead carnal men, who are only able to love carnally, to the healthful love of his flesh, and afterwards, little by little, to spiritual love."[3]

It is this sensible love which St Bernard knew so well how to rouse in souls. His sermons on the different mysteries of the mortal life of Jesus, so pathetic or so tender, move the feelings to the highest pitch. They are great aids to affective piety.

As regards spiritual love, it has, as we shall see, its most noble manifestation in the mystical union of the soul with God.

[1] St Bernard, like St Augustine, declares the state of pure love to be impossible here below. Only passing acts of this love are possible.

[2] St Bernard again distinguishes *reasonable* love, which is more perfect than sensible love and less so than spiritual. It is the love which rejects all error and clings firmly to the teaching of the Church respecting Christ. *In Cantica, sermo* XX.

[3] *In Cantica, sermo* XX, 6.

III—THE MEANS OF SANCTIFICATION—PERFEC-
TION THROUGH PRAYER, EXAMINATION OF
CONSCIENCE, DISCRETION AND SPIRITUAL
DIRECTION

It is through humility and charity that the soul is raised
towards God. This ascent is slow and laborious; the height
of perfection is not achieved suddenly; it is, in fact, reached
not by flying, but by climbing to the top of the mystical
ladder.[1] Our sanctification is truly, according to the expression of St Bernard, a " spiritual exercise."[2]

In order to accomplish this ascent, we have need to be
helped, even to be carried, by prayer and meditation, which
are compared to our two feet.

" Let us then ascend," he says, " with meditation and
prayer for our two feet. Meditation teaches us what it is
that we lack, and prayer obtains it. Meditation shows us the
way, and prayer makes us walk therein. Finally, meditation
lets us know the dangers which threaten us, and prayer
makes us avoid them by the grace of our Lord Jesus Christ."[3]

We must note the mutual and necessary help which prayer
and meditation give to each other. Bernard did not yet
foresee our modern exercise of mental prayer, for with him
meditation and prayer remain distinct. But we see arising
from his writings the two constituent elements of our present
prayer, and, when circumstances demand it, they have only
to be united in one single exercise and duly regulated in order
to create that means of sanctification rendered classical by
St Ignatius Loyola and St Teresa.

The teaching of St Bernard on prayer is inspired by the
Conferences of Cassian. We find therein the four kinds of

---

[1] *In festo S. Andreae apostoli, sermo* I, 10.

[2] *Sermo* XXV, *de diversis,* 4; *In Circumcisione Domini, sermo* III,
11. The same expression is found in other writings, contemporary or
almost so with St Bernard. Thus the *Epist. ad Fratres de monte Dei*
(*P.L.,* CLXXXIV, 297-300) calls prayer and meditation " spiritual
exercises " (lib. I, cap. x, 29; xi, 32; xiv, 44; lib. II, cap. iii, 17). The
Scala claustralium (*ibid.,* 475-484, and *P.L.,* XL, 997-1004, *Scala Para-
disi*) also calls reading, meditation, prayer and contemplation " spiritual
exercises " (cap. i).

[3] *In festo S. Andreae apostoli, sermo* I, 10 : *Ascendamus igitur, velut
duobus quibusdam pedibus, meditatione et oratione. Meditatio siquidem docet quid desit; oratio ne desit obtinet: Illa viam ostendit, ista
deducit. Meditatione denique agnoscimus imminentia nobis pericula;
oratione evadimus, praestante Domino nostro Jesu Christo.* See the
beautiful thoughts on prayer, *In Quadragesima, sermo* IV-VI. Our
prayers are never useless : *Sermo* XXV, 5 : *Nemo vestrum fratres parvipendat orationem suam. Dico enim vobis quia ipse ad quem oramus
non parvipendat eam. Priusquam egressa sit ab ore nostro, ipse scribi
jubet eam in libro suo. . . . Aut dabit quod petimus, aut quod nobis
noverit esse utilius. . . . Oratio tamen infructuosa non erit.*

prayer which the Abbot of Marseilles drew from a text in
1 Tim. ii, 1 : *supplication, prayer, intercession and thanksgiving.*[1] There is nothing of new interest to arrest our
attention. The advice given as to the precautions to be taken
to avoid distractions, and the necessary conditions in order
that our petitions may be granted by God, have been brought
to our knowledge elsewhere.

The personality of St Bernard. is more apparent when he
treats of meditation.

Like all the mystics of the twelfth century, he sees in it
a most effective means of acquiring human knowledge, and
of discerning divine teaching and becoming imbued with it.[2]
In this he is in perfect agreement with the school of St Victor.
He recommends and lays great stress on meditation on the
mysteries of the life of Christ,[3] and chiefly of his Passion.[4]
We shall see presently with what feeling Bernard made these
meditations himself, and how he could make others weep with
him over the sufferings of the Saviour, and not only those of
his time, but also of the generations which came after him. He
speaks in language full of enthusiasm to his former disciple,
Pope Eugenius III, in the celebrated treatise *De Consideratione,* of the sweetness, the consolation and the benefit
derived from meditation on heaven.[5]

Meditation is so important in the eyes of St Bernard that
he draws up a theory of it in this treatise *Concerning Consideration.*[6]

St Bernard calls *Consideration,* as does St Victor, all
seeking after truth. It is thus distinguished from contemplation, which is concerned with truth that has been found and
is known with certainty.[7] But truth may be sought either
within ourselves or outside ourselves. The word *consideration,* therefore, has different meanings according to whether
it signifies reflection on ourselves or meditation on supernatural realities. In fact, St Bernard uses it in these different
senses in regard to the counsels which he gives to the Pope.

First of all, he advises Eugenius to *examine* himself : as to
his condition as mortal man, his conduct, his moral tempera-

---

[1] *Sermones de diversis, sermo* XXV. Cf. Cassian, *Collatio,* ix. St
Bernard attaches a curious etymology to the Latin word *oratio,* which
he suggests might come from *oris ratio,* because when we pray our
mouths speak to God. *Sermones de diversis, ibid.*

[2] Cf. *Liber de diligendo Deo,* cap. iv.

[3] *In Nativitate B.V.M., De aquaeductu,* 11.

[4] *Sermones de diversis, sermo* XXIX.

[5] *De Consideratione,* lib. V, cap. iv.

[6] The book *De Consideratione* was written from 1149 to 1153.

[7] *De Consideratione,* lib. II, cap. ii. Cf. *De Imitatione Christi,* lib.
II ; the expression *consideration* is synonymous with *meditation* and
with *reflection.*

ment and the way in which he fulfils the duties of his state.[1]
Afterwards, the Pope ought to watch over his house, the
universal Church, the clergy, and even schismatics and
infidels.[2] But, above all, he should *meditate* on the divine
truths. He should think of God in himself, in the Trinity of
his Persons, of God in his dealings with the world, who
rewards goodness and punishes evil. He should also meditate
on the angels and especially on his guardian angel.[3]

But Bernard is unable to confine himself to pure theory.
When he speaks of the thoughts concerning God, his soul
immediately becomes inflamed, and, combining example with
precept, he himself makes the reflections which he recommends.

In some wonderful pages he answers the question, *Who
is God?* He touches upon the principal errors put forward
in his time on the divinity, the Trinity, and on creation. In
a word he frames his answer so as to confute such errors.
The very well defined idea which he gives of God is at once
changed to an act of love.

" Perhaps thou wilt be surprised if we ask once again who
God is, for we have already very often sought an answer,
and perhaps thou dost despair of ever knowing. Know, O
Eugenius, my Father, that God is the only being that is
never sought in vain, even though he cannot perfectly be
found. Thine own experience teaches thee concerning him,
and if it teach thee not, believe not my witness, but that of
the holy man who said : *The Lord is good to them that hope
in him, to the soul that seeketh him* (Lam. iii, 25). Who,
then, is God? He is the end of the universe, he is the salvation of the elect. . . . Who is God? He is the all-powerful
will, the power full of goodness, the light eternal, the unchangeable wisdom, the sovereign blessedness. He creates
souls in order that they may share in his life, he livens them
to give them feeling, he touches them to excite their desires,
he expands them that they may receive his good things, he
justifies them in order that they may merit, he enkindles them
to enflame their zeal, he fertilizes them that they may be
fruitful, he directs them in order that they may abide in
justice, he fashions them that they may be kind, he guides
them that they may be wise, he strengthens them that they
may be virtuous, he visits them to console them, he enlightens them that they may know, he preserves them for
immortality, he fills them with himself in order to make them
happy, he surrounds them to watch over their safety."[4]

Such consideration gives a deep knowledge of divine truths ;
it is necessary to piety. Bernard goes so far as to say that

---

[1] *id.*, lib. II, cap. iii-iv.   [2] *ibid.*
[3] *id.*, lib. I, cap. vii-viii ; lib. V, cap. iv-xiv.
[4] *De consideratione,* lib. V, cap. xi.

true piety consists in giving oneself up to consideration :
Quid sit pietas, quaeris?—Vacare consideratione. He continues to maintain the Augustinian definition of piety, which
makes it consist in the worship given to God by the fervent
Christian.[1] For without reflection the spiritual life drifts
away :

" It purifies the mind, it then directs the motions of the
soul, guides our actions, corrects our errors, regulates our
morals, renders life virtuous and well-ordered and finally
enables us to acquire knowledge of things divine and human.
Consideration it is which unravels that which is confused,
which combines that which is incongruous, which joins that
which is scattered. . . . It is consideration which foresees
what is to be done, which reflects on what has been accomplished, so that there is nothing left in us that has not been
examined or that has need of examination. Consideration it
is that in prosperity lets us foresee adversity, and in distress
enables us to sustain it."[2] Again, it is reflection or meditation which brings about that unity and magnificent harmony
between the four cardinal virtues which we so admire.[3]

St Bernard also constantly advises Pope Eugenius and all
those who have the desire for self-sanctification not to give
themselves up wholly to business without interruption, but
to keep a little of their time and a little of their soul for consideration,[4] a recommendation specially applicable to present-
day Christians, who run the risk of being carried away by the
feverish anxiety to do something, to the great detriment of
their interior life.

St Bernard, furthermore, counsels those who desire to
become perfect that, together with prayer, examination and
meditation, they watch carefully over their thoughts and
affections that they be holy, their hands that they be pure,
and their tongue that it speak no evil thing.[5]

He wishes also those who are novices in the religious life
to have a guide to teach them, to lead them and to encourage
them.[6] Without this direction they are inclined to lack discretion, " the mother of virtues," and to give themselves up
to excess of devotion, to the injury of their health and great
detriment of the religious life.[7] Besides, no one is able to
direct himself.

[1] *id.*, lib. I, cap. vii.   [2] *id.*, lib. I, cap. vii.
[3] *id.*, lib. I, cap. viii.
[4] *id.*, lib. I, cap. vii : *Non totum te, nec semper dari actioni, sed
consicerationi aliquid tui et cordis et temporis sequestare.*
[5] *De diversis, sermo* XVII.
[6] *De diversis, sermo* VIII, 7 : *Parvulis in Christo paedagogus vobis
. . . necessarius est, qui doceat, deducat, foveat vos.*
[7] *In Circumcisione Domini, sermo* III, 11 : *Discretio mater virtutum
est et consummatio perfectionis: haec nimirum docet quid nimis.*

" He who makes himself his own master," wrote St Bernard to Ogier, Canon Regular of Mont-Saint-Eloi, near Arras, " makes himself the disciple of a fool. As to this, I do not know what others think of themselves. I speak from experience, and declare that, for my part, it is easier and safer to command many others and to guide them than to rule myself alone. You have, therefore, shown prudent humility and humble prudence in recognizing your personal insufficiency in the matter of your salvation, and in the determination to live under the direction of another."[1]

Finally, St Bernard lays down the rule to be followed in order to make wise use of those sensible consolations which Christ usually employs, as caresses, to draw hearts that still hesitate to himself. We must not attach ourselves too much to these sweetnesses of devotion, which are shown rather than given to us. Many even seek them all their lives without ever having them. When we have them let us look forward to the time when we shall be deprived of them, and when they fail us let us think of joy experienced when we possessed them. Thus in the first case we shall not exaggerate our joy, and in the second we shall not be saddened beyond measure.[2]

St Francis de Sales gives similar advice. Let us repeat once more that in the writings of St Bernard we make long strides towards modern spirituality.

IV—ST BERNARD'S DEVOTION TO THE MYSTERIES OF THE LIFE OF CHRIST

This devotion is chiefly and admirably set forth in the *Sermons* for the liturgical year, or the *Proper of the Season* as it is now called.

The Cistercian Rule permits the abbot to give his monks an exhortation, sixteen times at most, on the principal feasts of the year. But the eloquence of St Bernard had such a charm, his monks had such a wish to hear him, that he was obliged to modify the custom of his Order on this point and to preach more frequently.[3] Thus he drew up a considerable number of sermons for the feasts of our Lord, the blessed Virgin and many of the saints.

The sermons were preached in the chapter hall before the choir monks and novices; the lay-brothers were preached to separately. To this select audience, Bernard was able to deliver a more exalted form of address. Mabillon states, in

---

[1] *Epist.* lxxxvii, 7 : *Qui se sibi magistrum constituit, stulto se discipulum subdit. . . . Facilius imperare et securius possum praeesse aliis multis quam soli mihi. . . .*

[2] *In Circumcisione Domini, sermo* III, 11.

[3] Cf. *In Septuagesima, sermo* III, 2; *Qui habitat, sermo* X, 6.

his preface to the *Sermons* of the Abbot of Clairvaux,[1] that, as a rule, the Homilies of the Fathers of the Church are those parts of their works prepared least carefully, because, being addressed to the people, to whom ordinary thoughts had to be suggested within the grasp of their lack of education, they were couched in a popular style. The sermons of St Bernard, on the contrary, are remarkable for their depth and for their form. They touched upon even the most lofty questions, which only those monks that were educated were able to understand.

Abundant teaching is more especially found there concerning the *mysteries* of the life of the Saviour. Bernard does not make use of this term, which was only used in this sense later on. But he well understood that every event in the life of Christ hides some lesson and merits for us some grace. With what power does he bring out this lesson! And in order to force us to implore the grace that corresponds with the mystery, Bernard knows how to stir up the feelings of the soul. It is in this that his sermons are chiefly remarkable. But to be properly appreciated, they should be read in the Latin text. The finest translation is powerless to bring out the freshness, the sweetness and the tenderness of the original.

In his sermons for Advent, St Bernard distinguishes a threefold coming of the Saviour into the world. In the first, he came in the weakness of the flesh in order to redeem us; in the second, he comes to us through his spirit and his grace to be our repose and consolation; in the third, he will appear at the end of time surrounded with glory and majesty to glorify our risen bodies.[2]

In order to touch the hearts of his hearers and to inspire them with grateful love for the divine Word, Bernard draws a picture of him in heaven, after the fall of Adam and Eve, offering himself to his Father as the Redeemer of the human race by means of his Incarnation:

" Our first parents, Adam and Eve, from whom has sprung all our race, became disobedient and guilty of theft, for at the suggestion of the serpent, or, rather, the devil, they endeavoured to take from the Son of God that which belonged to him—that is, the knowledge of good and evil. The heavenly Father did not leave unpunished the insult done to his Son, for he loves him, but immediately he inflicts chastisement on man and lays a heavy hand upon us. All we have sinned in Adam and have been condemned in him.

" What does the Son when he thus sees his Father avenge him in such a way without sparing any of his creatures?

---

[1] *P.L.,* CLXXXIII, 10.
[2] *In Adventu, sermo* V.

' Behold,' he says, ' because of me my Father loses his creatures. The leader of the angels envied my divinity, and has drawn into rebellion a multitude of his companions. My Father immediately chastised him, striking him and his adepts with an incurable wound and inflicting on them a most hard punishment. Man, in his turn, has desired to rob me of knowledge, which is, undoubtedly, my own possession; and my Father has not pardoned him and his eye has not spared him. . . . He had created two kinds of creatures gifted with reason, capable of happiness—angels and men, and behold on account of me he has condemned many angels and the whole human race. And so, that it may be known that I love my Father, I desire that he receive at my hands that which he has, in a way, lost, on account of me. . . . And so I come, and desire to show myself so that whosoever inclines towards me and desires to imitate me will perform a good work. I know that the faithless angels are chained to malice and evil, and that they did not sin in ignorance or from weakness. Moreover, those who refuse to repent must needs perish. . . . On account of this, my Father created man to take the place of the rebel angels. . . . But he hath not created any other creature in the place of man, denoting by this that man may still be redeemed. For it is the wickedness of another that has made him fall : the charity of another may, then, uplift him.' "[1]

Bernard thus loves to picture the redemption as a drama in the bosom of God. His tendency to this is still more clearly seen in the first sermon *On the Annunciation of the Blessed Virgin*. The text of this is taken from Psalm lxxxiv, *Mercy and truth have met each other; justice and peace have kissed,* as though there had been discord betwen Mercy and Truth and between Justice and Peace; a discord which the redemption had caused to cease.

" In creating man," says Bernard, " God surrounded him with these four virtues as with a vesture of salvation." Mercy was to be his companion (*pedissequa*). Truth was to instruct him and Justice to guide him. Finally, he was to enjoy peace both within himself, where the passions were in subjection, and outwardly with other creatures that obeyed him.

Through sin the first man was stripped of these divine gifts, and at the same time a serious breach of harmony arose between the virtues. Truth and Justice showed themselves pitiless towards the human race which ought to be severely chastised. Peace and Mercy, on the contrary, inclined towards indulgence.

All these were gathered together in heaven in a great con-

[1] *In Adventu, sermo* I, 4-5.

ference over which the heavenly Father himself presided,
and each one pleaded its cause. " He must be forgiven,"
said Mercy, " a creature endowed with reason deserves
pity."—" Not so," answered Truth, " the condemnation
decreed by God must be accomplished, and Adam and all
his descendants must die."—" It is all over with me," replied
Mercy, " if God never have pity on anyone."—" And with
me also," said Truth, " if the sentence of death pronounced
by God be not carried out."

The dispute being thus prolonged without coming to an
understanding, a cherub suggests submitting the matter to
the Son of God, *to whom all judgement has been given.*
Mercy and Truth thus are confronted before him and begin
to plead again with so much liveliness that Peace must needs
intervene : " It is not seemly," says Peace, " that virtues
should thus dispute." Meanwhile, the Judge, the Son of God,
stooping down, wrote with his finger on the ground. Peace
read out what had been written : " Truth says, ' I am lost if
Adam do not die,' and Mercy replies, ' I am lost if Adam be
not forgiven.' Let death become good, and both will be
satisfied." At this pronouncement heaven marvels at the
wisdom of the Judge and asks how the solution may be
reached. The Son of God answers : " Let one on whom
death has no claim die for the love of man."

Immediately Truth traverses the earth and Mercy the
heavens to seek the just Redeemer ; but he cannot be found.
Then says the Son of God, " Behold, I come ! This chalice
cannot pass unless I drink it." He sent the angel Gabriel on
earth to say to the daughter of Sion : " Behold thy King
cometh." Thus was the world saved. And on the night of
the Nativity, when the angels sang *Peace on earth to men
of goodwill,* Justice and Peace did kiss.

This dramatic staging of the dogma of the Redemption
made a wonderful impression on the minds of the Middle
Ages. This sermon of St Bernard became embodied in the
Mystery Plays as the famous " Trial in Paradise," which
ended the prologue to these religious dramas.[1] This is not
the only case in which dramatic authors have borrowed from
the works of the Abbot of Clairvaux. They also made use of
his thrilling descriptions of the crucifying of Christ and the
sorrows of his Mother at the foot of the cross. It was in
great measure in these that they found those pathetic touches
which drew tears from the witnesses of their pious tragedies.

When he speaks of the third coming of Jesus, at the end
of time, Bernard only stops at the glorification of the bodies

[1] *Meditations on the Life of Jesus Christ,* a work of the thirteenth
century wrongly attributed to St Bonaventure, reproduces this *sermon*
of St Bernard. Ludolph the Carthusian, *De vita Christi,* cap. ii, also
quotes it.

of the elect by means of the resurrection. His hearers, fervent monks, did not need to be stimulated by the terrors of the last judgement, but rather to be encouraged in the practice of bodily austerities. This body which the cloister uses so ill, which Bernard calls " the burden and prison of the soul,"[1] " the sick-bed on which we lie stretched with our moral infirmities,"[2] this body will finally be raised again at the last day.

Those who heard St Bernard had noticed with what partiality he loved to speak of Christmas night and the birth of Christ. On this subject, historians tell us,[3] he was inexhaustible and his loving soul gave vent to words of ineffable tenderness towards the divine Child. The mystery of Bethlehem was revealed to him in his early youth,[4] and it had ever since been the constant subject of his meditations.

When, on Christmas Eve, the reader of the Martyrology in the chapter hall proclaimed the birth of Christ : *Jesus Christus, Filius Dei, nascitur in Bethlehem Judae,* Bernard used to feel his soul melt, and would cry out :

" Hearken, O heavens, and thou, O earth, give ear ! Admire and sing praises, O universe, but chiefly thou, O man ! *Jesus Christ, the Son of God, is born in Bethlehem of Juda.* Must not he have a heart of stone who does not feel his soul melt at these words? What announcement can be more sweet, what more delightful can be told? *Jesus Christ, the Son of God, is born in Bethlehem of Juda.* O short words concerning the Word Incarnate, but how full of heavenly sweetness ! Love burns with the desire to express at greater length this truth, sweet as honey, but is unable to find utterance. The phrase of the Martyrology has so much charm that it would touch me far less if an iota of it were changed : *Jesus Christ, the Son of God, is born in Bethlehem of Juda.* O birth, full of honour for the world on account of its spotless sanctity, beloved of men on account of the greatness of the benefits which it gives, impenetrable even for the angels on account of the depth of the holy mystery which it hides, wonderful in every way on account of its sovereign and wholly unique novelty. For there has been nothing like it before, nor will there be again. O childbirth produced without sorrow, without shame, without corruption ; childbirth not violating, but consecrating, the temple of the virginal womb. O birth, higher than nature and taking place for the good of nature, birth high above all things on account of the greatness of the miracle which it performs, but restor-

---

[1] *In psalm. Qui habitat, sermo* VIII, 6.
[2] *In feria* iv *hebdomadae sanctae, sermo de passione Domini,* 14.
[3] *S. Bernardi vita prima,* lib. I, cap. ii, 4 (*P.L.,* CLXXXV, 229
[4] *ibid.*

ing all things by virtue of the mystery it contains.   By
brethren, who shall sufficiently proclaim for us this birth?"[1]

The Virgin brought her child into the world without pain,
as the burning bush of old threw out its flames and yet was
not consumed.[2]   In the same way that a star sends out its
luminous rays without losing its brightness, so Mary brought
forth the Word Incarnate without the least harm to her pure
virginity.[3]   The Child-God is a flower that bloomed in all its
beauty without lessening the vigour of its stem.[4]

Bernard contemplated untiringly the divine Child in his
cradle, and he makes use of every kind of tender language
to express his love for him.   " O little Child, desired of thy
little ones !"   *O parvule, parvulis desiderate!*

" This is not the time for us to proclaim the greatness and
the glory of the Lord, for the Lord has made himself small
and lovable beyond measure; yes, it is a very little child that
is born to us (*parvulus utique qui natus est nobis*).[5] . . .
Thy power, O Lord, was formerly made manifest in the
creation of the world, thy wisdom in the ordering of created
beings; but now thy merciful goodness is seen surpassingly
in thy humanity. . . .   Let thy goodness, O Lord, appear,
so that man, created in thy image, may be able to imitate
it; for we cannot imitate thy majesty, thy power, or thy
wisdom. . . ."[6]

The Abbot of Clairvaux does not weary in considering with
love beyond expression " the sweet kisses given by Mary to
the Child she nourished and smiled upon,"[7] and " the tenderness of the Babe's body (*infantilis corporis teneritudinem*)."
St Bernard sees his tears and hears his wailing (*parvuli
vagitus et lacrymas*).[8]   The stable, the manger, the swaddling
clothes, all move him to pity, and teach and edify him.

" Flee from pleasure . . . do penance," he says.   " It
is this that the stable preaches, this that the manger proclaims, this that is clearly told us by the Child's little limbs
and taught us by his tears and wailings.   For Christ weeps,
but not as other children, or not, at least, as they are wont
to do.   It is the senses that make children weep, but Christ
weeps through love. . . .   Children cry because they suffer,
Christ cries in compassion for us. . . .   He weeps for the
sins of the sons of Adam.   And, indeed, later on he will pour
out his blood for those who now draw forth his tears.   O
hardness of my heart !   O Lord, grant that as the Word has
taken our flesh, so also my heart may become a heart of flesh

---

[1] *In Vigilia Nativitatis Domini, sermo* I, 1.
[2] *Super Missus est, Homil.* II, 5.
[3] *ibid.*, 17.   [4] *ibid.*, 6.   [5] *In Cantica, sermo* XLVIII, 3.
[6] *In Nativitate Domini, sermo* I, 2.
[7] Cf. *In Assumptione B.V.M., sermo* I, 4.
In Nativitate Domini, sermo III, 1.

and melt with pity.[1] . . . It is not without mysterious reason that the Saviour was bound in swaddling clothes and laid in a manger, for these clothes are given by the angel as a sign by which we must recognize him. . . . Thy swaddling clothes, O Lord Jesus, are a sign, a sign of contradiction for many until this day. . . . I recognize thee clearly, I recognize Jesus the Great High Priest, bound in these coarse swaddling clothes."[2]

That which the infant Jesus teaches us above all things is to be afraid of God no longer. Ever since the first man fled from the presence of God and went and hid himself, we have dreaded him. Henceforth, before the manger fear yields to trustfulness.

" Why fearest thou, O man?" cries St Bernard. " Why dost thou tremble before the Lord because he comes? He does not come to judge the earth, but to save it. . . . Flee not, be not afraid. He does not come armed; he seeks thee not to punish thee, but to save thee. And now thou must no longer say, *I heard thy voice and I hid myself* (Gen. iii, 10). See, this Child cannot speak, and a wailing child prompts us much more to pity than to fear. . . . He has become a little Child, the Virgin his mother binds his little limbs in swaddling clothes, and dost thou yet tremble with fear? Know then well that he does not come to work thy ruin, but to save thee; he comes to free thee, and not to bind thee in chains."[3]

In fact, everything at the Crib speaks to us of our salvation. Doubtless the divine Child utters no word, but everything in him and around him consoles us and fills us with hope.

" *Be comforted, be comforted, my people, saith your God* (Isa. xl, 1). Emmanuel, God with us, repeats these words to us. The stable proclaims it, the Crib proclaims it, his tears proclaim it, his swaddling clothes proclaim it."[4]

The Word became a little child to heal our moral wounds and to teach us by his example to practise Christian virtue. His humility confounds our pride; his poverty, his want, and his sufferings are the condemnation of our refinement and unbridled love of pleasure. Our sickness was indeed very serious to need such a remedy in order to heal it.[5]

St Bernard gives special honour to the mystery of the Circumcision, because the Word Incarnate gave therein an extraordinary proof of his humility, he who was holiness itself, in thus submitting to a rite instituted as a remedy for the corruption of the human race.[6] He takes to himself not

---

[1] *In Nativitate Domini, sermo* III, 3. Cf. *Sermo* V, 1.
[2] *id., sermo* IV, 1. [3] *id., sermo* I, 3.
[4] *id., sermo* V, 1.
[5] *id., sermo* III, 5. [6] *In Circumcisione Domini, sermo* I, 1.

only the condition of man, as in the Incarnation, but also the condition of the sinner : *Qui non solum formam hominis sed formam habet peccatoris.*[1]

It was when he was circumcised that the Infant-God received the name Jesus. This is the real motive for St Bernard's affection for this mystery.

We know with what great love his heart was enkindled for the name of Jesus and with what sweetness he extolled it.

" My Jesus," he exclaims, " does not bear, as did his forerunners, a vain name, devoid of meaning. There is not in him the shadow of a great name, but the reality.[2] . . . When the Child which was born for us was circumcised he was called Saviour, because, in his circumcision, he began to bring about our salvation by shedding for us his most pure blood."[3]

The name of Jesus, like the name of the Spouse in the *Canticle of Canticles* (i, 2), is *as oil poured out,* able to heal our infirmities.

" Without any doubt," says St Bernard, " there are analogies between oil and the name of the divine Spouse, and it is not without reason that the Holy Spirit compares them one with the other. I find, for my part, that oil has three qualities : it gives light, it nourishes and it brings healing. . . . It feeds the fire, it nourishes the body, it eases pain. It is a light, a food, a remedy. Notice how similar is the name of the Spouse. When it is preached it enlightens us, when we meditate on it it nourishes us, when we invoke it it eases and softens our pain. Let us, then, dwell on each one of these thoughts."[4]

This beautiful theme fills Bernard with enthusiasm, and he allows his burning soul to escape in words of fire, capable of enkindling for ever the piety of the faithful.

" Whence, think you, comes the light of faith, which has shone so vividly and so rapidly throughout the world, if not from the preaching of the name of Jesus? Is it not in the brightness of this light that God has called us to his wonderful light? . . . The name of Jesus is not only a light, it is also a food. Have you not always been strengthened every time you have recalled it? What is it that satisfies the soul so much as the calling to mind of this name? What is it that invigorates once more the wearied heart, strengthens virtue, produces holy and pure morals, and inspires with chaste love? The food of the soul becomes dried up if it be not moistened with this oil; it is tasteless if not seasoned with this salt. If you write, I have no interest in your work if I read not there the name of Jesus. If you converse, if you discuss, it leaves

[1] *id., sermo* III, 3.   [2] *id., sermo* I, 2.
[3] *id., sermo* II, 3.   [4] *In Cantica, sermo* XV, 5.

me indifferent if I hear not spoken the name of Jesus.[1] The
name of Jesus is honey to my mouth, but it is also a remedy.
Which of you is in distress? Let the name of Jesus come to
his heart and from thence burst forth from his lips, and,
behold, when the light of this name appears, darkness is
dispelled and calmness restored. Should a man, fallen into
sin and despairing of the divine mercy, fling himself into the
meshes of death—if he but invoke this life-giving name, must
he not return to life? . . ."

" O my soul, thou hast enclosed within the vessel of the
name of Jesus a sure and healthful remedy, which applied to
every malady is ever effective. Let it be constantly on thy
breast, let it be always at hand, so that all thy thoughts and
all thy actions may be directed towards Jesus."[2]

The Gospel sums up the childhood, the youth and the
adolescence of Jesus in these few words : *He was subject to
them* (Luke ii, 51). Jesus was obedient to Mary and Joseph.

" Who is it that obeys, and to whom is he obedient?"
cried St Bernard, filled with admiration. " It is God that
obeys man; God, I say, to whom the angels are subject, to
whom the Principalities and Powers are obedient. God
obeyed Mary, and not only Mary, but also Joseph because
of her. Gaze with wonder at these two things, and find out
which of the two is the more admirable, the most goodly
condescension of the Son or the high dignity of the Mother.
Both astonish us, both surprise us. That God should be
obedient to a woman is a humility without parallel, and that
a woman should command God is an unequalled dignity. . . .

" Learn, O man, to obey; O earth, learn thou to submit;
learn, O dust, to be subject. The Evangelist, speaking of
thy Creator, says, *He was subject to them*—that is, to Mary
and to Joseph. Blush, O proud dust ! God humbles himself,
and thou exaltest thyself. God submits himself to man, and
thou, in thy impatient desire to lord it over man, liftest
thyself above thy Creator. . . . O man, if thou scorn the
example of other men, surely it is not beneath thy dignity to
imitate him who created thee. . . ."[3]

We must set a limit to the quotation of these passages,
however captivating they may be. In traversing the delightful
garden of the *Sermons* of St Bernard on the childhood of
Christ, we are tempted to delay. At every step we meet with
flowers more and more beautiful and with more bewitching
perfume.

[1] St Augustine (*Confessions,* lib. III, cap. iv) regrets not to find the
name of Jesus in Cicero's *Hortensius.* He adds : *Quoniam hoc nomen
secundum misericordiam tuam, Domine, hoc nomen Salvatoris mei Filii
tui, in ipso adhuc lacte matris tenerum cor meum praebiberat et alte
retinebat; et quidquid sine hoc nomen fuisset, quamvis litteratum et
expolitum et veridicum, non me totum rapiebat.*
[2] *In Cantica, sermo* XV, 6-7. [3] *Super Missus est, Homilia* I, 7-8.

Let us end with a saintly uplifting passage concerning the silence imposed by the Word Incarnate upon himself during the thirty years of his hidden life and finally broken at the beginning of his public ministry.

" Speak now, O Lord Jesus! How long wilt thou keep silence? How long wilt thou hide thyself? Thou hast held thy peace so long, yes, so very long, but now thou hast permission from thy Father to speak. How long, O Power of God, O Wisdom of God, wilt thou remain lost in the crowd like a feeble and foolish being? Until when, O noble King, O King of heaven, wilt thou suffer thyself to be known as and called the son of a carpenter? . . . O humility, virtue of Christ! O sublime humility, do thou abase our pride and vanity! Hardly do I come to know anything, or, rather, hardly does it seem to me that I know anything, but I put myself forward imprudently, and imprudently with ostentation, anxious to speak, impatient to teach others, and little inclined to listen to them. Did Christ, keeping silence so long, hiding himself for so many years, fear vainglory? What had he to fear from this, he who was the true glory of the Father? He feared, yes, but not for himself. He feared for us. . . . He warned us, he taught us. He kept his mouth closed, but he taught us by his action."[1]

Calvary had as great an attraction for St Bernard as did Bethlehem.

His biographers tell us that he used often to pray alone in his monastic church before a crucifix which he adored very devoutly and kissed with love. The hands of Christ were occasionally seen unfastened from the cross to embrace the fervent adorer.[2] This touching scene is a lively symbol of the compassionate love with which meditation on the sufferings of Christ filled the heart of St Bernard.

" For my part, my brethren," he once said to his monks, " ever since the outset of my conversion, in the place of those merits which I knew myself to lack, I have been careful to gather for myself a bundle of myrrh and place it on my breast (Cant. i, 12), a bundle formed of all the anguish and bitterness which my Lord hath undergone, first of all his privations as a child, then his labours and preaching, his

---

[1] *In Epiphania, sermo* I, 7.

[2] *S Bernardi vita prima,* lib. VII, cap. vii (*P.L.,* CLXXXV, 419-420). Among the apocryphal writings of St Bernard several are found in which devotion to the sufferings of the Passion of Christ are particularly remarkable : *Meditation on the Passion and Resurrection of the Lord* (*P.L.,* CLXXXIV, 741-768) ; *Lamentation on the Passion of Christ* (769-772) ; *Sacerdotal Instruction on the Passion, the Eucharist and Heaven* (771-792) ; *Liber de passione Christi et doloribus et planctibus matris ejus* or *De planctu Mariae* (*P.L.,* CLXXXII, 1133-1142). The influence of St Bernard is evident in all.

weariness and journeyings, his watchings in prayer, his temptation after his fast, his tears of compassion, the snares of his adversaries, his perils from false brethren, finally, the insults, spittings, blows, sarcasms and mockery, the nails and other like things, which, as the Gospel bears abundant witness, he underwent for our salvation. And among these slender stems of sweet-smelling myrrh, I have not thought fit to pass over the myrrh which was given him as drink on the cross, or that with which he was anointed for burial. He accepted the first for the remission of my sins, and by the second, he has proclaimed the future incorruptibility of my body.

" . . . To meditate on these mysteries is wisdom. For my part, I see in them the perfecting of justice, the fulness of knowledge, the riches of salvation, the treasures of merit. I sometimes draw therefrom a healthful draught of bitterness, and at other times a sweet oil of consolation. They sustain me in adversity, calm me in prosperity, and in the midst of the joys and sorrows of this present life they provide me with a sure guidance, since I walk in the royal way of the cross, avoiding the evils which threaten me from right and left. They gain for me the Sovereign Judge of the world. . . . Often also, as you know, are these mysteries in my mouth, and always in my heart, as God knoweth; my pen is quite familiar with them, as is seen. My highest philosophy is to know Jesus, and Jesus crucified."[1]

That which touches St Bernard, above all, when he meditates on the Passion of Jesus, is the extraordinary witness of love which is given therein to man.

" Perhaps someone may say : ' Might not the Creator have been able to restore his work, spoilt by sin, without imposing so much sorrow?' He could, no doubt, have done so, but he preferred to restore it at his own cost rather than provide mankind with the occasion for falling into the odious vice of ingratitude.[2] . . . Because of *his exceeding charity wherewith he loved us* (Eph. ii, 4) neither hath the Father spared the Son, nor the Son himself, in order to redeem the slave. Love truly excessive, for it surpasses all measure, it exceeds the ordinary rule, it is, indeed, superior to all. *Greater love than this no man hath,* says Jesus, *that a man lay down his life for his friends* (John xv, 13). Thou hast had, O Lord, a love still greater in dying even for thy enemies. For, whilst we were as yet thy enemies, by thy death thou hast reconciled us with thee and with our Father. What love, then, has there been or will be like to this?"[3]

---

[1] *In Cantica, sermo* XLIII, 3-4. Cf. *In Feria IV Hebdom. Sanctae, sermo de Passione Domini,* 11 ; *Sermo* XXII *de diversis,* 5.
[2] *In Cantica, sermo* XI, 7.
[3] *In Feria IV Hebdom. Sanctae,* 4.

The inconceivable abasements of the Saviour in his Passion strike the Abbot of Clairvaux with a kind of stupor. He does not know how to find words to express the emotion which the sight of so much humility causes him.

" *As many have been astonished at thee, so shall his visage be inglorious among men, and his form among the sons of men* (Isa. lii, 14). He had ceased to be *beautiful above the sons of men* (Ps. xliv, 3) in order to become the reproach of the world, and as a leper, the vilest of mortals, truly a man of sorrows, struck and humiliated by God so that he had no longer form or comeliness. O vilest of men, and, at the same time, most exalted ! O man humbled and yet so pre-eminent ! O reproach of men and still the glory of the angels ! There is none so great as he, and none more despised ; he is covered with spittle, wearied with insults, condemned to a shameful death and numbered among the wicked. What merit does not belong to such immeasurable humility ?"[1]

The forgiveness which Christ on the cross implores for his executioners brings the love of St Bernard to its highest point.

" When thou didst lift up thy hands, O Lord, and thy morning sacrifice became the burnt offering of the evening . . . thou didst cry : *Father, forgive them, for they know not what they do* (Luke xxiii, 34). O how generously dost thou pardon ! O how immeasurable is thy goodness, O Lord ! O how far are thy thoughts from our thoughts ! O how thy mercy extends even to the impious ! How can it not be admired ? Thou criest, *Forgive them,* and the Jews cry, *Crucify him.* . . . O patient and compassionate charity ! That charity should be patient is enough ; that it should be beneficent is the zenith of love."[2]

Finally, in what moving words does the Abbot of Clairvaux express his lively compassion when he speaks of Mary, whose soul was pierced at the foot of the cross, at the hour of her Son's agony and death.

" The martyrdom of the Virgin Mary took place both when the aged Simeon prophesied, and also during the passion of Jesus. *This child,* the old man said of the infant Jesus, *is set for a sign which shall be contradicted,* and addressing himself to Mary, he added, *and thy own soul a sword shall pierce* (Luke ii, 34, 35). Yea, O blessed Mother, a sword has truly pierced thy soul. It is only after having pierced thy soul that the sword of the executioner pierced the flesh of thy Son. In fact, when thy Jesus had rendered up his soul—thine, too, in a special way, although belonging to all—the cruel lance, furiously attacking a body which it could no

[1] *id.,* 3. [2] *id.,* 9.

longer cause to suffer, opened his side, without touching his soul, which had fled, but piercing thine own. His soul was no longer in his body, but thine was there, and was unable to tear itself away. A sword of pain has then pierced thy soul, O Mary, so that we may rightly proclaim thee greater than the martyrs, thee whom compassion for thy Son hath made to suffer more than all their corporal pains put together.

" Was not that word of Jesus more than a sword, piercing thy very soul even to the point of severing soul from mind? *Woman, behold thy son* (John xix, 26). What a change! John is given thee instead of Jesus, the servant in place of the Master, the son of Zebedee instead of the Son of God, a man in the place of God. How must this word have pierced thy soul, when our hearts, although hard as rock and iron, become overwhelmed by it in simply calling it to mind. Let us no longer be astonished, my brethren, to be told that Mary endured a real martyrdom in her soul. Let it astonish him who has forgotten the words of St Paul, when, speaking of the crimes of the Gentiles, he says that they were void of affection. It was not thus with the heart of Mary; grant also that it be not so with us who are her servants."[1]

The drama of the redemption ends with the glorious mystery of the resurrection and ascension of Christ. Bernard knows how to extol them in grandiloquent terms. Let us retain, by way of epilogue, this beautiful passage drawn from his second Sermon on the Ascension :

" O Lord Jesus Christ, in order to complete our faith and to render it perfect, it remains for thee to mount up to the highest heaven, in the presence of thine Apostles, lifting thyself in the air as Sovereign Master of the air. Then is it shown that thou art the Lord of all the universe, that thou hast accomplished all in all, and that henceforth at thy name every knee must bow in heaven, on earth and in hell, and every tongue proclaim that thou art in glory at the right hand of the Father. . . . In consequence of which the Apostle warns us *to seek the things that are above, where Christ is sitting at the right hand of God* (Col. iii, 1). For our treasure is in heaven, Christ Jesus, in whom are hidden all the treasures of knowledge and wisdom, *for in him dwelleth all the fulness of the Godhead corporally* (Col. ii, 9)."[2]

I have quoted at length the *Sermons* of St Bernard on the mysteries of the life of Christ, because they gave a new direction to piety. Henceforth the thoughts of faithful religious became occupied with meditation on the principal

[1] *Dominica infra octav. Assumptionis B.V.M. Sermo de duodecim stellis*, 14-15. This sermon of St Bernard inspired chapter xl of the *Augustini Meditationes* (*P.L.*, XL, 941), an apocryphal work of St Augustine, later than St Bernard.
[2] *In Ascensione Domini, sermo* II, 2.

events of the earthly life of the Saviour.[1] When devotion to
the rosary was fostered, it was only necessary to make use
of the method of St Bernard to honour the joyful, sorrowful
and glorious mysteries of the Christian religion. The mystics
of the following centuries, such as St Gertrude (1303) and
St Bridget (1373), were also inspired by St Bernard in
writing their *Revelations* on the Christian mysteries. A new
kind of writing, that of the Lives of Christ, came into being.
The preachings of the Abbot of Clairvaux, taken collectively,
form a kind of mystical biography of the Saviour. The
pseudo-Bonaventure, of the thirteenth century, in his *Meditationes vitae Christi*, and Ludolph the Carthusian, in the
following century, in his famous *Vita Christi*, were also
largely inspired by them. It may be said that all the
mysticism of the Middle Ages has yielded to the influence of
the great Cistercian orator.

V—ST BERNARD'S DEVOTION TO THE BLESSED VIRGIN

THE Abbot of Clairvaux was a most zealous servant of Mary,
a fact, perhaps, which greatly contributed to the development
of devotion to her in the Middle Ages.

Posterity has conceded to him this merit. It has looked
upon Bernard as Mary's " Cavalier." It is he who gave her
and rendered popular the beautiful name of *Our Lady*,[2] by
which since the twelfth century Catholic piety loves to invoke
the Mother of God.

Bernard has also been called the singer of Mary,
citharista Mariae, literally the *musician* of Mary ; for it may
well be called a music which he makes heard when he sings
the glories of the Queen of heaven. In his time, four feasts
of the blessed Virgin were kept—the Purification, the Annunciation, the Assumption and the Nativity. At each one of
these he showed forth to his monks the prerogatives of Mary
and her virtues. One of his first writings, *De laudibus
Virginis Matris, super verba Missus est,* was devoted to the
praise of the Virgin Mother.

When he celebrated a feast of the holy Virgin he was so
seized with rapture that he could think of nothing else.[3]

---

[1] The people in the twelfth century did not understand Latin. In
order that they might read the *Sermons* of St Bernard, translations were
made into the vulgar tongue. A translation into the dialect of Lorraine,
Li Sermon saint Bernard, made at the end of the twelfth century, has
come down to us. *Cf.* Vacandard, *Vie de S. Bernard*, t. i, p. 460.

[2] *Epist.* lxxxvi, 1 ; *In Adventu, sermo* II, 5 ; *Dominica infra oct.
Assump.,* 6, 15, etc.

[3] *Epist.* lxxxvi, 1 : *Natalis Dominae nostrae dies festus illuxerat, cujus
me totum jure sibi devotio vindicans, nihil aliud cogitare sinebat.*

The devotion of Bernard to the Virgin Mary was proverbial in the Middle Ages. The author of the *Divine Comedy* chose St Bernard to guide him near to the throne of Mary in heaven, for he knew that " the angelic Queen " would gladly welcome " her faithful Bernard."[1]

And having reached the Queen of heaven with his companions, Bernard chants a hymn in her honour, which is a heavenly echo of the sermons he formerly preached on earth.[2]

The Bernardine Mariology is summed up in his famous letter to the canons of Lyons on the Conception of Mary.

" Give as much honour as possible," the Abbot of Clairvaux recommends them, " to the virginity of the Mother of the Lord and to the holiness of her life. Admire in this Virgin her fruitfulness and reverence her infant God. Exalt her who has conceived without knowledge of concupiscence and who has brought forth without pain. Praise her whom the angels revere, whom the Gentiles desired, whom the patriarchs and prophets foretold, who was chosen from among all creatures and who is above all. Glorify the finder of grace, the mediatrix of our salvation, the restorer of the world. Finally, celebrate her who has been raised above the choirs of angels in heaven."[3]

The virginity and holiness of Mary, her divine maternity, the excellence of her virtue, her role as mediatrix between God and ourselves, finally, her glorification in the heavenly kingdom—these are the claims of the Virgin to our praise and devotion.

Mary is the first of the children of Adam who embraced virginity (*virginitatis primiceria*).[4] She is, therefore, the first to sing in heaven the new canticle reserved for virgins.[5] It is God who directly inspired her with the thought of making the vow of virginity of which the Old Testament offers no instance. The divine Word was her Master before becoming her Son.[6]

The holiness of Mary is higher than that of other saints. What is there astonishing in this, for the angel bears witness that the Lord himself was with her?

" What familiar intercourse, O my Queen, between Jesus and thee ! How greatly didst thou merit to be thus closely bound to him; indeed, more, to become his intimate friend. What signal grace hast thou found in his sight ! He abides in thee and thou in him. Thou clothest him, and he clothes thee. Thou clothest him with the substance of thy flesh, and

[1] *Paradiso*, Canto XXXI.   [2] *id.*, Canto XXXIII.
[3] *Epist.* clxxiv, 2.
[4] *In Dominica infra oct. Assumptionis*, 7.
[5] *Super Missus est, Homil.* II, 1.
[6] *id., Homil.* III, 7. Cf. *In Assumpt. B.V.M., sermo* IV, 6; *In Dominica infra oct. Assumpt.*, 9.

he clothes thee with the glory of his majesty. Thou clothest the sun with a cloud, and art thyself clothed with the sun."[1]

Mary has been so sanctified that, according to a pious belief, she never committed any personal fault. Penitence never had occasion to penetrate her most pure heart.[2] It is noticeable that this doctrine of the total exemption of Mary from all personal sin, although clearly affirmed by St Augustine, was still not regarded as certain in the twelfth century. But Bernard, full of so strong and tender a love for the Mother of God, does not hesitate to accept it.[3]

Why did he think it necessary to refuse to believe in the Immaculate Conception? He wrote his famous letter to the canons of Lyons to reproach them—and that in a very forcible manner—for having introduced the feast into their church. He considered it impossible for Mary to have been exempt from original sin; she was only sanctified from her birth, he said, like St John the Baptist, but surpassingly. For she could not be sanctified before she existed, and she did not exist before she was conceived : *Non valuit ante sancta esse quam esse, siquidem non erat antequam conciperetur.* The sanctification of Mary is, then, posterior to her conception.

To this sophism there is added, in the mind of St Bernard, a false notion—an Augustinian idea—concerning the transmission of original sin, which as yet obscured the doctrine of the Immaculate Conception. It was thought that original sin is transmitted by the concupiscence of the parents exercised in the generation of the child. Exemption from hereditary sin, therefore, could not be found except in virginal conception. Now Mary was conceived according to the ordinary laws of nature; how, then, could she be sheltered from original sin? *Quomodo peccatum non fuit ubi libido non defuit?*[4]

The perfect good faith of St Bernard is self-evident, but his error is, nevertheless, a cloud which casts a slight shadow on the reputation of this great servant of Mary. There is a pretty legend which, after his death, became current in the monasteries. At Clairvaux, St Bernard appeared one night to a very holy lay-brother in his sleep. He was clothed in brilliant whiteness, but with a black stain on his breast. The monk, very surprised and filled with sadness, said to him, " Father, what is it that I see? A black stain upon thee?"

---

[1] *In Dominica infra Oct. Assumpt.*, 6. Cf. *Super Missus est, Hom.* III, 2.   [2] *In Assumpt. B.V.M.*, *sermo* II, 8.

[3] *Ego puto quod et copiosior sanctificationis benedictio in eam descenderit quae ipsius* . . . *vitam ab omni deinceps peccato custodiret immunem, quod nemini alteri in natis quidem mulierum creditur esse donatum. Decuit nimirum Reginam virginum singularis privilegio sanctitatis absque omni peccato ducere vitam.*

[4] *Epist.* clxxxiv, 7.

" It is," he answered, " because I wrote concerning the conception of our Lady as I should not have written, that I bear thus a stain upon my breast, in token of my expiation."[1]

It must, doubtless, have cost St Bernard a great deal to have to refuse to our Lady the privilege of the Immaculate Conception, for he said that our thoughts and our words, however high they may be, are powerless worthily to express her prerogatives.[2]

In conformity with the teaching and tradition of the Catholic Church, St Bernard connects all the spiritual gifts with which the soul of Mary was endowed with the divine maternity.

This maternity was virginal, for God could only be born of a virgin, in the same way that a virgin mother could only bring forth a God.[3] Fruitful virginity is a unique privilege.

" If I extol the virginity of Mary," says St Bernard, " many other virgins that have followed her example present themselves before me. If I praise her humility, some faithful, perhaps few in number, are to be found, who, in accordance with the teaching of her Son, have become gentle and humble of heart. If I wish to glorify the extent of her mercy, there are merciful among both men and women. There is only one thing in which Mary has none like her and will never have—to taste the joys of motherhood whilst preserving her virginity."[4]

Mary's humility as well as her virginity had a preponderant part in the divine maternity. Bernard here is inspired by St Augustine :

" Wonderful blend of virginity and humility in Mary ! Her soul was pleasing to God because, in her, humility gives the prize to virginity and virginity is the ornament of humility. . . . I do not fear to say that without humility even the virginity of Mary would not have pleased God. . . . If Mary had not been humble, the Holy Ghost would not have rested on her, and if he had not thus rested, she would not have become fruitful. . . . It is then clear that before she conceived by the Holy Ghost, as she herself says, *God regarded the humility of his handmaid* (Luke i, 48) still more than her virginity. If she pleased by her virginity, it is, nevertheless, by her humility that she conceived. It is,

---

[1] Vacandard, *Vie de S. Bernard*, t. ii, p. 88.

[2] *In Assumpt. B.V.M., sermo* IV, 1 : *De ejus gloria nec silere devotio patitur, nec dignum aliquid sterilis concipere cogitatio, aut inerudita potest locutio parturire.*

[3] *Super Missus est, Homil.* II, 1; *In Assumpt. B.V.M., sermo* IV, 5.

[4] *In Assumpt. B.V.M., sermo* IV, 5. Cf. *Super Missus est, Homil.* I, 5-17.

then, true that her virginity is pleasing to God because of her humility."[1]

All the other virtues, together with virginity and humility, are in the soul of Mary in an exceptionally high degree (*caeteras quoque virtutes singulares prorsus invenies in Maria*).[2] This blessed soul is the most holy dwelling-place which the divine Wisdom has built for itself and in which it has raised seven pillars (Prov. ix, 1) which represent all the virtues. Uncreated Wisdom has so filled her with grace, that this grace overflowed from Mary's soul upon her flesh in order to render it fruitful. By a special privilege the Virgin clothed with flesh and gave to the world this wisdom itself which she had already conceived in her most pure heart.[3] God has truly set in Mary the plenitude of all goodness (*totius boni plenitudinem posuit in Maria*).[4]

The merits of Mary, then, are exceptionally great, and so also must be her glory in heaven—*Quantum enim gratiae in terris adepta est prae caeteris, tantum in coelis obtinet gloriae singularis.*

"If eye hath not seen nor ear heard nor the heart of man understood the reward which God hath prepared for them that love him, who can tell what he prepared for his Mother, for her who, without doubt, loved him more than all others?"[5]

Bernard knows not how to express himself when he speaks of the Assumption of the Virgin, the joy of the angels who receive their Queen while singing her praises, the happiness of Mary when she takes possession of her throne, and, above all, the love with which Jesus welcomes his mother.

"Is it possible to understand," he exclaims, "the glory with which the Queen of the world was surrounded when she advanced triumphantly on the day of her Assumption, the reverence and love with which the multitude of angelic legions went out to meet her, the chants they sang while they led her to her throne of glory, the joy, the calmness and the warm embraces with which she was received by her Son and placed above all creatures with the honour due to such a Mother, and in the glory suitable for such a Son to give?

"Those were sweet kisses which Mary formerly imprinted on the lips of Jesus, the child whom she nourished at her virginal breast and upon whom she smiled; but how much sweeter, must we not think, were those which she received from the lips of her Son, now seated at the right hand of the Father, on the day of her blessed reception into heaven, when

---

[1] *Super Missus est, Homil.* I, 5. Cf. *Homil.* IV, 9; *In Dominica infra oct. Assumpt.*, 11-12; *In Nativitate B.V.M. de Aquaeductu*, 12; *Tract. de moribus et offic. episc.*, cap. v, 17; *In Assumpt. B.V.M., sermo* IV, 7-8.

[2] *In Assumpt. B.V.M., sermo* IV, 6.

[3] *Sermo* LII *de diversis*, 4.   [4] *In Nativitate B.V.M.*, 6.

[5] *In Assumpt. B.V.M., sermo* I, 4.

she mounted her throne singing the canticle, *Let him kiss me with the kiss of his mouth* (Cant. i, 1)? Who can sufficiently proclaim the generation of Christ and the Assumption of Mary?"[1]

St Bernard had at heart the inspiring of his monks with a tender devotion to the Virgin, and this devotion he sums up in three principal duties—to honour the Mother of God, to pray to her with great confidence, and to imitate her virtues.

In point of honour rendered to Mary, Bernard is never satisfied. Nothing brings him greater pleasure than to speak of the merits of the Virgin Mother, yet nothing inspires him with so much fear.[2] How can we praise worthily that which is not only above human language, but even higher than thought? Also, we can never venerate Mary enough. Let us take here as our model the Son of God himself, who has so honoured his Mother, in crowning her with supernatural graces and by raising her in heaven to the dignity of Queen of the world—*Intueamini quanto devotionis affectu a nobis eam voluerit qui totius boni plenitudinem posuit in Maria.*[3]

But Bernard desires us, above all, to have filial confidence in Mary. To inspire us with this he expounds at length—and with what eloquence !—in his sermons, the doctrine of the mediation of Mary and her role in the dispensation of grace. Mary is the mediatrix between Jesus and us, between the Saviour and his Church.

Christ is doubtless the great Mediator between God and man. But we are, perhaps, afraid to go to him, for although he is man he is also God, and his humanity is somewhat absorbed by the brightness of his divinity. He is good and merciful, but he has been appointed by his Father to judge the world, and, in him, the severity of the Judge veils the clemency of the Saviour.[4]

It is not the same with Mary, who did not receive the empire of justice, but only that of goodness, gentleness and mercy. "Why, then, should frail humanity fear to have recourse to Mary? There is nothing severe, nothing terrible in her. She is all good, offering to all milk and wool. Examine the Gospel story with attention, and if you find there that Mary has been severe and hard or that she has shown anger, I grant that for the future you should beware of her and fear to approach her. But if, as I believe, everything about her

---

[1] *In Assumpt. B.V.M., sermo* I, 4.
[2] *id., sermo* IV, 5 : *Non est equidem quod me magis delectet, sed quod terreat magis, quam de gloria Virginis Matris habere sermonem.*
[3] *Dominica infra oct. Assumpt.,* 1-2. Cf. *Super Missus est, Homil.* II, 3; *In dominica infra oct. Assumpt. B.V.M.,* 15.
[4] *Dom. infra oct. Assumpt.,* 1.

speaks of affection, tenderness, meekness and mercy, thank God, who, in his kind compassion for you, has given you such a mediatrix in whom is found nothing to mistrust."[1]

Mary has given surety for Eve. The daughter has done away with the disgrace of the mother, and has paid her debt. If, indeed, man fell through woman, it is by woman also that he has been raised.[2] All creatures, moreover, have their eyes turned towards Mary, because in her and through her the merciful hand of the Almighty has remade all that he created. In Mary the angels find joy, the righteous grace, and sinners forgiveness.[3]

Mary is in every way our advocate. She is our advocate with Jesus, as Jesus is our advocate with the Father. The royal Virgin has been the way by which the Saviour came to us. We ought to strive to ascend towards him by the mediation of her through whom he came down to us.

"By thee," piously exclaimed St Bernard, "O blessed finder of grace, O Mother of life, O Mother of salvation, we have access to thy Son, in order that through thee we may be received by him who by thee was given. Let thy virginity justify us with him for the sin of our corruption, and thy humility which is so dear to God obtain us forgiveness for our pride. Let thy abundant charity cover the multitude of our sins, and thy glorious fruitfulness procure for us the fruitfulness of our merits. O our Sovereign, O our Mediatrix, O our Advocate, reconcile us with thy Son, recommend us to thy Son, present us to thy Son. Grant, O blessed Virgin, by the grace that thou didst find, by the prerogatives thou hast merited, by the mercy thou hast brought forth, grant that he who by thy mediation has deigned to participate in our weakness and our misery, may render us also by thine intercession partakers in his glory and his beatitude."[4]

The inexhaustible goodness of our heavenly mediatrix ought, then, to encourage us to have recourse to her with unlimited confidence. We cannot doubt her good will towards us, neither let us doubt her power. For, associated as she is with Jesus in the work of the redemption, she remains associated with him in that of the sanctification of souls. Mary is the dispenser of every grace.

Before St Bernard, the panegyrists had already caught a glimpse of this function of the distribution of grace. St Cyril of Alexandria taught that it was through Mary that "Christian Churches had been founded in the towns, villages

---

[1] *id., 2.* Cf. *In Nativitate B.V.M.*, 7.
[2] *Super Missus est, Homil.* II, 3 : *Curre Eva ad Mariam, curre mater ad filiam; filia pro matre respondeat, ipsa matris opprobrium auferat, ipsa patri pro matre satisfaciat: quia ecce si vir cecidit per feminam, jam non erigitur nisi per feminam.*
[3] *In Pentec., sermo* II, 4.   [4] *In Adventu, sermo* II, 5.

and islands . . . and that every faithful soul is saved."[1]
St John Damascene called the Mother of God "the dis-
tributor of the good things and the dispenser of the riches
of heaven."[2] But more precise details are lacking. In the
twelfth century the Abbot of Clairvaux expounded this
doctrine and made it popular, it may be said, throughout the
Church.

" It is the will of God that we have all things through
Mary," he says; *Sic est voluntas ejus qui totum nos habere
voluit per Mariam.*[3] And, first of all, " in view of the re-
deeming of the human race, he put in her all the price of our
redemption, which is Christ "—*Redempturus humanum genus,
pretium universum contulit in Maria.*[4] All the graces which
the Saviour has merited for us have been given us through
her mediation. She is the channel, the aqueduct (*aquae-
ductus*) by which the divine waters reach us.[5] God has made
of her in a manner a heavenly reservoir of grace, superabundant and overflowing, the overflow of which is poured
upon us.[6] Thus God has willed that nothing should be given
us that has not passed through the hands of Mary—*Nihil nos
Deus habere voluit, quod per Mariae manus non transiret.*[7]
The confidence of St Bernard is raised by this beautiful
doctrine.

" Have recourse to Mary," he recommends. ". . . My
dear children, she is the ladder of sinners, she is the motive
of my unconquerable trustfulness, she is my whole reason
for hope. What then? Can her Son reject her or suffer her
to be rejected? . . . Let us then seek for grace and seek it
through Mary, for what she seeks she finds, and she cannot
be deceived. . . .[8] Let us beseech the Mother of mercy
(*Matrem misericordiae*) to obtain for us the grace of devotion
and the fervour of charity. . . ."[9]

In our difficulties, in our sorrows and in our temptations,
let us lift our eyes to heaven towards Mary, towards the
star of the sea—*Maria . . . maris stella.* Let us again listen
to St Bernard :

[1] *Homil.* XI, *In sanctam Mariam Deiparam* (*P.G.*, LXXVII, 1033).
[2] *Homil.* I, *In Dormit. B.V.M.*, 3 (*P.G.*, XCVI, 701).
[3] *In Nativitate B.V.M.*, 7.
[4] *In Nativit. B.V.M.*, 6. Cf. *In Annuntiat. B.V.M.*, sermo III, 8;
Super Missus est, Homil. II, 7.
[5] *In Nativitate B.V.M.*, 3, 4, 8, 9, etc. This sermon is called *Sermo
de Aquaeductu.*
[6] *In Assumpt. B.V.M.*, sermo II, 2 : *Plena sibi, nobis superplena et
superfluens. In Nativit. B.V.M.*, 6 : *Si quid spei in nobis est, si quid
gratiae, si quid salutis, ab ea noverimus redundare, quae ascendit
deliciis affluens. id.*, 5 : *Nec suo potest esse contenta bono, sed . . .
petit supereffluentiam ad salutem universitatis.*
[7] *In Vigilia Nativitatis Domini, sermo* III, 10 : *Quia indignus eras
cui donaretur, datum ·est Mariae, ut per illam acciperes quidquid
haberes.*　　　　　　　[8] *In Nativitate B.V.M.*, 7.
[9] *In Dominica prima post Epiphaniam, sermo* II, 3.

" All you who feel that you are being tossed about in the current of this present age, in the midst of storms and tempests, rather than walking on the earth, turn not your eyes from this star if you do not wish to be shipwrecked. If the wind of temptation arise, if you should be cast upon the rock of trial, gaze on the star, call to Mary. If you are shaken by the billows of pride, ambition, evil-speaking or envy, gaze on the star, call to Mary. If anger, avarice, or the enticements of the flesh violently uplift the bark of your souls, look to Mary. If, dismayed at the enormity of your crimes, shamed by the hideousness of your consciences, frightened by the terrors of judgement, you begin to be engulfed in the abyss of sadness and the depths of despair, think of Mary. In danger, in anguish, in perplexity, think of Mary, invoke Mary. Let her be ever on your lips and in your hearts, and in order to obtain the help of her prayer do not fail to follow the example of her life."[1]

To imitate Mary, to follow her example, is, together with prayer, the best means of securing her protection.

" When we follow her we do not lose the way, when we pray to her we do not despair, when we think of her we do not wander. When she holds us we do not fall, when she protects us we fear nothing, when she guides us we do not weary, when she is favourable we reach the harbour."[2]

In the enthusiasm of his filial confidence Bernard does not hesitate to throw down this challenge :

" Let him never more speak of thy mercy, O blessed Virgin, who has invoked thee in his necessities without receiving thy help "—*Sileat misericordiam tuam, virgo beata, si quis est qui invocatam te in necessitatibus suis sibi meminerit defuisse.*[3]

In St Bernard's beautiful homilies are found a great number of prayers addressed to Mary; the highly emotional piety of the holy orator did not allow him to speak for long without expressing directly to the Virgin whom he loved so much the feeling which overflowed in his heart. These pious upliftings, more or less paraphrased, have become prayers that are universally used in the Church. The most famous is the *Memorare* or *Remember, O Virgin Mary.*[4] It is not

---

[1] *Super Missus est, Homil.* II, 17.
[2] *ibid.*
[3] *In Assumpt. B.V.M., sermo* IV, 8.
[4] The *Memorare*, as we now have it, was not composed by St Bernard. But it is inspired from his homilies, chiefly from the opening of No. 8 of the Fourth Sermon on the Assumption, and from the passage *Jam te, Mater misericordiae* in the middle of No. 15 of the Sermons for the Sunday within the octave of the Assumption. *Cf.* Vacandard, *Vie de S. Bernard*, t. ii, pp. 96-97. The phrase *Inviolata, integra et casta Mariae viscera* (*In Adventu, sermo* II, 4) brings to mind another well-known prayer to the blessed Virgin.

easy to say all that the Marian euchology owes to the Abbot of Clairvaux. It would be necessary to trace the pious formulas with which his heart was inspired and which passed by word of mouth for several generations until the time when they became fixed in a hymn or prayer in honour of the Virgin.

VI—ST BERNARD'S DEVOTION TO THE GUARDIAN ANGELS

In the twelfth century no one doubted the help which Christians received from guardian angels,[1] but so far Christian piety had hardly directed its attention to the subject.

The Abbot of Clairvaux, in homilies that have remained famous,[2] expounded with love and precision the ministry of the good angels in our regard, and also our duties towards them. He thus gave an impetus to devotion to the guardian angels, which only increased as time went on.

According to St Bernard, the Church herself is guarded by the angels: *O mater Ecclesia . . . custodes tui angeli sancti.*[3] Even more, each Christian edifice, each church, is entrusted to the care of the angels.[4] The heavenly spirits, in choir, blend with the psalmody of the monks.[5]

But it is the guardian angels who principally claim the earnest attention of the Abbot of Clairvaux.

God, in his infinite goodness to us, has given us angels to protect and assist us.

"*Lord, what is man,*" exclaims St Bernard, "*that thou art made known to him? or the son of man that thou makest account of him?* (Ps. cxliii, 3). Thou hast sent him thine only Son, thou hast given him thy holy Spirit, thou promisest him thy glory, and, so that nothing may be lacking in thy care for us, thou hast sent the angelic spirits to help us, charging them to protect us, ordering them to be our guides. . . . O admirable goodness of God! O love truly wonderful! . . . The Most High has commanded the angels, his angels, those sublime spirits so happy and so near his throne, his familiar and, we may say, his intimate friends. He has given his angels charge over thee. Who art thou, then? *Lord, what is man, that thou art mindful of him?* (Ps. viii, 5). . . . And what has he ordered them on thy account? . . . To protect thee."[6]

---

[1] *Cf.* Peter Lombard, *Sentent.*, lib. II, *dist.* XI (*P.L.*, CXCII, 673 ff.); *Summa Sententiarum, tract.* II, cap. vi (*P.L.*, CLXXVI, 88 ff.). St Bernard writes: *Si fidem consulas, ea tibi angelicam probat praesentiam non deesse. In ps. Qui habitat, sermo* XII, 6.

[2] *In psalm. Qui habitat, sermones* XI-XIV.

[3] *In Cantica, sermo* LXXVII, 4.

[4] *In Dedicatione Ecclesiae, sermo* IV, 2-3.

[5] *Epist.* lxxviii, *ad Sugerium Abb.*, 6; *In Cantica, sermo* VII, 5-7.

[6] *In psalm. Qui habitat, sermo* XII, 3-5.

The guardian angels constantly surround the souls of the faithful with their care.[1] They console them in their sorrow; they watch with deep attention and great charity over their interest—*Benigni siquidem sunt atque extenti in charitate . . . sedula circa nos et curam gerentes nostri.*[2] They have a great desire to lead us to the heavenly glory which they themselves possess. They defend us unceasingly against the devil and protect us from his attacks—*Adsunt ut protegant, adsunt ut prosint.* They are the intermediaries between God and us; they lay our fears before him, they offer him our vows and our prayers, and in return they bring us his grace and his gifts.[3] The faithful soul, in gratitude for so many benefits, owes his guardian angel respect, love and confidence. He should also constantly invoke him :

" *God hath given his angels charge over thee: to keep thee in all thy ways* (Ps. xc, 11). How these words should inspire thee with respect, love and confidence ! With respect for the presence of thine angel, love for his goodness, trustfulness in his care. . . . Wherever thou dost dwell, into whatsoever corner thou dost retire, have great respect for thine angel. Wouldst thou dare in his presence to do that which thou wouldst not do before me? Dost thou doubt his presence because thou dost not see him? . . . All that exists, nay, even all which is bodily, is not seen; for how much greater reason, then, do spiritual realities escape our senses, and need to be sought by the mind? If thou acceptest those things that are of faith, they prove to thee that the angels are present with us. . . ."

" Since God has given them orders in our regard, let us not be ungrateful to the angels who execute them with so much charity, and assist us in our needs, which are so great. Let us be filled with devotion and gratitude towards such guardians. Let us love them as much as we can and as we ought. . . . Let us love the angels of God, my brethren, as the future joint heirs with us in heaven, and as actually our guides and protectors, appointed by God, and our leaders. . . .

" Although we may be but little children, and the way that remains for us to pass over before we reach salvation be very long, and not only very long but also full of danger—for all that, what is there for us to fear, who are guided by such guardians? It is impossible for them to be overthrown or

---

[1] *In Cantica, sermo* XXXIX, 4-5. Cf. *De Consideratione,* lib. V, cap. v, 12 : *Angelus . . . cum anima . . . ut contubernalis animae inest.*

[2] *In Cantica, sermo* XXVII, 5. Cf. *In festo S. Michaelis, sermo* I, 3-4.

[3] *In Vigilia Nativitatis Domini, sermo* II, 5-6; *In Cantica, sermones* XXII, 5; XXXI, 5.

seduced, still less for them to seduce us, they who keep us in all our ways. They are faithful, they are prudent, they are powerful; wherefore fear? Let us follow them, let us cling to their footsteps, and we shall thus abide under the protection of the God of heaven. . . .

" Shouldst thou foresee a grave temptation or fear a great trial, invoke thy guardian, thy guide, thy refuge in oppression and in distress. Call on him and say, ' Lord, save us, for we perish.' He does not sleep, he does not slumber. . . . O my brethren, may your guardian angels be your intimate friends; be unceasingly with those who, when you often think of them and devoutly pray to them, guard and console you every moment."[1]

This pious homily, which the Church makes us read in the Breviary on October 2, has nourished, and will continue indefinitely to nourish, the devotion of the faithful towards the holy guardian angels.

VII—ST BERNARD AND ST JOSEPH

St Joseph, in the twelfth century, was not as yet the object of any devotion. In accordance with the point of view of the Fathers of the Church, he was looked upon as a personage of the Old Testament. Did he not die before the redemption was accomplished and the new law was established? His virtues were praised in the same way as those of Abraham, Jacob and Moses. St John Chrysostom, in particular, composed very eloquent homilies on the obedience of Joseph and his submission to the dictates of Providence and his devotion to the Holy Family.[2] But we nowhere find that the foster-father of Christ was given honour or prayed to by the faithful.

St Bernard began to direct thoughts and hearts towards the holy patriarch, by putting in prominent relief all his dignity and his virtues.

God, he said, honoured Joseph in the highest way by willing that he should be known as, and believed to be, the father of Jesus. This title and the responsibilities that it involved raised the holy patriarch to the highest dignity[3] and threw light on his faithfulness and prudence.

" There is no doubt that he was a good and faithful man, this Joseph, to whom the Mother of the Saviour had been betrothed. Faithful and prudent servant, I say, whom the Lord appointed as the supporter of his Mother, as the one

---

[1] *In psalm. Qui habitat, sermo XII, 6-10.*
[2] *Homilia IV in Matthaeum.*
[3] *Super Missus est, Homil.* II, 16; *Conjice . . . ex hac appellatione, qua, licet dispensatoria, meruit (Joseph) honorari a Deo, ut pater Dei et dictus et creditus sit; conjice et ex proprio vocabulo (quod augmentum non dubitas interpretari) quis et qualis homo fuit iste Joseph.*

to rear his body, and finally the one single man on earth who had been chosen to carry out the plans of his great resolve."[1]

Joseph was " the faithful guardian of the virginity of the Mother of his God." He reared the child Jesus and preserved him, " not only for himself but for the whole world " by withdrawing him from the anger of Herod. He was the " confidant of heavenly secrets " concerning the Incarnation. Is he not greater than Joseph of old who fed the Egyptians?[2]

The holy Spouse of Mary is of the race of David, whose virtues he possesses.

" He is wholly the son of David," says St Bernard, " not only according to the flesh, but by faith, by holiness, by piety. . . . Joseph, to whom, like another David, the Lord *hath made manifest the uncertain and hidden things of his wisdom* (Ps. 1, 8) and willed that he should know a mystery which no prince of the time knew; to whom it was given to see and to hear him whom many kings and prophets had desired to see and hear. It was given him not only to see and hear him, but also to carry him, guide him, embrace him, kiss him, rear him and protect him."[3]

St Bernard does not invite us to do honour to Joseph nor to pray to him. But he lays down principles which must soon prompt Christian piety to do so. If the greatness of St Joseph be such, if his virtues be so perfect, his influence in heaven must also be great. Why, then, not pray to him? Why leave in the shade one who took so considerable a part in the mysteries of the childhood of Christ? These conclusions were fully brought to light in the fifteenth century by John Gerson and by St Bernardine of Siena, and, in the sixteenth by St Teresa. Devotion to St Joseph after this could not do otherwise than increase, until its full expansion in the nineteenth century.

VIII—ST BERNARD'S MYSTICAL THEOLOGY

This is to be found, above all, in the *Sermons on the Canticle of Canticles*.

In the twelfth century, the *Canticle of Canticles* had many commentators. This book, indeed, provided a wonderful theme for mystical thought. The love of King Solomon for the Sulamite, his bride, is an expressive and graceful symbol of the love of God for the soul raised to the mystical state.[4] Moreover, the writers of the twelfth century, for whom

---

[1] *ibid.*   [2] *ibid.*   [3] *ibid.*

[4] It is not for me to deal here with the literary criticism and exegesis which have arisen in connection with the *Canticle of Canticles*. It is enough to state that this inspired book is symbolical. It expresses the love of God for the Christian soul, and the love of Christ for the Church, his mystical Spouse.

realities only counted in so far as they held hidden some divine teaching, were passionately attached to the great symbolism of the most excellent of Canticles.

Honorius of Autun wrote a commentary on this book, " of which the whole world is speaking," he says, " and few understand."[1] Richard of St. Victor, in his commentary, has very clearly explained that if the *Canticle of Canticles* contains words expressing carnal love, it is with a view to exciting us to divine love. The violence of this natural love teaches us what should be the fervour of our love for God.[2] The historians of St Thomas Aquinas tell us that his disciples, at the end of his life, begged him to explain to them the *Canticle of Canticles*.[3]

At this period, moreover, it was expected of every writer with any claim to distinction that he should write a commentary on this wonderful book, which was attracting so much attention.

William, Abbot of St Thierry, near Rheims, a disciple of St Bernard and his first biographer, visiting Clairvaux in order to recover from a long illness, expressed to his master, who was also ill, a desire to hear him explain the divine Canticle.[4] Bernard then began—it was about 1128—in private conference with his friend, his commentary. He was to develop it later and give it to his monks in eighty-four sermons. He died, in 1153, before having completed his work. Another of his disciples, Gilbert de Hoy, Abbot of Swinsed in the Diocese of Lincoln (1172), continued the commentary, without himself reaching the end of the *Canticle*.[5] It is because these orators, above all St Bernard, allowed themselves to be carried away by their eloquence and could not end. The Abbot of Clairvaux extemporized his sermon after having meditated on the text to be explained. On the spur of the moment it often happened that he abandoned his subject in order to develop a thought that came into his mind. His sermons on the *Canticle* also touch upon divers points in the spiritual life, the monastic state and even the sacerdotal ministry.

[1] *Expositio in Cantica Canticorum* (*P.L.,* CLXXII, 347).
[2] *In Cantica Canticorum Explicatio, prologus* (*P.L.,* CXCVI, 405).
[3] *Gulielmus de Thoco,* O.P., *Vita S. Thomae Aquinatis,* cap. x; *Acta Sanct. Martii,* vol. i, p. 675, Paris 1865.
[4] *S. Bernardi vita,* lib. I, cap. xii, 59; Migne, *P.L.* CLXXXV, 259. William of St Thierry made a summary of part of the *Sermons* of St Bernard on the *Canticle of Canticles* (*P.L.,* CLXXXIV, 407-436). He also wrote a treatise on the love of God and on contemplation (*P.L.,* CLXXXI, 379-408; 365-380).
[5] *Sermones in Canticum Salomonis* (*P.L.,* CLXXXIV, 11-252). Thomas the Cistercian, who lived at the end of the twelfth century, left a wordy commentary on the *Canticle of Canticles* (*P.L.,* CCVI, 21-863). *Cf.* Ch. de Visch, *Bibliotheca scriptorum ordinis cisterciensis,* Douai 1649.

St Bernard's ideas on the *Canticle of Canticles* are the same as those of Richard of St Victor. The Abbot of Clairvaux often corresponded with the monks of St Victor, and was in most things in perfect agreement with them in opinions.

The purely spiritual and allegorical sense of the book, in keeping with all the rest of their contemporaries, is the only one that they accept.[1] The *Canticle* is a little poem, a kind of mystical drama.

" We see represented there," says Richard of St Victor, " four personages or groups of personages which speak in turn—the bridegroom, the bride, the companions of the bride (*adolescentulae*), and the friends of the bridegroom. The bride is assuredly the Church; the bridegroom is Christ; the companions of the bride are those souls which enter into the spiritual life, and who, after a new development, become marriageable (*pubescentes*); the friends of the bridegroom are either the angels who dwell with him, or else perfect souls who are in the Church and who have known how to declare the truth to mortals. But the companions of the bride and the friends of the bridegroom are also the bride, because they form part of the Church. . . . Indeed, the soul which loves God perfectly is his bride."[2]

Nevertheless, the rank and dignity of bride of Christ are not bestowed at once. A preparation is needed.

" One who has newly entered into the way of happiness," adds Richard,[3] " is a companion of the bride. Let us strive to become the bride. If we are not yet able, let us at least be the friends of the bridegroom, and, if that be still too much for us, let us gather together near the nuptial bed. For, as we have said, the bridegroom and the bride are Christ and the Church. Let us imitate the friends of the bridegroom and the companions of the bride, let us listen to the words of the bride and learn from their discourse to increase in the fervour of love."

This interpretation of the *Canticle,* common in the twelfth century, is that of St Bernard. According to him also the bridegroom is Jesus, the bride is the Church and the fervent soul, the companions of the bride are those souls, still imperfect, which aspire to the rank of brides, the friends of the bridegroom are the angels.[4] Before becoming a bride it is necessary to begin by being the companion of the bride; the exercises of asceticism, in fact, must precede the sweetness of mystical union. In his commentary, the Abbot of Clairvaux also deals fairly often with Christian mortification, with

[1] St Bernard, *In Cantica, serm.* LXIII, 1; LXXV, 2; LXI, 2; XXXII, 1. Richard of St Victor, *In Cant. Cant., prologus.*
[2] Richard of St Victor, *ibid.*   [3] *ibid.*
[4] St Bernard, *In Cantica, serm.* I, 8; VII, 8; XIV, 5.

the destruction of vice and the development of virtue, in a word, with that which the companion of the bride must do in order to become herself a bride and enjoy the mystical embrace of the bridegroom.[1]

The mysticism of St Bernard is not presented in synthetic form; it is expounded in an oratorical way. It is, moreover, not scientific but essentially practical.

Contrary to that of St Augustine and of the pseudo-Dionysius, the neoplatonic theories are wholly absent, as likewise is scholastic philosophy. The Abbot of Clairvaux speaks of mystical facts according to his personal experience and that of the monks whose confidences he had received. He adapts this experience in his commentary on the *Canticle of Canticles,* the allegorical interpretation of which he accepts, as it was everywhere adopted in his time. His mysticism, therefore, is purely and simply his own. It is this which adds to its interest.

St Bernard first speaks of the preparation for mystical union through spiritual love, and then endeavours to describe this union itself.

According to the particular views of the Abbot of Clairvaux, mystical love passes through three phases. In the first it is sensible—*carnalis*—that is to say, it has for its object the humanity of Christ and the mysteries of his mortal life. This sensible love, in its progress, becomes rational—this is the second phase—by becoming absorbed in the teachings of the faith concerning the Saviour and by rejecting all error. Finally, it becomes spiritual when it has as its object God himself.[2]

We are aware of the great importance which this sensible love had in the spirituality of St Bernard, and how it wholly inspired his devotion to the mysteries of the mortal life of Christ. Is it not this love, above all, which nourishes affective piety, in which the Abbot of Clairvaux so excelled?

And yet this sensible love, which attaches itself to the humanity of Christ, is considered as an inferior love, as a ladder by which we are raised to spiritual love.[3] It is because man can only approach the spiritual through the sensible that he begins by loving the body of Christ.

" In reality," continues St Bernard, " although this devo-

[1] St Bernard expounds his mystical theology by commenting on the *Canticle of Canticles.* He thus makes use of daring expressions and images. True mystics, holy persons, are dead to the life of the senses and only live for God. He expresses the violence of divine love which consumes them by the aid of comparisons the startling nature of which might occasionally surprise the profane.

[2] *In Cantica, sermo* XX.

[3] *id., sermo* VI, 3 : *Obtulit carnem sapientibus carnem, per quam discerent sapere et spiritum.*

tion to the humanity of Christ be a gift, and a great gift, of the Holy Ghost, the love which inspires it is none the less sensible (*carnalem tamen dixerim hunc amorem*), as compared with that other love which is not so much connected with the Word made flesh as with the Word of Wisdom, the Word of Justice, the Word of Truth, the Word of Holiness."[1]

St Bernard admits that in the beginning of his conversion sensible love alone could move him. And even long afterwards he was filled with shame that someone who was dear to him touched him more than the thought of God.[2] But he strove with all his strength after spiritual love which has no longer the humanity of Christ as its object, but his divinity, and this love alone is able to bring about mystical union.

Cassian, in the fifth century, also taught that those who are raised to perfect prayer no longer contemplate, at the moment of union, the humanity of Christ, but " that they contemplate his divinity with most pure eyes "—*illi purissimis oculis divinitatem ipsius speculantur*.[3] He thus interprets the following text of St Paul : *Wherefore henceforth we know no man according to the flesh. And if we have known Christ according to the flesh: but now we know him so no longer* (2 Cor. v, 16).[4] Mystical contemplation, then, should not have as its object the humanity of Jesus. It unites the soul to God to the exclusion of everything else. Mystics are practically unanimous on this point.[5] When St Bernard describes mystical union, he does not speak of the humanity of Christ; it remains an object of sensible love. For, he says, this union is wholly spiritual.

" Be careful to think of nothing corporal or sensible in this union of the Word with the soul. Let us call to mind here what the Apostle says, *He who is joined to the Lord is one spirit* (1 Cor. vi, 17). The rapture of the pure soul in God or the holy entrancement of God in the soul is expressed by us as best we can in our poor words, *comparing spiritual things with spiritual* (1 Cor. ii, 13). It is in the spirit that this union takes place : *In spiritu fit ista conjunctio*, because

---

[1] *id., sermo* XX, 8.   [2] *id., sermo* XIV, 6.

[3] *Collatio* X, *de oratione*, cap. vi (*P.L.*, XLIX, 826-827).

[4] Cassian (*De Incarnatione Christi*, lib. III, cap. iii) interprets this text differently : " We no longer know Christ according to his flesh weak and mortal, but according to his flesh spiritualized and absorbed by the divine Majesty " (*P.L.*, L, 52-54). But he does not say that the humanity of the risen Christ may be the object of mystical contemplation.

[5] It is only at the actual moment of mystical contemplation that the humanity of Christ is excluded. At other moments mystics ought to perform their duty towards the humanity of Christ. There exists no spiritual state, however perfect it may be, in which the humanity of Christ ceases to be the necessary means of approaching God. *Cf.* Bossuet, *Instruction sur les états d'oraison*, second treatise, chap. ix ff., Paris 1897.

God is a spirit and because he is enamoured of the beauty of
a soul which he finds walking according to the spirit and not
following the desires of the flesh, and, above all, wholly on
fire with divine love.[1]

When the soul after being completely purified is solidly
established in spiritual love, it is able, if called by God,[2] to
be raised to mystical union. It is *nubile: Ad nubiles quodam
modo pervenerit annos;*[3] it becomes the bride of the Word,
Conjugem Verboque maritatam; it contracts with him a
spiritual marriage, *spirituale matrimonium.*[4]

" Having reached this degree of love, the soul may venture
to think of spiritual marriage. And why should it not? It
is so much the more nubile as it sees itself the more like God.
That soul that is brought near to him by resemblance, united
to him by love, and whom the bridal state marries to him, is
not afraid of the greatness of the bridegroom. . . . When,
then, you see a soul, having left all, united to the Word,
living by the Word, guided by him, conceiving through the
Word what it should bring forth for him (*de Verbo concipere
quod pariat Verbo*), one who is able to say, *For to me to
live is Christ and to die is gain* (Phil. i, 21), know that that
soul is the bride of the Word and that it has contracted a
spiritual marriage with him."[5]

St Bernard makes use of most forceful images from the
Canticle of Canticles in order to describe this extraordinary
union of the holy soul with God.

Like all spiritual writers, he teaches that this union is
brought about by love which has reached such a degree that
the will of the Christian is fully identified with the divine will :

" Such conformity with the divine will marries (*maritat*)
the soul to the Word, to whom it is like by its spiritual
nature, and to whom it is not less like by its will, loving him
as it is loved by him. Then, if it love perfectly, it is a bride.
What is there sweeter than this conformity of wills? What
more desirable than that love which makes thee, O soul,
discontented with the teachings of men, to go with confidence
to the Word? Thou remainest united with him, thou dwellest

---

[1] *In Cantica, sermo* XXXI, 6. St Bernard always speaks of the Word,
and not of Christ, in connection with mystical union. St Augustine
and Dionysius also speak of God and not of Christ.

[2] *De diversis, sermo* LXXXVII, 2. St Bernard clearly teaches the
necessity of a special call in order to be raised to mystical contemplation : " *Osculetur me osculo oris sui.*" *Ac si diceret: ego non viribus
meis, non industria, non meritis ad contemplanda gaudia Domini mei
assurgere valeo; sed ipse " osculetur me osculo oris sui "; id est ejus
gratia fiat; non per doctrinam, non per naturam, sed per gratiam suam
" osculetur me osculo oris sui.*"

[3] *In Cantica, sermones* I, 12; LXXXV, 12.

[4] *id., sermones,* LXXXV, 12, 13; LXXXIII, 3.

[5] *id., sermo* LXXXV, 12.

familiarly with him, thou consultest him on all things, daringly desirous of knowing as much as thy intelligence is able to understand. This contract of marriage is always spiritual, always holy. To say *contract* is not enough, it is an *embrace (complexus)*, a veritable embrace, in which the identification of the two wills makes of the two minds one only same thing."[1]

This identification, brought about through love, renders everything common between the Word and the soul, as between bride and bridegroom, " who have nothing belonging to them singly, but who have one and the same table, one and the same bed, and also one and the same flesh."[2] The soul may truly say with the bride in the *Canticle of Canticles,* however bold it may seem, *My beloved to me and I to him (Cant.* ii, 16).[3]

Such is the state of the soul raised to the dignity of the bride of the Word, and most closely united to him.

It remains for us to speak of the extraordinary and supernatural manifestations of this union which usually accompany his spiritual marriage with the soul, and which are, in the words of the *Canticle of Canticles,* like the kisses of the bridegroom. By this is meant mystical contemplation, rapture and ecstasy.

St Augustine, raised to the mystical state, passionately desired to see God and to contemplate him. The bride of the Word, according to St. Bernard, also ardently sighs after the kiss of the bridegroom : " *Let him kiss me with the kiss of his mouth (Cant.* i, 1) she says. Who says this? The bride. What bride? The soul who has a burning thirst for God. . . . She asks for neither freedom, reward, inheritance any more than knowledge, but for a kiss. . . . Notice the urgency of her request. She begs a great favour from a high personage, yet does not make use, as in the ordinary way, of flattering words and roundabout speeches. No preamble, nothing in the way of ingratiation, but in fulness of her heart, in all freedom and daring, these words suddenly burst forth, *Let him kiss me with the kiss of his mouth.*"[4]

Then is the soul brought into the chamber of the King, into that mysterious retreat in which she is wholly retired within herself. All intercourse between her and the outer world is suspended. There is perfect tranquillity within and about her—*Tranquillus Deus tranquillat omnia.*

" If perchance anyone among you," said Bernard to his

---

[1] *In Cantica, sermo* LXXXIII, 3.
[2] *id., sermo* VII, 2. Cf. *sermo* XLVI, 4.
[3] *id., sermo* LXVIII, 1, 2. St Gertrude spoke of the spiritual marriage in similar terms (*Revelations,* Book IV, chap. xxix, etc.).
[4] *In Cantica, sermo* VII, 2.

monks, " has been drawn into this secret place, this sanctuary of God, and hidden there for one hour in such manner as neither to be in any way distracted, nor disturbed by the needs of the senses or the sting of anxiety or the remorse of conscience, nor, which is still more difficult, by the phantom of sensible images; such an one when he will have returned to us will be able to glorify himself and to say, *The king hath brought me into his storerooms (Cant.* i, 3)."[1]

St Augustine, the pseudo-Dionysius, and all the mystics also describe this suspension of the faculties of the soul at the moment of ecstatic contemplation. The soul is so wholly absorbed that it is oblivious to what is going on around it. All activity is concentrated on God who is possessed within it.

It is, indeed, this sensible possession of God in the soul, flooding it with joy, in which lies the essential manifestation of mystical union. It is the kiss of the bridegroom. St Bernard makes an attempt, in halting words, to show us something of the bride thus reposing in the arms of the bridegroom :

" *I adjure you, O daughters of Jerusalem . . . that you stir not up, nor make the beloved to awake till she please (Cant.* ii, 7). The heavenly Spouse, in his ardent desire not to disturb the repose of his beloved, leaves her to sleep in his embrace, and suffers nothing to interrupt this most sweet slumber. I cannot contain myself for joy at the sight of the divine majesty deigning to stoop to our weakness in so familiar and delightful a union, in which the supreme God contracts marriage with the soul exiled here below and desires to bear witness to that love towards her with which he is smitten. Thus, I doubt not, thus is heaven ! I read in holy Writ—and the soul, the bride of Christ, realizes the whole truth of these words—that it is impossible to express the happiness that is experienced there. But the soul is also incapable of telling the joy that she feels now united to the bridegroom. What more shall that soul receive, I ask you, that here below enjoys God so familiarly that she feels herself clasped in his embrace, warmed on his breast, and so carefully guarded lest her sleep be broken before she awake?"[2]

But if the bride sleeps, her heart watches (*Cant.* v, 2). This sleep of the senses and the imagination is ecstasy— *Dormitio est quae tamen sensum non sopiat sed abducat. Est et mors. . . . Proinde et ego non absurde sponsae ecstasim vocaverim mortem (illam).*[3] The mind of the bride remains active. It receives an interior brightness which enlightens it—*Vitalis vigilque sopor sensum interiorem illuminat,*[4] and causes it to acquire an extended knowledge of

---

[1] *In Cantica, sermo* XXIII, 16. Cf. *sermo* XLV.
[2] *In Cantica, sermo* LII, 2.   [3] *ibid.,* 3-4.   [4] *ibid.,* 3.

Christian mysteries.[1]   St Augustine and the pseudo-Dionysius
also said that in contemplation the truths of faith are shown
to the soul with so great certainty that it is impossible to doubt
them.

This activity of the mind is occasionally raised to a state
of paroxysm; the divine light becomes superabundant and the
vision of God takes place.   This vision is produced without
the help of the imagination, which remains completely inactive.[2]   It is of short and rapid duration, like lightning—
*Cum autem divinitus aliquid raptim et veluti in velocitate
corusci luminis interluxerit menti spiritu excedenti.*[3]

We here again find that famous contemplative vision of
God of which St Augustine and the pseudo-Dionysius spoke
so much.   But St Bernard does not picture it in their way.

As opposed to their teaching, he believes that this vision is
not direct nor immediate.   He makes use of certain expressions of St Paul, and declares that this vision takes place as
in a mirror and in an obscure manner, and not face to face—
*Per speculum siquidem et in aenigmate, non autem facie ad
faciem intuetur.*[4]   The bride, he says, who would see her well-
beloved has need to be decked with those chains of gold
of which the *Canticle of Canticles* speaks (i, 11)—that is to
say, with the resplendence of the divinity, *Aurum divinitatis
fulgor,*[5] which allows her to contemplate God.   It is nothing
other, as I think, he adds, than spiritual images,[6] suggested
to the soul by the angels, the heavenly goldsmiths, and these
images allow of the contemplation of the divine Wisdom
through their mediation.   Bernard goes so far even as to
think that the images may be sensible.   But they are produced
through celestial spirits and not through the imagination,
which is always inactive; the soul is thus less blinded by the
brightness of this dazzling vision.[7]

The Abbot of Clairvaux, then, rejects the teaching of the
ancient mystics, according to which the vision of God in
contemplation is purely intellectual and is produced without
the help of any image or any mediation.   According to him,
it is only in heaven that God is seen; here below he is only

[1] *id., sermones VII-VIII.*

[2] *id., sermo LII, 5 : Moriatur anima mea morte etiam (si dici potest)
angelorum, ut praesentium memoria excedens, rerum se inferiorum cor-
porearumque non modo cupiditatibus, sed et similitudinibus exuat,
sitque ei pura cum illis conversatio, cum quibus est puritatis similitudo.
Talis (ut opinor) excessus aut tantum, aut maxime contemplatio dicitur.*

[3] *id., sermo XLI, 3.*   Cf. *sermo XVIII, 6.*

[4] *In Cantica, sermo XVIII, 6.*   [5] *id., sermo XLI, 2.*

[6] *ibid., 3; Spirituales similitudines.*

[7] *ibid., Adsunt imaginatoriae quaedam rerum inferiorum similitudines, infusis divinitus sensis convenienter accommodatae, quibus
quodam modo adumbratus purissimus ille ac splendidissimus veritatis
radius et ipsi animae tolerabiliter fiat. . . . Existimo tamen ipsas
formari in nobis sanctorum suggestionibus angelorum.*

contemplated by faith : *Auditus ad meritum, visus ad praemium.*[1] The light of faith, no doubt, casts extraordinarily
vivid enlightenment on the soul of the contemplative; but God
does not show himself unveiled as regards the mind; he
remains at least in part obscured. This is why mystical contemplation is not an act of vision of God, properly so called.
It still belongs to the domain of faith, though bordering on
sight.

Furthermore, St Bernard makes use of the expression *vision*
in order to explain the phenomenon of contemplation. It is the
term which best expresses that act by which the contemplative,
flooded with divine light, apprehends supernatural realities.

The soul that is favoured with this *vision* enjoys a great
calm and a sweet peace.

" This vision," says St Bernard, " does not startle, but
calms; it does not over-excite through curiosity, but satisfies;
it does not tire, but brings repose. It is quietude in a true
sense."[2]

During mystical union, whether accompanied by the vision
of God or not, the soul is inebriated with delights. It
sings the canticle of love. It sings without motion of the
lips, without employing words, for this canticle consists in
the mutual joy of the bridegroom and the bride.

" This canticle," says Bernard, " is taught only by *grace,*
and the idea of it can only be obtained by experience. Those
who have felt it know, those who do not know burn with
desire not so much to understand as to experience it. It
consists not in words of the mouth, but in a song of the heart;
nor is it a sound with the lips, but a movement of joy. It is
the harmony not of voices but of wills. It is not heard from
without, for it resounds not in public. They alone, the one
who sings it and he to whom it is sung, that is, the bride and
bridegroom, are able to hear it. For it is indeed a nuptial
song, expressing the chaste and sweet embrace of minds, the
concord of feeling and mutual and loving harmony of desire."[3]

Cassian[4] and the Fathers of the desert also experienced this
silent prayer of the heart, produced by the Holy Spirit and
expressed without utterance, without movement of the tongue
or pronouncement of words.

St Bernard, together with all mystical writers, teaches that
mystical union is a phenomenon of short and intermittent
duration. According to his personal experience it is rare.
Heu! rara hora, et parva mora.[5] How he yearns for it to be
renewed !

[1] *In Cantica, sermo* XXVIII, 5.
[2] *In Cantica, sermo* XXIII, 16.
[3] *id., sermo* I, 11.   [4] *Collatio* IX, 25, 15.
[5] *In Cantica, sermo* XXIII, 15. Cf. *sermo* LXXXV, 13.

" When the Word withdraws, the soul has but one only cry which it constantly utters, but one yearning which it expresses unceasingly, but one word which it ever repeats until he returns—*revertere,* come back !"[1] Such moments are most sweet : the joy experienced is so great—*Subito tanta mihi . . . infusa laetitia est !*[2] There we are sheltered from temptations and from sin. " For the soul in rapture, even though it do not depart this life, departs from the life of sense ; temptation can be felt no longer."[3] In the same way, St Augustine said that in contemplation the vanity of earthly things becomes clearly apparent to the soul, and their beauty was ugliness and disenchantment. Also, he desired to die in order to enjoy God without interruption ; and Bernard, after similar heavenly favours, wished to die for the same reasons.

" Here the soul experiences the vicissitudes of the visits and absences of the Word, as he formerly said : *I go away, and I come again unto you* (John xiv, 28). *A little while and now you shall not see me: and again a little while and you shall see me* (xvi, 16). O this little while, this little while ! O this little while that is so long ! Sweet Lord, thou findest the time short which we must wait before we see thee. With all respect for thy word, it is long, yea, very long. But it is both short and long ; short as regards my merits and long as regards my desire."[4]

St Bernard seems to feel a kind of shame in speaking publicly to his monks of the spiritual favours granted him by God. Moreover, he does not explain them completely. He has even the fear of being deceived in describing such exalted phenomena, and he listens to the accounts of what others have experienced by way of counter-proof.

" Who is wise enough to understand these things," he once said to his religious, " to the extent of being able to distinguish them as we should from one another, to state precisely each of them and to explain them to others in such a way as to give a clear idea of them? If I were asked that, I should decline, preferring to hear the explanation from one who had made trial of them and had had a long experience. But since such a one, no matter who he may be, through modesty and reserve (*verecunde*) would rather hide what happened in the inwardness of his soul, and thinks it better to keep the secret to himself, I, who speak through duty and because I am not able to keep silence, state that which I know from my own experience and by that of others, and many might easily experience, leaving the higher mystical states to those who are able to understand them."[5]

---

[1] *In Cantica, sermo* LXXIV, 2, 3-4. Cf. *sermo* XXIII, 15 : *O si durasset! iterum, iterum visita me Domine!*
[2] *id., sermo* XXIII, 15.   [3] *id., sermo* LII, 4.
[4] *id., sermo* LXXIV, 4.   [5] *In Cantica, sermo* LVII, 5.

That which Bernard knows full well is how to speak of the love of God, of that mystical love which produces such incomprehensible marvels in souls. His commentary on the *Canticle of Canticles* is, it may well be said, a continuous hymn in celebration of heavenly and divine love. Listen to this :

" Love receives its name from loving and not from honouring. We honour when we are astonished, when we are dazzled, when we fear or admire; all that disappears when we love. Love suffices for all things in itself. When it enters into a heart it absorbs and captivates all other feelings. That is why the bride that loves, just loves and knows nothing else. The bridegroom, doubtless, deserves to be honoured, to be greatly admired; nevertheless, he prefers to be loved. This is to be bride and bridegroom. What other duty and what other bond do you seek between them if not to love and to be loved? This bond of love is stronger than all others that nature has formed, such as that which unites parents with children; since *man shall leave father and mother and shall cleave to his wife* (Gen. ii, 24). . . .

" To this may be added that the bridegroom, here, not only loves but is love itself . . . for God is love (1 John iv, 8). . . . Love seeks neither its source nor its fruits outside itself. The fruit of love is love. I love because I love. I love in order to love still more. Love is great provided that it always return to its cause, that it go back to its starting-point, that it be driven towards its source, ever to draw thence the waters which it pours out unceasingly. Love is the only one of all the motions, affections and feelings of the soul by means of which the creature is able to treat with the Creator, if not on an equal footing, at least by giving him something resembling what is given. For, if God be angry with me can I be as angry with him? . . . If he accuse me, I cannot in turn accuse him without being overwhelmed. . . . Behold how otherwise it is with love. When God loves he only wishes to be loved; he only loves in order to be loved, knowing that love will render all those that love him happy.

" O how great is love ![1] . . . O divine love, impetuous, vehement, all on fire and irresistible, which gives not a thought to anything other than thyself, disdaining all the rest, despising all, provided that thou thyself be satisfied! By thee is distance suppressed, custom ignored, moderation unknown. . . . It is love that speaks throughout this *Canticle of Canticles*. If we would understand what is read there, we must love. In vain should we read this song of love, in vain listen to it, if we love not; a cold heart cannot understand words full of fire, just as we cannot understand discourses in Greek, Latin, or any other language without knowing those

[1] *In Cantica, sermo* LXXXIII, 3-5.

languages. Thus the language of love for the one who loves not is a barbarous tongue. . . . Those that have received the Holy Spirit of grace love to understand its language, and, to its words of love which are so well known, they at once answer in the same language—that is to say, by works of love and piety."[1]

IX—THE PRIESTHOOD: QUALITIES IT CALLS FOR

In those sermons on the *Canticle of Canticles* in which he speaks of mystical love, St Bernard often speaks of the sacerdotal apostolate, and particularly of the ministry of preaching. And, assuredly, the exercise of the pastoral office is indeed a work of love; it is, according to the idea of St John Chrysostom, a great witness of affection for Christ and of charity towards the faithful.

The teaching of the Abbot of Clairvaux on the pastoral ministry may be found summed up in this beautiful passage from one of his sermons, in which he speaks of zeal :

" May charity fire thy zeal, knowledge enlighten it, and strength render it secure. Let thy zeal be ardent, let it be prudent, let it be unconquerable. Let it be active, let it be discreet, let it be fearless. Note well that these three qualities of thy zeal are expressed in this precept of the law. God said, *Thou shalt love the Lord thy God with thy whole heart, and with thy whole soul, and with thy whole mind, and with thy whole strength* (Mark xii, 30). It seems to me—at least, until a better explanation of this triple distinction be found— that the love of the heart refers to the zeal of charity, the love of the soul to its being ruled by reason, and the strength of love to its constancy and solidity."[2]

Divine love is, indeed, the nourishment of pastoral zeal. Pastors and those who have the care of souls should be the very dear friends of the heavenly bridegroom : *Amici sponsi . . . at parum dixi amici, amicissimi sint oportet, qui privilegio tantae familiaritatis donantur.*[3]

---

[1] *id., sermo* LXXIX, 1. Cf. *De Imitatione Christi*, lib. III, cap. v, 23 : *Si quis amat, novit quid haec vox clamat.* The whole of this chapter would seem to be inspired by St Bernard. The Abbot of Clairvaux also calls to mind the ecstatic virtue of love when he says that the soul is much more in that which it loves than in the body which it animates : *Neque enim praesentior spiritus noster est ubi animat quam ubi amat* (*De praecepto et dispensatione,* cap. xx).

[2] *In Cantica, sermo* XX, 4 : *Zelum tuum inflammet charitas, informet scientia, firmet constantia. Sit fervidus, sit circumspectus, sit invictus. Nec teporem habeat, nec careat discretione, nec timidus sit.* Cf. *sermo* XLII, 4. St Bernard says the same in his *Sermon on the Nativity of St John the Baptist,* 3 : *Est enim tantum lucere vanum, tantum ardere parum et lucere perfectum.*

[3] *In Cantica, sermo* LXXVI, 7.

They should be men of prayer, devoted to meditation on divine truths; they should pass from the restfulness of mystical contemplation to the duty of preaching : *Nitendi ad contemplationis quietem labor praedicationis imponitur.*[1] It is during these intimate communings with the Lord " that grace comes, that the bosom expands, that the breast is filled with a torrent of piety, from which there flows in abundance an excellent milk "[2] for the nourishment of souls.   The apostle, then, should be at once a contemplative and a man of action.

St Bernard in proffering this counsel gives a picture of himself :

" It is characteristic of true and pure contemplation," he says, " for the soul that is kindled thereby with divine fire to be occasionally so filled with ardent zeal and with so lively a yearning to give to God souls that love him fully, that it most willingly abandons the repose of contemplation for the labour of preaching.   Then, when its ardour is satisfied, it goes back to contemplation with so much the more eagerness in that it remembers to have left it with greater fruit.   In the same way, after having tasted anew the charms of contemplation, it sets itself with fresh courage to make further conquests for God."[3]

For the sweetness of these communings with God ought to incline the preacher always to prefer the state of Mary to that of Martha.[4]   But he must also go to souls.   Pastors have to guard the city of God, to deck and adorn the bride of Christ, to tend and to direct his sheep.[5]   They must not live for themselves, but for all : *Nec cuiquam sibi, sed omnibus vivendum.*[6]   They should not think of their own comfort but of the salvation of their flock, for they are physicians and not lords—*Medicos se et non dominos agnoscentes;*[7] also they should love souls much and treat them with great gentleness.

"Know," St Bernard tells them, " that you must be mothers to those that are submitted to you and not masters.   If, from time to time, severity must be employed, let it be fatherly and not tyrannical.   Show yourselves mothers in encouragement and fathers in correction. . . .   Why make heavy the yoke of those whose burdens you ought rather to carry?   Why should this little child, bitten by the serpent, avoid the priest, when he ought to fly to him as he would to the breast of his mother?"[8]

As to the knowledge which the zealous preacher ought to possess, St Bernard recommends that it be sought in prayer and in meditation.   Strictly speaking, this knowledge is that

---

[1] *id., sermo* XLI, 5.
[2] *id., sermo* IX, 7.
[3] *In Cantica, sermo* LVII, 9.
[4] Cf. *sermo* LVII, 11.
[5] *id., sermo* LXXVI, 8-9.
[6] *id., sermo* XLI, 6.
[7] *id., sermo* XXV, 2. Cf. *serm.* XXIII, 12 ; XXXIII, 15; LXXVII, 1.
[8] *id., sermo* XXIII, 2.

of contemplation; the profane writers are not able to give it.[1]
We are acquainted with the ideas of the Abbot of Clairvaux
on this point. In this contemplative prayer, the mind receives
the light which it needs and the heart is filled with love; an
irresistible eloquence is thus prepared.

But this prayer should be incessant, for the true preacher
gives only of his overflow.

Bernard here expounds an important teaching by the help
of a most expressive image. The pastor of souls, he says,
if he properly understand his mission, will make of himself
a reservoir and not a canal—*si sapis, concham te exhibebis et
non canalem.*[2] For the canal pours out all that it has as it
receives it; the reservoir, on the contrary, waits until it is
full, and then gives of its overflow without hurt to itself.[3]
The Abbot of Clairvaux thinks, rightly, that it is necessary
to begin with the sanctification of one's own soul before thinking of sanctifying those of others. Those pastors who set
aside no time for prayer and meditation soon become dried
up and incapable of spreading the waters of salvation to
others.

If the roots of zeal are to be found in charity, and if it be
nourished by contemplative prayer, it must of necessity be
disinterested and solid. It should also be discreet, and this
is provided for it by true knowledge.

" Zeal without knowledge is insufferable. When love is
very ardent, discretion, which regulates charity, is specially
needful. Zeal unenlightened by knowledge always loses its
force, and at times becomes harmful. . . . Discretion,
indeed, regulates all virtues, and thus renders them moderate,
beautiful and lasting. . . . It is not so much a virtue itself
as the chastener and guide of the other virtues . . . take it
away, and virtue is changed to vice."[4]

St Bernard not only spoke of the qualities required for
pastoral zeal; he also pointed out, on several occasions, the
virtues necessary for those who are called to exercise it.

The future bishop must be pious and versed in the study of
holy Scripture; piety should always be greater than knowledge.[5]

Innocence preserved, or, at least, recovered by sincere
repentance, appears to be essential for him who would aspire
to the guidance of souls. Should he not begin by taking care
of his own conscience before being occupied with those of
others? *Rectus ordo requiret ut prius propriam deinde alienas
curare studeas conscientias.*[6]

[1] *In Cantica, serm.* XLI, 6, 8; XXIII, 6; XXXVI, 4.
[2] *id., sermo* XVIII, 3.   [3] *ibid.*
[4] *In Cantica, sermo* XLIX, 5. Cf. *sermo* XXIII, 8.
[5] *Epist.* ccl, 2.   [6] *Epistola* viii, 1.

Before undertaking the episcopal office, it is necessary to consult God by prayer in order to learn the *secret of his counsel* and to find out if one is called to this high estate. For " who can know whether he be called or no, except the Holy Spirit who knows the divine secrets, or he to whom they have been revealed by this same Spirit?" *Utrum vero vocatio Dei sit, an non sit, quis scire possit excepto Spiritu qui scrutatur etiam alta Dei, vel si cui forte revelaverit ipse?*"[1]

He who is raised to the episcopate should be humble, without ambition, an enemy of luxury, chaste.[2] For that refrain (*canticum*) may be applied to the bishop which Bernard repeated to Pope Eugenius III :

" It is, indeed, a monstrous combination to have the highest dignity joined with a soul that is base, the highest place with conduct that is vile, pompous speech with an idle hand, much talk without result, a solemn exterior with frivolous actions, a huge authority with little strength."[3]

When he deals with the lower clergy, priests, deacons and subdeacons, the Abbot of Clairvaux deplores their incontinence, an evil then pretty general.[4] In the preceding century, St Peter Damian also deplored it, and Pope Gregory VII undertook a rigorous reform of the morals of the clergy. This reform ended in a more precise and definite legislation respecting ecclesiastical celibacy. The œcumenical Council of the Lateran in 1123 laid down that admission to major orders (priesthood, diaconate and subdiaconate) should be no longer an impediment that prohibited marriage, but one that nullified it. This is the actual law.[5]

---

[1] *id.*, viii, 1, 4. St Bernard also sees the need of a vocation for the other ministers. Cf. *De conversione ad clericos,* cap. xix.

[2] *De officio episc.*, cap. i, iii, v, vii.

[3] *De consideratione*, lib. II, cap. vii : *Monstruosa res gradus summus et animus infimus; sedes prima et vita ima; lingua magniloqua et manus otiosa; sermo multus et fructus nullus; vultus gravis et actus levis; ingens auctoritas et nutans stabilitas.*

[4] *De conversione, ad clericos,* cap. xix-xx.

[5] It is desirable here to point out spiritual writers among the Cistercians who were the contemporaries of St Bernard. I have already mentioned William of Saint-Thierry, Gilbert de Hoy, Thomas the Cistercian. Blessed Aelred, Abbot of Rievaulx, in the Diocese of York (1166), composed *Sermons* for different feasts, the *Speculum caritatis,* the *De spirituali amicitia* (*P.L.,* CXCV, 209-792). To him are also attributed the *De Jesu puero duodeni,* among the works of St Bernard (*P.L.,* CLXXXIV, 849-870), the *Regula sive institutio inclusarum,* among the works of St Augustine (*P.L.,* XXXII, 1451-1474), which treats of the eremitical life. He also wrote several *Lives* of English saints, published in Migne, *P.L.,* CXCV, and in the *Memorial of Hexham Priory,* London 1864. Serlon, Abbot of Savigny (1158) has left a *Collection of Moral and Allegorical Thoughts* in *Bibliotheca cisterciensis,* vol. vi. Gonthier, who died in Alsace about 1210, wrote a treatise, *De oratione, jejunio et eleemosyna* (*P.L.,* CCXII). Helinand, a monk of Froidmont (1223), has left ascetical writings, *De cognitione sui et de bono regimime principis* (*P.L.,* CCXII).

CHAPTER III
THE BENEDICTINE SCHOOL
AFTER ST BERNARD
JOACHIM OF FLORA IN ITALY—BENE-DICTINE MYSTICISM IN GERMANY—THE CISTERCIAN MONASTERY OF ALVASTRA IN SWEDEN (ST BRIDGET)—BLOSIUS.

AT the end of the twelfth century the Benedictine school had as principal centres in Italy, Fonte Avellana—which St Peter Damian had rendered famous—and, above all, Flora, in Calabria.

At Flora there was a Cistercian monastery. It was there that the movement of prophetic mysticism began, which was destined to grow to such importance and to be prolonged until the Great Schism. Its beginnings were rather extravagant and troubled the Church. But very soon the mystics who led it grew prominent on account of their sanctity and became powerful helpers of the leaders of the Church.

During the twelfth century, the Abbot of Clairvaux and many other holy persons had preached the need of a renewal of the Christian spirit and of ecclesiastical life. The irregularities of the clergy were looked upon as the chief cause of the evils from which the Church was suffering. A wise reform was ardently desired.

And with the voice of the preachers there arose that of the mystics to cry out for it.

I—JOACHIM OF FLORA

JOACHIM,[1] Abbot of the Cistercian monastery of Flora, in Calabria, was one of the most exalted of these mystics. He foretold terrible punishments which were to burst over the Church, and at the same time put forward, in a kind of apocalypse, his views as to the future. The world, he said, was divided into three periods : that of the Old Testament or of God the Father ; that of Christianity or of God the Son ; and that of the Holy Spirit which was to begin in 1260. This third period was to be that of the Eternal Gospel (Apoc. xiv, 6), in

[1] Joachim died in 1202. His chief work is a commentary on the Apocalypse. *Cf.* Gebhart, *Italie mystique,* chap. ii ; *Archiv für Littera-tur und Kirchengeschichte des Mittelalters,* 1885, pp. 48-142.

which the Church of the Spirit would triumph over the carnal Church and would convert almost all mankind to God.

During his life, Joachim was looked upon as a saint,[1] and he had considerable influence. He was honoured with the confidence of several Popes, on account of his deep compassion for the ills of the Church, and of his impatient desire for a reform.

But after his death, when his disciples had developed his system and spread his ideas,[2] it was quite otherwise. Considerable agitation was produced in Italy and even in Germany by the spreading abroad of the Joachimite prophecies. Bands of terror-stricken penitents were to be seen, going from town to town, giving themselves the discipline, in order to avert the justice of God. They were called the *flagellants*. These practices soon caused serious disorders, which the Church had to suppress.

The ideas of Joachim, as we shall see, deeply troubled the Franciscan Order, which had but recently come into being. The works and the ideas of the Abbot of Flora were condemned at the Council of Arles in 1263, yet the mystical exaltation which they had brought about subsided but slowly.

II—BENEDICTINE MYSTICISM IN GERMANY: ST HILDEGARDE, ST ELIZABETH OF SCHOENAU, ST GERTRUDE THE GREAT, ST MECHTILDE OF HACKBORN AND ST MECHTILDE OF MAGDEBURG

St Hildegarde, Abbess of Rupertsberg, near Bingen, and St Elizabeth, Abbess of Schoenau, also exercised what might be called, if the expression is allowable, a " prophetic ministry."

Hildegarde was born in 1098 at Bäckelheim, in the Diocese of Mainz. The dispute as to investitures which had arisen between Henry IV, Emperor of Germany, and Pope Gregory VII was just about to come to an end. The Church gained the victory, and remained mistress of the spiritual power she had received from Christ, which the Emperor had wished to abolish. But she had been deeply disturbed by the struggle she had sustained in order to succeed. And in these political and religious troubles—which were to be renewed again under Frederick Barbarossa (1152-1190)—ecclesiastical discipline was not restored as quickly as so great a reformer as Gregory VII had wished. Hildegarde, in a manner, played the role

---

[1] Dante gives him a special place in his *Paradiso*, xii.
[2] Particularly by the *Commentaries on Isaias and Jeremias*, which appeared about the middle of the thirteenth century.

of prophetess in this difficult period in the history of the Church.

From the age of eight years, she had been accepted as an oblate of the Benedictine monastery of Disenberg, in Mount St. Disibode. In 1147, she left this house in order to found the monastery of Rupertsberg, near Bingen, not far from Mainz on the Rhine, that river on the banks of which, during the Middle Ages, there was such a beautiful mystical blossoming. There it was that the great ones of the time came to consult her; there also she pronounced her " oracles," listened to with religious dread, which more than once kept princes and bishops in the path of duty when 'in danger of forsaking it. She died on September 17, 1179.[1]

The *Works*[2] of St Hildegarde consist of letters, visions, and revelations or prophecies. They are in Latin, although the saint did not know that language; she spoke the German dialect of the period. But her historians tell us that she had a monk as her secretary, and that he put into correct Latin what she dictated. She herself, however, wrote in Latin those revelations which happened to be made to her in that language.[3]

The number of St Hildegarde's letters is considerable.[4] Among those with whom she corresponded we find four Popes, two emperors, a great number of princes and princesses, saints, such as the Abbot of Clairvaux, many bishops, and abbots and abbesses of monasteries. In her letters, she speaks unceasingly of the needs of the Church and of its dangers. She adopts the tone of prophetess, and, after the manner of St Bernard, uses a freedom which, to ears of modern refinement, seems rather crude.

But it was her visions and prophecies which rendered St Hildegarde famous. She was, in very truth, a visionary, taking the word in its etymological sense. From the age of three, she possessed the gift of vision, and, as she grew older, the supernatural light shone more clearly and with new enlightenment. It is, however, permissible to think that this gift was also due to the temperament of Hildegarde. At first she was afraid of this light which enveloped her soul; she hid it as much as possible. But God, she said, forced her at length to speak and to unveil to the world what had been

---

[1] The *Martyrology* gives her the title of Saint, although she was never officially canonized.

[2] These are to be found in Migne, *P.L.*, CXCVII, and in Card. Pitra, *Analecta sacra Spicilegio Solesmensi parata; Nova S. Hildegardis Opera*, Paris 1882, vol. viii. The text given by Migne is defective. *Cf.* F. Vernet, *loc. cit.*

[3] *Vita S. Hild.,* lib. II, 14; lib. I, 2.

[4] Migne (cols. 145-382) gives 145 letters. Card. Pitra published a like number of new letters.

revealed to her.[1] Hildegarde had a mission; she must not withdraw herself therefrom;[2] it was a teaching and a prophetic mission, rather like that of the author of the *Apocalypse,* whom the saint appears to follow.

Her visions are symbolical. Beneath the allegorical form of a landscape, a building, a man or a monster, she puts forward some dogmatic, moral or prophetic teaching. We see in her choice of symbols and in her descriptions the influence of a German imagination tending, like German epic poetry, towards the mysterious, the huge and the terrible.

This is how, in a vision, she describes the Church unceasingly bringing forth new children through baptism :

"After that I saw as it were an image of a woman as great as a great city. Her head wore a crown marvellously worked; rays of glory, like sleeves, enveloped her arms and cast radiance from heaven to earth. Her body was like a net with a thousand meshes through which a multitude might enter. She had neither legs nor feet, but remained prostrate before the altar which is in the presence of God, and she embraced it with extended hands. Her eyes gazed intently on the immensity of heaven. I was not able to examine her clothing, for she was resplendent with brightness and wholly surrounded by glory. On her breast was seen a sparkling aurora of a brilliant red, and I heard varied music singing in her honour the song of the shining aurora.

" And this image enfolded her splendour like a vesture and said, ' I must conceive and bring forth children.' And immediately there ran, like lightning, a multitude of angels, preparing places within her for human beings whose coming was to be accomplished. Then I saw children, all black, moving on the ground and in the air, as fish swimming in water, and entering into her womb through the meshes, which were open for all who wished to enter. And she, trembling, drew them up and caused them to pass out through her mouth without suffering. And behold, in a serene light there appeared to me again the figure of a man, brilliant as a

---

[1] *Vita*, lib. II, 16. St Elizabeth of Schoenau, according to her biographers, was soundly whipped by an angel for having hesitated to speak of her revelations (*Acta Sanct.,* June 18). The monk entrusted with the translation of the *Revelations* of St Bridget into Latin also received a severe blow from a heavenly spirit for not having done this quickly enough (*Acta Sanct.,* October, vol. iv). Such facts are not matter for criticism.

[2] The revelations of St Hildegarde are contained in the *Scivias* (*Scivias Domini* : thirteen visions concerning God, the Angels, Hell, the Fall, the Old and New Testaments, the Eucharist, the Church, the End of the World); in the *Book of the Divine Works* (ten visions concerning the works of God, natural and supernatural); and in the *Book of the Life of Merits*, published by Card. Pitra, which describes the ravages of the passions and their remedies, and also treats of Purgatory, Hell and Heaven.

burning flame, like a vision that I had already had, who
removed from each one of these children its black skin, which
he threw far off out of the way; then she reclothed them with
a white tunic, made their eyes glisten with a shining light,
and said to each of them, ' Cast away this old rag of sin
and reclothe thyself with this new vesture of holiness, for the
gate of thy inheritance is opened to thee. . . .' "[1]

And the Saint explains this image of a great woman to be
the Church, the bride of Christ. The crown that adorns her
head symbolizes the Apostles, the Martyrs and the Saints,
her greatest claim to glory. Her womb, like a net, calls to
mind the maternity of the Church. The children, all black,
who enter there are the aspirants for baptism whom Christ
cleanses with the water of holiness and renders white as
snow.

The visions are, as a rule, explained. But there nevertheless remains enough obscurity to qualify them by the term
Sibylline. Has not, indeed, St Hildegarde been surnamed
the Sibyl of the Rhine?

Sibyl she was, above all, in her prophecies. Neither the
latter nor her visions have been ratified by the authority of
the Church;[2] acceptance of them is not imposed as of obligation for the faithful. It is even very doubtful as to whether
they are truly prophetic. Nevertheless, the contemporaries
of the Saint were deeply impressed by them.

Hildegarde made prophecies concerning Antichrist and the
end of the world.[3] They were believed with terror by generations of Christians who had often been startled before by
these kinds of predictions. We cannot know what they are
worth, since as yet they have not been fulfilled, and because
the value of private prophecy can only be recognized in its
accomplishment.

Is the case different as regards announcements respecting
Protestantism? Are we to think that the Seer of Bingen predicted that violent storm, particularly in the three letters that
she wrote to the clergy of Cologne, to the Church of Treves,
and to the Abbot Werner of Kirchheim?[4] This prophecy was
like a cry of alarm which she sent forth unceasingly, and a
solemn warning to the members of the clerical state in view
of the evil which their conduct was to bring upon the Church.
Hildegarde also seized the occasion to lash their vice. For
the sorrow, according to her, which was to bring affliction

[1] *Scivias,* lib. II, *visio* 3 (*P.L.,* CXCVII, 453-454).
[2] The visions of St Hildegarde have never been approved by the
Church. The Pope who had her writings examined (Eugenius III, at
the Council of Treves in 1147) simply declared that they contained
nothing contrary to Catholic doctrine. St Bernard wrote the Saint a
favourable letter, *Epist.* ccclxvi.
[3] *Scivias,* lib. III, *vis.* 11 and 12 (709-730).
[4] *Epist.* xlviii (244-253); xlix (254-258); lii (269-271).

on Christian society was looked upon, in the prophecy, as chastisement for the sins of unfaithful priests. These letters of Hildegarde recall the warnings at the beginning of the Apocalypse, addressed to the Churches of Asia :

" Princes and a reckless people, O priests, will fall upon you who have forsaken me till now [it is the Church that is speaking]. They will drive you out and put you to flight. They will take away your riches because you have neglected your sacerdotal office. . . . And in thus acting they will think that they serve God because you have dishonoured me."[1] To plunderings and persecution will be added suppression of convents, for obedience and other monastic virtues are not observed there.[2]

Nevertheless, there will be true pastors and saints who will resist the false reformers and will not allow themselves to be deceived by them. They will be subjected to a severe persecution. The persecutors of the Church, moreover, will be thorough hypocrites.

" The people who will accomplish these things profess holiness; deceived by the devil and sent by him, they will come with pale countenance, perfectly counterfeiting holiness, and will unite themselves with the powerful princes of the earth. . . . All, however, will not be seduced by them, for there are pastors, most stout soldiers of God who are righteous. There will also be some congregations of saints whose lives are pure who will not allow themselves to be carried away. Then the enemies of God will counsel the princes and the rich to compel with whip and cudgel these pastors of the Church, and other spiritual men their disciples, to obey them."[3]

These strictures can only be applied to Protestantism in a very vague way. But we can well understand how, after the event, they were associated with it. It is, nevertheless, true that, during the lifetime of Hildegarde, these predictions were known in Germany and made a deep impression there. Holy persons, pastors and monks, who were labouring towards a wise reform of the Church, often quoted them by way of menace.

St Hildegarde remains one of the most interesting figures of mystical reform.[4]

St Elizabeth,[5] Benedictine Abbess of Schoenau, in the Diocese of Treves (1165), also prophesied against the laxity

---

[1] *Epist.* lii (270-271). [2] *Epist.* xlix (256).
[3] *Epist.* xlviii (250-251).
[4] St Hildegarde also composed works on physics; that is to say, on natural history as applied to medicine : *Book concerning the Subtleties of the Nature of Divers Creatures; Book concerning Simple Medicine and Compound Medicine,* published by Pitra.
[5] *Acta Sanctorum,* June 18. Her brother, D'Eckbert, Abbot of St Florinus of Schoenau (1185), has left a treatise, *De laude sanctae crucis.*

of the clergy. But her influence did not equal that of the Seer of Bingen, with whom she had frequent intercourse.

The mysticism of the Cistercians of Helfta, near Eisieben in Saxony, was, on the contrary, wholly interior. The Cistercian reform at the beginning of the thirteenth century was widely spread in the north-east of Germany. The monasteries of women for the most part followed the Benedictine Rule as it was understood at Cîteaux,[1] and mystical life there blossomed forth wonderfully. The influence of St Bernard and the reading of his writings tended to prepare for exceptional divine graces. Towards the end of the thirteenth century the famous mystical school of German Dominicans, with which we shall deal at length, saw the light. The sons of St Dominic, especially at the beginning of their Order, were zealous mystical propagandists. These various causes contributed to the formation of the mystics of Helfta. But their piety remained wholly Benedictine in character.

Three amongst them stand out as being particularly famous : St Gertrude the Great, St Mechtilde of Hackborn and another St Mechtilde, the Beguine of Magdeburg.[2]

St Gertrude must not be confused, as is sometimes done, with Gertrude of Hackborn, Abbess of the monastery of Helfta, her contemporary and her superior. The Cistercian author of the *Revelations* remained a simple nun all her life.

She was born on January 6, 1256, in Germany. The chronicler who speaks of her has neglected to tell the place of her birth and the social position of her parents.[3]

At the age of five years[4] she left her father's house in order to enter the convent of Helfta, where she was to pass her life. Intellectual culture was particularly well developed there. St Bernard was fully honoured there; he is often quoted in the

---

[1] *Cf.* Franz Winter, *Die Cistercienser des nordöstlichen Deutschlands,* Gotha, 1867-1871, 3 vols.

[2] The revelations of these three saints have been published by the Benedictines of Solesmes : *Revelationes Gertrudianae ac Mechtildianae,* Poitiers and Paris 1875-1877, 2 vols. Vol. i. contains the *Revelations* and the *Spiritual Exercises* of St Gertrude. Vol. ii. includes the *Revelations* of the two Mechtildes. The *Revelations* of St Gertrude have also been published, under the title *Héraut de l'amour divin,* a French translation, made by the Benedictines, Poitiers and Paris 1878, 2 vols. Another title of the *Revelations* is : *Insinuation de la divine piété, ou la Vie et les Révélations de Ste Gertrude,* French translation by a Benedictine, new edition, 2 vols., Paris 1918. For a more complete bibliography see F. Vernet, *Dict. de Théol. cath.* (art. *Gertrude la Grande, Sainte*).

[3] The biography of St Gertrude is found in the first book of the *Revelations,* written by one who knew the Saint intimately. The second book was written by the Saint herself. The last three were edited from notes taken at her dictation. *Cf.* G. Ledos, *Ste Gertrude,* Paris 1919.

[4] *Revelationes,* lib. I, cap. i.

Revelations. St Gertrude was filled with admiration for his " sweet eloquence." She saw him, in her visions, with hands filled with " bracelets of gold and with precious stones." The gold symbolized " the inestimable price of his most rare teaching," and the stones " all that he had said or written on the love of God." Devotion has reaped the greatest benefit from his pious works.[1]

Gertrude, in the early days of her religious life, allowed herself to be rather too much absorbed by study, to the detriment of spiritual exercises. The consequence was a certain lukewarmness. She was " converted " after a vision that she had on January 27, 1281. The Saviour appeared to her under the figure and aspect of a young man of sixteen, asking her " to come back to him in the end."[2] From that day Gertrude was transformed. She received most vivid light whereby to know her imperfections, and felt an intensely burning desire to correct them and to grow in virtue. At the same time God revealed to her that he was pleased to take up his abode in her.[3] Henceforth her life was nothing but an uninterrupted continuance of extraordinary mystical happenings.

St Gertrude had a special devotion to the humanity of Christ, conformable with the Cistercian tradition created by the Abbot of Clairvaux. The fourth book of the *Revelations* consists of meditations on those feasts of the liturgical year which celebrate the mysteries of the life of the Saviour. The upliftings on the sorrowful mysteries give touching expression to the compassionate love of Gertrude for the sufferings of Jesus.

The liturgical prayers of the divine Office also nourished the piety of the Cistercian nuns of Helfta. When we read the *Revelations* we are met on almost every page with lofty thoughts suggested by the phrases chanted in choir, in accordance with the well-known bent of Benedictine piety.

Theories must not be sought in the writings of St Gertrude, nor anything suggestive of speculative spirituality. Her piety, entirely affective, is expressed in the form of a dialogue between God and the soul, in simple words which in no way suggest the language of theology.

Like St Francis of Assisi, St Gertrude also loves to be raised towards God by the spectacle of nature. Her mind, untrammelled by speculation, joyfully contemplates the beauty of created things, above all of plants and flowers, and sees in them a reflection of divine perfection. The German mystics, in the following century, for the most part lose this sense of nature and shut themselves up, as in a dark and stifling prison, in the philosophical theory of mystical union,

---

[1] *id.,* lib. IV, cap. li.   [2] *id.,* lib. II, cap. i.
[3] *id.,* lib. II, cap. ii-iii; lib. I, cap. vi.

Gertrude does not venture to explain this union. She experiences it and endeavours to describe, at times in delightful language, what she feels. What she realizes most is the presence of God within her. She is careful to note the moment when, for the first time, she received this grace. It was between the feast of Easter and that of the Ascension, after a day in which she felt inwardly attracted by God :

" In the evening, before going to bed," she says, " as I was on my knees in prayer, this passage from the Gospel suddenly came into my mind : *If any man love me, he will keep my word, and my Father will love him, and we will come to him, and will make our abode with him* (John xiv, 23). Inwardly, my heart of clay felt, O God infinitely sweet, that thou wert about to come within it."[1]

This sense of the presence of God in her soul was permanent. Gertrude states that it was only absent for eleven days; the Lord seems to have separated himself from her during that period as a punishment for her having undesirable intercourse with worldly people.[2] But this was only a passing eclipse. Mystical union in Gertrude became more and more perfect, and assumed various forms.

During one Christmas night the Child Jesus became united with the heart of the Saint, producing a most heavenly beatitude there :

" It seemed to me," she said, " that there was offered me and that I received as in my heart, a tender child, born at that moment, who contained within himself the gift of highest perfection, the gift excelling all things. And as my soul kept him within it, it appeared suddenly to be wholly changed into the same colour with him, if indeed that can be called colour which cannot be compared to any visible object. Thence my soul perceived an ineffable understanding of those words so full of sweetness : *That God may be all in all* (1 Cor. xv, 28), so that it felt as though it possessed its well-beloved in its very depths and that it rejoiced to see that it was not deprived of the sweet presence of the Spouse whose caresses have so great a charm. Also it drank with an unquenchable eagerness the delicious draught of the following words divinely proffered to it : ' As I am the figure of the substance of God the Father in the divinity, thus shalt thou be the figure of my substance in the humanity ; and thou shalt receive in thy soul the emissions of my divinity, as the air receives the rays of the sun. Penetrate therefore into the innermost of that ray that must unite us, and thou shalt become capable of a more familiar union with me.' "[3]

On the feast of the Circumcision Gertrude invoked the name of Jesus with so much piety that the Saviour, " leaning

[1] *Revelationes,* lib. II, cap. iii.   [2] *ibid.* and cap. xxiii.
[3] *Revelationes,* lib. II, cap. vi.

towards her with affection, and as though carried away by the impetuosity of his love, impressed upon the *lips of her soul,* so to speak, a kiss the sweetness of which surpassed that of honey beyond compare."[1]

On the feast of the Purification her soul, " all softened like wax exposed to the heat of the fire," received the imprint of the Holy Trinity.[2]

Most worthy of notice are the graces of union with the Heart of Jesus with which Gertrude was favoured. Her soul, she declares, " was presented one day before the Heart of her divine Spouse in order to receive therefrom the mark and impression of a seal. . . . It was received in this blessed Heart in the form of a piece of wax softened by fire," as if it " were melted by the excess of heat which was hidden in the depths of that Heart." Another time the Saviour presented himself to Gertrude offering his left side, " from which there came out from the depths of his blessed Heart a spring as pure and as solid as a river of crystal."[3] The Heart of Jesus, like a lamp, was as though suspended in the heart of the saint. She perceived therein marvellous beatings and an extreme sweetness. These beatings were two in number : one brought about the salvation of sinners, and the other that of the just.[4]

For devotion to the Heart of Jesus is not only a source of consolation for the soul, it is also a fountain of grace. It makes up for our deficiencies and shortcomings. Gertrude is invited to refer with trustfulness to this most sweet Heart, " the organ of the adorable Trinity," all that she was not able to accomplish perfectly of herself; so that the eyes of Christ should see nothing in her that was not perfect.[5] Sinners and the faithful, tried by temptation, will also find in the divine Heart repentance and comfort.[6]

This devotion to the Heart of Jesus characterizes the mysticism of St Gertrude and is peculiar to it. Certain pages of the *Revelations* would not be out of place in the writings of St. Margaret Mary, the modern apostle of the Sacred Heart, so clearly did our Saint define the object and ends of this devotion.

Besides St Gertrude, the Heart of Jesus was revealed to two others of her contemporaries at the monastery.

One, Mechtilde of Hackborn (1298), our Saint's mistress,

---

[1] *id.,* lib. IV, cap. v. St Gertrude personifies the soul that receives on its mouth *os animae,* the kiss of Christ.

[2] *id.,* lib. II, cap. vii.

[3] *id.,* lib. II, cap. vii-ix.

[4] *id.,* lib. III, cap. xxvi, lii.

[5] *id.,* lib. III, cap. xxv.

[6] *id.,* lib. III, cap. vii. *Cf.* lib. IV, cap. xliii. The Heart of Jesus is like a musical instrument in order to sing the glories of the Blessed Trinity.

also felt the beatings of the Heart of Jesus.[1] Like Gertrude,
she was raised to the highest mystical union by the contact
of the divine Heart with her soul.[2]

The other who was thus privileged by the Heart of Jesus
was a Beguine of Magdeburg, also named Mechtilde (1280),
who spent the end of her life with the mystics of Helfta.[3]

It is not too rash to think that the writings of St Bernard
drew the attention of St Gertrude and her companions to the
wounds of the Saviour, and chiefly to that of his side. In a
beautiful passage on the wounds of Jesus the Abbot of Clairvaux exclaims :

" Goodly openings which establish faith in the resurrection
and in the divinity of Christ. . . . In them the sparrow
finds a resting-place and the turtle-dove a nest where she may
lay her young; in them the dove takes shelter and looks without fear on the hawk that flies round about. . . . They have
pierced his hands and his feet and thrust a lance into his side,
and through these openings I am allowed to suck honey from
the stone and to draw oil from the most hard rock—that is to
say, to taste and see how sweet is the Lord. . . . The iron
has pierced his soul and penetrated to his Heart to the end
that he may know how to have compassion on our wretchedness. The holes of the body let escape the secrets of the
Heart, the great mystery of love, the bowels of the mercy of
our God."[4]

St Bernard was the first to point out to the mystics the way
that leads to the Heart of Jesus. We have seen how ardently the Cistercian nuns of Helfta took it up. Like St Bonaventure, they went " to the most humble Heart of the most
high Saviour through the door of his side opened by the
lance. There undoubtedly lies a hidden and ineffable and
much to be desired treasure of charity; there is found a new
love; there is to be sought the gift of tears."[5]

Devotion to the Heart of Jesus in the Middle Ages was not
only a privilege of mystics, it spread among the faithful of
Germany.[6]

[1] *Revelationes Gertrudianae et Mechtildianae,* Poitiers and Paris
1875, vol. ii, p. 18. The visions and revelations of St Mechtilde of
Hackborn have been collected in the *Book of Special Grace,* inserted in
the *Revelationes,* vol. ii.

[2] *id.,* ii, pp. 80, 179, 230.

[3] Cf. *Revelationes,* vol. ii, p. 464. The work of Mechtilde of Magdeburg is entitled *The Light of the Divinity,* or *The Torch of God.*

[4] St Bernard, *In Cantica, sermo* LXI, 3-4. Devotion to the wounds
of the Saviour was widespread towards the end of the fourteenth
century. Cf. *De Imit. Christi,* lib. II, cap. i; *Augustini meditationes,*
xli; *Manuale,* xxiii, etc. (*P.L.,* XL, 940, 961).

[5] St Bonaventure, *Vitis mystica* or *Lignum vitae,* cap. xliv (among the
apocryphal writings of St Bernard, *P.L.,* CLXXXIV, 726).

[6] *Cf.* Karl Richstätter, *Die Herz-Jesu-Verehrung des deutschen
Mittelalters,* Paderborn 1919.

St Gertrude in her *Revelations* gives evidence of a very great devotion towards the blessed Eucharist. Her *Exercises,* both for hearing Mass and also in preparation for Holy Communion, have been preserved to us. We know from other sources that devotion to the blessed Sacrament developed greatly in the thirteenth century.[1] Writers on spirituality at this time laid stress in their writings on that immense movement in Eucharistic devotion which culminated in the institution of the feast of *Corpus Christi* and the composing of the wonderful fourth book of the *Imitation.*

Devotion to the Heart of Jesus, to his Eucharistic Body, and also to the Virgin Mary[2] rendered the mystical union in St Gertrude more and more perfect. This union was on several occasions accompanied by extraordinary phenomena which we would do well to remark.

One of these was the intellectual vision of God :

"On the Second Sunday in Lent," says Gertrude, " as in the procession before Mass we were singing the respond : *Vidi Dominum facie ad faciem . . . I saw the Lord face to face . . .* my soul found itself suddenly surrounded with a wondrous burst of light which was no other than that of thy revelation, O Lord. I seemed to see against my face another face, which, according to the expression of St Bernard, *was not contained under any form, yet gave form to all else; which did not strike the eye of the body, but charmed that of the soul; which was lovable, not through the brightness of its colour, but through the gifts of its love.* It is but thou, my God, who canst know how not only my soul, but also all the powers of my heart found pleasure in this happy vision, in which the brightness of thine eyes, like two suns, looked straight into my own. . . .

"When then, as I have just said, thou didst approach thine adorable face, in which is found an abundant source of all joy, close to my own, so greatly unworthy to touch it, I perceived a gentle light proceeding from thy divine eyes and passing through mine, spreading itself in every secret part of me, and seeming to fill all my members with a wonderful power and strength. At first it was as though it had dried up the marrow of my bones, and then, destroying the flesh and bones themselves, as if my whole substance were nothing else but this divine splendour which shone within it with greater allurement and beauty than is possible to tell, filling my soul with joy and incredible calmness."[3]

St Gertrude experienced ecstasies also, but not, it seems,

---

[1] In the preceding century St Hildegarde often wrote concerning the Sacrament of the Altar and the dignity of the priest who celebrates it. *Scivias,* lib. II, *visio* vi (*P.L.,* CXCVII, 507 ff.).

[2] St Gertrude, *Revelationes,* lib. II, cap. xvi ; lib. III, cap. xix.

[3] *Revelationes,* lib. II, cap. xxii.

in great number. In one of these she was rapt in so close a union with God that she asked herself how it was she did not die.[1] The spiritual favours with which she was loaded, moreover, produced in her a violent yearning to be separated from the body in order to go to God.[2]

Another extraordinary grace which St Gertrude received was the imprint of the Stigmata of Christ upon her heart. One day, when she was earnestly begging for this grace, she recognized that the adorable marks of the sacred wounds, such as they are on the body of the Saviour, were imprinted in the depths of her heart.[3] They rendered the Saint most compassionate for the suffering Christ and overflowing with love for him.

The mystical intercourse of St Gertrude with the Saviour is a living commentary on the *Sermons* of St Bernard *on the Canticle of Canticles*. Gertrude was, in truth, the bride of Christ, living in sweet familiarity with him. She was transformed into him, and had no other desire than to accomplish in all things his holy will.

Although she had not, strictly speaking, any outward mission, as had St Hildegarde, and later on St Bridget and St Catherine of Siena, God willed her, nevertheless, to write down the favours of which she had been the object. Gertrude hesitated, temporized, so great was the repugnance she felt at unveiling such intimate secrets. But the Lord repeated the command: "I desire," he told her, "in thy writings to give a certain and incontestable proof of my divine goodness in these latter days in which I am prepared to heap my graces on a great number."[4] The Saint carried this out. Her writings were, during her lifetime, submitted to the censure of theologians. This scrutiny was wholly favourable to them; they contain nothing contrary to the teaching of the Church and are capable of developing devotion.[5]

They were not, however, well known till the beginning of

---

[1] *id.*, lib. II, cap. xxiii. Mystical contemplation weakened the health of St Gertrude. Mystics admit that supernatural states impair physical strength. "If we love God truly," said St Hildegarde in this connection, "we should not be in such good health."

[2] *id.*, lib. I, cap. xi. St. Gertrude died in 1303.

[3] *id.*, lib. II, cap. iv-v.

[4] *Revelationes*, lib. II, cap. x. *Cf.* lib. I, cap. xvi.

[5] The *Exercises,* often issued separately, sanctified many souls. They are seven in number, and their object is the renewal of fervour in nuns. They are : renewal in the grace of baptism; the anniversary of taking the holy habit; the anniversary of the holy profession; the renewal of the religious profession; exercise to excite divine love; exercise of praise and thanksgiving; reparation for sins and preparation for death. There is a French translation of the *Exercises* by Dom Emmanuel (Librairie de l'Art Catholique, Paris 1919). English editions of both the *Prayers* (1919) and the *Exercises* (1921) are to be had (London, Burns, Oates and Washbourne).

the sixteenth century.[1] Blosius (1556) derived inspiration
from them for his works. St. Teresa also owes something
to the great German mystic. In the last century the
Oratorian Faber cited her as a beautiful example of the
liberty of mind inherent in true piety.[2]

III—THE CISTERCIAN MONASTERY OF ALVASTRA
(ST BRIDGET)

St Bridget of Sweden may be connected with the Cistercian
school to which she belonged by her training, if not by her
profession. She lived for some time in the monastery of
Alvastra in Sweden, where her husband became a Cistercian
and also died.

Like St Hildegarde, the famous mystic of Northern
Europe fulfilled the role of prophetess. She seemed to have
been raised up by God at the beginning of the Great Schism,
with St Catherine of Siena, in order to give counsel to Popes
in that difficult period, and to endeavour to avert the crisis
which brought about so much evil to the Church.

Bridget or Birgit (Birgitta)[3] was born in 1302. Her father
belonged to the royal family of Sweden. When about fourteen she married a noble, Ulf Gudmarson, Prince of Nericia.
She had eight children.

In the desire to lead a more perfect life, with her husband's
consent she took a vow of continence. On their return from
a pilgrimage to Compostella in Spain the married couple
formed the project of entering the religious life. Ulf decided
to become a Cistercian in the monastery at Alvastra. He
died in 1344, a short while after he had carried out his
intention. Having thus become a widow, Bridget had an
intuition of what God required of her. Henceforth she was
to be the bride of Christ and his confidante. The revelations[4]

---

[1] Through the Latin edition, prepared by J. Lansperg, Carthusian of
Cologne, and published in 1536, by the Carthusian Thierry Loher.

[2] Faber, *All for Jesus*.

[3] We have two *Vitae* of St Bridget. The first was written by a contemporary of the Saint, Birger, Archbishop of Upsala, in Sweden.
The second is by Berthold, a monk of the Order of St Saviour, founded
by St Bridget. They are in the *Acta Sanctorum, Octobris*, vol. iv,
pp. 485-533, Paris 1866.

[4] The writings of St Bridget consist of eight books of *Revelations*.
To these must be added one supplementary book (*Revelationum Extra-
vagantium liber*). This last book was written by the Cistercian Prior
of Alvastra, Peter Olafsson (1390). It was he who translated the greater
part of the *Revelations* of Bridget from Swedish into Latin, for the
Saint did not know Latin. It was revealed to her that her *Revelations*
should be translated into that language by the Prior of Alvastra, who
was supernaturally smitten for not having done them quickly enough
(*Revelat. Extrav.*, cap. xlviii). The first edition of the *Revelations* was

which she received were to be of use not only for her own salvation, but also for that of others.

"A short time after the death of her husband, . . ." say her biographers, " she was enraptured in her mind. She saw a luminous cloud, and she heard, as did formerly the children of Israel on Mount Sina, the Lord saying to her : I am thy God, who desires to speak with thee. Terrified, she was afraid that she was deceived by an illusion. But she heard the Lord once more : Fear nothing, he said, for I am the creator of all things and not a deceiver. I speak not for thee alone but also for the salvation of others. Hearken to what I say to thee, and go, find Master Mathias, who has the gift of discerning spirits, and tell him from me that thou art to be my bride and my word-bearer. Thou wilt hear and see spiritual things, and my Spirit will dwell with thee until thy death."[1]

God prepared the Saint for her mission by giving her the prestige of high sanctity and by raising her to extraordinary mystical states.

Her piety is Cistercian in character. The passion of Christ and the glories of the Virgin Mary are its principal objects. At the age of ten she had a vision of the Saviour crucified. The memory of it ever remained with her.

"Bridget," says Birger, "once heard a preacher on the passion of Christ, and his words became engraved with love upon her heart. On the following night Christ showed himself to her as he was at the moment of his crucifixion, and said to her : Behold, this is how I was wounded. Bridget, thinking that the Saviour had just been crucified again, answered him in mind : O Lord, who has treated thee thus? Those that despise me and disdain my love, he replied. On coming to herself Bridget henceforth retained such a memory of the passion of Christ that she could not think of it without weeping. She suffered such great pain from the contemplation of the wounds of her Spouse that sometimes she

---

published in Rome in 1475. The editions of Lübeck (1492), of Nuremberg (1600) and of Rome (1628) were widely circulated. This last contained : (1) A *prologue* by Cardinal John of Turrecremata (Torquemada), the Dominican who, at the Council of Bâle, defended the *Revelations* of Bridget against her adversaries; (2) a preliminary treatise by Gonsalvo Durand, Bishop of Montefeltro; (3) a Prologue to Bk. VIII, by Alfonso de Vadatera, Austin hermit and former Bishop of Jaen. The Comtesse de Flavigny published a biography of *Sainte Brigitte de Suède,* Paris 1892. The *Revelations* of St Bridget have often been translated into French and English.

[1] Birger, *Vita S. Birg.*, 19. This first vision of St Bridget's ministry is mentioned in Bk. I, cap. ii, of the *Revelations* and in the *Supplement* (*Revel. Extrav.*), cap. xlvii. Mathias of Sweden, Canon of Linköping, doctor of theology, directed Bridget when she began to have revelations.

was wholly on fire with love of them, and her sorrow caused her to shed tears."[1]

A most beautiful prayer on the passion and on the life and prerogatives of the most glorious Virgin Mary, Mother of Jesus, was revealed to her. She recited it every day.[2] Her spirituality is, in other respects, much more affective than speculative.

Bridget had frequent ecstasies, during which she would seek from God what she was to say to the great ones of the world. Alfonso de Vadatera informs us that she saw and heard, in her rapture, all that is set forth in the fifth book of the *Revelations*. Her mind was extraordinarily active during the ecstasy. Whilst her body was "asleep" and realized nothing of what was passing, her soul was "awake to the seeing, hearing and feeling of supernatural things."[3] When she came out of ecstasy, like St Catherine of Siena, she had authority, fully divine, to employ even the most forcible language to those who were neglecting their duty.

It was by this authority that she founded the Order of St Saviour. The Rule which she gave to this new order was, she stated, dictated to her by Christ.

There is a noteworthy tendency on the part of the great mystics to look upon all their inspirations as revelations properly so called. But we must not take their declarations too literally. The contemporaries of the Saint, in fact, do not hesitate to modify some of her views. The Rule that was approved by Urban V differed on more than one point from that which Bridget drew up.[4]

The Bridgettine Order, moreover, possesses nothing completely original. It is a reproduction of that of Fontevrault, near Angers, founded in 1100 by the Benedictine Robert d'Arbrissel. Every community of this Order comprised two convents, one for monks and the other for nuns. The church was used in common; the nuns said the Office in the upper part, and the monks in the lower. The abbess of the nuns was always the superior-general of the double monastery. Urban V desired that the two monasteries, although subject to the abbess, should be entirely distinct; each must have its church and its own possessions.

The details of St Bridget's Rule are borrowed from the

---

[1] Birger, *Vita S. Birg.*, 6. Bridget belongs to the number of those mystics of the Middle Ages who have described in realistic terms the sufferings of Christ.

[2] *id.*, 12.

[3] *Revelationes*, lib. IV, 77; lib. VI, 52. Berthold (*Vita altera S. Birg.*, lib. II, cap. i, 82-83) narrates that Bridget was at times raised up in the air in ecstasy when she was praying in the churches of Rome. She had also the gift of perceiving an evil smell at the approach of sinners (*ibid.*, 101-103).

[4] For a comparison of the two rules see *Acta Sanctorum, Oct.*, vol. iv, pp. 419 ff.

Benedictine Rule as it was interpreted at Cîteaux.[1] The
Cistercian spirit exercised a real influence on the famous
foundress, who had such frequent dealings with the
monastery of Alvastra.

The first convent of the Order was founded about 1363 at
Wadstena, near Linköping, in Sweden. Urban V approved
its Rule in 1370. After the death of the Saint, Urban VI
placed the Order on a definite footing, and it became widely
spread throughout Norway and Denmark.

St Bridget is as famous in the role of prophetess as in
that of foundress of an Order. Her prophecies were made
principally in Rome, where she went in 1346, when she
formed the project of founding the monastery of Wadstena.

"Go to Rome," Christ said to her during a sojourn at the
monastery of Alvastra, "and remain there until thou hast
seen the Pope and the Emperor. Thou shalt tell them from
me what I shall reveal to thee."[2]

The Popes were then residing at Avignon. The mission of
Bridget, and also that of her contemporary St Catherine of
Siena, was to exhort them to return to the Eternal City.

At Rome Bridget visited the tombs of the holy martyrs,
and lived an austere life and practised charity. She lashed
the evil courses of the cruel and dissolute Romans, whose
incessant outbreaks had forced the Sovereign Pontiffs to
become exiled in France. Thus, too, she drew their hatred
upon her. The prophetess spared nobody, neither kings nor
clergy nor Popes. She was in truth the voice of God, which
sought out evil wherever it was to be found. So great was
her desire to restore to her Spouse a Church *without spot or
wrinkle* (Eph. v, 27).

This desire is made manifest on every page of the
Revelations. The warnings and the prophecies contained
there have no other end in view but that of bringing recal-
citrants back to their duty. The enraptured descriptions of
the beauties of Christ and the Virgin Mary are destined to
rekindle or revive divine love in souls. In order to frighten
hardened sinners Bridget depicts the punishments which
await them in hell in fearful colours. When she speaks of
the last judgement it is to inspire terror. Her descriptions
of purgatory cause even the most holy among the faithful to
tremble.

No doubt we need not accept all the revelations of Bridget
as dictated by God himself.[3] In dealing with personal revela-

---

[1] The rule which was approved by Urban V, however, seems also to
be inspired by that of St Augustine. That approved by Urban VI in
1379 is almost entirely the same as that of St Augustine.

[2] *Revelat. suppl. (Revelat. Extrav.)*, 8. *Cf.* Birger, *Vita*, 24.

[3] St Bridget (*Revelat.*, lib. IV, cap. xiii) appears to give some credence
to the legend, widely spread in the Middle Ages, concerning the deliverance from the flames of hell of the Emperor Trajan at the intercession
of St Gregory the Great.

tions it is almost impossible to draw the line between what comes from God and what belongs properly to the mystic. The Church alone is able to undertake this with success. In the ordinary way she is content to give a negative approval by declaring that the revelations submitted to her contain nothing contrary to her teaching. Bridget, however, obtained more. In the Bull of canonization, in 1391, Pope Boniface IX declared that the books of the *Revelations* contained several predictions inspired by the prophetic Spirit.[1]

How flattering soever this judgement may be, it remains very vague, and we can understand that it has not prevented critics from raising a very delicate problem respecting the writings of Bridget. The Saint, as we know, did not know Latin. Like St Hildegarde, she had to have recourse to translators, the Cistercian Peter Olafsson and another Peter, confessor of the Saint and monk of the monastery of Wadstena. The former Bishop of Jaen, Alfonso de Vadatera, compiled all the revelations and divided them into eight books. Did the translators and compiler add nothing to the thoughts of Bridget? Have we the discourse that God caused her to hear in the exact form in which it was communicated?[2]

We may admit that we possess substantially the Saint's thought, and that this thought is admirable. It is expressed in a most picturesque style which captivates even the unbelieving reader. The prophecies, particularly, possess a powerful poetic inspiration.

" The Son of God thus speaks to his bride," she said respecting Pope Clement VI. " Write these words on my behalf to Pope Clement : I have raised thee up and brought thee to the highest degree of honour. Arise, therefore, and reconcile the Kings of France and England,[3] those dangerous fools that cause souls to be lost. Come afterwards to Italy to proclaim the divine word, the year of salvation and divine love.[4] Thou wilt see the places red with the blood of my saints. After that I shall give thee endless reward."[5]

Like the prophets of Israel of old, Bridget adds threatening to her invitations. Christ again bids her say to the same Pope :

---

[1] *Acta Sanctorum*, p. 408. It was St Catherine of Sweden, daughter of St Bridget, who was most active in the canonization of her mother. She died in 1391 at the Abbey of Wadstena, of which she was Abbess.

[2] See the dissertation in which the Bollandists deal with the problem. *Acta Sanctorum*, p. 412. The same question occurs with regard to St Catherine of Siena, who did not know how to write and employed secretaries to draw up her dialogue.

[3] The Hundred Years War between France and England began in 1337.

[4] That is to say a jubilee.   [5] *Revelationes*, lib. VI, cap. 93.

"Reflect how in time past thou didst daringly provoke my anger and I kept silence. Thou didst then what thou wouldst and not what thou oughtest. I was patient as though I were no judge. But my time draws near, and I shall ask thee to account for thy neglect and the evil of the epoch in which thou livest. . . . Neither shall I forget how, during thy pontificate, avarice and ambition have flourished and have increased in the Church. Thou mightest have reformed and corrected many disorders; but thou hast allowed thyself to be hindered by human considerations. . . ."[1]

These complaints were everywhere expressed in the time of Bridget. All ardently yearned for a reform of the Church, and looked impatiently for the Pope who should realize it. In one of her visions Bridget saw the Leonine City of Rome, and heard a voice crying :

"The Pope who will love the Church as I have loved it myself, and as my friends love it, will take possession of these places in order that he may call his counsellors together there more freely and more quietly."[2]

Clement VI took no notice of the prophecy of Bridget. He died in December, 1352, and had as successor Innocent VI (1362), "of a better metal than his predecessor . . . but the malice of men demanded that he should soon leave this world," in order that he might keep the merit of his good will intact.[3] Urban V, who succeeded him, recognized that he must go and reside in Rome. He reached there in 1367, but he very soon manifested his intention of returning to Avignon, in spite of the prophecy of Bridget foretelling his early death if he should do so.[4] He died at Avignon in 1370.

It was Gregory XI, elected in December, 1370, who was destined to bring the Papacy back to Rome. Bridget sent him message after message foretelling most terrible punishment for him if he remained at Avignon.[5] She died in 1373[6] before her most cherished desire had been realized. Gregory only entered Rome in January, 1377, at the instance of St Catherine of Siena.

Bridget and Catherine of Siena were undoubtedly animated by the Spirit of God, since the Church has raised both of them to her altars. Their policy was not actuated by human considerations. It was inspired by a passionate love for Holy Church. Nevertheless, we can understand the hesitation of the Popes in following it. For it was not evident to the contemporaries of the two Saints, as it is to us, that their revelations had a well-authenticated supernatural character.

[1] *id.* Cf. cap. 96.   [2] *id.,* lib. VI, cap. 74.
[3] *id.,* lib. IV, cap. 136.
[4] *id.,* lib. IV, cap. 138.   [5] *id.,* lib. IV, cap. 140-143.
[6] The year before her death she made a pilgrimage to the Holy Land.

Moreover, the return of the Popes to Rome was full of danger; it might even, as things were then—the event proved it—bring about schism;[1] also we know what a bitter feeling there was at the beginning of the fifteenth century against those mystics who set themselves up as counsellors of the head of the Church.

Jean Gerson deplores that those to whom the duty of government was confided should so easily have given credence to the visions of pious women (*muliercularum*) when they had to come to serious decisions. "Pope Gregory XI," he tells us, "realized when too late the truth of what I say. When on the point of quitting this world, holding in his hands the Body of Christ, he advised all that were assisting him to beware of those men and women who, under the shelter of piety, tell their imaginary visions. He had allowed himself to be caught, and despising the wise advice of his counsellors, had acted in such a way as to expose the Church to the danger of imminent schism, had not Christ in his mercy provided against it. Alas!" continues Gerson, "the horrible reality of the schism proved only too well the truth of the Pope's words!"[2]

It is not, then, surprising that at the Council of Constance (1414-1418), which put an end to the schism, and later at that of Bâle (1431-1443), some rather lively attacks were directed against the *Revelations* of Bridget. It was even asked that they might be censured.[3] But the Bishops of the North of Europe, and the Dominicans, whose chief representative at the Council of Bâle was Cardinal Turrecremata, defended them with success. Moreover, Gregory XI and Urban VI had already passed favourable judgement upon them,[4] and Boniface IX, before canonizing their author in 1391, had caused them to be seriously examined. But since this examination, as well as the canonization of the Saint, was the work of a Pope who had only a portion of the Church under his obedience, it was thought desirable to ratify them by the Councils. That is why, at both Constance and Bâle, the question as to the writings of Bridget arose.

[1] But for the return to Rome, the party of Cardinals which elected Clement VII the Pope of Avignon would have had no motive for effecting this election.

[2] Gerson, *De examine doctrinarum, Consid.* III. *Gersonii opera omnia*, Antwerp 1706, vol. i, p. 16. Catherine of Siena is here referred to, and doubtless Bridget also.

[3] Cf. *Acta Sanctorum, Oct.*, vol. iv, p. 419. *Cf.* Gerson, *De Probatione Spirituum, Consid.* V, vol. i, p. 38. Hefele, *Histoire des Conciles* (French translation by Leclercq), vol. vii, pp. 184-185.

[4] *Acta Sanctorum*, pp. 406, 416.

IV—BLOSIUS, BENEDICTINE ABBOT OF LIESSIES

LOUIS DE BLOIS, or Blosius, Abbot of Liessies in Belgium, does not belong to the Middle Ages, but to modern times : he was born in 1506.[1] If attention is drawn to him here it is to point out that with him Benedictine spirituality ceased to be exclusively affective and began to be also speculative. Scholastic theology, the glory of which shone with such splendour in the Middle Ages, ended by transforming the spiritual teaching of the sons of St Benedict.

Blosius, nevertheless, retained in a great measure the old affective style. He owes much to St Gertrude, in whose writings he greatly delighted. Like her, he had a special devotion to the humanity of our Lord, above all to his passion. When he meditates on the life of the Saviour he is far more affective than speculative; reasoning has but a very small part therein.[2]

But the Abbot of Liessies studied the German mystics of the fourteenth century. He frequently quotes Tauler, and even defends him against Ekkius. He is conversant with Ruysbroeck. Blosius is influenced by their theory of mystical contemplation, above all in his *Book of Spiritual Instruction* (*Institutio spiritualis*),[3] which is a treatise on scientific mysticism. It denotes a certain change in the Benedictine school. In Blosius there is found the fusion of the two kinds of spirituality—the affective with the speculative.

[1] Blosius was born in Hainault in Belgium. He was descended, through his father, Adrian de Blois, from the Counts of Blois and of Champagne. For some time he was page to Charles V. When he was fourteen he entered the Benedictine Abbey of Liessies on the banks of the Helpe in Belgium. He became Abbot in 1530, and effected its reform. He died in 1566. His *Works* were published at Louvain in 1568 in folio, then at Cologne in 1572. The best edition is that of Antoine de Winghe, Abbot of Liessies, published at Antwerp in 1632. The Benedictines of St Paul de Wisques have undertaken the French translation of the *Spiritual Works* of Blosius. Two volumes have appeared, Paris and Poitiers 1911, 1913.

[2] This may be seen by reading the *Prayers and Rules of Life,* especially the *Colloquies (Cimeliarchion),* Antwerp edition, 1632, pp. 40 ff., and vol. i of the Benedictine translation.

[3] Vol. ii of the Benedictine translation contains *L'Institution spirituelle; Le Miroir de l'âme; La consolation des âmes craintives,* which deals mostly with scruples.

CHAPTER IV
SPECULATIVE SPIRITUALITY
AND PLATONISM OF
THE TWELFTH CENTURY

THE DIVERS CONCEPTIONS OF THEOLOGICAL SCIENCE—THE SCHOOL OF ST VICTOR OF PARIS : ITS MYSTICAL THEOLOGY — HETERODOX MYSTICISM AT THE END OF THE TWELFTH CENTURY

THE Benedictine Order favoured the cultivation of affective spirituality. They did not, however, monopolize it. We shall find, later on, certain Orders, doubtless not so famous, where the spiritual teaching is put forward in a simple and practical way with piety alone in view.

We have found it necessary to follow the Benedictine school rather far in order to have a clear conception of it.

Let us now retrace our steps, in order to study the beginning of speculative spirituality at the commencement of the twelfth century, and to follow its development. Its history is somewhat involved with that of theology, for, in the Middle Ages, those who formed theories respecting spiritual teaching did not separate it from dogma or from morals. Every theologian was to some extent a spiritual writer, who, however, understood the science differently from those that were affective.

It was the Platonic philosophy that served, first of all, as a basis for mystical speculation.

I—DIFFERENT CONCEPTIONS OF KNOWLEDGE IN THE MIDDLE AGES

THE dawn of the twelfth century in the West discovered among minds in the domain of theology two very distinct standpoints.

The one—that of St Bernard—disdained theories. It appreciated only what was practical. Writers with this tendency looked upon reasoning as little able to lead to true science, which to them was the science of life. Knowledge of that which had to do directly with the salvation of the soul alone claimed their attention.

" It is necessary to note with great care," counsels St Bernard, who was opposed to speculation, "what above all and before all we ought to learn, for life is short. If all knowledge, considered in itself, be good if it rest on truth, nevertheless, thou who, on account of the shortness of life, art eager to work out thy salvation with fear and trembling, have a care to learn first of all, and more completely than the rest, that which relates most closely to the salvation of thy soul."[1]

The only knowledge worthy of esteem is that which teaches one to live a Christian life. The Apostles have taught us nothing more.

"They are our masters," again declares the Abbot of Clairvaux; "they have deeply learnt from the sovereign Master the ways of life, and these they have taught us until to-day. What have they taught us and what is it that they still teach? . . . They have not taught us to read Plato, nor to unravel the subtleties of Aristotle. They have not taught us to study without ever arriving at the knowledge of truth. They have taught us to live. And think you that to know how to live is little knowledge?[2] Christ did not draw his Apostles from the schools of rhetoricians and philosophers."[3]

All science which does not make us acquire the knowledge of God and of ourselves puffs up and tends to pride.[4] How great is the number of those who study through vainglory, out of curiosity, or to gain money, without troubling themselves to seek in their knowledge a means of becoming better and of growing in the love of God! St Bernard, in his *Sermons,* frequently inveighs against them so far as to incur the reproach of contemning science[5] and warning his disciples against it :

"There are those," he says, " who desire to know simply in order to know : this is shameful curiosity. Others seek instruction in order to have the reputation of being learned : this is shameful vanity. They cannot avoid the sneer of the satirist who addressed these lines to the vain : *Thy know-*

---

[1] St Bernard, *In Cantica, sermo* XXXVI, 2 (*P.L.,* CLXXXII, 968). Cf. *sermo* XXXVII, 2.

[2] *In festo SS Petri et Pauli, sermo* I, 3 (col. 407). Cf. *In festo Pentecostes, sermo* III, 5.

[3] *In Cantica, sermo* XXXVI, 1.

[4] *In Cantica, sermo* XXXVII, 2-5.

[5] *In Cantica, sermo* XXXVI, 2 : *Videar forsitan nimius in suggillatione scientiae et quasi reprehendere doctos, ac prohibere studia litterarum. Absit. Non ignoro quantum Ecclesiae profuerint et prosint litterati sui sive ad refellendos eos qui ex adverso sunt, sive ad simplices instruendos.*

ledge is nothing if it be not known that thou possess it
(Persius, *Satire* I, v. 27). There are others again who
desire to know in order to sell their knowledge, either for
money or for honours : this is a disgraceful traffic. But
there are some who wish to become instructed in order to
edify their neighbour, which is charity, as there are those
who desire instruction that they may edify themselves, which
is prudence. In all these groups of scholars the last two
alone do not abuse science, since they desire to be instructed
in order to do good."[1]

Writers from the other standpoint, the tendency to
speculation, delighted, on the contrary, in learned abstractions. They set forth spiritual teaching by means of
dialectics and syllogisms. They appealed almost exclusively
to reason, without attempting to excite the affective part
of the soul. Their end was to expound the principles of
theology and spirituality in an abstract manner, in synthetic
treatises, all the parts of which should be bound together and
to each other according to the strict rules of logic. They
gave but little attention to evolving practical consequences
in order to apply them to the divers circumstances of life.
For the object of speculative science is knowledge pure and
simple : *Scientia speculativa vocatur cujus finis proprius non
est nisi scire*. It is thus distinguished from practical science,
the immediate object of which is action : *Scientia practica est
cujus proprius finis est operari.*[2]

Speculative science was fostered in the twelfth century
above all by Abelard, and we know to what perfection it was
brought by the great scholastic theologians in the century
that followed. Mystics were at first distinctly unfavourable
to it. They were unwilling to allow, in the search after
truth, that the intelligence alone should be employed; the
heart, according to them, ought always to take the principal
part. True science is not that which renders a man learned,
but that which makes him virtuous.

St Bernard did not think it permissible to study solely in
order to know what was to be known concerning divine
truths, in order to explain them as far as possible and to
draw up for them a rational theory. He rose up against
Abelard, who made so bold as to reason on Christian
mysteries much more than to meditate on them and to make
them the rule of his life :

"Master Abelard," he wrote to a Cardinal in Rome, " exceeds the limits set by our fathers. Disputing and writing
on matters of faith, the Sacraments, and the blessed Trinity
he changes all at will, adds or minimizes as it pleases him

---

[1] *In Cantica, sermo* XXXVI, 3-4.
[2] Cajetan, *In Summa Theolog.*, pars I, Q. I, art. 4.

. . . there is nothing in heaven or earth that he does not know unless it be himself."[1]

In spite of this opposition, speculative theology ended by commanding respect on account of its clearness, its precision and the services it rendered to the Church. St Thomas Aquinas, at the beginning of his *Summa Theologica,* was able to lay down that theology is a science much more speculative than practical.[2]

But many mystics were never reconciled to it. In the course of the Middle Ages the author of the *Imitation of Christ*[3] and many others were unable to tolerate ascetic and mystical speculations. According to their way of looking at it, theological systems, painfully elaborate, only ended in opinions without stability or in useless subtleties. They are more often than not the result of pride, and lead to a sort of intellectual paganism. We take pleasure in them and consecrate our life to them, and forget the one thing needful—to struggle against vice and to practise virtue. Never will a man, infatuated with the conceptions of his mind, have sufficient humility to despise the vanities of the world and to imitate the life of Christ. The soul, then, that desires to labour after inward perfection will turn away from this futile science.

Nevertheless, intelligent minds were of opinion, not without reason, that speculative theology ought not to be condemned under the pretext of piety. They thought, on other grounds, that pure speculation was full of danger and likely to dry up the life of the soul. Would it not be possible to unite the science of the heart with that of the mind, to transform speculative theology into affective theology by way of preparation for mystical contemplation?

In the twelfth century the school of St Victor strove to popularize this twofold conception of knowledge, which would be both speculative and affective, theoretical and practical. Hugh, the great theologian of this school, had much greater sympathy than the Abbot of Clairvaux with the science of the mind,[4] whilst insisting on the necessity for the science of the heart, the science which teaches us to love God.

"There are some," he says, "who love to hear the word of God and to study his works, not because they are healthful for the soul, but simply because they are wonderful.

[1] *Epist.* cxciii. Cf. *Tractacus de erroribus Abaelardi,* cap. i.

[2] *Sum. Theol.,* pars I, Q. I, art. 4 : *Sacra doctrina non est scientia practica sed magis speculativa.*

[3] See chapters i, ii, iii of the first book, and chapter xliii of the third book.

[4] *Cf.* Hugh of St Victor, *Eruditionis didascaliae,* lib. V, cap. vi (*P.L.,* CLXXVI, 794). Lib. VI, cap. iii : *Omnia disce [in Scripturis]. Videbis postea nihil esse superfluum. Coarctata scientia jucunda non est* (800-801).

They desire to pry into divine mysteries and to learn things out of the common, to know everything and to do no good work. . . . In my opinion they should be helped rather than troubled; for they are thoughtless rather than of evil intent. There are others, again, who study Holy Writ in order to be, according to the apostolic precept (1 Pet. iii, 5), *ready to satisfy everyone that asketh a reason of the hope which is in them*—that is to say, to refute the enemies of truth, to instruct the ignorant, and to know more perfectly themselves the way of salvation; in a word, in order to have a higher understanding of divine mysteries and to love God more ardently. Their piety deserves to be praised and imitated . . .[1] For the Christian philosopher study ought to lead to good, and not only occupy the mind, but enkindle good desires and not extinguish them.''[2]

At St Victor it was hoped to find in the idealism of Plato a means of rendering theological science both speculative and affective. They thus imitated St Augustine, the great Platonist, who knew how to fathom the divine mysteries deeply without ever hindering the marvellous flights of his soul towards God.

In the twelfth century—and it was thus throughout the Middle Ages—there were therefore three conceptions of knowledge : practical knowledge, which touches the heart without reasoning, speculative knowledge, which reasons without touching the heart, and knowledge which is both speculative and practical, appealing alike to the reason and to the affections. The first is that of the mystics—it is that of the Benedictine school; the second belongs to the scholastics, the last was that of the theologians of St Victor and a great number of teachers like St Bonaventure and Gerson, whom we shall meet with later.

II—THE ABBEY OF ST VICTOR IN PARIS—THE REPRESENTATIVES OF ITS SCHOOL—ITS PLATONIC IDEALISM

The founder of the school of St Victor was William of Champeaux, a friend of St Bernard.[3] William first taught at Notre-Dame de Paris with great renown. Abelard was one of his disciples and afterwards became his most ardent opponent. In 1108 William gave up his chair at Notre-Dame, together with the office of Archdeacon, in order to retire to

---

[1] Hugh of St Victor, *Eruditionis didascaliae*, lib. V, cap. x (*P.L.*, CLXXVI, 798).
[2] *ibid.*, cap. vii.
[3] *Cf.* Michaud, *Guillaume de Champeaux et les écoles de Paris au XIIe siècle*, Paris 1867 ; Feret, *La faculté de théologie de Paris et ses docteurs les plus célèbres*, Paris 1894 ; Mignon, *Les origines de la scolastique et Hugues de Saint-Victor*, Paris 1895.

St Victor, near Paris, where he became a Canon Regular of St Augustine. In this retreat he was invited to undertake once more the teaching which had been so much appreciated. This he did, and thus was founded the famous school of St Victor.[1]

The Canons Regular of St Victor followed the Rule known as St Augustine's.

This Rule, largely inspired by Letter CCXI of the Bishop of Hippo, chiefly came into vogue in the eleventh century. At this time, in fact, many of the clergy who were living in community renounced the possession of private property which had been allowed by the Canonical Rule of St Chrodegang of Metz, and took religious vows.[2] They usually adopted the Rule of St Augustine, more or less modified. Thus arose the Order of Canons Regular (*canonici regulares*).

At first each house of the Canons Regular was independent. But in the twelfth century they formed themselves into proper congregations embracing several convents, attached to one of them either by the bond of foundation or by that of reform. The most famous congregation of Canons Regular is that of the Premonstratensians, founded by St Norbert of Xanten, who came from the Rhine Provinces. Norbert settled at Laon, where in 1120 he formed the convent of Premontré (Praemonstratum).[3] St Bernard ceded to Norbert the rights which he had over this place.[4] He had, moreover, a great veneration for Norbert and his work,[5] in spite of certain difficulties which arose between the Premonstratensians and the Cistercians.[6] The Order of Premonstratensians developed enormously, and was one of the most famous of the Middle Ages.[7]

The Rule of St Augustine varied in severity according to the houses.

[1] William of Champeaux became Bishop of Chalons-sur-Marne in 1112. It was then that he became the friend of St Bernard, whom he consecrated Abbot (*Bern. Vita*, lib. I, cap. viii). He died in 1121.

[2] The author of this reform was Pope Gregory VII, who desired to restore canonical discipline in the cathedral and collegiate chapters. The canons often held their title from feudal overlords and lived contrary to the laws of the Church. Many bishops made their chapters adopt the Rule of St Augustine. The work of William of Champeaux and that of St Norbert helped them considerably in their endeavours to reform their canons.

[3] *Acta Sanctorum, Junii*, vol. i, June 6. See Godefroi Madelaine, *Histoire de S Norbert*, 1886.

[4] Bernard, *Epist.* ccliii, n. 1.

[5] This is shown from the letters of St Bernard. Cf. *Epist.* lvi; viii, 4; clxxviii, 2.

[6] *Cf.* Bernard, *Epist.* ccliii, 10.

[7] Similar congregations were founded at the same period. They are less important. Thus the Canons Regular of the Lateran, those of the Holy Sepulchre at Jerusalem, those of S Rufus at Avignon, etc.

It laid down as essential the community life with the three vows of poverty, chastity and obedience. The night Office also was always prescribed, but it was shorter than that of the Benedictines. The day was taken up by prayer and work which was either that of parochial duties, study or manual labour. Fasting and mortifications varied considerably between one congregation and another. With the Premonstratensians, austerity as regards food, clothing and sleep were as great as in the Cistercian monasteries. On the other hand, meat was allowed three times a week, and fish, eggs and milk products were not forbidden at other times.

The Rule of St Augustine, then, was variable; unlike the other great Rules, it had no single type.

At St Victor the observance was almost as severe as that of the Benedictine Rule. Only those that were ill were allowed meat. The life laid down was as near as possible that of the Cistercian monasteries.[1] The religious devoted the greater part of their day to study. Thus did the school of St Victor become in the twelfth century an important intellectual centre where mystical theology was held in high repute. The chief figures of this school were Hugh, Richard and Adam.

The native country of Hugh is not known. It is thought that he was born in Saxony.[2] He was the great theologian of the school and the one who did most to render it famous. He died in 1140. Richard (1173) seems to have made mystical theology his special study. He synthesized the teaching of St Victor concerning ecstatic contemplation. He is looked upon as representing the mysticism of the Victorines. Adam (1177) is the mystical poet of the school. He has left hymns or rhymed *proses* for divers feasts of the liturgical year.

In the same way that the dialectics of Aristotle formed the necessary basis for scholasticism, so the idealism of Plato was the foundation of the mysticism of St Victor.

Platonic philosophy became the vogue in the Middle Ages by means of the writings of St Augustine, which were largely studied at St Victor; and also, above all, through those of Dionysius the Areopagite.

The writings of the pseudo-Dionysius appeared, as we know, at the end of the fifth century, real erratic masses, the origin of which it is difficult to determine. They first

---

[1] Hugonin, *Essai sur la fondation de l'école de Saint-Victor de Paris,* chap. ii (*P.L.,* CLXXV, 24-40); Hugh of Saint-Victor, *Expositio in regulam B. Augustini* (*P.L.,* CLXXVI, 881-924); *De institutione novitiorum* (925-952).

[2] *Cf.* Hugonin, *id.,* chap. iii; B. Hauréau, *Hugues de Saint-Victor, Nouvel examen de ses œuvres,* Paris 1859.

gave inspiration to the Greek mystics, of whom the most famous was Maximus the Confessor, in the eighth century.

In the West the works of Dionysius were chiefly known through the Latin translation by the Irish philosopher, John Scotus Eriugena (877).[1]

This translation appeared at the time when the legend respecting the apostolic authority of Dionysius was current, which gave to the writings of the Areopagite a weight almost equal to that of the Bible. The great theologians of the twelfth and thirteenth centuries often cite them. They made commentaries on them with a view to rendering popular a teaching inspired, as it was thought, by the Apostles themselves.[2] Dante's Divine Comedy, which is a faithful echo of the religious thought of the Middle Ages, sang the praises of Dionysius the Areopagite.[3]

Attentive and also religious study of writings with such authority must inevitably have led the Middle Ages to mysticism. The disdain for theoretical science shown by a great number of writers of this period, their preference for intuition and the direct intercourse of the soul with divine Truth came principally from the Areopagite.

It will be remembered how little Dionysius thought of that rational knowledge of God which we are able to acquire. Reason gives us so imperfect an idea of the divinity that in reality it is not one.[4] A true knowledge of God is obtained less by speculation than by the light of grace. Moreover, intuitive mystical theology is incomparably superior to rational and abstract theology. It is by contemplation that we arrive at truth. These were the ideas that inspired the theology of the school of St Victor.

[1] John Scotus Eriugena was head of the school of the palace of Charles the Bald, about 847. His chief works are his translation of the works of the pseudo-Dionysius; a scarcely orthodox commentary (*Expositiones*) on these writings which has come down to us incomplete; *De divisione naturae libri quinque; De praedestinatione* (*P.L.*, CXXII). He explains the Catholic dogma by the help of Neo-platonism. His theories, above all that of the return of all things into God, were disastrous to some mystics of the Middle Ages. *Cf.* F. Vernet, *Erigène*, in the *Dict. de Theol. cath.* of Vacant.

[2] Hugh of Saint-Victor has written a commentary on the book of Dionysius on the *Celestial Hierarchy* (*P.L.*, CLXXV, 923-1154). St Thomas Aquinas often quotes Dionysius in his *Summa*. He wrote a commentary on the treatise of *The Divine Names*. His master, Albert the Great, did so on the book of the *Celestial Hierarchy*. St Bonaventure drew inspiration from the *Ecclesiastical Hierarchy*, etc.

[3] *Paradiso, canto X.*

[4] St Bernard appears to be acquainted with the Dionysian principle (*In psalm. Qui habitat, sermo X*, 1) : *nec nostra est, nec nova vobis, sed nota omnino sententia, in praecipuis quibusque partibus nostrae fidei, quid non sit quam quid sit et sciri posse facilius et periculosius ignorari* (*P.L.*, CLXXXIII, 221).

III—THE MYSTICAL THEOLOGY OF THE SCHOOL
OF ST VICTOR[1]—THE SYMBOLIC CONCEPTION
OF THE WORLD—MYSTICAL INTUITION—CON-
TEMPLATION AND ECSTASY

THE word mystical, with the Victorines, as with the greater
number of the writers of the Middle Ages, was not used in
the precise sense in which it is employed to-day, when we
distinguish it from the term ascetic. It was synonymous
with *symbolic* or with *affective*.

At St Victor, by mystical, in accordance with its etymology,
was meant that which was hidden beneath a symbol.
Mystical contemplation, then, was that which enables us to
find, under the symbolism of material realities, the truths
which lie hidden there. The spirituality of St Victor, as we
shall see, postulates a symbolic conception of the world,
which comes from Platonism.

The object of contemplation—this ought also to be noticed
—was not at St Victor supernatural truth alone. It was all
truth. The soul begins with the contemplation of scientific
truth that has been discovered by intellectual effort. Then,
little by little, under the influence of grace, it is raised to
the vision of divine truth.

For the mystics of the twelfth century there was no such
thing as profane science; all science is religious, for it
enables us to know what God teaches through creation.
The Victorines do not clearly distinguish between the natural
and the supernatural, nor the object of philosophy from that
of faith, although this distinction is in their mind.[2] Has
not the whole of the universe been restored by Christ?
Also, according to them, contemplation of revealed truth is
the continuation, the perfecting of natural truths. The
mystical writers of the fourteenth and fifteenth centuries
carefully distinguished between mystical contemplation and
the contemplation of scientific truths. They deal exclusively
with the first. The theologians of St Victor proceeded
differently.

[1] Principal sources : Hugh of St. Victor, *De sacramentis christianae fidei, De vanitate mundi; Eruditionis didascaliae libri septem; Expositio in regulam S Augustini; De institutione novitiorum; Soliloquium de arrha animae; De laude charitatis; De modo orandi; De amore sponsi ad sponsam; De meditando seu meditandi artificio; De modo dicendi et meditandi; De fructibus carnis et spiritus* (*P.L.*, CLXXVI). Richard of St Victor, *De praeparatione animi ad contemplationem liber dictus Benjamin minor; De gratia contemplationis, seu Benjamin major; Expositio in Cantica Canticorum; De eruditione hominis interioris* (*P.L.*, CXCVI). Adam of St Victor, *Sequentiae* (*P.L.*, CXCVI).

[2] John Scotus Eriugena, who made no distinction between the object of faith and that of philosophy, seems in this to have inspired the school of St Victor.

The mystical system of the Victorines comprises three parts : the symbolic conception of the universe, which is the basis; intuitive meditation, which is its method; and contemplation, which completes it.

Scholastic science, Aristotelian—as we shall see—studies things in themselves as realities. It proceeds by induction in tracing back from the effect to its cause, or by deduction in passing from the principle to its consequence. It makes use of the syllogism as the means by which it strives to attain to reality.

The Victorines, on the contrary, are intuitive : they go directly to the true by meditation and contemplation without passing through the series of more or less complicated discursive acts of the syllogism; for they looked upon created beings less as realities than as symbols of divine teaching. The sensible world hides invisible realities; what should be studied is not sensible beings in themselves but the teaching which they contain.

1. The Symbolistic Conception of the Universe.

The mysticism of the Middle Ages, in fact, looks upon the world as a symbol.

The Christian school of Alexandria, which in the third century was directed by Clement and Origen, had already accustomed minds to seek, beneath the literal sense of a writing or the appearances of an object, deeper and more mysterious realities.

This symbolism was first of all employed in biblical exegesis, and then applied a little to everything. St Ambrose, St Augustine, St Gregory the Great, to mention only the principal allegorists, see in almost all things symbols of vice or virtue. Material beings are like words that express a divine thought to be discovered. It is unnecessary to state that this symbolism is that of the pseudo-Dionysius, the oracle of the Middle Ages. From the twelfth century, also, there were many who looked upon the world as a symbol and each being as expressing an idea of the Word, an idea which it was necessary to evolve by means of mystical contemplation.[1]

Here, for example, is the conception of the universe that was formed at St Victor.

The works of God in the world were narrowed to the creation and to the restoration of creatures through the in-

---

[1] M. Emile Male, in his charming work, *L'art religieux du XIII*ᵉ *siècle en France,* Paris 1910, pp. 43-44, well observed that this symbolic conception of the world inspired the artists of the cathedrals as well as mystical theologians. See also the *Monographie de la cathédrale de Lyon*, Lyons 1880, by M. Lucien Bégule, Parts III and IV, *Vitraux* and *Sculpture.*

carnation. The creation is the work of the Word, it is his outward utterance. Every creature is the sensible expression of a thought of the Son of God; it is a word which signifies this thought. Each being then contains hidden a divine thought. The whole of created beings together is like an immense book which contains the teachings of God. In a book two things may be considered : the beauty of the letters and the thoughts which they express. Our eyes admire the competence of the calligrapher, and our reason takes pleasure in the ideas which the writer has expressed. Our sight and our intelligence are thus equally charmed. Material beings are the words which make manifest the thoughts of God, they are the marvellous symbols which hide the heavenly teachings.

The Creator has endowed the human soul with a twofold sense; an outward sense capable of seeing and admiring the beauty of material realities, and an inward sense wholly spiritual, which is able to penetrate beyond material things in order to discover the idea which they conceal.[1] Man alone is so constituted as to be able to contemplate visible realities and those which lie hidden from the senses. The angel is able to see only that which is immaterial. The animal perceives only the sensible. Man, who is both matter and spirit, knows material beings, discerns their beauty and understands also what they signify. He can both admire the wonderful art with which the Creator has formed the letters of the great book of creation, and disclose the thoughts which are expressed by them. Man, therefore, ought to praise God in his work, praise him because of the magnificence of the material world, and because of the wonderful teaching which can be discovered there.[2]

Thus should man, by this spectacle of the universe, be moved to glorify and love the Lord. If, indeed, our first parents had not sinned we should have been raised without effort or difficulty from the sensible to the intelligible. We should easily have discovered, beneath the material envelope of creatures, the truths which lie hidden therein. The symbolism of the world would not have been a secret for us, and our hearts, filled with acknowledgement and love, would have ascended towards God by means of sensible beings.

But sin disturbed this primitive plan. Since the fall man became the slave of his senses. His intelligence had weakened. It was no longer able to be raised to the divine idea which creatures expressed. It was almost always arrested at the material element, the sensible symbol, with-

---

[1] Hugh of St Victor, *De sacramentis christianae fidei,* lib. I, pars VI, cap. v. Cf. *Eruditionis didascaliae,* lib. VII, cap. iv.

[2] Hugh of St Victor, *De sacramentis christ. fid.,* lib. I, pars VI, cap. v.

out attaining to the truth symbolized. Creation thus
became a dangerous book because wrongly read, and far
from guiding the soul to God it misled it by inclining it to
remain fixed in the sensible as though it were its final end
instead of only a means of approaching the Creator.
The work of God, then, required to be restored, to be,
so to speak, remade. The divine Word remade his work by
becoming Incarnate.

By the Incarnation God offered to man a new sign by which
to arrive at the knowledge of invisible realities. The
humanity of Christ was added to the world in order to show
God to man. Through it we approach the Word which it
hides. It enlightens our ailing sight with the light of faith,
and thus it brings us out of the darkness into which sin has
plunged us.[1] It proffers itself as an admirable model to be
imitated, which our outward senses are able to study, and it
leads our inward senses, illumined by faith, to the divinity
which it conceals.

The Incarnation then redresses the fall by teaching us to
raise ourselves to God by the help of the sensible.

" The Word took flesh without losing the divinity, and he
offered himself to man like a book written within and without : externally by the humanity, and internally by the
divinity, in order that he might be read outwardly by
imitation, and inwardly by contemplation; outwardly in
order to heal us, and inwardly to lead us to happiness. . . .
Inwardly we read, *In the beginning was the Word* (John i,
1); outwardly, *The Word was made flesh and dwelt among
us* (John i, 14). This book then is unique, written once
within and twice without : first, by the creation of the visible
world, and then by the Incarnation; the first time in order to
afford us a pleasurable sight; the second, to heal us; the
first, in order to create nature; the second, to redress the
fall."[2]

The Word Incarnate has completed this restoration of fallen
humanity by the institution of the Sacraments. These
accustom man to perceive with the eyes of faith beneath the
material appearances of rites, the invisible reality of which
is hidden, like remedies in vessels. They thus teach him to
raise himself from the sensible to the spiritual. The sacra-
mental rite is not only, like ordinary sensible beings, a
symbol which hides the divine thought, it is also a vessel
which contains grace (*vasa sunt spiritualis gratiae sacra-
menta*).[3] It possesses in itself wherewith to heal man
wounded by original sin; it is filled with that which is divine.

[1] Hugh of St Victor, *Expositio in Hierarchiam caelestem S Dionysii,*
lib. I, cap. i (*P.L.*, CLXXV, 926).
[2] Hugh of St Victor, *De sacramentis,* lib. I, pars VI, cap. v.
[3] *id.*, lib. I, pars IX, cap. iv.

The efficacy of the Sacraments is the triumph of mysticism which strives to find God through sensible beings.

The world is not only a great book written by the very hand of God; it is also a mirror which reflects the divine thought and in which it may be contemplated. The mystical writers of the Middle Ages loved to make use of the term mirror (*speculum*) as a title for their works. The symbolical explanation of ecclesiastical rites, and of the prayers and ceremonies of the Mass, placed in the appendix to the works of Hugh of St Victor, bear the name of the *mirror,* " because we may there contemplate the mystical image of each rite of the Church."[1] The great encyclopædia of the Middle Ages, the work of the famous Dominican, Vincent of Beauvais, is entitled the *Great Mirror (Speculum Majus).*[2] In fact, is not the whole world a great mirror in which is seen the thought of God?

The divine thought is to be sought, first of all, in Holy Writ, by allegorical interpretation. The Middle Ages are in no way inferior to the patristic period in their exaggerated attachment to the mystical sense of the sacred text. The word of God does not appear to them to be expressed by the literal meaning of the words; they must be discerned by an allegory. Hugh of St Victor notices, as well as censures, those " doctors of the allegorical sense " who entirely despise the literal study of the Bible.

" We read the Scriptures, they say, but without being bound to the letter. We take no heed of the literal sense; that which we teach is the allegorical sense. . . . We read, no doubt, the letter of the text, but without stopping at the grammatical sense of the words. For it is the allegory which we are seeking, and we explain the expressions not according to their literal meaning but their allegorical. . . . Thus the word *lion* literally indicates an animal, and allegorically it indicates Christ. For us, therefore, the word lion denotes purely and simply Christ."[3]

It is not astonishing to find, side by side with most interesting mystical commentaries, such as those of Hugh on different parts of the Bible[4] and of Richard of St Victor on the Psalms,[5] others in which the allegorical subtleties surprise us much more than they edify.

Honorius of Autun remarks, for example, that the

---

[1] *Speculum de mysteriis Ecclesiae (P.L.,* CLXXVII, 335).

[2] *Speculum Majus,* Douai 1624, 4 vols. Vincent of Beauvais, so called from the place of his birth, belonged to the Order of St Dominic. He lived in the time of St Louis, King of France. His work is divided into four parts : The Mirror of Nature, the Mirror of Knowledge, the Mirror of Morals, and the Mirror of History.

[3] Hugh of St. Victor, *De Scripturis et scriptoribus sacris,* cap. ▼ (*P.L.,* CLXXV, 13).

[4] *P.L.,* CLXXV, 10-634.

[5] *Adnotationes mysticae in psalmos (P.L.,* CXCVI, 265-402).

Psalter contains one hundred and fifty psalms, for, he says, "as at the time of the deluge the world was washed from its sins by one hundred and fifty days of flood, so is the penitent Church cleansed in tears from its faults by reciting the hundred and fifty psalms."[1] It is useless to multiply quotations of this kind.

Since the material world as a whole is looked upon as a discourse of the Word, each being of which is a word,[2] the task of the mystic then is to discover the eternal truths which God has willed each thing to express.

With this end in view there was drawn up in the Middle Ages a regular mystical *Natural History*[3] which the preachers and the artists who adorned our cathedrals turned to account. Minerals, plants and animals are there represented as symbols of Christian realities.

St Francis de Sales must surely have read these curious writings. He discovered there naïve and charming comparisons, drawn from real or imaginary properties of minerals and plants, as well as from true or legendary habits of animals, which delight the reader of the *Introduction to the Devout Life* and the *Treatise of the Love of God*.

Among minerals are the precious stones which, by their varied colours, best symbolize supernatural realities. Marbod, Bishop of Rennes (1123), at the end of his book *Liber de gemmis,* explains the mystical symbolism which he finds in the twelve precious stones which were part of the outer wall of the new Jerusalem (Apoc. xxi, 19-20).[4] Jasper, green in colour, signifies living faith, vigorous and full of verdure. Sapphire, the colour of the sky, represents Christians who think unceasingly of their heavenly country. Every stone is the symbol of a Christian virtue.

Plants and their fruits also provide easy and abundant themes for mystical writers. Roses call to mind the blood of the martyrs, when red, and when white the purity of virgins.[5] Honorius of Autun, in a sermon on the Purification of the Blessed Virgin, explains the symbolism of the

---

[1] *Expositio in psalmos selectos* (*P.L.*, CLXXII, 272). Honorius of Autun, priest of the Church of Autun, lived at the beginning of the twelfth century. He was a prolific writer who had a great influence in his time. He then became so forgotten that nothing is known of his life. His works are in Migne, *P.L.*, CLXXII. The most famous is the *Speculum Ecclesiae,* a collection of sermons for the principal feasts of the year, into which preachers delved for a long time.

[2] E. Male, *op. cit.*, p. 50.

[3] One of the most celebrated is the *De bestiis et aliis rebus,* wrongly attributed to Hugh of St Victor (*P.L.*, CLXXVII, 13-164).

[4] *Lapidum pretiosorum mystica applicatio* (*P.L.*, CLXXI, 1771-1774). These mystical explanations are reproduced in the *De bestiis et aliis rebus,* lib. III, cap. lviii.

[5] Petrus de Mora, Cardinal and Bishop of Capua, *Rosa Alphabetica,* in the *Spicilegium Solesmense,* vol. iii, p. 489; E. Male, *op. cit.*, p. 45.

nut *à propos* of the rod of Aaron placed by Moses in the tabernacle of the testimony, miraculously budding and blossoming and bringing forth fruit (Num. xvii, 8).

"The rod of Aaron," he said, "is an image of the Virgin Mary, who produced a sweet almond by bringing into the world a God-Man. The almond is, in fact, the symbol of Christ. The green envelope which covers it is his flesh; the shell is his bones; the kernel is his soul. The sweet savour of the inside of the nut, with which man is nourished, is his divinity. The nut is divided by means of a partition in the form of a cross which symbolizes the separation of the soul and body of Christ on the cross. This mystical nut is the food of the elect, it constitutes the banquet of all the choirs of angels."[1]

The poor man in his cottage and the monk in the refectory of his convent were equally edified, whilst taking their meal, by this symbolic teaching which they had heard explained in the sermon on Sunday.

But it is zoology which most took the fancy of the mystics of the Middle Ages. The marvellous and more or less legendary habits which the ancient naturalists[2] attributed to animals were singularly favourable to moral reflections. In the Bestiaries the animals of creation, real or fabulous, are like so many symbols of the Christian virtues or of the truths of faith. It was, in a measure, a method of teaching by image, so useful to the unlettered.

"Do not accuse me of levity," we read in the Prologue to the *De bestiis et aliis rebus,*[3] "because I describe the vulture and the dove. . . . What writing is to the scholar, the image is for the ignorant. In the same way that the learned man enjoys the elegance of style, so are the simple captivated by the simplicity of image." "One of the faithful, while assisting at Mass in a cathedral, kneeling near a column, sees sculptured there at the base a reptile with one ear placed against the ground and stopping the other up with the end of his tail: It is the asp, the emblem of prudence." The asp is a kind of very venomous viper that lives in caves. In order to kill it it must be charmed and thus lured from its hole. "It is related," says a Bestiary, "that when the asp begins to hear the charmer who desires to draw it out of its cave with his chanting, in order not to run the risk of

---

[1] Honorius of Autun, *Speculum Ecclesiae* (*P.L.,* CLXXII, 850); Adam of St Victor, *Sequentiae,* iii, 45 (*P.L.,* CXCVI, 1433-1434).

[2] Among others, Pliny the Elder, and a famous bestiary of the second century of the Christian era, the *Physiologus,* of which the Greek text has been edited by D. Pitra, *Spic. Solesm.,* vol. iii. The *De Universo* of Rabanus Maurus (*P.L.,* CX) was also drawn upon. Hildebert, Archbishop of Tours, at the beginning of the twelfth century, also composed a *Physiologus* (*P.L.,* CLXXI, 1217-1224).

[3] *P.L.,* CLXXVII, 15.

going out it leans one ear down on the ground and stops up the other with the end of its tail. It thus renders itself insensible to the magical accents and does not surrender to the charmer. . . .[1] We must imitate the asp and close our ears to the songs of the sirens—that is to say, to the solicitations of pleasure and the deceitful charms of the passions in order to be, according to the advice of the Lord, as prudent as serpents.''[2]

If from the base of the columns the worshipper should raise his eyes to the windows he would see represented there the symbolic legend of the bird called *caradius* or *charadius*.

" This bird is entirely white,'' says Honorius of Autun in his sermon for the Ascension. " It is allowed to know if sick persons are to be cured or not. When it approaches a sick man, if he is to die, the bird turns away its head. If he is to live the caradius fixes him with a solemn eye, places his beak close to his mouth and breathes in the sickness.[3] He then flies into the air, is exposed to the rays of the sun and discharges, by perspiration, the malady that he has absorbed. The sick man rejoices at his return to health. The white caradius symbolizes Christ, born of the Virgin, who has been sent by his Father to the human race that is sick. The Saviour has turned his face away from the Jews whom he has left in death, and he has turned towards us. He has snatched us from death by bearing our malady on the cross and shedding his sweat of blood. He has afterwards flown with our humanity to his Father in the highest heaven, giving us all eternal life.''[4]

Not far from the caradius is seen another window in which a young girl is represented mounted on an animal;[5] it is the fabulous history of the unicorn used as a symbol of the Incarnation. The unicorn is an animal possessing great strength, with a horn in the middle of its forehead, and it is very wild. Only a virgin can master it. As soon as the unicorn sees the young maiden who calls it, it comes to her and allows itself to be taken. In like manner the Virgin Mary alone was able to draw down the Son of God who

[1] The Psalmist (Ps. lvii, 5-6) also speaks of the " deaf asp that stoppeth her ears : which will not hear the voice of the charmer : nor of the wizard that charmeth wisely.''

[2] *De bestiis et aliis rebus,* lib. II, cap. xxx. Honorius of Autun explains this same symbolism of the asp in his Sermon for Palm Sunday (*P.L.,* CLXXII, 914-915).

[3] See the coloured glass in the cathedral of Lyons. L. Bégule, *op. cit.,* p. 120.

[4] Honorius of Autun, *Spec. Eccles.* (*P.L.,* CLXXII, 958). Cf. *De bestiis et aliis rebus,* lib. II, cap. xxxi.

[5] Coloured glass in the cathedral of Lyons. L. Bégule, *op. cit.,* p. 117.

assumed human form, rested on her breast, and thus allowed himself to be taken by man.[1]

The greater number of animals were thus put before Christians as clever symbols representing the truths of faith.[2]

Finally—and this does not surprise us—it was in the Middle Ages that there appeared the symbolical interpretation of liturgical ceremonies. Amalarius of Metz, in the ninth century, inaugurated these mystical studies of the liturgy.[3] But in the twelfth century liturgists[4] entirely forgot the historical meaning of Christian rites; they were willing only to admit the mystical sense. It seems hardly necessary to state that it often happened that they were inclined to accentuate the subtleties of liturgical symbolism. This exaggeration itself tends once more to show the state of mind at this period. Reality is nothing in itself; it is only a veil which must be raised, an envelope which must be broken, in order to attain to that which is spiritual and catch a glimpse of God.

Let us see, for example, the mystical teachings which Honorius of Autun finds in the sequence of the different hours of the canonical office:

" The day," he says, " represents the life of each one of us; the different ages correspond with the divers hours at which man, taught by the law of God, labours in the vineyard of the Lord (Matt. xx, 1-16).

" *Lauds* reminds us of infancy when we emerged from the night in order to see light when our mothers brought us into the world. It is right to praise God at this hour when we rejoice at having passed, through baptism, from the darkness of error to the light of truth. *Prime* makes us think of youth, the period when we began to study. Very rightly do we praise God at this time when we were initiated in the divine service. *Terce* is adolescence, the age for the reception of minor orders. With good reason do we glorify God at this hour when we became his ministers. *Sext* is the strength of early manhood at which we were promoted to the orders of the diaconate and the priesthood. At this hour, above all, should we bless God for having established us as heads and masters of his people. *None* makes us think of the decline of life,

---

[1] Honorius of Autun, *Speculum Ecclesiae* (*P.L.*, CLXXII, 819); *De bestiis et aliis rebus*, lib. II, cap. vi.

[2] For further information on this interesting subject, see the works of E. Male and L. Bégule already quoted.

[3] *De ecclesiasticis officiis* and *Eclogae de officio missae* (*P.L.*, CV).

[4] Rupert de Tuy, *De divinis officiis* (*P.L.*, CLXX, 11-332); Honorius of Autun, *Gemma animae, Sacramentarium* (*P.L.*, CLXXII, 541-806); Hugh of St Victor (?), *Speculum de mysteriis Ecclesiae, De officiis ecclesiasticis* (*P.L.*, CLXXVII, 335-456); Sicard of Cremona, *Mitrale sive Summa de officiis eccles.* (*P.L.*, CCXIII, 13-436). In the thirteenth century, William Durand, Bishop of Mende, summarized the works of his predecessors in his *Rationale divinorum officiorum*.

the age when most of us are laden with some ecclesiastical
dignity as with a heavy burden. Is it not meet to glorify
God at this hour in which it has pleased him to set us over
his people? *Vespers* represents old age in which many
among us, as though living in vanity, having rested all the
day idle, begin to be more fervent (Matt. xx, 6). Should we
not praise God and thank him for having placed us among
those that celebrate his glory? At *Compline* we prepare for
the end of life by confession and penitence in which we hope
to be saved."[1]

Similar mystical reflections are made concerning the sacred
vestments of the ecclesiastical ministers *à propos* of the
ceremonies and prayers of the Mass, the different objects of
devotion, and furniture of the church. For sacred things,
even more than ordinary material things, are the expression
of some divine teaching.

2. *Intuitive Meditation.*

What is the method to be followed in order to raise ourselves from the visible to the invisible, and to discover in
created beings the mind of God, so that we may profit by it
and reach perfection?

This cannot be, surely, by pure dialectics. The idea of
the world that is suggested by syllogistic deduction is
different from that of the mystics. Intuition and contemplation are better means of finding, beneath the material surface
of creatures, the thought that God has desired to express
through them.

The Christian who is desirous of knowing God, of loving
him and of attaining to holiness should act then in regard
to created things as does the artist before a work of art.

The artist begins by examining the work in front of him
in order to notice its details; in a word, to read it.[2] Then
he reflects, meditates and endeavours to discover, with an
intuitive eye, the idea which the painter if it be a picture,
the sculptor if it be a statue, or the architect if it be a
building, has wished to express. When this idea has been
found he contemplates it with love; he is in ecstasy, so to
speak, at the happy manner in which it has been expressed.

Created beings are the *chefs d'œuvre* through which God
has made manifest his thoughts. We must read them and

---

[1] Honorius of Autun, *Gemma animae*, lib. II, cap. liv (*P.L.*, CLXXII,
633).

[2] Hugh of St Victor, *De modo dicendi et meditandi; De meditando
seu meditandi artificio* (*P.L.*, CLXXVI, 877-880); *Eruditionis didascaliae*, lib. V, cap. ix; lib. III, cap. x-xi. Richard of St Victor, *De
gratia contemplationis*, lib. I, cap. iii-iv (*P.L.*, CXCVI, 66-68). See
also St Bernard, *De consideratione*, lib. II, cap. ii-iii.

examine them with attention. Reading is the beginning of knowledge; it is also the first condition for mystical yearning. It gives to the intelligence the first notion as to the meaning of a writing; it is by means of it also that sensible images of creatures penetrate the soul and incite the mind to seek the truth which they conceal. Reading precedes meditation and renders it possible.

In meditation the mind makes an effort to discover the divine thought hidden beneath the veils of sensible images or the surface of holy writings. The truth is presented to us, imprisoned, as it were, in the sensible and enveloped in darkness—we must free it and bring it fully to light. This results from the meditative effort of the soul. It is thus that we learn what it is that God commands us to do in order to avoid vice and practise virtue.[1]

But before we reach contemplation it is necessary that we should conform our life to the teachings discovered in meditation.

The vision of the truth is the work of moral purification and the perfecting of the soul, as much as of intellectual activity. The knowledge of the true ought to be transformed into love and the practice of goodness. Moreover, is not study itself a kind of pious exercise by which we become detached from evil in order to attain to God and to be united to him? To be instructed and to be edified is all one. Did not Plato say that to know leads of itself to goodness and virtue?

In order to become better, doubtless we have need of grace, but we obtain it through prayer. Therefore, after meditating we should pray; then, by the help of God we shall devote ourselves resolutely and without ceasing—for to stop is to go back—to the practice of what is good.[2]

We thus arrive at contemplation, in which our souls are enkindled with the flames of divine love.

According to Hugh of St Victor, therefore, there are five mystical stages to be surmounted in order to reach perfection such as he conceives it : *reading, meditation, prayer, progress in goodness,* and finally *loving contemplation.*

In this spiritual ascension towards God the soul experiences a work of purification which at times is very difficult.

The first step in meditation coincides with a violent agitation of the passions, which casts a shadow over truth and renders the seeking of it toilsome. Then, when the soul has succeeded in mastering its senses and has arrived at the discovery of truth, it is seized with joy at finding it and quivers with admiration. Finally, in contemplation it feels

---

[1] *De modo dicendi et medit.,* 6; *Erud. did.,* lib. III, cap. xi.
[2] *Erud. did.,* lib. V, cap. ix; *De meditando (P.L.,* CLXXVI, 993).

a great calm and tastes the inebriating joys of divine love.[1]

Hugh of St Victor understands how to find striking comparisons in order to show forth this teaching :

"In meditation," he says, "there is a kind of struggle between ignorance and knowledge. The light of truth is still obscured by the smoke of error, like fire which catches green wood with difficulty, but when fanned by a strong wind flares up and begins to blaze in the midst of black volumes of smoke. Little by little the burning increases, the moisture of the wood is absorbed, the smoke disappears, and the flame, with a sudden outburst, spreads, crackling and conquering, to the whole log. . . . But when all is burnt and the wood has entirely assumed the appearance and properties of the fire, all noise and crackling are arrested. . . . This violent and devouring flame, after having reduced everything to submission and assimilated all, maintains a deep silence and great peace, because it finds nothing different from itself or contrary to its nature. We thus see first fire with flame and smoke, then fire with flame and no smoke, lastly fire with neither flame nor smoke.

"Our carnal heart is like green wood; it is still soaked with the moisture of concupiscence. If it receive some spark of the fear of God or of divine love the smoke of evil desires and rebellious passions first of all arises. Then the soul becomes strengthened, the flame of love becomes more ardent and more bright, and soon the smoke of passion disappears, and the mind, thus purified, is lifted up to the contemplation of truth. Finally, when by constant contemplation the heart has become penetrated with truth, when it has attained to the very source of the sovereign truth in all its ardour, when it has been kindled by it, and when it has become transformed into the fire of divine love it feels neither distress nor agitation any more. It has found tranquillity and peace.

"Thus, at the beginning, when, in the midst of dangerous temptations, the soul seeks enlightenment in meditation, there is the smoke and flame. Afterwards, when it is purified and begins to contemplate the truth, there is flame without smoke. Then, when it has fully found the truth and charity is perfected within it, it has no longer anything to seek; it rests sweetly in the tranquillity and in the fire of divine love. It is the fire without either smoke or flame."[2]

The author of the *Imitation of Christ* recommends a similar method of reaching to the knowledge of goodness and to the love of God.

[1] Hugh of St Victor, *De modo dic. et medit,* 9.
[2] Hugh of St Victor, *In Ecclesiasten, homilia* I (*P.L.,* CLXXV, 117-118).

" Happy," he says, " is he whom Truth himself teaches, not in figure and passing words, but as he himself is. Our reason and our senses often fail us and perceive but little. . . . He to whom the Eternal Word speaks is set free from many opinions. All things come from the only Word and all things speak of him. *He is the beginning who also speaks unto us* (John viii, 25). Without him no man understandeth or judgeth rightly."[1]

Every truth, he teaches, springs from the Eternal Word. We can only have a knowledge of it by participating in the uncreated light of the Son of God. But in order to participate in this light of the Word, to discover easily the truth, we must purify ourselves, free ourselves from all unruly affection and from all self-seeking. For the more we are recollected within and free from outward things the greater the number of lofty truths that we comprehend without effort, because we receive the light of understanding from on high.[2] The soul, thus purified and detached from itself, may be united to the Word and become one with it. " O Truth who art God, grant me to be one[3] with thee in love eternal. Often am I weary of reading and hearing many things; in thee is all my will and my desire. Let all teachers hold their peace. Let all creatures keep silence before thee. Do thou alone speak to me !"[4]

3. *Mystical Contemplation and Ecstasy according to the School of St Victor.*

It is in the writings of Richard[5] that the theory of contemplation and ecstasy is completely synthesized. The elements of it were constructed by Hugh, but they remained scattered through his works.

According to the Victorines—as we have already noticed—contemplation is first of all philosophical : the natural faculties alone of man have worked towards it. Then, little by

---

[1] *De Imitat. Christi,* lib. I, cap. iii, 1-2, 7-9. The *Imitation,* as is often seen, contains many thoughts similar to those of the mystics of the twelfth century. We may therefore think that, if it may be clearly shown to belong to the fifteenth century, many of the elements belonging to it are older.

[2] *De Imitat. Christi,* lib. I, cap. iii. 14.

[3] The author of the *Imitation* is here inspired by the doctrine of the return of beings to unity so much employed by the pseudo-Dionysius (*De eccles. hier.,* i; *De myst. theol.,* i; *De Divin. nomin.,* xiii). I shall speak of this theory later on.

[4] *Imit.,* lib. I, cap. iii, 11-13.

[5] Especially in the *Benjamin major, de gratia contemplationis libri quinque* (*P.L.,* CXCVI, 63 ff.) Richard looks upon Benjamin, the son of Jacob, as the symbol of ecstatic contemplation, from verse 28 of Psalm lxvii : *Ibi Benjamin adolescentulus in mentis excessu.* This allegorical interpretation of this verse was quite common in the Middle Ages.

little, beneath the action of grace, the soul is raised to the consideration of the truths of faith until it reach mystical union and ecstasy, if called thereto.

At St Victor, as we know, there was no division, as is the case to-day, between the domains of philosophy and theology. Mysticism was the final goal of all knowledge. Science, in fact, properly understood, turns into love.

In a very general sense, contemplation is a clear insight into truth, accompanied by lively sentiments of joy which the perception of the beauty of this truth brings to the soul. Exact knowledge of truth and the blissful admiration which it brings about, such are the essential elements of contemplation.

It is thus distinguished from simple reflection (*cogitatio*) and from meditation (*meditatio*), the object of which is the seeking of truth. One who meditates labours to find the true, the contemplative rejoices in the possession of it. In meditation the mind reflects on a particular point; in contemplation it embraces in one glance a great number of truths; and when perfection is reached it lovingly contemplates the Creator himself.[1]

Richard endeavours to describe the divers motions of the mind which contemplates truth.

He compares them to the varying flight of different birds. It is noticed, he says, that there are some birds that rise very high in the air and then plunge, a moment later, towards the earth; they renew this double movement continuously. Others incline successively right and left. Some go backward or forward. Some there are that describe circles varying in circumference. Finally, some are seen to rest, as it were, suspended in the air in a motionless state, or have the appearance of remaining still.

In contemplation the mind has movements as varied. Sometimes it goes from the genus to the species or from the whole to the part—this is the movement up and down; or it goes from a point to its opposite—this is the movement to right and left; or it passes from cause to effect—this is the movement backwards and forwards; or it surveys the accidents that surround the substance—this is the circular movement; or finally it becomes fixed in a motionless and silent consideration of the truth. The mind of each contemplative is impressed with the movement which is most in keeping with his nature and his temperament.[2]

The degree of contemplation is so much the higher as its

---

[1] Hugh of St Victor, *De modo dicendi et med.*, 8-9; *In Ecclesiasten, homilia* I; Richard of St Victor, *Benjamin major,* lib. I, cap. iv.
[2] *Benjamin major,* lib. I, cap. v.

object is the more perfect and its admiration the more increased.

Richard counts six degrees or six species of contemplation, which correspond, according to him, to the six stages of the sanctification of the soul, and appear to him to summarize the whole spiritual life.

The first degree of contemplation, and the lowest, consists in the consideration and the admiration of corporeal beings which strike the senses. The ignorant, those that are at the beginning of Christian life, are hardly capable of contemplating the material world and of admiring the power and wisdom of the Creator. If they have the good will they will rise little by little to the higher degrees of contemplation.

From considering the spectacle of nature man comes to find the reason for the existence of material things. He discerns the cause of them, their order and their use. The plan of the world becomes apparent to him, and he is enraptured with its beauty. Such is the second degree of contemplation.

In the third man is raised to a knowledge of the immaterial by the aid of reason. Visible things are the reflection of invisible realities; they make us know, according to the words of St Paul, that *the invisible things of God, from the creation of the world, are clearly seen, being understood by the things that are made* (Rom. i, 20). The mind makes use of the images of material beings as a kind of " ladder " in order to mount to the consideration of spiritual realities. Man, having reached this degree of contemplation, begins to become spiritual; he strives to free himself from that which is earthly in order to fly towards that which is heavenly. The divine light *which enlighteneth every man that cometh into this world* (John i, 9) sends its rays on him, illumines him and makes him to know the spiritual world that lies beyond the world of matter.

Continuing his ascent, man is raised to the fourth degree— that is to say, to the region of invisible and incorporeal substances, which are the soul and the angelic spirits. The imagination is nothing here, for the intelligence no longer makes use of material images in order to reflect. The spiritual soul studies itself, retires within itself, gains knowledge of itself, and admires the beauty with which the Creator has adorned it. It forms for itself an idea, as exact as possible, of the angels, always without the help of any image, but with the help of the reason alone.[1]

Until now we have not met with mystical contemplation, properly so-called. That which has just been set forth is concerned rather with the preparation of the soul for contemplation than with contemplation itself. Those which Richard calls degrees of contemplation are in reality only the approach to it.

[1] *Benjamin major*, lib. I-III.

" In the two first degrees," he explains, " we are instructed in outward and corporeal things; in the two following we reach a knowledge of invisible and spiritual creatures; in the last two we are finally raised to the perception of super-celestial and divine realities."[1]

St Thomas Aquinas is more precise in that he reserves the term *contemplation* for the consideration of the one divine truth exclusively. The consideration of created beings may lead to contemplation, but does not constitute it.

It is therefore when he treats of the fifth and sixth degrees of contemplation that Richard really expounds his mystical theology.

Raised at length to these heights "we come to know, through divine revelation, truth which no human reason can fully understand and no reasoning can enable us to dis-cover with certainty. Such are the teachings of the divine scriptures on the nature of God and the simplicity of his essence."[2]

Those truths, the contemplation of which belongs to the fifth degree, are simply beyond reason. In the sixth degree the truth contemplated is not only above reason, but it seems to be opposed to it, like the mystery of the Trinity. Here the divine light makes us to know realities which, in ap-pearance, are repugnant to human reason.[3]

This kind of contemplation demands that the human mind should become in a manner angelic.[4] It necessitates in the contemplative, above all, great purity of heart.

" In my opinion," Richard declares, " in order to reach this contemplation compunction of heart is more needed than deep investigations of the mind, yearning of the soul more than reasoning, groanings more than proofs. We know, indeed, that nothing renders the heart more pure, nothing brings greater purity of soul, nothing more effectively drives away the clouds of error, nothing gives greater calm than true repentance and compunction. What in fact does the Scripture say? *Blessed are the clean of heart, for they shall see God* (Matt. v, 8). Let him, therefore, who desires to see God and to reach the contemplation of things divine, strive to purify the heart."[5]

To contemplate the truths of faith, to fathom them and to take sweet delight in their beauties and sublimities is a

[1] *id.,* lib. IV, cap. v.
[2] *id.,* lib. I, cap. vi; lib. IV, cap. ii-v.
[3] *Benjamin major,* lib. I, cap. vi. The two Cherubim who over-shadow the ark of the covenant with their wings symbolize, according to Richard, the two last degrees of contemplation. The Cherub on the right represents truths that are simply above reason; the one on the left those that seem opposed to reason. *Cf.* lib. IV, cap. viii.
[4] *id.,* lib. IV, cap. vi.
[5] *id. Cf.* Hugh of St Victor, *De arrha animae.*

wholly supernatural favour reserved for the perfect, and is the fruit of a special grace which is not given to all.[1] One of the conditions is an extended acquaintance of the mind with heavenly matters. And even he who is thus prepared for it cannot attain to it by his own effort. God himself must raise him to this sublime state.[2] We may have an earnest desire to experience these signal benefits; we shall obtain them if it please God by prayer. In any case we must always hold our souls ready to receive them.[3]

Richard makes mystical contemplation consist in the vision of God and in the intimate and beatific union of the soul with him. The object of this contemplation is God himself : God considered in the unity of his nature and in his attributes, God considered in the Trinity of his persons. The divine Trinity, according to Richard, is shown to those that have reached the last degree of contemplation, in which the mind, supernaturally enlightened, perceives truths contrary in appearance to human reason.[4]

In contemplation the intelligence is raised to a means of knowledge higher than that which is natural to it : *Intelligentiae vivacitas divinitus irradiata humanae industriae metas transcendit.*[5] It is enlightened by the divine light itself, which, like a dazzling sun, transforms the pale dawn of reason into the light of day.[6]

Richard makes use of the term "revelation" to indicate this manifestation of divine light in the soul.[7] He compares it to the prophetic illumination so frequent in the Old Testament.[8] He also uses the expression " divine inspiration " to describe the illuminating action of God in the contemplative. At the moment of contemplation " the breath of divine inspiration " (*divinae inspirationis aura*) drives away the darkness of the mind and makes "the rays of the true sun to shine."[9] And when " the intelligence is opened by means of this divine inspiration the prophetic grace is, in a way, renewed."[10]

[1] *id.*, lib. IV, cap. v, xi, xiii.

[2] *id.*, lib. IV, cap. vii ; lib. V, cap. xv-xvii.

[3] *id.*, lib. IV, cap. x, xiii.

[4] *id.*, lib. IV, cap. xvii-xix.   [5] *id.*, lib. V, cap. ii.

[6] *id.*, lib. V, cap. ix. *Cf.* lib. IV, cap. x : *Debemus et nos cordis nostri alas per desiderium extendere . . . ut quacumque hora divinae inspirationis aura mentis nostrae nubila deterserit, verique solis radios, remota omni caliginis nube, detexerit . . . mens se ad alta elevet, et avolet, et fixis obtutibus in illud aeternitatis lumen. . . . Cf.* lib. V, cap. xi ; lib. IV, cap. xxii, etc.

[7] *id.*, lib. IV, cap. xxi, xxii. *Cf.* lib. V, cap. xi : *Cum inaccessibilis illius et aeterni luminis revelatio cor humanum irradiat, humanam intelligentiam supra semetipsam . . . levat. . . .*

[8] *id.*, lib. V, cap. xviii : *Tu quaecumque es anima, quae soles . . . quasi quibusdam propheticis intellectibus vel revelationibus divinitus. sublimari, prophetico disce exemplo quid tu facere debeas.*

[9] *id.*, lib. IV, cap. x.   [10] *id.*, lib. V, cap. xviii.

Doubtless, inspiration and revelation do not teach the contemplative new truths which were not already in the deposit of Christian revelation; but there is revelation in the etymological sense. Divine truths are unveiled to the contemplative much more completely than to those that know them by the ordinary means of faith. And even occasionally the veil may fall altogether, and *vision* of divine realities be produced. This vision is purely intellectual. Imagination would only be a hindrance, for all sensible representation is essentially unfitted for perception of the divinity. Besides, contemplative vision is ecstatic; it requires the alienation of sense and the suspension of the faculties of the soul.[1]

The Patriarch Abraham, seated at the door of his tent ready to receive the visit of the angels (Gen. xviii), and the prophet Elias at the entrance of his cave *awaiting the passing of God* (3 Kings xix) are types of the contemplative who sighs after the coming of the Lord.[2] When he feels him approach " he goes out of his tent [by ecstasy] and casts himself down before the Lord, and being outside he sees him face to face, and rapt outside of himself in ecstasy he contemplates the light of the sovereign wisdom unveiled, unshadowed by figures, not as *through a glass in a dark manner,* but in plain truth, if I dare to speak thus."[3]

Often enough Richard contrasts the knowledge acquired by faith with that which is brought about by ecstasy.[4] Faith perceives things through a mirror, contemplation sees them without shadow.

" Although contemplation and speculation (*speculatio*) are taken one for the other, and the language of Scripture confuses them, nevertheless our expressions are more appropriate and become more precise when we call speculation the seeing of truth through a glass and contemplation the vision of truth in its purity without veil or shadow."[5]

The hills which, according to the Psalmist (Ps. cxiii, 4), skip like lambs, symbolize the speculatives who consider the heavenly mysteries only in a glass in a dark manner. But the mountains which skip like rams are the contemplatives

---

[1] *id.*, lib. IV, cap. xxii.

[2] *id.*, lib. V, cap. x.

[3] *id.*, lib. IV, cap. xi : *Sed ille quasi de tabernaculo in advenientis Domini occursum egreditur, egressus autem quasi facie ad faciem intuetur, qui per mentis excessum extra semetipsum ductus, summae sapientiae lumen sine aliquo involucro figurarumve adumbratione, denique non per speculum et in aenigmate, sed in simplici, ut sic dicam, veritate contemplatur.*

[4] *id.*, lib. IV, cap. xxii : *Possumus quaedam ex divina revelatione cognoscere et per mentis excessum contemplationis oculo cernere. Cf.* lib. V, cap. ix : *Novitas itaque visionis et rei vix credibilis adducere solet admirationem mentis quando aliquid incipit videri quod vix possit credi.*

[5] *id.*, lib. V, cap. xiv.

who, in their ecstasy, see the divine realities in their pure and simple truth (*in pura et simplici veritate vident quod minores . . . vix per speculum et in aenigmate videre valent*).[1]

Richard differs then markedly from St Bernard, to whom the mystical vision takes place through the veil of images. He maintains the tradition of St Augustine and of the Areopagite, according to which the mystic sees the sovereign Truth directly, without mediation. Later on we find, in St Thomas Aquinas, a strong reaction against this claim of the mystics to the direct vision of God in their raptures.

Man, in this vision, learns many things which he is powerless to express when, the mystical state having ceased, he returns to his ordinary condition.[2]

At the moment when it sees God the soul becomes united with him in the intoxication of love inexpressible. The terms made use of by Richard in order to express the charm of this union yield nothing in strength to those of St Bernard.[3] Contemplation is the work of charity. Like all mystics, the Victorines sang the praises of divine love. Within the cloisters of the Abbey of St Victor, as in those of Clairvaux, ardent hymns in honour of heavenly charity resounded.[4] The twelfth century perhaps is the period in which the celebration of mystical love reached its highest point.

Contemplation is specially helpful in averting evil, in making rapid progress in virtue, in becoming detached from the world in order to restore a yearning for heaven.[5]

It is very uncertain. Sometimes God grants this favour to the soul, at others the blessing is withdrawn, only to be granted again afterwards in greater measure.[6]

According to Richard, true contemplation is ecstatic.

In the last two books of *Benjamin major,* also, he treats of ecstasy at length in connection with the two highest degrees of contemplation.

In fact, there is a certain amount of ecstasy in all rather intense contemplation. When the soul is in the presence of a beautiful sight, whatever it may be, it is seized with admiration; it is as though outside itself and insensible to things around it. Thus understood, ecstasy may be produced

---

[1] *id.*, lib. V, cap. xiv.
[2] *id.*, lib. IV, cap. xii.
[3] *id.*, lib. IV, cap. xv-xvi.
[4] See the wonderful *De laude charitatis* of Hugh of St Victor (*P.L.*, CLXXVI, 969-976), and his short treatises *De amore sponsi ad sponsam* (987-994), *Soliloquium de arrha animae* (951-970).
[5] *Benjamin major*, lib. IV, cap. ix-x.
[6] Richard of St Victor, *De eruditione hominis interioris*, lib. I, cap. i : *Contemplationis gratia quandoque divinitus datur, interdum subtrahitur, tandemque multiplicius reparatur* (*P.L.*, CXCVI, 1231).

by the sight of a lovely landscape or by any other vision of nature.[1]

But what is important for us to know is what Richard thought of true ecstasy, of that supernatural ecstasy which God grants to holy souls, raised to mystical contemplation. He looks upon it as a state in which the soul becomes a stranger to itself (*alienatio mentis*) :

"Contemplation," he says, " takes place occasionally by the alienation of the soul, which is produced when the soul loses the remembrance of things present and, transformed by divine action, acquires a new and unwonted state, that is naturally inaccessible."[2]   In ecstasy the soul is outside itself, *mentis excessus,* to the extent of forgetting not only outward things but also what is passing within during this supernatural phenomenon.

" When," adds Richard, " we are violently raised to the contemplation of divine realities in ecstasy, immediately we forget all that is around us and that is within us.   And when we return to ourselves from this sublime state we are incapable of recalling that which we have contemplated in the brightness of the heavenly truth."[3]

Mystics favoured with ecstasy have all declared, like St Paul (1 Cor. xii, 4), that they heard in their raptures words ineffable.

Alienation of the soul in ecstasy admits of degrees.   The lowest of these is that in which the use of the corporeal senses is suspended.   The ecstatic is so absorbed by the contemplation that he does not see anything in front of him and hears nothing when spoken to.   The imagination, nevertheless, retains the power of producing images.   At times—in the second degree—the imagination is completely bound and incapable of action.   Finally, the intelligence itself may find it impossible to reflect or to exert itself.   Flooded with the heavenly light it can only receive what God lets it know. Richard states that he is unable to be more precise as regards this highest degree of ecstasy.[4]

He describes, on the other hand, at some length, the causes, or rather the occasions, of ecstatic contemplation, for the true cause can only be divine grace.   Ecstasy is produced sometimes through intensity of love, at others through the greatness of admiration, at others, lastly, by the extreme joy experienced by the soul.

" Intense love," he says, " produces ecstasy when the soul is so enkindled with the fire of heavenly desire that the flame of divine love, growing within it in an unusual way, liquefies

---

[1] *Benjamin major,* lib. IV, cap. xxii.
[2] *id.,* lib. V, cap. ii.
[3] *id.,* lib. IV, cap. xxiii.
[4] *id.,* lib. V, cap. xix.

it like wax,[1] renders it light like smoke and causes it to rise to the heavenly regions."

Admiration is ecstatic when the soul, penetrated by the rays of divine light and seized with surprise at the sight of celestial beauty, is smitten with such stupor that it is wholly thrown outside itself. The sight of the beauty which it sees brings about, by way of contrast, a great contempt of itself and inclines it at first to humble itself. But soon the desire for the joys of on high causes it to rebound, raises it above itself and carries it to the sublime regions.

Finally, intense joy throws a man into ecstasy when his heart, overwhelmed by inward sweetness, inebriated even by it, entirely forgetting what it is and what it has been, is rapt outside itself by the fulness of the intoxication and finds itself suddenly filled with divine love, feeling at the same time an ineffable joy.[2]

. The gift of ecstasy is bestowed very unequally among fervent souls. With some the ecstatic phenomena are most rare; they are only produced after long waiting. Others experience them almost at will.[3] I am inclined to think that on this last point Richard somewhat exaggerates. Is not ecstasy a state to which we are unable to attain by our own effort?

Richard is one of the mystical writers who has given the greatest number of details as to contemplation and ecstasy. It has therefore been felt necessary to assign him an important place in this history of spirituality.

It is to be regretted that the reading of his works is no easy task. His style is strained. In fact, the description of mystical states is always laborious. The expressions often lack the power to make us grasp those realities which come within the experience of but a small number of Christians. Above all, Richard is a subtle symbolist, like all the mystics of his time. He sees figures and symbols of contemplation in the least details of the Old Testament, even at the risk of tiring the reader. Here is an example:

" It seems to me," he says, " that Moses gave a mystical description of the six degrees of contemplation when, from instructions from the Lord, he disclosed the plan of the ark of the old covenant. The first degree is typified by the making of the parts of the ark, which were of wood; the second, by the gildings with which they were adorned; the

---

[1] *Ad cerae similitudinem liquefactam.* This expression, drawn from Psalm xxi, 15, and from Cant. v, 6, is often used by mystics in order to express the violence of the fire of divine love in the soul. *Cf.* St Bernard, *In Vigilia Nativitatis Domini, sermo* I, 1, etc.

[2] *Benjamin major,* lib. V, cap. v.

[3] *id.,* lib. IV, cap. xxiii.

third, by the crown round about the ark; the fourth, by the mercy seat; the fifth and sixth, by the two Cherubim which overshadowed the mercy seat."[1]

In spite of these three undoubted imperfections Richard was looked upon, in the Middle Ages, as a great mystic. St Thomas Aquinas often quotes him as an incontestable authority, as great as Dionysius the Areopagite or St Gregory the Great.

IV—HETERODOX MYSTICISM OF THE TWELFTH CENTURY

THE adapting of any philosophy to Christian teaching is always a delicate task, as we shall have several opportunities of showing. The school of St Victor made most correct use of Platonism in order to expound its mysticism. Others were less happy.

The pseudo-Dionysius was greatly indebted, in his mystical theology, to the Neoplatonic theory concerning the return of beings to the divine unity. God is the One whence have sprung the many; the many must return again to the One. This return is brought about through mystical contemplation.

Dionysius understood how to explain this return to unity without falling into Pantheism. Many mystics of the Middle Ages emulated his prudence.

Some, like the author of the *Imitation*,[2] were content to point out this return to unity and to desire it for themselves, but they were very careful to specify its nature. Others understood by it the moral transformation of the soul through the consuming action of mystical love which renders it entirely spiritual and celestial.

" In the same way," says the *Scala Claustralium*,[3] " that with the debauchee the soul is so engrossed by the concupiscence of the flesh that it loses the use of reason, and man becomes, it might be said, wholly carnal, so in heavenly contemplation the carnal passions are consumed and absorbed by the soul to such a degree that they are no longer opposed to it, and man is, in a way, entirely spiritual."

The passions are not, however, deadened in the sense that

---

[1] *Benjamin major,* lib. I, cap. xi.

[2] Lib. I, cap. iii, 10-11 : He to whom everything is the One, who refers all to that Unity, who sees all things in that Unity, is able to possess a stout heart and to rest in God in a deep peace. O Truth which is God, grant that I may be one with thee in an eternal love. Lib. III, cap. v, 16 : [He who loves] reposes above all things in the One highest from whom proceeds and flows all goodness.

[3] *Benjamin major,* lib. I, cap. v. This work, falsely attributed to St. Bernard, deals with the contemplative life (*P.L.*, CLXXXIV, 479).

they cannot be awakened or place the soul in danger of offending God.

But all mystics were not content with that. Certain writers of the twelfth century thought that it was not giving mysticism its full due. They considered that man, when raised to contemplation, was no longer exposed to the attacks of his passions because he had become all one with God. And this identity was not simply moral in the sense that the human will was perfectly subordinated to the divine will, willing only what God willed and not willing what he did not. It was an identity that implied the impossibility of committing sin. This strange teaching is found particularly in the famous *Letter to the brethren of Monte Dei*,[1] against which Jean Gerson[2] warned his contemporaries. The author appears to be inspired by the commentary on the writings of the pseudo-Dionysius by John Scotus Eriugena.[3] He lays rather too much stress on the return of the mystical soul to the divine unity.

" There is," we read in the *Letter*, " another resemblance with God which is much more perfect than that which is effected through the practice of virtue. It is that which has already been to some extent spoken of, which is so special that it is no longer the resemblance but the unity of the mind with God, since man becomes one same thing with God, one same mind, not only through the unity of the same will, but by a certain closer union of the will (as has already been said), which removes from the soul the power of willing otherwise than God. This union is called unity of the mind, not only because the Holy Spirit brings it about and guides therein the mind of man, but because it is the Holy Spirit himself, God-love. It is through this Spirit, who is the love of the Father and the Son, that are produced the sweetness, the gentleness, the caresses and embrace, and all that there may be in common between these two divine Persons in this

[1] By an unknown writer. Jean Gerson attributed it to St Bernard; Mabillon, to William of St Thierry, a friend of St Bernard; Massuet, to Guignes, fifth Prior of the Grande Chartreuse (*P.L.*, CLXXXIV, 297-300). The *Letter* is addressed to the monks of a Carthusian monastery, just founded, in the twelfth century. On several points, especially on that of love of God, its teaching greatly resembles St Bernard's. This is its definition of piety, which consists " in the continual remembrance of God, and in the incessant effort of the mind to know him, of the heart to love him, so that the servant of God will never remain, I do not say a day, but even a single hour, without giving himself up to spiritual exercise and to the desire of perfecting himself, or to the sweetness of tasting and possessing God " (lib. I, cap. iv).

[2] *Sermo de humilitate factus in coena Domini* (*Joannis Gersonii opera omnia*, Antwerp 1706, vol. iii, p. 1125).

[3] John Scotus Eriugena teaches this doctrine of the return of the soul to divine unity in all his works, especially in Book IV of the *De divisione naturae* (*P.L.*, CXXII, 741 ff.).

sovereign unity of truth and truth of unity.   The same thing
happens, in a manner, in the union of man with God, as in
that which unites the Son substantially with the Father and
the Father with the Son.   In the embrace and caress of the
Father and the Son it is, as it were, the Holy Spirit which
is the intermediary.   In this ineffable and unthinkable way
man merits to become of God yet not God, for that which
God is by nature man is by grace.''[1]

This explanation of the unity of the perfect man with God
has a suspicion of Pantheism which the uncertainty as to
the text of the *Letter,* no doubt altered, does not tend to
remove.   In any case what is quite certain is that according
to our writer mystical union causes the soul to lose the
faculty of willing otherwise than God; in other words,
renders it impeccable.   This idea is expressed several times
in the *Letter:*

" The unity of the mind with God, in the man who keeps
his heart raised to heaven, is the state of the perfection of
the will which tends towards God.   It is realized when not
only does he no longer will other than God wills, but is so
advanced in love that he is not able to will other than God
wills.   For to will what God wills is to be like him; to will
only what he wills is to be already what God is, in whom to
be and to will are one and the same thing."[2]

This impossibility of willing otherwise than God was not
a passing phase.   It was not to last merely during the
moments of ecstasy.   It was to be permanent and to constitute the specific note of the state of the Christian perfected
in love.

[1] *Epist. ad fratres de Monte Dei,* lib. II, cap. iii, no. 16 (*P.L.,*
CLXXXIV, 349) : *Alia est adhuc similitudo Dei. Haec est de qua jam
aliquanta dicta sunt, in tantum proprie propria, ut non jam similitudo,
sed unitas spiritus nominetur; cum fit homo unum cum Deo, unus
spiritus, non tantum unitate volendi idem, sed expressiore quadam
unitate virtutis (sicut jam dictum est) aliud velli non volendi. Dicitur
autem haec unitas spiritus, non tantum quia efficit eam, vel afficit ei
spiritum hominis Spiritus sanctus, sed quia ipsa ipse est Spiritus
sanctus, Deus charitas; cum per eum qui est amor Patris et Filii, et
unitas, et suavitas et bonum, et osculum, et amplexus, et quidquid
commune potest esse amborum in summa illa unitate veritatis, et
veritate unitatis; hoc idem homini suo modo fit ad Deum, quod cum
substantiali unitate Filio est ad Patrem, vel Patri ad Filium; cum in
amplexu et osculo Patris et Filii mediam quodammodo se invenit beata
conscientia; cum modo ineffabili inexcogitabilique fieri meretur homo
Dei non Deus, sed tamen quod Deus est ex natura, homo ex gratia.*

[2] *Epist. ad fratres de Monte Dei,* lib. II, cap. iii, 15 : *Unitas vero
spiritus cum Deo homini sursum cor habenti, proficientis in Deum
voluntatis est perfectio, cum jam non solummodo vult quod Deus vult,
sed sic est non tantum affectus sed in affectu perfectus, ut non possit
velle nisi quod Deus vult. Velle autem quod Deus vult, hoc est jam
similem Deo esse; non posse velle nisi quod Deus vult, hoc est jam esse
quod Deus est, cui velle est esse, id ipsum est.*

We can see the consequences of such teaching. A false mystic influenced by it would take his own will for the very will of God, and would consider all his whims as divinely inspired. Errors in mysticism have very terrible consequences. [1]

[1] I say nothing concerning the false mysticism of the *Cathari* and of the *Waldenses*. Their errors have to do with the history of the heresies of the twelfth century much more than with that of its spirituality.

CHAPTER V
SPECULATIVE SPIRITUALITY
AND ARISTOTELIANISM
THE TEACHING OF ST THOMAS
AQUINAS

THE authority which the school of St Victor had acquired contributed to the success of speculative theology.

This success, nevertheless, became great in a different way in the thirteenth century, when Aristotelianism was substituted for Platonic philosophy. The scholastic method created by St Anselm and vigorously taken up by Abelard then reigned supreme. Its unrivalled prestige enabled it to absorb everything, even spiritual doctrine.

It was, as we shall see, the school of St Dominic, above all, that fostered speculative spirituality. Albert the Great and St Thomas Aquinas were not content with the dialectics of Aristotle, they also borrowed from him doctrines wherewith to expound and defend Catholic theology. It became the more urgent a matter to win Aristotle to the side of orthodoxy in that Siger of Brabant,[1] the great leader of Averroism in the thirteenth century, endeavoured to capture his writings on behalf of error. The great leaders of the Dominican school performed their work with a master hand. This cannot be said of all the writers of this school, especially of certain mystics of the fourteenth century.

The thirteenth century was the age of great religious syntheses. All Catholic doctrine was expounded in a systematic form in the *Summae* of theology. Spirituality was found included in these synthetic works. At that time it did not as yet constitute a distinct branch of theology. The formal distinction between dogmatic, moral, and

---

[1] *Cf.* Mandonnet, *Siger de Brabant et l'Averroïsme latin au XIIIe siècle*, Fribourg (Switzerland) 1899. Averroes, a celebrated Arabian physician and philosopher, was born at Cordova in 1128, and died in Morocco in 1198. He held a high position in his own country. He made a great study of Aristotle, and used him in order to attack the Christian and Jewish religions. It was through him that Aristotle became known in the West, and in a bad light. The sum of the errors of Averroes is called Averroism; its great champion was Siger of Brabant. The chief of its errors, that which did the most harm to certain mystics, is that of the oneness of the human intellect. It taught that in all mankind there was only one intellect. St Thomas Aquinas refuted this heresy in his treatise *De unitate intellectus contra averroistas*.

spiritual theology was a development which belonged to the sixteenth century.

Among the scholastics of the Middle Ages spirituality was incorporated with the other sections of theology.

In the *Summa* of St Thomas Aquinas it is found a little everywhere, but principally at the end of the treatise concerning theological and cardinal virtues, of which it is, in a measure, the crown.[1] Is it not by the practice of Christian virtue that we attain to perfection and, if it please God, reach contemplation and rapture?

Scholastic theologians were content to expound and demonstrate the principles of spirituality. Their manner of doing so was rather dry, for they are much more philosophers than mystics. When we study them the mind receives abundant light, but the heart remains cold. Furthermore, they were never looked upon as spiritual writers properly so called.

Their theories as to spirituality are connected with the virtue of charity, for they clearly saw that charity is the centre of the Christian life. Moreover, the mystics of the twelfth century sang the praises of divine love to such an extent that they forcibly drew the attention of the speculatives thereto.

The school of Abelard, which has the merit of having inaugurated the scholastic method, places the virtue of charity in high relief. The very first theological *Summa,* the *Epitome theologiae christianae,* of Abelard, is divided into three parts, one of which is devoted to charity.[2] In this connection the writer treats of Christian virtues and the vices that are opposed to them. The great theologian of the twelfth century, Peter Lombard, accepted the views of Abelard and perfected them. In the third book of the *Sentences*[3] he deals at some length with the theological virtues, the cardinal virtues and the gifts of the Holy Ghost, and he touches on the principles of the spiritual life. William of Auvergne, Bishop of Paris (1249), one of the creators of scholastic theology, does the same.

In the thirteenth century theologians, in commenting on the *Sentences* of Peter Lombard, were brought to include spirituality in their theological syntheses. The most famous

---

[1] The *Treatise on Prophecy,* which deals with rapture, and the *Treatise on the State of Perfection and the Contemplative Life,* are placed after the cardinal virtues (II-II, Q. clxxi-clxxix).

[2] *Epist. theol. christ.,* cap. i : *Tria sunt ut arbitror, in quibus humanae salutis summa consistit, scilicet fides, charitas et sacramentum (P.L.,* CLXXVIII, 1695). The same doctrine is found in the *Introductio ad theologiam,* lib. I, 1 (*id.,* 981), in Roland Bandinelli, the future Pope Alexander III, a disciple of Abelard, and in Gietl, *Die Sentenzen Rolands,* p. 16, Freiburg im B. 1891.

[3] *P.L.,* CXCII, 809-830.

doctrine among them, that of St Thomas Aquinas,[1] will be summarized here under these different headings : *The principle of the spiritual life—Christian perfection and the state of perfection—Christian virtues—meditation and prayer —the passions—contemplation and rapture.*

The principle of the spiritual life is grace, that grace the excellence and efficacy whereof the author of the *Imitation of Christ*[2] extols in such poetic terms.

The Christian possesses within him a double principle of action; his natural activity and grace. By means of the first he acts as man and performs actions suitable to his nature; by means of the other he produces supernatural acts meriting eternal life.

Man acts with his faculties. These proceed from the substance of the soul, and are put in motion by natural divine concurrence, yet without compulsion. For the Christian is endowed with a supernatural organism, set above his natural organism but somehow adapted to it, and capable of producing divine acts. This comprises grace which adheres to the substance of the soul which it deifies, grace being a participation in the divine nature.[3] From this grace flow the infused virtues and the gifts of the Holy Ghost, the end of which is to make perfect the powers of the soul and to communicate to them a supernatural power. The infused virtues are in a way the supernatural faculties of the Christian.[4] This supernatural organism, consisting of grace which adheres to the substance of the soul, of virtues and gifts which render its faculties supernatural, has need of help and impulse from God, of actual grace, in order to pass from power to act so that evil may be avoided and good produced.[5]

The infused virtues which render the powers of the soul supernatural are the three theological virtues : faith, hope and charity, and the moral virtues which are attached to all the cardinal virtues of prudence, fortitude, temperance, and justice. They are called *infused* because they are given to the soul at the same time as grace, without there being any other efforts to be made in order to acquire them than those which are necessary to obtain the grace itself. By this they

[1] His biography is well known. He was born about 1225 at Aquinum, a small town of Campania. He began his studies at Monte Cassino; then, in 1244, he joined the Friars Preachers at Naples. He taught in Paris with great success. He died in 1274, in the Cistercian monastery of Fossa-Nova in the diocese of Terracina, on his way to the second Council of Lyons. Cf. *Acta Sanctorum*, 7 Martii, vol. i, Gulielmus de Thoco, *Vita S Thomas Aq.*

[2] Lib. III, cap. lv.   [3] I-II, Q. cx, art. 4.

[4] III Pars, Q. vii, art. 2 : *Sicut potentiae animae derivantur ab ejus essentia, ita oportet quod virtutes sint quaedam derivationes gratiae.*

[5] I-II, Q. cix, art. 9.

are distinguished from acquired virtues. These latter are engendered by prolonged and laborious repetition of the same acts. They may exist without grace, for they simply place man in the order desired by his nature, whereas the infused virtues place him in a higher order and direct him towards his supernatural end. The acquired virtues also are less easily lost. They are habits; contrary and repeated acts alone are able to uproot them from the soul. Infused virtues, on the other hand, depart as easily as does grace when grievous sin is committed.[1]

The soul that possesses grace together with the infused virtues participates in the very life of God; it is also the temple of the three divine Persons who take full possession of it.[2] Thus endowed with supernatural energy it is able to carry out the duties of Christian life.

Christian duty is accomplished with greater or less perfection. Some act like hirelings who perform strictly what is laid down. Others are faithful to a heroic degree. Whence proceeds this variety in the accomplishment of good? Doubtless according to the generosity of each one, but also from the higher perfections (*altiores perfectiones*)[3] which are called the gifts of the Holy Ghost. The Angelic Doctor means by these gifts the works of holiness which go beyond the common order and mark the Church of Christ.

Like the infused virtues, the gifts flow from grace poured out on the soul. They are distinguished from them in that the virtues tend to make man follow the dictates of reason, whilst the gifts incline him to be guided by the motions and inspirations of the Holy Ghost. The gifts prompt the soul to something better, to that which is more perfect. To them are attributed the ascent towards the arduous heights of sanctity, such as illuminations and other phenomena of the mystical life.[4]

According to St Gregory the Great (*Ezechiel,* lib. II, homil. vii), and in conformity with an interpretation of a passage in Isaias (xi, 2-3), there are seven gifts of the Holy Ghost: wisdom, understanding, counsel, fortitude, knowledge, piety, and the fear of the Lord. St Thomas strives to define the nature and the end proper to each of them.[5] One

[1] I-II, Q. cx, art. 3. *Cf.* Q. lv, lx, lxiii. Solid Christian virtue is formed by the union of acquired virtue and infused virtue. Acquired virtue alone is simply human, it is not Christian. Infused virtue alone is fragile; by itself it does not render the Christian solidly virtuous. These principles are most important in the ordering of serious Christian life.

[2] I Pars, Q. xliii, art. 3 and 5.   [3] I-II, Q. lxviii, art. 1.

[4] I-II, Q. lxviii, art. 2 and 3. St Thomas is very cautious respecting the connection between the gifts of the Holy Spirit and mystical phenomena.

[5] I-II, Q. lxviii, art. 4 and 5.

of their fruits is, especially, the striving of the Christian soul towards perfection.

The Angelic Doctor, in agreement with the traditional and most clear teaching in the books of the New Testament and in the writings of St Augustine, estimates the value of Christian perfection by charity, the virtue which unites us to God.

" For," he says, " a being is perfect in so far as he attains to his proper end, which is his highest perfection. Now it is charity that unites us to God, the last end of the human soul, since, according to St John (iv, 16), *he that abideth in charity abideth in God and God in him.*"[1]

The other virtues only tend to perfection in a relative way, in so far as they contribute to the growth of charity, whereas of itself charity constitutes Christian perfection by uniting us to God. But what degree of charity is needed in order to attain to perfection? St Thomas answers this question as does St Augustine, by drawing a distinction between absolute and relative perfection.

The first, which cannot be attained here below, demands a charity such that " the affection of the soul inclines towards God, in a real manner, to the full extent of its power and without ever failing." Now we know that even the most fervent Christian still commits many venial faults. The only perfection possible in this life is, then, relative. It is that " which tends to exclude what is opposed to charity and would prevent the soul from tending to God."[2] Charity is perfect in him who " habitually puts his whole heart in God, so that he neither thinks nor desires anything contrary to divine love."[3]

St Augustine further defined the nature of perfect charity by declaring that it brought about habitual avoidance of grave sin and gradually lessened the lighter faults. Furthermore, the commentators of St Thomas have thought well to crown his definition of Christian perfection with his teaching as to devotion.

Devotion is coupled, in the *Summa Theologica*,[4] to the virtue of religion, as opposed to the point of view of many writers according to whom it is related rather to charity.[5] It is, according to the Angelic Doctor, " a special act of the will, ready to give itself up to all which concerns the service

---

[1] *Summa Theol.*, II-II, Q. clxxxiv, art. 1. Cf. *Opusculum* lx; *De dilectione Christi et proximi.*
[2] *Summa Theol., ibid.,* art. 2.
[3] *id.*, Q. xxiv, art. 8.
[4] II-II, Q. lxxxii, art. 2.
[5] St Francis de Sales, *Introduction to the Devout Life*, Part I, chap. i : Charity and devotion are no more different from each other than is the flame from the fire. See chap. ii.

of God."[1] This promptitude in serving the Lord would be characteristic of perfection, which should finally consist in ardent charity, prompt and zealous, in the service of God.[2] We are able to distinguish three stages in the development of divine love. When the soul resolutely keeps away from sin, love is at its beginning; when it develops within itself virtue, love increases; and, finally, when it aspires to union with God and to possess him, love reaches its perfection.[3] This perfection being only relative here below, charity is capable of indefinite increase, for " in proportion as charity makes progress in the soul, it becomes more and more qualified for greater love."[4] St Thomas here comments on St Augustine :

" Charity," he says, " that we possess here below is able to grow. For, if it be said that we are travellers on this earth, it is because we are going towards God. Now the nearer we draw to God the more we advance," and we approach to him, as St Augustine says (*Tract.* XXXII, n. 1, *In Joan.*), not by the motion of the body, but by the outbursts of the soul. " But it is charity which brings about this approach, since charity it is that unites our soul to God. The power to increase is then essential to the charity which we have here below. If it ceased to do so we should ourselves be unable to continue our journey on this earth."[5]

It is the exercise of charity which renders it more perfect in this sense, according to St Thomas's explanation, " that each act of love renders man more eager to act by love." This disposition to do all through love, in the measure in which it grows, makes the soul more and more fervent and causes it to advance in charity.[6]

The formula which St Thomas makes use of in order to particularize the role that belongs to the counsels of perfection has not been fully accepted by his commentators.

" The perfection of charity," he says, " chiefly and essentially consists in the observation of the precepts," for the precepts " have as their end the avoidance of what is contrary to charity," that which would be opposed to its existence in the soul, " whilst the counsels have as their end

---

[1] II-II, Q. lxxxii, art. 1.
[2] This is the definition of St Francis de Sales, *loc. cit.*, and of Suarez, *De Statu relig.*, lib. I, cap. iv, n. 5.
[3] II-II, Q. xxiv, art. 9.
[4] *ibid.*, art. 7.   [5] II-II, Q. xxiv, art. 4.
[6] *ibid.*, art. 5 : *Quilibet actus charitatis disponit ad charitatis augmentum, in quantum ex uno actu charitatis homo redditur promptior ad agendum iterum secundum charitatem; et habilitate crescente homo prorumpit in actum ferventiorem dilectionis, quo conetur ad charitatis profectum; et tunc charitas augetur in actu.* Theologians generally teach that every act of charity directly increases this virtue within us.

simply the removing of that which would be an obstacle to the act itself of charity." " Perfection, therefore, only consists in the counsels in a secondary and instrumental manner."[1]

The *effective* practice of the counsels, doubtless, is not essential to perfection, for there are found persons in the world who are far advanced in charity. Nevertheless, does not perfection require that each one should observe the counsels in the measure in which his position allows of it?[2] It will never be said of one who is just content to avoid grave sin that he is in the way of perfection. His charity languishes, and he does not love God as much as he is able, if he do not, at least from time to time, more than is due. Active and fervent charity necessarily includes also the disposition to place the love of God before all earthly lawful affection, and a willingness to abandon riches, relations and all things if this total abandonment were demanded. He who lacked this disposition would not love God truly. Thus the *spiritual effective* observance of the counsels is essential to perfection, it is not merely a means.[3]

The incomplete formula of the Angelic Doctor is explained by the distinction, so well brought out in the *Summa,* between perfection and the state of perfection.

It is very true that the practice of the counsels, such, for example, as is required among religious, does not constitute perfection, but is only a means, an instrument of perfection. It is possible to find " perfect men who are not at all in the state of perfection and men that are very imperfect that are in the state of perfection—that is to say, in the religious state."[4]

It was particularly opportune in the thirteenth century to recall this teaching at a time when there were so many monks, and when violent discussions as to the lawfulness of the mendicant orders were raised, as we shall see later, by William of Saint-Amour. No doubt all the religious were not sufficiently preoccupied with the interior perfecting of the soul. " The habit and tonsure," says the author of the

---

[1] II-II, Q. lxxxiv, art. 3 : *Charitatis perfectio principaliter et essentialiter consistit in praeceptis; secundario autem et instrumentaliter in consiliis.*

[2] This is the teaching of St Francis de Sales, *Devout Life,* Part I, chap. i : " Devotion adds nothing to the fire of charity unless it be the flame which renders charity prompt, active and diligent, not only in the observance of the commandments of God, but also in the exercise of the counsels and heavenly inspirations." Suarez teaches the same in *De statu relig.,* lib. I, cap. xi, 16.

[3] See St Catherine of Siena, *Dialogue,* 47 : " Those who possess, observe the commandments and follow the counsels only in spirit, not in reality. But as the counsels are bound up with the commandments, no one can observe the commandments without observing the counsels at least spiritually."

[4] II-II, Q. clxxxiv, art. 4.

Imitation,[1] "give little and are of little use; it is the re-formation of morals and the entire mortification of the passions which make the true religious." St Thomas[2] also declares that "there are some that are in the state of perfection and who have not in any way either charity or grace."

This state of perfection is established by the entrance into the religious life. He who pledges himself by vow to practise poverty, obedience and perpetual chastity in a religious congregation places himself in a state of perfection, for he consecrates himself wholly and sacrifices himself, with all that belongs to him, to the service of God.[3] He is not perfect on that account itself, for he may possess only the lowest degree of charity. But he makes a profession of tending towards perfection; he has bound himself to the perfect way. Should he neglect to increase charity within him he would be lacking in a serious duty.[4]

According to St Thomas, bishops also are in the state of perfection, not only, like the religious, in the way which leads to it, but at the final end of perfection. This teaching is based on the authority of the pseudo-Dionysius, according to whom (*De eccles. hierarch.* v) " the episcopal order is the term of perfection, the sacerdotal order is illumination and brightness, the order of ministers is purification and separation."[5] Simple priests and deacons are not in the state of perfection, although, as we shall see, interior perfection is needful in order to perform their functions worthily.

The Angelic Doctor makes this teaching clearer by comparing, from the point of view of perfection, the religious state with that of bishops and with that of priests who have the cure of souls.

There is no doubt that the state of bishops is the most perfect in every respect.[6] As to that of priests having the care of souls, it is inferior to the religious state by the kind of life—which is the secular life—but it is superior to it by dignity and functions. The sacerdotal dignity greatly excels that of the simple religious profession, and the pastoral ministry affords an excellent opportunity for the exercise of charity towards the faithful. Moreover, the priesthood calls for sanctity in those that are clothed with it, otherwise they would not worthily exercise its functions. Also priests and

---

[1] Lib. I, cap. xvii, 6.
[2] II-II, Q. clxxxiv, art. 4. St Bernard said in the twelfth century (*Epist.* xcvi) : *Multo facilius reperias multos saeculares converti ad bonum quam unum quempiam de religiosis transire ad melius.*
[3] II-II, Q. clxxxvi, art. 1.
[4] II-II, Q. clxxxiv, art. 4, 5.
[5] *ibid.*, art. 6. See art. 5 and 7. St Thomas groups prelates—that is to say, abbots of monasteries and superiors of religious orders—with bishops as regards perfection.
[6] II-II, Q. clxxiv, art. 7.

other clerks in holy orders should already have attained to interior perfection,[1] whilst simple religious are only under the obligation to strive to reach it. For, according to the mind of St Thomas, " a clerk who is in holy orders and who acts contrary to holiness commits a more serious sin, all other things being equal, than a religious not in holy orders, even though this lay religious be bound to the regular observances to which those who have received holy orders are not bound."[2]

This excellent teaching, so well founded on the very nature of things, has been reproduced by all the commentators of the Angelic Doctor. It has been thus condensed : the lay religious is in a state in which he should acquire perfection (in statu perfectionis acquirendae); the priest in one in which he should already have acquired it (in statu perfectionis acquisitae).

St Thomas sums up, with greater precision, the traditional teaching concerning the three perpetual vows of obedience, poverty and chastity which essentially constitute the religious life. He also deals with the obligations and the prerogatives of religious of the divers religious orders and with the conditions required for entrance into the religious life.[3] He is much less strict than the Fathers of the desert or St Benedict in requiring manual labour of monks. For in the thirteenth century many religious gave themselves exclusively to study or to the pastoral ministry and lived on alms.[4]

He accepts, on the contrary, the point of view of the ancients respecting the superiority of the eremitical life, which, in itself, must be more perfect than the common life.[5] Finally, St Thomas, more cautious than St Jerome and St Bernard, recognizes that when the parents have urgent need of the help of their children the latter ought not to abandon them in order to enter religion. They are under the obligation of deferring the execution of their project as to the religious life.[6]

Asceticism—as the Fathers of the desert and the earlier writers have taught us—is based, for the greater part, on

---

[1] ibid., art. 6 : Ex hoc quod aliquis accipit sacrum ordinem, non ponitur simpliciter in statu perfectionis, quamvis interior perfectio ad hoc requiratur quod aliquis digne hujusmodi actus exerceat. Simple laymen do not sin by neglecting their perfection, provided that this negligence does not imply contempt for the things relating to perfection. II-II, Q. clxxxvi, art. 2.

[2] II-II, Q. clxxxiv, art. 8. St Thomas groups archdeacons with priests having the cure of souls. The duties of an archdeacon, as they were in the Middle Ages, no longer exist to-day.

[3] II-II, Q. clxxxvi-clxxxix. There are allusions to the attacks of William of Saint-Amour.

[4] id., Q. clxxxvii, art. 3, 4; Q. clxxxviii, art. 5.

[5] id., Q. clxxxviii, art. 8.   [6] id., Q. clxxxix, art. 6.

the theology respecting the virtues, on the way in which good habits are acquired and developed, or lost. Moral theology and spiritual theology completely intermingle here, as is clearly shown in the Angelic Doctor's remarkable treatise concerning the virtues.

After stating the theory of virtue and vice in general,[1] St Thomas examines at length the theological virtues and the sins that are opposed to them. Then, passing on to the study of the cardinal virtues, he analyzes each one of them with care, determines precisely the intrinsic virtues that are attached to them more or less directly, and finally the vices opposed to them.[2]

This classification of virtues and vices can hardly avoid being arbitrary; the link which attaches one virtue to another seems sometimes artificial. But the subject is thrashed out thoroughly and the teaching set forth is very valuable. Theologians and ascetics may draw indefinitely on this section of the *Summa Theologica*. The placing together of virtues and vices, moreover, was a question with which minds were preoccupied in the Middle Ages. Already in the twelfth century Hugh of St Victor had endeavoured to draw up a genealogical tree " of the fruits of the flesh and of the spirit.'' The tree of the old Adam, the tree of vices, he explains, has pride as its root. Its trunk is divided into seven parent branches, which are the seven capital vices : envy, pride, anger, sloth, avarice, gluttony, and lust. Each of these branches produces secondary branches which are the vices born of the first. The second tree is that of the new Adam, it springs from humility. The seven principal branches are the three theological virtues and the four cardinal virtues. Each branch in turn subdivides and produces the virtues which form its necessary accompaniment.[3]

However attractive were these attempts, St Thomas's classification was not slow in causing them to be forgotten. It was accepted without contradiction in the schools. It enters into the *Speculum Majus* of Vincent of Beauvais, the third part of which, the *Moral Mirror,* remained unfinished at the author's death. Finally, this classification inspired the artists of the Middle Ages who so often carved the virtues and vices on the façades of our cathedrals.[4]

---

[1] I-II, Q. xlix-lxvii, lxxi.

[2] II-II, Q. xlvii-clxx. I would point out (Q. clxi, art. 6, and clxii, art. 4) the remarks which St Thomas makes on the twelve degrees of pride described by St Bernard, and which correspond with the twelve degrees of humility enumerated in the Rule of St Benedict.

[3] Hugh of St Victor, *De fructibus carnis et spiritus (P.L.,* CLXXVI, 997-1010).

[4] E. Male, *L'art religieux du XIIIᵉ siècle en France,* bk. III; L. Bégule, *Monographie de la cathédrale de Lyon,* p. 131 ff.

Meditation and prayer are excellent means of developing divine love within us, and thus advancing in perfection.

Meditation, in the writings of St Thomas, is very different from that of the Victorines, for it postulates a different conception of knowledge. Scholastic theologians inaugurated a distinction between scientific meditation and religious meditation; the first does not necessarily encourage divine love in us, as occasionally it can be an obstacle to devotion.[1] For speculative science has as its end the knowledge of truth. Now deep, abstract, subtle reflections often paralyze the outbursts of the heart towards God.[2]

Therefore, it is not all meditation that sanctifies, as the school of St Victor taught, but only "meditation on that which can produce the love of God within us."[3] Meditation thus understood brings to man the thought of giving himself to God.

"First of all, by considering the divine goodness and its benefits, in accordance with the words of the Psalmist: *It is good for me to adhere to my God, to put my hope in the Lord God* (Ps. lxxii, 28); this thought leads to love which is the proximate cause of devotion. Afterwards, by the consideration of human weakness and its failures, which make us feel the need of leaning on God, as says Psalm cxx: *I have lifted up my eyes to the mountains, from whence help shall come to me. My help is from the Lord, who made heaven and earth;* this consideration banishes presumption from the soul which would prevent us from submitting ourselves to God and would incline us to lean on our own strength and on our own virtue."[4]

This knowledge of God and of ourselves, the fruit of meditation, is rightly regarded by St Thomas as the best foundation for fervour. In the Middle Ages, moreover, there was a form of spirituality based on the knowledge of God and of the soul. It had considerable success and a great number of spiritual writings were inspired by it.

Meditation, as it is recommended by the Angelic Doctor, must not be likened to our "mental prayer," an exercise that did not exist in the thirteenth century. It consists in pious reflection on Christian truths, made without any previous fixed method and without being necessarily accompanied by prayers. With regard to prayer itself, St Thomas admirably explains the theological teaching concerning it, without adding anything that has any particular connection with spirituality.[5]

The causes of temptation are, as we know, of two kinds: outward causes, the world and the devil, and inward causes

---

[1] St Thomas, II-II, Q. lxxxii, art. 3, *ad* 1.   [2] *ibid.*
[3] *ibid.*   [4] *ibid.,* art. 3.   [5] II-II, Q. lxxxiii.

—that is to say, the concupiscence of the flesh, the concupiscence of the eyes, and the pride of life, which finally bring about inordinate love of self, the source of every sin.[1]

St Thomas analyzes this love of self and deduces therefrom his fine theory of the passions, which was to be so drawn upon by the spiritual writers of the future, and differed palpably from the pessimistic doctrine of St Augustine as to concupiscence. He teaches that the inordinate love of self implies the desire, " the inordinate love " of good, of pleasure. For to say that a man loves himself is to say that he has a passion for what he thinks is a good and an enjoyment for him. Self-love, in fact, is to desire good for oneself.[2]

But the love of self is not necessarily inordinate; it is part of the nature of man, it is the affective side of him. This natural inclination towards that which to us is good is called by the Angelic Doctor, in agreement with Aristotelian philosophy, an appetite, the delectable appetite or the appetite of pleasure. It is concupiscence, understood in the philosophic sense, without implying any worse idea : *concupiscentia est appetitus delectabilis*.[3]

The object of this inclination is the good things of the body and of the soul. But because in man, on account of the unity of complex humanity, everything has its counteraction in sensibility, this inclination is always sensible in some way. Moreover, concupiscence has its seat, properly speaking, in the sensible appetite and in the concupiscible appetite from which its name is derived.[4]

From the sensible appetite are born the passions, those violent movements of the soul which prompt it to seek what it desires or to fly from what it fears. The passions which impel towards the desired object proceed from the concupiscible appetite; those that bring about the struggle against the obstacles that are opposed to the possession of the object coveted come from the irascible appetite. The concupiscible appetite and the irascible appetite are two powers of the sensible appetite that are specifically distinct and cannot be reduced to a single source. But St Thomas, who clearly recognizes these two tendencies and their motions, does not disregard their close relationship. He remarks several times that the passions of the irascible appetite have their origin in the concupiscible appetite. We only become angry because we wish to possess at any cost that which we desire for

---

[1] I-II, Q. lxxvii, art. 5 : *Inordinatus amor est causa omnis peccati.*
[2] *ibid.*   [3] I-II, Q. xxx, art. 1.
[4] I-II, Q. xxx, art. 1 : *Bonum secundum sensum est bonum totius conjuncti. Talis autem delectationis appetitus videtur esse concupiscentia quae simul pertineat et ad animam et ad corpus, ut ipsum nomen concupiscentiae sonat. Unde concupiscentia, proprie loquendo, est in appetito sensitivo et in vi concupiscibili, quae ab ea denominatur.*

ourselves in order to enjoy it. Love engenders all the passions.[1]

But it behoves us here to know the different passions of the soul even more than their genesis; to determine the way they act within us and the treatment to which they must be subjected so that they do not harm the Christian life. On these divers points St Thomas has set forth most sound principles from which the writers of the centuries that followed deduced useful consequences for the guidance of souls.

The Angelic Doctor enumerates eleven passions—six belong to the concupiscible appetite and five to the irascible. We know that Bossuet, in his *Treatise on the Knowledge of God and of Self*,[2] has accepted this classification.

The six are opposed to each other two by two : *love* or the inclination towards a known good, and *hate* or the movement to repudiate that which is displeasing; *desire* to obtain what is coveted, and *aversion* from that which we hate; *joy* obtained by the possession of some good, and *sadness* which tends to grieve over present evil. The five others imply a difficulty that has to be overcome, for which reason they belong to the irascible appetite. These are : *hope* to acquire some possible though difficult good, and *despair* when the acquisition of it seems impossible; *fear* which makes us avoid some terrible evil, and *boldness* which enables us to face difficulties bravely; finally, *anger* which has no opposite.[3]

Considered in themselves in so far as they are motions of the concupiscible and irascible appetites, the passions are neither good nor bad. They become praiseworthy or blameworthy according to whether they be ruled by reason or not; but in themselves they are indifferent. We must see in them deep forces of human nature which may be employed either for good or evil.[4]

The Stoics, as we know, laid it down as a first principle that all passion of the soul is bad. According to them, perfection consisted in the destruction of the passions so effectively that man reached *apatheia* or the passionless state.

[1] I-II, Q. xxv, art. 1. See art. 2 : *Omnes in potentia concupiscibili passiones ex amore causantur.* Cf. *De veritate*, Q. xxvi, art. 4.

[2] Chap. i, n. 6.

[3] I-II, Q. xxiii, art. 4 and Q. xxv. St Thomas elsewhere classes them all under four principal passions, which comprise all the others : joy and sadness, which are produced by the concupiscible appetite; and hope and fear, by the irascible appetite. Q. xxv, art. 4.

[4] I-II, Q. lix, art. 1 : *Passiones ex seipsis non habent rationem boni vel mali ; bonum enim vel malum hominis est secundum rationem. Unde passiones, secundum se consideratae, se habent et ad bonum et ad malum secundum quod possunt convenire rationi vel non convenire.* Cf. Q. xlv, art. 1 and 2; Q. xxiv, art. 1 and 2; II-II, Q. xxxv, art. 1; Q. cxxv, art. 1 and 2, etc.

St Augustine looked upon the claim to free ourselves from passion as chimerical. He considered that fallen human nature, even with the fervent Christian, contains a virus which nothing can stamp out, which is concupiscence. This is an evil in itself : it is a sickness, a weakness, a vice of humanity, the consequence of original sin.

St Thomas is more optimistic. He accepts the teaching of Peripateticism, according to which the passions, when ruled by reason, are good; they may exist in the soul side by side with virtue, because in themselves they are indifferent.[1] The passions and concupiscence, which is the seat of them, are only an evil in so far as they are irregular—that is, out of harmony with reason and with the law of God.

Original sin, in fact, consists precisely in " the privation of original justice " which Adam possessed before the fall.[2] The supernatural gifts, which established this original justice, were the bond which kept all the forces of the human soul in order. This bond was broken by sin, and immediately the faculties of the soul were borne forward, with violence and in disorder, towards their object.[3] Concupiscence, in the theological sense, consists in this disorder of the motions and the passions of the soul. It is this disorder that is bad; the passions considered in themselves are not so.

Thus fallen man has only been stripped of the supernatural gifts; his natural qualities have not been lessened. The Thomists held the *homo gratuitis spoliatus* as opposed to the *homo vulneratus in naturalibus* of the Augustinians.

The Angelic Doctor, by this teaching, directed spirituality towards more moderate views than those of St Augustine. According to him, thus differing from certain disciples of the Bishop of Hippo, sensibility is not in itself a thing to be distrusted, or one of which every manifestation without distinction is to be condemned.

If the Thomist doctrine knows how to avoid rigorism, nevertheless it does not suppress asceticism or mortification. The passions are two-edged swords; they may be suggestions of evil as well as helps towards goodness.[4] Wisely controlled, they enable man to give himself forcefully to that which is good; undisciplined, they cast him into evil with frenzy. It, therefore, behoves the faithful Christian to watch attentively over his passions; for, on account of their spontaneity and their violence, they often forestall the

---

[1] II-II, Q. cxxiii, art. 10 : *Stoici enim et iram et omnes alias passiones animae ab animo sapientis et virtuosi excludebant. Peripatetici vero, quorum princeps fuit Aristoteles, et iram et alias animae passiones attribuebant virtuosis, sed moderatas ratione.*
[2] I-II, Q. lxxxii, art. 3.
[3] *ibid.*, art. 4. *Cf.* IV *Sent. Dist.*, 40, Q. iii, art. 5, sol. 1 *ad* 4.
[4] I-II, Q. xxiv, art. 3; Q. lix, art. 2, etc.

judgement of reason.[1] So by means of mortification and asceticism they are curbed and kept in the path of duty.

Later spiritual writers will be found to point out that, among the passions, there is in each one of us one that predominates. It is the ruling passion. It is that which controls the others and is the most ordinary cause of our falls. It is a matter of importance to know it well in order to attack it with vigour.

Thus the theory of St Thomas ·respecting the passions provides spirituality with a moral remedy not entirely new, for the Fathers of the desert had carefully studied the nature of vice; but one more precise, more reasonable and equitable than that of the preceding ages.[2]

None of the questions which were discussed in his time escaped the genius of St Thomas. It is, then, not surprising to find that he had studied the phenomenon of contemplation, about which so much was written in the twelfth century. He was inspired by the mystical theories of Dionysius the Areopagite, of St Gregory the Great and of Richard of St Victor; but, as usual, he brings notably greater preciseness to bear on the views of his predecessors.

Human life, looked upon from the mystical point of view, is divided into the active life and the contemplative life. St Gregory the Great (*Moral.,* lib. VII, n. 61) perceived symbols of these two lives in the two wives of Jacob. Lia, who was fruitful, represents the active life, and Rachel the contemplative. In the Middle Ages these two biblical symbols were made use of by mystical writers as much as the gospel types of Martha and Mary.[3]

Like Hugh of St Victor and the mystics of the Middle Ages, the Angelic Doctor teaches that reading, prayer, meditation, and consideration are the preparation for contemplation.[4] His enumeration is intentionally incomplete, for writers were not agreed as to the number and nature of these preparatory acts. With St Gregory and all spiritual writers the Angelic Doctor requires, as a necessary disposition for the contemplative life, the practice of moral virtues; for this life calls for calmness of the passions and freedom from absorbing outward occupations.[5] Then, the preparation accomplished, the soul effects the ascent towards mystical contemplation.

[1] *ibid.,* Q. xxiv, art. 3; lix, art. 2, etc.
[2] On the relationship of the faithful to Christ, see *Summa Theologica,* Q. viii; Q. xlviii; *Opusculum De Humanitate Jesus Christi.*
[3] II-II, Q. clxxix, art. 2; Q. clxxxi, art. 1.
[4] *ibid.,* Q. clxxx, art. 3: *Variis . . . animi operibus ad eam [contemplationem] homines ascendunt, ut auditione, lectione, oratione, meditatione, consideratione, cogitatione,* etc.
[5] *ibid.,* art. 2.

The steps that must be mounted before arriving at this height are, according to Richard of St Victor, six. St Thomas does not reject[1] them, but prefers to simplify; he reduces the stages that have to be passed in order to reach the contemplative life to four : the practice of virtues; the preparatory acts of contemplation; the consideration of the divine works, which lead to the knowledge of the Creator; finally, the contemplation of divine Truth itself.[2]

St Thomas is very precise as to the object of contemplation. It is divine truth revealed and known by faith, to the exclusion of scientific truth discovered by reason. The Angelic Doctor, contrary to the Victorines, clearly distinguishes between the object of faith and the object of science. The latter is alien to contemplation. But though the mystic contemplates divine truth, he is not able to perceive the divine essence itself. This remains outside the reach of Christians here below.

" To the contemplative life," declares St Thomas, "chiefly belongs the contemplation of divine truth, since such contemplation is the whole end of human life. This is why St Augustine says (De Trinitate I, cap. viii) that ' contemplation of God is promised us as the end of all our actions and the eternal perfecting of all our joys.' It will only be perfect in the future life when *we shall see God face to face,* which will render us perfectly happy. Here below we only attain to the contemplation of divine truth imperfectly, *as in a glass in a dark manner* (1 Cor. xiii, 12). This is the reason that it only gives us a beginning of beatitude which will be completed in the future life."[3]

Henceforth the precise theological sense of the word contemplation is determined.

St Bernard and Hugh of St Victor give different meanings to this term, especially that of the perception of what is true, without error or uncertainty, as opposed to consideration and meditation, which are the seeking after truth. Richard of St Victor makes use of it without distinction in order to signify consideration of the works of God as well as the clear vision of divine truth. After St Thomas, contemplation is exclusively understood as the act by which the mind clearly perceives divine truth. Other acts of the faculties of the soul have as their end that of preparing for contemplation; they do not constitute it.

" For there is this difference between man and the angels, as Dionysius teaches (De Divin. nom. VII), that the angel sees the truth by a single act of the intelligence, whilst man only reaches it by a long and progressive advancement. That

---

[1] *ibid.,* art. 4, *ad* 3.
[2] *ibid.,* art. 4.
[3] II-II, Q. clxxx, art. 4. Cf. *Opusculum* lx; *De dilectione,* cap. xxv.

is why, if the contemplative life has but one act by which it is formally constituted and which forms its unity, that is the contemplation of truth, it comprises many others by which it is reached."[1]

In contemplation, as it has been just explained, the soul considers divine truth, but it is unable to be raised to the immediate vision of the divine essence. This vision, according to St Thomas, cannot be produced here below. That which the contemplative perceives is not God himself, seen directly, but a sign, a "created effect," of a supernatural order by which God becomes known.[2]

Like St Bernard, the Angelic Doctor teaches that the vision of God in contemplation is brought about by an intermediary by means of a sign belonging to the order of grace. The nature of this sign remains a mystery.

This vision of God being only mediate, it is necessarily obscure. It is a knowledge *per speculum et in aenigmate*. Contemplation is doubtless a very perfect knowledge of God, but it is a knowledge through faith, such as man may have here below. It is only in this sense that the Christian may be said to contemplate God, and, in accordance with the expression of the Angelic Doctor, " the contemplative life consists chiefly and essentially in the contemplation of God."[3] The mind of the contemplative is flooded with quickened enlightenments of faith by which he excels in the knowledge of God, but he does not participate in the light of glory through which the intuitive vision of the divinity is produced.

St Thomas clearly specifies the character of this knowledge of God acquired in contemplation. It is not a discursive knowledge like that obtained through reasoning. Neither is it the result of abstraction by which the mind draws its ideas from images. It approaches in semblance to the angelic mode of knowledge. The contemplative perceives the divine truth by a single act, by a simple look, by a kind of intuition.[4] The more perfect the contemplation the more perfect the unity towards which the actions of the contemplative must tend. This remark of the Angelic Doctor is in full accordance with the testimony of mystics.

Contemplation procures for the soul a happiness higher than earthly joys. For the knowledge of truth, being natural to man, is only able to delight him when it has been acquired with evidence and full certainty. Moreover, con-

---

[1] II-II, Q. clxxx, art. 3.
[2] St Thomas seems to have specified this point *à propos* of the contemplation of Adam before the Fall. *Summa Theol.*, I, Q. xciv, art. 1. See *Quaestiones disputatae, De Veritate*, Q. xviii, art. D; *Recherches de science religieuse*, May-September, 1919, pp. 147 ff.
[3] II-II, Q. clxxx, art. 7. *Cf.* art 4.
[4] *ibid.*, art. 3, *ad* 1: *Contemplatio pertinet ad ipsum simplicem intuitum veritatis.*

templation is an exercise of love, and love when it acts in the soul always produces some happiness.[1] Thomist contemplation is far from being the same as that expounded by St Augustine, Dionysius the Areopagite and Richard of St Victor, according to whom the soul, when in mystical ecstasy, is favoured with the direct vision of God.

The Angelic Doctor refuses to go so far as that :

" It is impossible," he says, " in the state of this present life and as long as the use of the senses continues for us to be raised in contemplation to the vision of the divine essence, although in rapture, such as that experienced by St Paul, this may take place (2 Cor. xii, 2-4).[2] The mortal body, indeed, is opposed to the direct vision of God by the soul. This vision could only be produced exceptionally, in a state intermediate between this life and the future life, in which the soul, whilst remaining united to its body, becomes momentarily freed from it to the extent of making use neither of the senses nor of the imagination.[3] This happened to St Paul, perhaps to Moses. No one else seems to have been favoured with so extraordinary a blessing.[4]

Is St Thomas too strict in this? It is not for me to decide. Nevertheless, it may be asked why the direct vision of God, which took place in the rapture of St Paul, should not be reproduced for a brief instant of time in the raptures of other saints? In any case, the characteristics which the Angelic Doctor finds in the rapture of St Paul, are exactly the same as those of the mystical states, implying the vision of God, described by St Augustine, Dionysius the Areopagite and Richard of St Victor; but there I leave it.

Rapture is produced by the Holy Spirit, who, "abstracting the soul from sensible things, raises it to supernatural things."[5] A certain violence is done to him who is rapt in God, and it is this which distinguishes rapture from ecstasy. The latter signifies simply that the soul is outside itself, that it has departed from its ordinary state.[6] Total alienation of the senses occurred in the rapture of the Apostle; for, when the intelligence is raised to this most high vision of the divine essence, it must abandon all sensible images and all ideas in order wholly to concentrate its powers and yield itself entirely to God.[7] This is why St Paul declares that he does not know

[1] II-II, Q. clxxx, art. 7. See the studies by P. Garrigou-Lagrange on the mysticism of St Thomas, in the review *La Vie Spirituelle,* January, April, May, 1920.
[2] *ibid.,* art. 5. *Cf.* Q. clxxv, art. 3; I, Q. xii, art. 11.
[3] *ibid.*
[4] St Thomas, like all theologians, teaches that the soul of Christ enjoyed the beatific vision here below; but this case is wholly different from mystical rapture. Also St Thomas considers the cases of St Paul and of Moses as entirely exceptional.
[5] II-II, Q. clxxv, art. 1.
[6] *ibid.,* art. 2.   [7] *ibid.,* art. 4.

whether it was in the body or out of the body that he was rapt to the third heaven, so complete was the suspension of his faculties.[1]

In order to perceive the divine essence the human mind needs to participate momentarily in the light of glory; for God can only be seen in his own light, as the Psalmist declares : *In thy light, O God, we shall see light* (Ps. xxxv, 10).[2]

Finally, rapture brings an intense joy to the soul. St Paul makes this understood when he relates that he was rapt to the third heaven. For the love which closely unites one to the Lord is undoubtedly found in the soul rapt to heaven. On this subject St Thomas cites and comments on the words of Dionysius the Areopagite : *Divine love produces ecstasy and rapture.*[3] Mystical phenomena are the effects of love; that is why they inebriate the soul with a great joy.

The Angelic Doctor is a perfect theorist of spirituality. From the fourteenth century his teaching was generally followed, not only by writers of the Dominican school, but also by all speculative theologians.

The affective aspect of piety is little found in his writings. Spiritual doctrine does not throb beneath his pen as with St Augustine, St Bernard, Hugh of St Victor or St Bonaventure. Even his commentary on the *Canticle of Canticles* allows the abstract direction of his mind to be perceived. The affective side of his soul is made manifest only in the beautiful hymns of the Office of the Blessed Sacrament.

But we must not expect of speculative theology that which belongs to affective theology. Dante, who gave St Thomas Aquinas so high a place in his *Paradiso*, has characterized in a word the distinction between the affective and the speculative writers represented by St Francis of Assisi and St Dominic :

> " The one was all seraphical in ardour ;
> The other by his wisdom upon earth
> A splendour was of light cherubical."[4]

---

[1] *ibid.*, art. 6.
[3] *ibid.*, art. 2; I-II, Q. xxviii, art. 3.
[2] *ibid.*, art. 3, *ad* 2.
[4] *Paradiso*, xi.

CHAPTER VI

ST FRANCIS OF ASSISI AND THE FRANCISCAN SCHOOL

ST FRANCIS AND HIS COMPANIONS— ST BONAVENTURE AND THE FRANCISCAN SPIRITUAL WRITERS OF THE XIII, XIV AND XV CENTURIES —BLESSED ANGELA OF FOLIGNO AND ST CATHERINE OF BOLOGNA

ST FRANCIS OF ASSISI had a thorough scorn for speculative knowledge, and he strove to inspire the Friars Minor with it.[1] He is eminently a mystic in the full sense of the word. The Franciscan Order, faithful to the spirit of its founder, has always preserved its preference for affective spirituality. From this point of view it differs greatly from the Dominican school.

At the time of its birth, however, scholastic theology began to exercise such a sway that it was not possible to hold aloof from it. Friars Minor, therefore, were perforce allowed to study at the Universities. Famous theologians, such as Alexander of Hales (1245) and Duns Scotus (1308), were soon found amongst them. But the need of studying science, without departing too much from the desire of St Francis, brought about a kind of fusion between speculative and affective theology. This union of the science of the mind with that of the heart is particularly noteworthy in St Bonaventure, who may be looked upon as the great representative of Franciscan spirituality.

---

[1] Thomas of Celano, *Legenda* II, 195 (Edouard d'Alençon's edition, pp. 315-316): " My brethren," said Francis one day, " those who are guided and inspired by curiosity and knowledge will have empty hands at the day of judgement. I should rather see them grow in virtue, so that when the time of tribulation come, they may find the Lord in their distress. For this tribulation will come, when books, henceforth useless, will be cast out of the window as rubbish."

I—ST FRANCIS OF ASSISI[1]—HIS LOVE OF POVERTY—HIS CONCEPTION OF THE FRIAR MINOR—HIS DEVOTION TO THE PASSION OF CHRIST—HIS MYSTICAL LOVE OF NATURE

THOMAS OF CELANO, the first historian of St Francis of Assisi, remarks that, the gospel teaching having become forgotten almost everywhere, the blessed Francis was sent by God in order to show forth the folly of worldly wisdom, and that by his preaching he might bring men to the wisdom of God.[2]

The Franciscan Order, perhaps unknown to its founder, certainly responded to this need. It is this which in part accounts for its extraordinary success; it is this also which enables us to understand the characteristics of its spirituality; for religious Orders are almost always destined to provide against the dangers of the period which gives them birth. Their Rule and the spirit which inspires them respond to such needs.

St Francis of Assisi left rather a spirit than a teaching; but through this spirit he had a much deeper influence on spirituality than many who have written books.

At the end of the twelfth century, when Francis was born,[3] the Church had, through a sequence of circumstances, acquired immense wealth and great secular power. The Bishops, as feudal lords, often possessed vast territories, and owing to their numerous vassals they were in a measure

---

[1] Principal sources : Wadding, *B. P. Francisci Assisiatis opuscula*, Antwerp 1623. *Cf.* Wadding, *Annales ordinis fratrum minorum*, vol. i. A critical edition of the *Opuscula* has been produced, Quaracchi 1904. They contain the Rule of 1223, the Testament of St. Francis, the Canticle of the Sun, etc. Giles of Assisi, *Aurea dicta*, Quaracchi, 1905. Thomas of Celano, 1 *Beati Francisci Legenda prima*, in *Acta Sanctorum, Octobris*, vol. ii, pp. 683-723, Paris 1866 (this edition is cited here); 2 *Beati Francisci Legenda secunda, pars prima et secunda*, published by Rinaldi, Rome 1806. The edition cited is that of Edouard d'Alençon, Rome 1906, pp. 153-338. *The Legend of the Three Companions* or *Life of St Francis*, by the three Friars Minor, Leo, Angelus and Rufinus (*Acta Sanctorum, Octobris*, vol. xxxiii, pp. 723-742 (cited as *L.T.C.*). St. Bonaventure, *Legenda S Francisci* (*Acta Sanctorum, Octobris*, vol. ii, pp. 742-798); *Speculum perfectionis, primum edidit* P. Sabatier, Paris 1898. *Fioretti*. See Le Monnier, *Histoire de Saint François d'Assise*, Paris 1890. Paul Sabatier, *Vie de St François d'Assise*. J. Jörgensen, *Saint François d'Assise*. Fr. Cuthbert, O.S.F.C., *St Francis of Assisi*. Mention will be found in these biographies of secondary sources, and also a critical study of the sources.

[2] *Legenda* I, 89 (*Acta Sanctorum, Oct.*, ii, 707-708). It is in an analogous sense that the dream of Innocent III was interpreted, in which Francis sustained on his shoulders the Roman basilica of the Lateran, which was threatened with ruin. Celano, *Leg.* II, pars i, 17 (Edouard d'Alençon, p. 182).

[3] In 1181 or 1182. He died on October 3, 1226.

temporal princes. The exercise of their rights, and still more the recovery of these when in dispute, obliged them to have recourse to force, to the great detriment of their pastoral ministry. The monasteries held numerous properties, and this superabundance of possessions brought with it, almost inevitably, laxity in discipline. The lure of riches was too often the sole motive that induced men to embrace the ecclesiastical state when they had no intention of practising its virtues.

Moreover, there were many who thought and said that the riches of the Church were the chief cause of the evils from which she was suffering.[1] The remedy lay in bringing the clergy back to the poverty of the apostolic ages, and many attempts were made in this direction.

Amongst these reformers were heretics influenced by an exaggerated and false mysticism. Peter Waldo of Lyons, the founder of the sect of the Waldenses, claimed, about 1177, to revive the apostolic life.[2] He preached poverty by word and by example.[3] His adepts were known as the Poor Men of Lyons. They were particularly numerous in Northern Italy.

The preaching of the revolutionary monk Arnold of Brescia was much less pacific. Strongly impressed by the difficulties which the Bishop of his native town met with in the maintenance of his temporal power and in the suppression of abuses among the clergy, Arnold desired to strip the clerks and monks of all their possessions. Would not poverty be a better means of causing virtue to reign in the Church? In order to achieve his end Arnold set himself to teach in his sermons and his public lectures that the civil authority alone had the right of possession.

"The clerks who have property," he said, "the Bishops who retain temporal power, and the monks who have possessions are quite unable to work out their salvation. All this belongs to the prince who can only dispose of it in favour of the laity."[4]

Arnold was not content to preach that the Church ought not to have possessions. He sought to strip her of them by violence. Gifted with the temperament of a tribune he raised up the populace. About 1138 there arose a tumult in Brescia which almost succeeded in dispossessing the Bishop of his

---

[1] See Dante, *Inferno*, vii; *Paradiso*, xxii.

[2] The Waldenses taught many heresies, among others the non-existence of Purgatory, the uselessness of prayer for the dead, the illegality of indulgences. Driven out of Lyons, they took refuge in Italy. They were condemned in 1184 by Pope Lucius III.

[3] The success of the heresy of the Albigenses was also due to the fact that they preached poverty.

[4] Otto Frisingensis, *Gesta Frederici*, ii, 20. *Cf.* Vacandard, *Revue des questions historiques*, vol. xxxv, 1884, pp. 52-114.

see. Condemned at the Lateran Council of 1139 by Pope Innocent II, denounced without rest or mercy by St Bernard,[1] Arnold was executed in 1155 at Rome, where he had fomented revolutionary troubles and placed the temporal power of the Papacy in danger.

Such excesses could only compromise the much-desired reform. Happily there were other faithful servants of the Church who laboured for this with wisdom, and were more efficient in another way. They, too, considered that the superabundance of possessions was most hurtful to both clergy and monks.

"Who will grant me," wrote St Bernard to the new Pope, Eugenius III, "who will grant me before I die to see the Church of God such as it was in that far-off epoch in which the Apostles threw their nets, not for fishes of gold and silver, but for souls? How I long that you might make your own the cry of him whose see you occupy : *Let thy money perish with thee !* (Acts viii, 20). O cry of thunder ! O cry of courage and of virtue ! grant that all those that hate Sion be filled with terror, confounded and overturned by it ! The Church impatiently awaits this, your mother the Church urgently begs it of you; they also, the sons of your mother, desire it; great and small, weeping, they ask *that every plant which the heavenly Father hath not planted shall be rooted up* (Matt. xv, 13) at your hands. . . . Many have exclaimed on hearing of your being thus raised : at last *the axe is laid to the root of the trees !*"[2]

St Bernard, in his famous book *On Consideration,* in bold terms, which to-day we should consider somewhat daring, recommends Eugenius III to use moderation in the exercise of his power,[3] humility in the midst of grandeur,[4] and, above all, detachment from the things of this world.[5]

St Francis of Assisi surpassed even St Bernard with all his eloquence, in making men love poverty. He himself loved this virtue as his bride. Dante has sung the espousals of Francis with Lady Poverty :

---

[1] *S Bernardi, Epistolae,* cxcv, 19.   [2] *Epistolae,* ccxxxvi, 6.

[3] *De Consideratione,* lib. II, cap. vi, 10-11; lib. III, cap. i, 2: *Praesis ut prosis, non ut imperes. Nullum tibi venenum, nullum gladium plus formido quam libidinem dominandi.* Power is *non dominium sed officium,* lib. II, cap. vi, 10. According to St Gertrude (*Revel.,* III, lxxiv), God asks of those who have been raised to some high command, " that they hold such dignities as though they did not possess them at all—that is to say, that they should make use of the authority bestowed on them by their rank as something that has been granted them but for a day or for an hour, and that they should be ready to relinquish all at any moment, without ceasing, however, to do all and to act with all their strength for the glory of God."

[4] *De Consideratione,* lib. II, cap. ix, 18.

[5] *id.,* lib. III, cap. v, 14; cap. ii, 8-9; cap. iv, 14.

A dame, to whom none openeth pleasure's gate
More than to death, was, 'gainst his father's will.
His stripling choice : and he did make her his,
Before the spiritual court, by nuptial bonds,
And in his father's sight : from day to day,
Then loved her more devoutly. ˙She, bereaved
Of her first husband slighted and obscure,
Thousand and hundred years and more, remained
Without a single suitor, till he came.
Nor aught availed, that, with Amyclas she
Was found unmoved at rumour from his voice.
Who shook the world : nor aught her constant boldness
Whereby with Christ she mounted on the cross,
When Mary stayed beneath. But not to deal
Thus closely with thee longer, take at large
The lovers' titles—Poverty and Francis.
Their concord, and glad looks, wonder and love
And sweet regard gave birth to holy thoughts.[1]

Son of a rich draper of Assisi, Francis passed his youth in dissipation.[2] Converted during a serious illness, he grew fully to understand the vanity of earthly possessions. He made rapid strides in contempt of self and of all he had loved up till that time so passionately.

" One day when praying fervently to God he heard a voice saying to him : ' Francis, if thou wouldst know my will thou must despise and detest all that thou hast loved according to the flesh and all that thou hast desired to possess. When thou hast begun to do thus, that which seemed before to thee to be sweet and agreeable will become to thee bitter and insupportable, and that which thou dreadest thou shalt find pleasing and of unspeakable sweetness.' "[3]

Francis, without delay, strove to realize this project.

He had an instinctive horror of lepers which he thought was impossible to be overcome. In order to conquer himself he set himself to visit them and even kissed their hideous wounds.[4]

He had been noticeable at Assisi by the richness of his dress and the folly of his extravagance. He triumphed over this pride by forcing on himself the humiliation of wearing the coarsest clothing, which drew upon him the contempt of all, and of begging the bread needful for life.[5]

Persecuted by his father on account of this wonderful conversion, Francis, in a scene which has remained famous, stripped himself of all, even his clothing, gave back every-

---

[1] *Paradiso* xi : *Cf.* Thomas of Celano, *Legenda* II, pars ii, 55 (Edouard d'Alençon, 213).
[2] Thomas of Celano, *Legenda* I, 3 : *Cum adhuc vir iste juvenili calore in peccatis fervesceret, et ubrica aetas ad explenda juvenilia jura ipsum impelleret insolenter. . . .*
[3] *Legend of the Three Companions*, chap. i, 11 (*Acta Sanctorum, Oct.*, II, p. 726).
[4] *L.T.C.*, chap. i, 11 ; Celano, *Leg.* I, 17.
[5] *L.T.C.*, ii, 21-22 ; Celano, *Leg.* I, 11.

thing that he possessed, and left his family. Henceforth he would call Peter Bernardone his father no more. He would have no longer any other father than the heavenly Father, and Poverty would be his consort.[1] To this poverty he would bind himself more and more closely. He called it sometimes his mother, sometimes his bride, always his mistress.[2]

After he had totally abandoned the world Francis lived as a hermit close to the Church of St Damian in the environs of Assisi. He wore a poor habit and walked about girded with a strap, with feet shod and a staff in his hand. " But one day at Mass he heard read the words which Christ addressed to his disciples when he sent them to preach throughout the world—that is, that they should possess neither gold nor silver, nor scrip nor staff, and that they should carry neither shoes nor two coats (Matt. x, 9-10). Having had these words explained by the priest himself, Francis was filled with unspeakable joy, and exclaimed : ' That is what I wish to accomplish with all my heart !' "[3]

He carried out the words of Christ to the letter. From that day he took neither shoes nor staff nor scrip. He had but one tunic, coarse and ugly, and he replaced his girdle with a cord.[4] The Franciscan habit had been found and the ideal of poverty achieved.

Like the disciples of Jesus, Francis began to preach. In the spring of 1209 he came to Assisi and preached penitence and peace. His very simple yet extremely ardent words penetrated hearts like a fiery dart. Conversions quickly resulted and disciples joined him in order to live his life and preach.[5]

One of his first cares was to train them in the practice of poverty. His companions were only allowed to possess one tunic, often patched within and without, a cord and short breeches.[6] When the number of his brethren had increased, he took anxious care lest they should have in their dwellings any object, vessel or utensil that was not absolutely necessary. " It is impossible," he said, " to satisfy simple necessity without letting oneself lapse into comfort."[7]

He insisted on a similar poverty in the dwellings. His first twelve companions lived, about 1209, in a shed they had built in the valley below Assisi, near the Chapel of St Mary

---

[1] *L.T.C.*, ii, 19-20; Celano, *Leg.* II, pars i, 7 : *Amodo, inquit, dicam libere: Pater noster qui es in coelis, non pater Petrus Bernardonis . . . Nudus igitur ad Dominum pergam* (Ed. d'Alençon, p. 177-178).

[2] St Bonaventure, *Leg. S Francisci*, vii, 93 (*Acta Sanctorum, Oct.*, ii, 761) : *Quam [paupertatem] modo matrem, modo sponsam, modo dominam nominare solebat.*

[3] *L.T.C.*, ii, 25; Celano, *Leg.* I, 22.

[4] *L.T.C.*, ii, 25; Celano, *Leg.* I, 22.

[5] Celano, *Leg.* I, 25-30.   [6] *ibid.*, 39.   [7] *ibid.*, 51.

of the Portiuncula. " Heaven is more quickly reached from a shed than from a palace," he said. He often repeated to the brethren that they must imitate Christ, " who had not where to lay his head."

Later, when the Franciscan Order developed, it became necessary to build houses. Francis never resigned himself to it. One day, when passing through Bologna, and learning that his religious had constructed a rather fine convent, he refused to enter it and commanded the brethren to leave it at once. Even the sick were put out. Only the intervention of Cardinal Ugolino, who happened to be at Bologna, was able to bend the terrible defender of " Lady Poverty."[1]

The town of Assisi, taking advantage of the absence of Francis, had the sheds of the Portiuncula replaced by a house roofed with tiles. On his return Francis was wroth, and mounting on the roof began to throw the tiles down to the ground. He only ceased on a protest being made by the soldiers of Assisi, who pointed out that the building belonged to the town.[2] The race of reformers has almost always exhibited a tendency to excess; it is frequently a condition of the success of their mission.

St Francis's horror of money surpassed anything that he could express. One of his religious, having presumed to touch an offering in money found in the chapel of the Portiuncula, in order to dispose of it elsewhere, was harshly reprimanded before the assembled community. Francis punished him by obliging him to take up the money " in his mouth " and to go and throw it on the first ass droppings that he should find in the road.[3] The master seems to have lost his customary meekness when he foresaw the least danger of his disciples enriching themselves. From this it will be seen that he intended at all costs to make it impossible for his convents to acquire possessions.

With a view to making poverty supreme he directed that his Friars should possess no resources, but that they should live from day to day by their work[4] or on alms. They were often obliged to beg for food. To those to whom it was repugnant to ask for an alms he said : " The Son of God was much more noble than we, he who was made poor in this world for our sake. Through love of him we have chosen poverty, we must then not feel ashamed to go and ask for alms. It is unfitting that the heirs of heaven should be ashamed to receive the offerings which are a pledge of the heavenly heritage."[5]

[1] Celano, *Leg.* II, pars ii, 58. [2] *ibid.* 57.
[3] *id., Leg.* I, 65.
[4] St Francis was severe on the idle. Celano, *Leg.* II, pars ii, 161-162.
[5] Celano, *Leg.* II, pars ii, 74 (E. d'Al., p. 227). Cf. *Leg.* II, pars ii, 75.

This seeking after poverty, pushed to its extreme limits, was not intended as a reflection on the clergy, nor on those who had possessions. His object was to obey the Gospel strictly and to imitate Christ as closely as possible.[1] Thus, indirectly, he gave a great lesson to the world. But he respected the sacerdotal dignity too greatly to censure those who were clothed with it.

" The Lord," he says in his *Testament,* " has given me and gives me so great a confidence in the priests who live according to the customs of the Holy Roman Church, on account of the Orders that they have received, that though they were to persecute me I should nevertheless have recourse to them. Even though I had the wisdom of Solomon, were I to find unworthy secular priests I should not preach against their consent in the churches where they dwell. I desire to respect them like all the others, to love them, to honour them as my lords. I do not wish to think of their sins, for I see in them the Son of God and they are my lords. I act thus because I regard nothing corporally here below which pertains to the most high Son of God, unless it be his most holy Body and Blood which they receive and which they alone administer to others."[2]

It was his wish that the hands of priests, on which had been conferred the power of consecrating the Body of Christ, should be held in great veneration.

" If I were to meet at the same moment one of the Blessed come down from heaven and a poor priest I should go first to the priest in order to honour him, and I should hasten to kiss his hands because they handle the Word of life and are something superhuman."[3]

A mendicant religious order forbidding in an absolute manner all possession was a beautiful novelty. But was it possible? Was it livable? Pope Innocent III asked himself this when, about 1210, Francis with eleven of his companions went to Rome to have the first Rule of his Order approved.[4] So many preachers of poverty had arisen in recent years, and they had only succeeded in troubling the Church. Would it not be the same with the attempt of the poor man of Assisi, whose intentions were excellent, but whose gifts of organization appeared as yet uncertain?

In order to calm the fears of the Sovereign Pontiff, Francis

---

[1] *id., Leg.* I, 22, 24-25.

[2] *Testamentum S Francisci (Acta Sanctorum, Oct.,* 4, p. 636, Paris 1866). The authenticity of this testament has been wrongly contested. *Cf.* Celano, *Leg.* II, pars ii, 116.

[3] Celano, *Leg.* II, pars ii, 201 (E. d'Al., 319); *L.T.C.,* iv, 57.

[4] Celano, *Leg.* I, 33; *L.T.C.,* 49. The Rule of 1210 was hardly more than an outline. Francis drew up another in 1221, then a third in 1223, the period when the Franciscan Order became developed and organized.

proffered him the famous parable concerning poverty which had come to him in his prayers :

"There was once a woman, very poor and very lovely," he said, " who dwelt in a desert. A great king, admiring her beauty, desired to take her as his bride, because he hoped through her to have beautiful children. The marriage having taken place, many sons were born to him. When they were grown their mother said to them : ' My children, you have no cause to be ashamed of yourselves, for you are the sons of the king. Go then to his court and he will give you all that you need.'

"When they reached the court the king, admiring their beauty and recognizing their resemblance to himself, said to them : ' Whose sons are you?' They answered that they were the sons of a very poor woman who dwelt in the desert. Then the king pressed them to his breast with joy, saying : ' Have no fear, for you are my sons. If strangers are fed at my table, for greater reason you also, for you are my legitimate offspring.' Then the king commanded the woman to send all the children she had conceived to his court that they might be fed.

" I, most holy Father, am this poor woman whom the Lord hath loved, and whom in his mercy he has rendered beautiful and of whom it has pleased him to have lawful children. The King of kings has declared to me that he will nourish all the sons that he will have by me, for if he feed strangers he must also feed his lawful children. If God grants temporal blessings to sinners, because he would nourish all his children, he will grant more to evangelical men who deserve it better."[1]

God had so inflamed the heart of Francis with an ardent love for holy poverty that he could not pronounce the name of it without his soul being flooded with joy. He used to sing, says Thomas of Celano,[2] the Psalms that spoke of poverty, such as, *The patience of the poor shall not perish for ever* (Ps. ix, 19) and *Let the poor see and rejoice* (Ps. lxviii, 33), with inexpressible fervour and consolation.

He carried the love for his dear virtue almost to fastidiousness. When he was invited to the table of a rich man, on his way to fulfil the engagement he would beg for pieces of bread at the doors of the houses and keep these with him as witnesses to his alliance with Poverty.[3]

Like a noble knight, he took umbrage at once when he thought that the honour of his Lady Poverty was wounded. One day, at Sartiano, a religious asked one of his Friars whence he came. " I come from the cell of Francis," he replied. The Saint on hearing these words at once answered : " Since

---

[1] *L.T.C.*, 50, 51 ; Celano, *Leg.* II, pars ii, 16-17 (E. d'Al., p. 181-182).
[2] *Leg.* II, pars ii, 70 (d'Al., 225).   [3] *ibid.,* 72.

thou hast given the name of Francis to a cell and hast thus made it mine, seek another occupant for it, for I shall not enter it in future any more. When the Lord went into the desert to fast and pray for forty days and forty nights he had no cell made for him, nor a house, but he sheltered himself beneath the mountain rocks. We may follow his example according as it is laid down, by having nothing of our own, even though we might be obliged to have some shelter."[1]

" It is Poverty," he said again, " and not your false riches, that makes the heirs and kings of the kingdom of heaven !"[2] . . . The world will turn away from the Friars Minor in the measure that they turn away from Poverty; they will then seek their food and will not find it. But if they embrace Lady Poverty the world will feed them, because they are sent to save the world."[3]

The love of the *Poverello* of Assisi for the virtue he loved so well sometimes drew from him most passionate cries, especially when he saw it set aside and despised by any of his disciples.

"O Lord, my sweet Jesus Christ," he then exclaimed, " have pity upon me and Lady Poverty. . . . Behold she is in distress, rejected of all . . . seated on a dunghill, she who is the queen of virtues. She complains that her friends have scorned her and have become her enemies. . . . Do thou remember, Lord Jesus, that Poverty is so far the queen of virtues that thou didst abandon thy dwelling with the angels in thine unchangeable affection for her in order to receive her as thy bride, and in order to possess a great number of perfect children. . . . She it is that received thee at thy birth, in the stable and in the crib, and, accompanying thee all through life, was careful so to strip thee of all that thou hadst not where to lay thy head. When thou didst begin the war of our redemption Poverty attached herself to thee to accompany thee as a faithful attendant. She took her place at thy side during the conflict of thy passion; nor did she withdraw when the disciples fled and denied thy name. . . . Finally, whilst thy mother, who at least followed thee to the end and took her part with such compassionate love in all thy sorrow; whilst such a mother, because the cross was high, was not able to reach thee, at that moment Lady Poverty embraced thee more closely than ever; thou wast so dear to her in thy fearful destitution. She would not let thy cross be fashioned with care, nor, as we think, the nails be in sufficient number, pointed and polished; but providing only three, she made them hard, wrinkled and clumsy, better to serve the intention of thy death. And while thou wast

---

[1] *Leg.* II, pars ii, 59.   [2] *ibid.*, 72.
[3] *ibid.*, 70.

dying of thirst, as a faithful bride, she refused thee a drop of water. . . . So that it was in the close embrace of this bride that thou didst let thy soul go forth. Oh! Who then would not love Lady Poverty above all things?"[1]

This passion of Francis for poverty is again shown in his *Testament* by earnest and precise recommendations addressed to his Friars, which sum up his whole thought.[2]

Finally, this passionate lover of poverty desired to render up his soul to God in the arms of " his Lady." When at the point of death he had himself stripped of his clothing, and asked to be laid on the ground in the extreme destitution which had been that of Christ upon the cross. " His heart tasted an unspeakable joy," says Thomas of Celano, " in being thus faithful until death to his Lady Poverty." His disciples having replaced him on the bed, he begged that at his last gasp they would lay him once more on the ground without clothing, and that his body should be left thus for a long time.[3] As though he wished, even in death, to bear witness to his favourite virtue, to the extraordinary love that he had for it, he requested " that he might have no other coffin for his body than poverty."[4]

Francis laid down that the practice of this absolute poverty was to be the characteristic of his Order. But his intentions in this regard were not fully respected by all his disciples. Was it not to be expected when we consider how rapidly the new Order developed? Was it not, moreover, too much to ask of human nature to oblige it to live in such complete destitution?[5]

The holy founder suffered cruelly on seeing his prescriptions violated. It seemed to him sometimes that his work had been a failure.[6] During his lifetime, and even more so after his death, controversies arose as to the interpretation of his prohibition of possessions.[7] Two parties were formed

---

[1] *Oratio pro paupertate obtinenda,* Wadding, *B. Francisci opuscula,* Antwerp 1623, pp. 110-111. *Cf.* Ozanam, *Les poètes franciscains,* pp. 55-56, Paris 1859.

[2] *Acta Sanctorum, Oct.,* pp. 663-664. Cf. *Mirror of Perfection,* II.

[3] Celano, *Leg.* II, pars ii, 214-217 (E. d'Al., 275).

[4] Dante, *Paradiso,* xi.

[5] About 1264, thirty years after the death of St Francis, the Franciscan Order numbered about two hundred thousand religious.

[6] Cf. *Mirror of Perfection,* chap. i : " We have learnt," said several ministers of the Order, " that brother Francis is making a new Rule, and we fear that he may make it so harsh that we shall not be able to observe it. . . . Then Francis, turning up his face to heaven, began to speak to Christ, ' Lord,' he said, ' did I not well say to thee that these would not believe in me?' " See chap. ii. *Cf.* Celano, *Leg.* II, pars ii, 156-157 (E. d'Al., 286-288) ; S Bonaventure, *Leg. S Francisci,* viii, 104-105.

[7] At the Chapter held September 29, 1220, Francis resigned his office of Superior of the Order in favour of Peter of Catania. He consented slightly to soften his prescriptions regarding poverty, as may be seen

among the religious—that of the strict observance and that which called for certain mitigations.

The Friars Minor, according to the intention of their founder, were to be humble as they were poor.

Francis loved humility much. "Humble in his bearing," says Thomas of Celano,[1] "he was still more humble in what he thought of himself, and desired to be looked upon as the last of all: *Humilis habitu, humilior sensu, humillimus reputatu.*" His success did not make him proud.

"I should like to know," one day Friar Masseo said to him, "why doth all the world follow after thee, and why doth every man seem to desire to see thee and to hear thee and to obey thee? Thou art not a man beautiful of body, thou art not greatly learned, thou art not noble : wherefore then should all the world follow after thee?" Hearing this St Francis rejoiced greatly in spirit, and raising his face to heaven stood for a long time with his mind uplifted to God, and thereafter, returning to himself, knelt down and gave praise and thanks to God, and then with great fervour of spirit turned to Friar Masseo and said : ' Wouldst thou know why after me? Wouldst know why after me? Why all the world follows after me? This have I from those eyes of the most high God, which in every place behold the good and the wicked : because those most holy eyes have not seen among sinners any more vile, or more insufficient, or a greater sinner than I am; and since to do the marvellous work which he meaneth to do, he hath not found a viler creature upon earth; therefore hath he chosen me to confound the nobility and the pride and the strength and the beauty and wisdom of the world.' "[2]

Francis carried contempt of self to the extent of seeking humiliations. He was never happier than when insulted or subjected to abuse. He sometimes insisted on his religious treating him as a man unworthy of esteem.[3] The Franciscan tradition has preserved the memory of the delightful conversations of Francis with Friar Leo on the subject of bearing with humiliations and ill-treatment. He considered that it is in the bearing of these that perfect joy is to be found.[4]

One is not truly a Friar Minor, he said, if unable to hear reproaches and insults with a face of joy.[5] In fact, the

---

in the Rule of 1221 which was drawn up after the Chapter. These concessions appear to have been dragged out rather than consented to. Elias of Cortona, Vicar-General of the Order, was the leader of the opposition.

[1] Celano, *Leg.* II, pars ii, 140 (E. d'Al., 275).
[2] *Fioretti*, viii (*alias* x). Ozanam's translation, *op. cit.*, pp. 256-257.
[3] Celano, *Leg.* I, 53, 103.
[4] *Fioretti*, vi-vii (*alias* viii-ix).
[5] Celano, *Leg.* II, pars ii, 145. *Cf.* 142-144 (E. d'Al., 278, 276-277);
L.T.C., iii, 40.

Franciscan preachers were not spared mockery and even blows when they passed through the villages of Umbria for the first time in their strange habit. The very name of *Friars Minor* which Francis gave to his religious was, for them, a constant exhortation to look upon themselves as the last of all, as belonging to the *minores* who were the least important among the people at that time;[1] honours and power must never be their portion.[2] "We call ourselves Friars Minor," he often said, "in order to be more humble in name, in works and by example than all men of the period."[3]

Charity, mortification, piety, and chastity were prominent among the disciples of the penitent of Assisi.[4] Perfect obedience was also required of them. The exhortations of Francis in this connection yielded nothing to those of the Fathers of the desert. In order to be a true disciple of Christ, he said, we must renounce everything we possess. But all is not given up if we do not put ourselves entirely in the hands of our superior by obedience.

"One day," relates Thomas of Celano, "he was seated with his companions, when lamenting he said : 'There is scarcely a religious in the whole world who obeys his superior perfectly.' His companions, much astonished, said to him : 'Teach us then, Father, in what perfect and sovereign obedience should consist.' Then, comparing the obedient to a corpse, he replied : 'Take a dead body and put it where you will. You will see that it offers no resistance to your action, it will not complain of the place which you give it, nor if you take it away. If you place it on a chair it will not look up but down ; if you clothe it in purple it will seem doubly pale. This is how one that is truly obedient acts. He does not ask why his position is changed, nor is he troubled concerning his fresh one, nor does he insist on being removed. Raised to a post of responsibility he retains his habitual humility ; the more he is honoured the more does he judge himself unworthy.' "[5]

The famous formula : We must obey *perinde ac cadaver* is earlier than St Ignatius Loyola. This perfect obedience which he recommended to others Francis practised admirably himself. After he had resigned the position of Superior of the Order, in 1220, he humbly obeyed the new General.

[1] Celano, *Leg.* I, 38. The *majores* were the rich and powerful.
[2] St Francis refused Cardinal Ugolino to allow his religious to be made bishops. Celano, *Leg.* II, pars ii, 148 (Ed. d'Al., 280-281).
[3] *Mirror of Perfection*, chap. ii.
[4] Celano, *Leg.* I, 38-41.
[5] Celano, *Leg.* II, pars ii, 152 (E. d'Al., 284). Cf. *ibid.*, 51 : *Fratres mei, primo verbo praeceptum implete, nec expectate iterandum quod dicitur. Leg.* I, 45.

And in order to combine the merit of obedience with every one of his actions he desired to place himself under the guidance of a brother who was his guardian and to whom he submitted in all things.[1]

The Friar Minor ought to serve God with joy, not the foolish joy which springs from vanity, but spiritual joy which is one of the fruits of divine love. The devil, said St Francis, exults when he is able to rob the servant of God of inward joy, for it is then easy to incline him to worldly pleasures. He can do nothing, on the contrary, against him who has his heart full of joyful ardour in the practice of virtue. Again, Francis could not tolerate sadness in his companions, he reproved them when their countenance was downcast and melancholy.[2]

He strove to have in abundance himself that joy which he inspired in others. If he happened to lose it he began to pray until he recovered it. Usually his soul overflowed with it. "A most sweet melody of mind sang within him and sometimes burst forth outwardly," says Thomas of Celano, "and the divine murmur of his soul used to break out in transports, furtively, in a canticle in the French language." The French manner of speaking was suitable to his expansive joy, to his gaiety so fully Italian.

This need which he felt to turn his joy into song showed itself sometimes in a childlike way. He used to pick up a piece of wood from the ground, place it on his left arm and then taking another in his right he would rub it on the first like a bow on a hurdy-gurdy, singing at the same time in French. He would sing of the Lord Jesus. Presently tears of compassion for the sufferings of Christ would run down. The song would melt away in sighs and lamentations, and the scene would end in an ecstasy in which Francis would be, as it were, held suspended in heaven.[3]

The counsels on the religious life which the penitent of Assisi gave to his companions, with the exception of that which concerned preaching, were followed by St Clare and her companions who lived in community at St Damian in the strictest poverty.[4]

It will be noticed that the Friar Minor, as understood by the poor man of Assisi, had not much resemblance to the Benedictine or Cistercian monk.

He was in the beginning a religious quite outside the

[1] Celano, *Leg.* II, pars ii, 151 (E. d'Al., 283); *Mirror of Perfection,* chap. iv.

[2] Celano, *ibid.*, 125, 128.

[3] *ibid.*, 127 (E. d'Al., 267); *Mirror of Perfection,* chap. viii.

[4] Celano, *Leg.* I, 18-20. Respecting St Clare, see *Acta Sanctorum,* 12 *Augusti*, vol. ii. *Histoire abrégée de l'ordre de Sainte Claire d'Assise,* Lyon 1906, vol. i, pp. 1-128.

traditional system, without noviciate,[1] who did not recite the
Ecclesiastical Office,[2] and who went about from village to
village preaching repentance and peace. Francis had not the
intention of founding a new Order, and he was rather
frightened by the rapidity with which the Minors multiplied.
He would have been incapable of disciplining and organizing
the immense religious movement which his burning soul had
excited if he had not had as counsellor and guide Cardinal
Ugolino, the future Pope Gregory IX.[3]

In reality, his first idea was to form travelling preachers,
men practising the Gospel literally, and going, two by two,
like the disciples of Jesus (Luke x, 1), to preach peace and
repentance to the world.[4] Francis was one of these
preachers. He began all his sermons by the peaceful
greeting : *Dominus det vobis pacem.*[5] It was our Lord himself who showed him how to go about it in this way, and
he obliged his disciples to do the same.

The Franciscan preachers preached in the churches; more
often in public places or at the corners of streets. First of
all they caused astonishment. But soon their message of
peace, delivered by men who had voluntarily stripped themselves of everything, produced an extraordinary impression.
There was a much felt need of peace at that time in Italy,
divided, as it was, between the Guelphs and the Ghibellines,
the party of the Pope and that of the Emperor. The towns
were almost always at war with each other and torn asunder
internally by rival factions. The preaching of Francis was
remarkably effective in procuring the cessation of enmity,
bringing about reconciliations and producing startling and
numerous conversions.[6] There was also a great personal
devotion to him. Men and women in crowds ran after him
and considered it a happiness to touch his habit.[7]

It is difficult for us to picture the enthusiasm which the
Franciscan sermons produced. Convents of Friars Minor
sprang into being on every side. Even more, both clergy
and laity came to ask of Francis rules of life, in order to
follow the precepts of the Gospel in the world and work out
their salvation. He gave counsel to all, and pointed out to

---

[1] It was in 1220 that Pope Honorius III imposed a year's noviciate
on the Order of Friars Minor. *Cum secundum*, Potthast, *Regesta
Pontificum Romanorum*, 6361.

[2] Celano, *Leg.* I, 45 : *Fratres tempore illo . . . ecclesiasticum
officium ignorabant.*

[3] Celano, *Leg.* I, 73 ; *L.T.C.*, iv, 65-67.

[4] Celano, *ibid.*, 29.   [5] *ibid.*, 23.

[6] Francis also endeavoured to evangelize the infidels. He started for
Morocco but was arrested by illness in Spain (1214-1215). In 1218-1220
he went on a mission to Egypt. His religious quickly spread throughout the world.

[7] Celano, *Leg.* I, 23, 36. Cf. *L.T.C.*, iv, 54.

each one the course he should follow in order to get to heaven.[1] Such was the origin of the Third Order, or, as it was then called, the Brotherhood of Penitence.[2]

The Brothers and Sisters of Penitence were called upon to live in great harmony with all, a harmony which at that time was greatly needed. They retained their possessions and remained in the world, in the state in which Providence had placed them. But they had to perform alms deeds as often as possible, to practise inwardly renunciation and to pray. It was, in a measure, the religious life adapted to the secular state.

The passion for poverty, zeal and virtue does not wholly sum up the seraphic soul of Francis. The penitent of Assisi is identified as much with the love of God and of Christ crucified as with the love of poverty. In this we are reminded of St Bernard.

Like the Abbot of Clairvaux, Francis possessed freely the gift of emotion. This sensitiveness, which was natural to him, had been excited by the troubadours of Provence,[3] and after his conversion it was directed with all its energy towards the mysteries of the Christian religion. The piety of the seraphic one of Assisi is filled with poetry, with that sunny poetry found in the rustic ways of Umbria where the Franciscan movement first saw light. For, as we shall see, Francis's piety was associated with all creatures, which he invited to join with him in praising God.

His love for God was so intense that, when divine love was spoken of in his presence, his soul would be melted, and the following burning cry would escape him : " Heaven and earth ought to bow down with respect when the name of the Lord is uttered."[4] His commonest exclamation was : " My God and my all !" *Deus meus et omnia!*[5] He was wont to pray almost continuously. Often he passed the night in churches that had been abandoned. He loved to withdraw into solitude, where, alone with God, wrapped in inexpressible transport, he would contemplate heavenly truths. He had in truth become a living prayer : *Totus non tam orans quam oratio factus.*[6]

[1] *ibid.*, 36-37 ; *L.T.C.*, iv, 60.
[2] The Third Order probably began about 1210, after the first journey of Francis to Rome. The first Rule which Francis gave them has not been preserved. The Brotherhood was called the Third Order. The First Order was that of the Friars Minor, the Second that of the Poor Clares.
[3] Pietro Bernardone, the father of Francis, often travelled in Provence. His mother was probably a Provençale.
[4] *L.T.C.*, v, 68 ; Celano, *Leg.* II, pars ii, 196 (E. d'Al., 316-317).
[5] Wadding, *B. Francisci Ass. opuscula*, p. 119.
[6] Celano, *Leg.* I, 71 ; *Leg.* II, pars ii, 94-140 (E. d'Al., 210-246).

His brethren noticed with what tenderness he spoke of the Saviour Jesus. The love of Christ overflowed from his soul and was shown outwardly by sweet words and canticles.

" How many times," exclaims Thomas of Celano, " when he was sitting at table and heard the name of Jesus spoken or pronounced, or simply called it to mind, would he not forget to take his meal? He was like the holy one of whom it is said that *seeing he saw not and hearing he heard not*. Even more, very often, when he was on the road and thought of Jesus and sang in his honour, he would forget his way and invite all created beings to praise Jesus."[1]

That which touched him the most was the humility of the Word Incarnate and the love which Christ showed for us in his passion.[2]

Like St Bernard, he tenderly wept when contemplating the infant God in his crib. On December 23, 1223, Francis celebrated the Feast of Christmas at Greccio by producing a representation of the scene of the birth of Christ; thus inaugurating a custom which very quickly became general. The Chevalier John of Greccio prepared a crib, not forgetting the ox and the ass. The people of the surrounding country, as well as the Friars of the neighbouring convents, were invited to the feast. The Saint, full of sweet joy, moved to tears, felt himself at Bethlehem before the crib, mingling with the shepherds. Mass was sung, Francis acted as deacon and sang the gospel. When he named the infant God in his gentle and thrilling voice, it was with an unspeakable tenderness that touched every heart.[3]

The love of Christ crucified, above all, filled his soul. It was not simply a love, but a compassion for the suffering Jesus, a veritable participation in his pain. Not long after his conversion, Francis felt himself pierced through with the love of the divine crucified one, in the Church of St Damian, then in ruin. While he prayed before a crucifix he heard the voice of Jesus saying to him : " Go, Francis, and repair my house, thou seest clearly that it is fallen in ruins." At the moment that he gave his servant a mission Jesus imprinted his wounds deeply on his soul.[4] From that day Francis was not able to think of the passion without weeping. " He filled the highways with lamentations," says Thomas of Celano, " and refused all consolation in meditating on the wounds of Christ."[5] He would occasionally withdraw into the woods and desert places in order to lament by himself over the sufferings of Jesus.

[1] *id., Leg.* I, 115.   [2] *id., Leg.* I, 84.
[3] *id., Leg.* I, 84-87 ; S Bonav., *Leg. S Fran.,* 149.
[4] Celano, *Leg.* II, pars i, 10-11 ; *L.T.C.,* i, 13-14.
[5] Celano, *Leg.* II, pars i, 10-11. *Cf.* S Bonaventure, *Leg. S Fran.,* x, 143.

" One day," as is related by the companions of Francis,
" he was walking alone near the Church of St Mary of the
Portiuncula weeping and lamenting aloud. A holy man heard
him and thought he was suffering. Seized with pity he asked
him why he wept. Francis answered : ' I bewail the passion
of my Lord Jesus Christ, and I ought not to feel ashamed
to go throughout the world thus weeping.' " The man then
began to weep with him. It was often noticed that when he
had just been praying his eyes were filled with blood because
he had wept so much and so bitterly. " Not content with
shedding tears, he used to deprive himself of food at the
memory of the passion of the Lord."[1]

He taught his religious this prayer with the intention of
making them do unceasing honour to the passion of the
Saviour : " We adore thee, O Christ, in all the churches of
the whole world, and we bless thee because by thy holy
Cross thou hast redeemed the world."[2]

Francis had so constant a memory of the passion present
in his heart that it might be thought that he desired to
participate actually in the pains of Christ. The *Fioretti*
attribute the following prayer to him, which expresses the
sentiment of his soul in this regard towards the end of his
life, a little while before the apparition of the Stigmata :

" O my Lord Jesus Christ, two graces do I beseech thee to
grant me before I die : the first that, during my lifetime, I
may feel in my soul and in my body, so far as may be
possible, that pain which thou, sweet Lord, didst suffer in
the hour of thy most bitter passion ; the second is that I may
feel in my heart, so far as may be possible, that exceeding
love whereby thou, Son of God, wast enkindled, to bear
willingly such passion for us sinners."[3]

His prayer was heard by the impression of the Stigmata of
Christ in his flesh. " About two years before his death," his
companions tell us, " at the approach of the Feast of the
Exaltation of the Holy Cross, he was praying one morning
on the slope of Mount Alvernia. He was uplifted to God
by desire and by seraphic ardour and felt himself transformed by a tender compassion for him who, in the excess of
his charity, willed to be crucified. A six-winged seraph then
appeared to him, bearing between his wings the form, of
great beauty, of one crucified, having the hands and feet
stretched on the cross, and clearly a figure of our Lord
Jesus. Two wings were folded so as to hide his head ; two

[1] *L.T.C.*, i, 14. Cf. *Mirror of Perfection*, chap. vii. St Francis
often had ecstasies when he prayed. *Cf.* St Bonaventure, *id.*, x, 139 ff.
[2] Celano, *Leg.* I, 45.
[3] *Fioretti, Third Consideration on the Sacred Stigmata.* No doubt
this prayer is not authentic, but it is a true expression of the soul of
St Francis.

others veiled the rest of his body, and the other two were extended to sustain the flight of the seraph. When the vision had disappeared a wonderful ardour of love rested in Francis's soul; and, more wonderful still, in his body there appeared the impression of the Stigmata of our Lord Jesus Christ. The man of God hid them as much as possible until his death, not wishing to make public the mystery of the Lord; but he was not able so to conceal them from his companions, at least from those that were most familiar. But after his happy departure from this world all the brethren who were then present and many of the laity saw his body gloriously marked with the Stigmata of Christ."[1]

Francis of Assisi bequeathed to his Order, as a precious heritage, a special devotion to the passion of Jesus; a devotion which very soon spread and became general throughout the Church.

The mystics of the twelfth century, it will be remembered, made use of creatures in order to rise to the state in which they could contemplate the Creator, but they regarded them from a metaphysical standpoint. The sensible world was a discourse of the Word of God; every creature was an expression, in word or phrase, of that sublime discourse. The mission of man was to discover the thought of the Word which lay hidden beneath the symbolism of sensible realities. The attitude of St Francis of Assisi with regard to creatures is very different. He does not look upon them as symbols, but as living realities. The creatures of God form an immense family; they spring from the same heavenly Father and are nourished by the same providence. All show forth the wisdom, the power and the goodness of the Creator, and all praise him after their kind. The fatherhood of God, spreading over all creation, was deeply realized by St Francis, who looked upon every being as, in a measure, of the same family as himself. He loved them with a fraternal love. He used, as Thomas of Celano tells us, to call them brethren.[2]

This view, arising from faith and the natural kindness of his soul, inclined Francis to be almost as compassionate towards animals as he was towards men.[3] He purchased the lambs that were being taken to the butcher in order to save their lives. He fed the bees in winter that they might not

---

[1] *L.T.C.*, v, 69-70; Celano, *Leg.* I, 94-95; *Leg.* II, pars ii, 135-136; S Bonaventure, *Leg. S. Francisci*, xiii, 188 ff.

[2] Celano, *Leg.* II, pars ii, 165 (E. d'Al., 294).

[3] *id.*, *Leg.* I, 77: *Affluebat spiritu charitatis, pietatis viscera gestans, non solum erga homines necessitatem patientes, verum etiam erga muta, brutaque animalia, reptilia t caeteras sensibiles et insensibiles creaturas. Cf. 78-81.*

perish. Thousands of anecdotes of this kind are told of him by his biographers.

The animals seemed to understand the affection for them which Francis had.[1] They submitted to him and carried out his commands. Swallows would stop singing so as not to disturb his preaching. Fire, at his bidding, gave him no pain when one day the doctor found it necessary to cauterize his face.[2] The Saint of Assisi possessed something of the power of Adam, in the earthly paradise, over created beings.

Like the first man before the fall, Francis was easily uplifted towards God by the consideration of creatures; he used to contemplate the Creator in each one of them with inexpressible joy. The beauty of the flowers enraptured him, for in them he saw a reflection of divine beauty.[3] Fire reminded him of the brightness of eternal light; moreover, his affection for it was so great that he would never put it out, even when it burnt his clothing. He would walk on stones with the greatest respect, for the love of Christ who is the rock upon which we have been exalted (Ps. lx, 3). When he found little worms on the road he would remove them that they might not be trodden under foot, for Christ, suffering, is spoken of as a worm of the earth (Ps. xxi, 7). He specially loved water, which is chaste, and symbolizes the purification of the soul.[4] Francis understood, in the highest degree, the mission given to man, of praising God in the name of all creation. The *Canticle of the Sun,* quoted further on, is a magnificent expression of his soul in this regard. He addressed himself to creatures as though they had the gift of reason and invited them to glorify the Lord.

One day when he was travelling in the Valley of Spoleto he saw a great number of birds gathered together in one place. Urged by his love of animals, Francis approached them, and, as they did not fly away, he began to preach to them :

" My brethren the birds," he said, " you ought greatly to praise your Creator and always to love him, who has given you feathers to clothe you and all else that you need. God has made you the most noble of his creatures; he has given you the air as a dwelling-place, and although you neither sow nor reap, he protects and guides you so that you lack nothing."[5]

When the sermon was ended the birds began to lift up

---

[1] *id., Tractatus de miraculis,* 20 : *Nitebantur ipsae creaturae amoris vicem rependere sancto Francisco et gratitudine sua pro meritis respondere* (E. d'Al., 355). *Leg.* II, pars ii, 166.

[2] *ibid.,* 20-32; *Leg.* II, pars ii, 166.

[3] *id., Leg.* I, 81.

[4] Celano, *Leg.* II, pars ii, 165 (E. d'Al., 293-294) ; *Mirror of Perfection,* xii.

[5] Celano, *Leg.* I, 58 ; *De miraculis,* 20.

their heads and spread their wings and open their beaks, at the same time looking at Francis as though approving of his words. The Saint reproached himself for not having preached sooner to the birds, which had listened with so much respect to the divine word.

This holy sentiment regarding nature was one of the strongest experienced by Francis. He translated it into song in that wonderful *Canticle of the Sun* which was composed by him two years before his death, when he was ill at St Damian.

"Most high, all-powerful and good Lord, to thee belong praise, glory and all benediction. To thee only are they due, and there is no man worthy to name thee.

"Praise be to thee, O Lord, on account of all creatures, but especially for our brother messire the sun, to whom we owe the light of day! He is beautiful and sends forth rays of great splendour, and bears witness to thee, O my God!

"Praise be to thee, my Lord, for our sister the moon and for the stars! It is thou who hast placed them in the heavens, bright and beautiful.

"Praise be to thee, my Lord, for my brother the wind, for the air and the clouds, and the calmness of every season, whatever it may be! For it is by means of them that thou sustainest all creatures.

"Praise be to thee, my Lord, for our sister the water, which is most useful, humble, precious, and chaste!

"Praise be to thee, my Lord, for our brother the fire! By means of it thou dost illumine the night; it is pleasant to see, unconquerable and strong.

"Praise be to thee, my Lord, for our mother the earth, which sustains us, nourishes us, and brings forth the variegated flowers and herbs, and every kind of fruit!

"Praise be to thee, my Lord, for those who forgive for the love of thee, and patiently bear infirmity and tribulation! Happy those who continue in peace! For it is the Most High who will crown them.

"Be praised, my Lord, because of our sister the death of the body, which no man living can escape! Woe to him who dies in mortal sin! Happy those who, at the hour of death, are found conformable to thy most holy will! For the second death shall not harm them.

"Praise and bless my Lord; return him thanks and serve him with great humility."[1]

With no other saint, not even St Francis de Sales, is there

---

[1] Wadding, *B. Francisci Ass. opuscula*, Antwerp 1623, pp. 398-399, where the Italian text is to be found (French translation by Ozanam, *Les Poètes franciscains*, pp. 71-73). The last verse but one was added a few days after the *Canticle* was composed, on the occasion of a dispute between the Bishop of Assisi and the magistrates of the city. The last was composed when St Francis learnt by a revelation the moment of

this mystical love of nature to such a degree. The seraphic Friar of Assisi used to be raised without effort towards God, even to the extent of ecstasy, by the contemplation of creation. No one is better able than he to make us understand what must have been the relations of man in a state of innocence with the created beings.

II—FRANCISCAN WRITERS OF THE XIII AND XIV CENTURIES—THE BIOGRAPHERS OF ST FRANCIS AND ST BONAVENTURE

THE first Franciscan writers were the biographers of their saintly founder.

We already know the work of Thomas of Celano and the *Legend of the Three Companions* of Brothers Leo,[1] Angelo and Rufinus. These historians had been the disciples of Francis and had lived in intimacy with him. A little later Bartholomew de Rinonico of Pisa (1401) wrote the *Book of Conformities*,[2] in which, as is indicated by its title, he strove to show, not without some exaggeration, that the life of the penitent of Assisi was conformed in all its details to that of Christ.

These biographies reflect the anxieties of that party among the Friars Minor who were desirous of remaining faithful to the primitive spirit of the Order. These anxieties produced an abundant literature. *The Chronicle of the Seven Tribulations* of Angelo Clareno (1337) is the best known work.[3] Angelo, in a fierce tone, expresses the indignation of the *Zelanti* or *Spirituals* against the Friars of the Common Observance or *Conventuals* who were directing the Order and softening the Rule contrary to the wishes of the founder.[4]

Animated with excellent intentions, the *Spirituals* or rigid observants were unable to remain faithful to religious obedience. They considered that the Order had swerved, and, yielding to a kind of mystical defiance, under the

---

his death. This chant is called *Laudes creaturarum,* the *canticle of creatures.* It is better known as the *Canticle of the Sun,* because the sun, for which Francis had a particular affection, is mentioned in the first place. Bartholomew of Pisa is one of the first to mention this chant in his *Liber conformitatum Vitae B. ac S Patris Francisci ad vitam J.C.D.N.,* lib. II, *Conformitas* xi.

[1] M. Paul Sabatier also attributes to Friar Leo the *Speculum Perfectionis, seu S Francisci A. legenda antiquissima,* Paris 1898.

[2] *Liber aureus inscriptus Liber Conformitatum Vitae B. ac Seraphici Patris Francisci ad vitam Jesu Christi Domini nostri,* Milan 1510, Bologna 1590. I omit other less important biographies.

[3] Published in part by F. Ehrle, in the *Archiv für Litteratur und Kirchengeschichte des Mittelalters,* Berlin 1885-1887, vol. i-iii.

[4] On all this, see Ed. d'Alençon, art. *Frères Mineurs* in the *Dict. de theol. cath.*

leadership of John of Parma (1247-1257), a large number of them clung with enthusiasm to the apocalyptic reveries of Joachim of Flora. They foretold a third revelation—that of the Holy Ghost, who, with the help of the Friars Minor Spiritual, was about to transform the world. Francis of Assisi was the new Messiah whose coming had been predicted by Joachim, and his Friars were to be the workers of this universal transformation of Christian society.

The monastery of Greccio, where John of Parma lived, was the centre of the Spirituals. The Joachimites accentuated still more the division from which the Franciscans were suffering, and they placed the orthodoxy of the whole Order in danger. It became necessary to remedy this.[1] On February 2, 1257, John of Parma was dismissed from his position as Minister-General, and St Bonaventure was elected in his stead.

Bonaventure,[2] hardly thirty-six years old, was placed at the head of the Franciscan Order in extremely difficult circumstances. He was not unworthy of his mission. He strove to arrest the Joachimite movement among his religious, and its principal leaders were imprisoned. Nevertheless, aspirations towards excessive severity in the Franciscan Rule were continued, especially by the famous Ubertino da Casale, author of the *Arbor Vitae*,[3] Peter of John Oliva[4] and Jacopone da Todi.

These most regrettable agitations furnished the adversaries of the mendicant Orders with weapons. The novelties introduced into the monastic life of St Francis of Assisi, and very soon afterwards by St Dominic, were not long in finding opponents. The most celebrated among them, in

---

[1] The Order was all the more compromised in that a Friar Minor, one Gerard di Borgo San Donnino, published the *Introductorius in Evangelium aeternum,* a kind of introduction to the chief works of Joachim, which laid the sons of St Francis open to violent attack, particularly by William de St Amour.

[2] St Bonaventure was born in 1221 at Bagnorea, in the Viterbo district, in Italy. He took the Franciscan habit about 1243, studied in Paris, and had as his master the famous Franciscan, Alexander of Hales. He afterwards taught in Paris at the same time as St Thomas Aquinas. He was General of the Order until 1273, when he was created Cardinal and Bishop of Albano. He assisted at the Council of Lyons of 1274, during which he died on the night of July 14. Cf. *Acta Sanctorum, Julii,* iii, dies 14.

[3] Ubertino da Casale joined the Carthusians in 1312. His works are tainted with illuminism. *Arbor vitae crucifixae Jesu,* Venice 1485, Ulm 1492; Italian translation, Foligno 1564. *De septem statibus Ecclesiae juxta septem visiones quae leguntur in Apocalypsi,* Venice 1515, 1525. He was in touch with Bl. Angela of Foligno, as he tells us in the prologue to the *Arbor Vitae.* Cf. *L'idéalisme franciscain spirituel au XIVe siècle. Etude sur Ubertin de Casale,* par Frédégand Callaey, O.M. Cap., University of Louvain, 1911.

[4] Peter of John Oliva or Olivi (1298), Franciscan of Béziers, taught that Christ and the Apostles never possessed anything. This teaching was declared heretical by Pope John XXII.

the thirteenth century, was William de St Amour, doctor of the Sorbonne.

The University of Paris, jealous of its privileges, put forward a claim to forbid the mendicant Orders—that is, the Franciscans and Dominicans—the right of erecting chairs for the public teaching of philosophy and theology. William de St Amour was charged with the duty of defending its interests. In a celebrated work[1] he transferred the dispute to questions of doctrine, and denied the religious the right to teach and to preach. He also put forward doubts as to the lawfulness of the practice of poverty such as it was understood by the mendicant Orders.

But in the question of doctrine he met his match. The two great theologians of this period, St Thomas Aquinas and St Bonaventure, were sent to Anagni to Alexander IV to take up the defence of their respective Orders. The Angelic Doctor, in the presence of the Pope, delivered an apology for the religious life, as conceived by Francis of Assisi and Dominic, which annihilated the theories of William.[2]

The thesis of the doctor of the Sorbonne was too faulty to succeed. This is not, however, to say that it contained nothing but error. The new religious, intoxicated by their success and rendered bold by the Bulls which they had received from Rome, sought at times—or at least some of them did—to withdraw themselves from the authority of the ecclesiastical rulers. William showed up these cases of insubordination. He also knew how to turn to account the Joachimite tendencies of the *Zelanti* Franciscans. But he drew up his criticisms with so much violence and in such exaggerated terms that he entirely compromised his cause, even on points in which it might have had some appearance of truth.

St Bonaventure well understood that the best refutation of the accusations of William de St Amour would be the irreproachable lives of his religious. Also, whilst repressing the faults of the Joachimites, he did not hesitate to deal rigorously with the party of lax Franciscans who were greatly responsible for the reactionary excesses of the *Zelanti*. Even from the morrow of his election he drew up a programme of reforms to be put into operation at once.

[1] *De periculis novissimorum temporum,* composed in 1255. William was born at the beginning of the thirteenth century in the town of St Amour, in Franche-Comté. He became Canon of Beauvais. His famous work against the mendicants was condemned at Anagni, where Pope Alexander IV then lived, by the Bull *Urbi et Orbi*. William died in Paris in 1272. His works were published in Paris in 1632, one vol.

[2] Echoes of this controversy are to be seen in the writings of S Thomas: *Quodlibetum* VII, art. xvii, xviii: *Contra impugnantes Dei cultum et religionem.* S Bonaventure, *De perfectione evangelica,* Opera S Bonav., vol. v, Quaracchi. An anonymous French writer, *Manus quae contra Omnipotentem tenditur,* published by M. Bierbaum, *Franziskanische Studien,* Beiheft 2, Munster i. W., 1920.

It has been noticed that the numerous biographers of Francis, from the spirit which animated them, were not unacquainted with the divisions in the Order. Bonaventure was commissioned by the Chapter at Narbonne in 1260 to draw up a Rule to replace all others and bring tranquillity to all minds. His work was hardly other than a compilation, in which, however, is shown, in an exquisite manner, the grateful love of the son for his father—in his childhood he had been healed of a serious illness by the intercession of St Francis.[1]

It is not so much as biographer only of the Poverello of Assisi that St Bonaventure is of interest to the history of spirituality. He himself is a spiritual writer, a mystic worthy of notice.

St Bonaventure,[2] without prejudice to his natural gifts, which were of the highest order, belongs, from the point of view of spirituality, to the family of St Bernard and to that of St Victor, as much as to the family of St Francis.

Like St Bernard, whom he often quotes, he is affective, and much more inclined to love than to speculation. No doubt he was less disdainful than was the Abbot of Clairvaux of theoretical knowledge. He has left *Commentaries* on the four books of the *Sentences* of Peter Lombard, comparable to those of the great theologians of his time. But, for him, knowledge had interest only in so far as it renders us better, leads us to love, and unites us with God. What is the value of pure knowledge?

---

[1] *Leg. S Francisci, prolog.,* 3.

[2] The best edition of his works is that which was published at Quaracchi 1882-1902, by the Franciscan fathers, *S Bonaventurae opera omnia.* The ascetic and mystical works are in vol. viii. The chief of these are—*De triplici via* (entitled *Incendium amoris, Stimulus amoris,* in the Venetian edition, 1754, vol. v). The triple way of meditation, prayer and contemplation leads to union with God by love. *Soliloquium de quatuor mentalibus exercitiis,* an imitation of the *Soliloquy* of Hugh of St Victor. The soul asks questions on spiritual subjects and the inward man replies. *Lignum vitae,* containing meditations on the life and passion of Christ. *De perfectione vitae ad sorores,* a small treatise on religious perfection. *De sex alis seraphim,* or the six chief duties of superiors. *Vitis mystica,* Christ is the mystical Vine. Vol. viii also contains the writings of St Bonaventure concerning the defence of the Order of Friars Minor and of poverty against the attacks of William de St Amour. The Quaracchi edition places the *Itinerarium mentis ad Deum* among the theological works, vol. v. It is a mystical as much as a theological work, in which is shown how the soul may be raised from creatures to the contemplation of God. *De quinque festivitatibus pueri Jesu,* vol. viii, treats of the relations of the soul with Jesus. The *Sermons* of St Bonaventure, vol. ix. The *Breviloquium* is a theological treatise which contains ascetic and mystical surveys, vol. v. *Cf.* E. Smeets, *Dict. de théolog. cath.,* art. *S Bonaventure.* In vol. viii of the Quaracchi edition will be found the apocryphal writings attributed to St Bonaventure.

Moreover, at the beginning of his *Commentaries on the Sentences,*[1] he declares that theology is chiefly affective, and in his explanation of doctrines he dwells in preference more on those which favour greater piety. He is not then an intellectual in the strict sense. Whilst a great number of theologians make heavenly beatitude consist in the act of intuitive vision, St Bonaventure makes it consist above all in the act of the will by which God is loved with a beatific love. His constant care to render the intelligence subservient to piety and devotion of heart caused him, from the fourteenth century, to be known as the Seraphic Doctor.[2]

St Bonaventure, on account of this special bent of his mind, felt himself more in sympathy with Plato than with Aristotle.[3] Affective piety—as is shown from the history of spirituality—prefers the idealism of Plato to the realism of Aristotle, and mystics are found to frequent the Academy more willingly than the Lyceum. St Augustine, the pseudo-Dionysius, the Victorines are Platonists, and the Seraphic Doctor drew his inspiration, in preference, from them.

That which is also to be noted in his writings is a great devotion to the Holy Trinity. The memory of the divine Persons is constantly in his mind and in his heart. He seeks everywhere for traces of images of the Trinity, and this prepossession inspires his theory of contemplation and even influences his style. Bonaventure develops his line of thought according to a tripartite literary process, which in the end becomes monotonous and artificial. In honour of the divine Persons each idea is divided into three parts, and each assertion put forward and supported by three reasons.

What is important in the spirituality of St Bonaventure is : (1) His theory as to the three ways of the spiritual life; (2) his views on contemplation; (3) his considerations on the passion of Christ, in which he shows himself a true disciple of the stigmatisé of Assisi.

It is in the works of the Seraphic Doctor that there is found—doubtless for the first time—a complete exposition of the famous distinction between the three ways of the spiritual life : the purgative way, the illuminative way, and the unitive way;[4] and this is put forward as responding

---

[1] 1 *Sent., proem.*, Q. iii.

[2] Gerson—who was not a lover of speculation—was specially devoted to the writings of St Bonaventure. *Opera Omnia,* Antwerp 1706, vol. i, p. 21.

[3] *Cf.* 2 *Sent., Dist.* I, pars I, quest. I; *In Hexaemeron, collatio* 3.

[4] *Hic triplex intellectus respondet triplici actui hierarchico, scilicet purgationi, illuminationi et perfectioni. Purgatio autem ad pacem ducit, illuminatio ad veritatem, perfectio ad charitatem; quibus perfecte adeptis, anima beatificatur. . . . In horum igitur trium cognitione dependet scientia totius sacrae scripturae et meritum aeternae vitae. De triplici via (vel de accendio amoris), cap. i, prologus.*

fully to the thought of the pseudo-Dionysius. In the purgative way, the soul is purified from its faults; in the illuminative way, it is enlightened as to God, Christ and itself; in the unitive way, it is united to God by charity.[1] In order to bring about its ascending progress in these three ways the soul employs three means : meditation, prayer and contemplation.

During the period of purification man, through meditation, awakens his conscience, stimulates it and guides it. He awakens it by examination of sins committed through negligence, passion or malice. He stimulates it by the consideration of the nearness of death, the sorrowful passion of Christ and the severities of the Sovereign Judge. He guides it in the way of goodness by correcting negligence with fervour, passion by renunciation, malice by rectitude. It is thus that the Christian renders his conscience pure and virtuous.[2]

Prayer proper to the purgative way consists in bewailing our wretchedness. These groanings call for sorrow at the remembrance of our sins, shame at the sight of our moral downfall, fear at the thought of inevitable judgement and hell, to which we lay ourselves open. To these feelings, which should enliven the soul whilst purifying it, should be added the desire to mortify evil inclinations and trustfulness in Christ the Redeemer, in the Virgin Mary and in the saints in heaven. It is by this means that man attains to complete peace of soul.

Once purified and calmed, the Christian enters the illuminative way. He acquires vivid enlightenments by reflecting on the faults which God has forgiven, and on those which he might still have committed if grace had not restrained him, by recognizing the natural and supernatural benefits he has received, and by thinking of the heavenly reward promised to the good. He implores the divine mercy with an ardent desire inspired by the Holy Ghost, with great confidence based on the merits of Christ, with persevering persistence encouraged by the prayers of the saints. It is in the illuminative way that the Christian strives to imitate Jesus the Saviour, above all the Saviour suffering and dying for us. He has compassion on his sorrows, he admires, contemplates, embraces his cross. The divine light thus leads the faithful soul into the fulness of truth.

At this stage of the spiritual life perfection is reached. The way of the perfect is called the unitive way because it admits of union with God through charity. Here the soul

---

[1] *De triplici via,* cap. i. *Cf.* cap. iii, n. 1 : *Necesse est . . . ascendere secundum triplicem viam: scilicet purgativam quae consistit in expulsione peccati; illuminativam quae consistit in imitatione Christi; unitivam quae consistit in susceptione Sponsi.* Cf. *Itinerarium mentis in Deum,* cap. i.

[2] Cf. *De perfectione vitae ad sorores,* cap. i.

is trained to love. This training consists in freeing the soul from the love of creatures, in inflaming it with the consideration of the beauties of the heavenly Spouse, in rendering it as spiritual as possible because God is above our senses and beyond our imagination. He is also above our intelligence, for he is indeterminable, unending, incomprehensible, but always wholly desirable. Here we see the influence of the Areopagite in the repeated assertion of the incomprehensibility of God.

As regards the unitive way, the Seraphic Doctor expounds his theory of divine love which is linked with that of prayer. True prayer, he says, consists in three acts : to lament our wretchedness, to implore divine mercy, and to pay divine honour to God. If one of these be lacking it is imperfect.

We bewail our faults in order to receive forgiveness, we implore the divine mercy to receive grace. It is in the paying of divine honour above all that love is to be found. This divine honour comprises the respect which becomes transformed into adoration, the love of goodwill which expresses itself in thanksgiving and the love of complacency which is made manifest in the mutual and intimate colloquies between the bridegroom and the bride of which the *Canticle of Canticles* speaks. This love is able to lead man even to ecstasy.

In order to reach this love in perfection, the Seraphic Doctor states that it is necessary to ascend by six mystical steps : sweetness, eagerness, satiety, inebriation, security, and tranquillity.

In the first degree the soul learns how the Lord is sweet and delightful. This knowledge produces within it such eagerness, so great a hunger for God that nothing in the world is able to sate it unless it be the more and more perfect possession of the Sovereign Good. The soul, in order to grasp God more fully, is often thrown out of itself in ecstasy. This eagerness which consumes it causes the soul to rise to the third degree, which is that of satiety. In this state all that is not God has no attraction for it and becomes distasteful. It resembles one who is replete and is unable to look upon material food without nausea. Then comes mystical inebriation. He who is intoxicated does not feel pain, he becomes foolishly exalted. Divine love, having reached this degree, with God's aid, seeks suffering and rejoices in it as though it felt it not. It is the folly of the cross ; the pain seems to bring pleasure.

The soul thus enamoured of God feels security. It drives away fear from itself. It has so great a confidence in the divine help that it thinks that nothing can separate it from the Lord. It was the state of St Paul, who felt the certainty that neither death, nor life, nor anything else was able to separate him from the love of God (Rom. viii). The sixth and last degree is that of tranquillity and perfect peace. Here we have the *apatheia* of the ancient ascetics. The soul enjoys such repose, such a silence, that nothing can disturb it. It is in a kind of mystical sleep which neither passion nor fear can trouble. This state is the fruit of love. When it is attained all is easy, even suffering and death. Oh! how we should strive towards this supreme charity![1]

St Bonaventure's theory of contemplation owes much to Hugh of St Victor. The world is a book in which the thoughts of God are traced in sensible characters, imperfect and perishable. The heavenly Trinity is made manifest therein more or less completely according to the perfection of created beings. It has left *vestiges* of itself in material creatures, an *image* of itself in beings endowed with reason, and finally a *resemblance* to itself in the soul deified by grace.

The world is, therefore, a kind of mystical ladder, the steps of which must be ascended by man in order to raise himself through contemplation to God. Before the fall the human soul was easily uplifted to the Creator; at present it is needful for its powers to be readjusted by grace in order to be capable of attaining to heaven. These powers are three in number: the corporeal senses which obtain glimpses of the divine in sensible beings, the mind which bears within itself the image of the Trinity, and a supernatural light which resides in the summit of the soul (*apex mentis*) or *synteresis*, which enables us to contemplate the likeness of the divine Persons within us.[2] Thus constituted, man rises progressively towards God, first of all by means of sensible beings, then through the mind of the soul, and afterwards by God considered in the unity of his essence and the Trinity of Persons.

It is with his whole being and with outbursts of love that the Christian contemplates the sovereign beauty resplendent in creation. The study of the universe enables us to discover marks of the heavenly Trinity, and, as it were, traces of his passage. The number three is everywhere found. Beings have been regulated by *measure, number and weight* (Wisd. xi, 20). They are born, they grow and die. Among them are found those that have being, others that have life as well as being, and finally others that have in addition intelligence. If we regard the manner of man's relationship with creatures we again meet with the number three. Thus man grasps the objects through perception by means of the five bodily senses; he is arrested by the pleasure which their beauty and goodness cause him, he obtains knowledge of them through

[1] *Breviloquium,* pars II, cap. xii.
[2] *Itinerarium mentis ad Deum,* cap. i.

judgement which, disregarding accidental conditions of time and place, fixes itself on that which is permanent and absolute.[1]

If we now set aside outward things and enter within ourselves, we discover in our souls no longer merely signs but an image of the Trinity. The human soul has some similarity with the divine Persons. It possesses three faculties : the memory, the understanding, and the will. From the memory proceeds understanding, by which thought is produced; from the memory and the understanding proceed love, which is related to the will.[2] How great then is the dignity of the human soul which thus resembles the Trinity and presents an image of the mysterious way in which the divine Persons proceed from one another !

" Consider above all, O my soul," exclaims St Bonaventure in this connection, "how generous nature has been toward thee ! This generosity consists, it seems to me, in that which has been imprinted in thy natural being in order to bring out the beauty and image of the Blessed Trinity. Also as St Anselm says in the Proslogion : ' I confess, O Lord, in blessing thee, that thou hast created me in thine image in order that I may be mindful of thee, that I may study thee, and that I may love thee.' And Bernard adds : ' When I look into man I find within myself three powers by which I think of God, know him, and love him. These are the memory, the understanding and the will. When I am mindful of God I delight in him. . . . By means of my intelligence I contemplate him in himself and see how incomprehensible he is ! he is the beginning and the end of all things. I understand that he is to be desired in the angels, for the angels desire to contemplate him; that he is to be enjoyed in the saints, for it is in him that they are happy for ever; that he is admired in all his creatures, for he has created all by his power, he rules all with wisdom and he distributes all freely. These thoughts make me love God, and when my will loves God it is transformed in him. Such, indeed, is the force of love that we must become such as that which we love.' "[3]

But since the fall man, left to his own strength, is not capable of entering into himself in order to contemplate the image of the Trinity. That is why Christ merited for us the grace by which the image of the Trinity is restored and made perfect in us. The human soul is reclothed with the three theological virtues of faith, hope and charity. It thus acquires

[1] *id.*, cap. i-ii.

[2] *id.*, cap. iii. The psychology which divides the faculties of the soul into memory, understanding and will was current in the thirteenth century. It is found in St Thomas Aquinas.

[3] St Bonaventure, *Soliloquium*, cap. i, n. 3. The work quoted is the *Bernardi meditationes*, chap. i, which is apocryphal.

a most perfect likeness to the divine persons with the life of whom it becomes associated. It is deified; it becomes possessed of the divine light by which it is able to contemplate God, not only in creatures and in itself, but in himself, in the unity of his essence and the Trinity of his Persons.[1] This contemplation is effected through faith, which is the supernatural life of the soul.

It has, as its primary object, the existence of God with its essential characteristics : pure being, simple, absolute, original, eternal, perfect, unique, unchangeable, everywhere present. " God may be pictured to the imagination as a sphere, the centre of which is everywhere and the circumference nowhere."[2] The ultimate object of contemplation is the Trinity itself : the distinction and equality of the Persons, the relationship between them and the manner in which they proceed one from the other. It comprises also the hypostatic union of the Word with human nature in Christ.[3]

It will be noticed that this contemplation is dogmatic rather than mystical. But, according to St Bonaventure, theology is an affective science which should lead to love. We must, then, not be surprised that he should suggest theological study in order to draw near to God or even to attain to ecstasy if we are called thereto.

St Bonaventure does not describe ecstasy. He calls to mind those of St Francis of Assisi; he quotes the pseudo-Dionysius. According to him this mystical phenomenon is most mysterious; it must have been experienced in order to recognize it. And it does not depend on us to be favoured with it, for it is a gift which God bestows on whom he pleases.[4]

Devotion to the passion of Christ, already so greatly advocated by St Anselm and St Bernard, received a considerable impetus from St Francis of Assisi and his Order. The writings of St Bonaventure mark a stage in the development of the love of the faithful for the suffering Jesus. Tender compassion, pity and compunction are shown forth

---

[1] *Itiner. mentis in Deum,* cap. iv.

[2] *id.,* cap. v. See *Soliloquium,* cap. iv. A beautiful contemplation of the joy of heaven.

[3] *Itiner. mentis in Deum,* cap. vi.

[4] *id.,* cap. vii : *In hoc autem transitu* [*in Deum per excessum*] *oportet quod relinquantur omnes intellectuales operationes et apex affectus totus transferatur et transformatur in Deum. Hoc autem est mysticum et secretissimum quod nemo novit nisi qui accipit, nec accipit nisi desiderat, nec desiderat nisi quem ignis Spiritus sancti medullitus inflammat . . . Quoniam igitur ad hoc nil potest natura, modicum potest industria, parum est dandum inquisitioni et multum unctioni . . . parum dandum est verbo et scripto et totum Dei dono, scilicet Spiritui sancto; parum aut nihil dandum est creaturae et totum creatrici essentiae, Patri et Filio et Spiritui sancto.*

there in a touching manner. The Seraphic Doctor meditated unceasingly on the sorrows of Christ crucified, and he exhorted all Christians to do the same.

"The true Christian," he says, ". . . who desires to resemble the crucified Saviour completely, ought to strive above all to carry the Cross of Christ Jesus either in his soul or in his flesh in order to feel himself, like St Paul, truly *nailed to the cross with Christ* (Gal. ii, 19). Now he alone is worthy to experience the ardour of such a feeling who, calling to mind with thankfulness the passion of the Lord, contemplates the labour, the sufferings and the love of Christ crucified with a memory so faithful, an intelligence so piercing and a will so loving, that he may exclaim with the bride of the *Canticles: A bundle of myrrh is my beloved to me, he shall abide between my breasts* (Cant. i, 12)."[1]

With a view to assisting meditation on the sufferings of Christ, Bonaventure composed a beautiful work called the *Tree of Life.* Jesus is this mystical tree. His mortal life is represented by the lower part of the trunk, his passion by the middle, and his glory by the top. The branches of the tree produce fruits which symbolize the prerogatives of Christ, such as the different happenings of his life, especially his passion. These fruits form nourishment full of delight for the inward soul. Each of them provides the Seraphic Doctor with an occasion for exaltation.[2] The most beautiful are those which treat of the sufferings of the Saviour.

We are moved to pity at the cry of pain which escapes the soul of Bonaventure at the sight of Mary at the foot of the cross; and tears flow when the pious writer asks us to contemplate Christ, tormented by pain and pallid in death, breathing his last. He then turns to the heavenly Father and, inspired by St Anselm, addresses him thus :

"Look down, then, O heavenly Father, from thy sanctuary and from the height of thy heavenly dwelling; look, I say, upon the face of thy Christ (Ps. lxxxiii, 10). Look at this most holy Victim which our High Priest offers thee for the expiation of our sins, and be thou appeased as to the malice of thy people. Do thou also, O man who hast been redeemed, consider the Person, the dignity and the greatness of him who is suspended for thee upon the cross; of him whose death gives life to the dead, whose death is lamented by heaven, by earth and by the hard rocks that are burst asunder as though moved with compassion. O human heart,

---

[1] *Lignum vitae,* n. 1, *prologus.* In the *Perfectione vitae ad sorores,* cap. vi, Bonaventure recommends meditation on the passion of Christ as an excellent means of sanctification.

[2] The tree has twelve branches. Four prerogatives of Christ, or circumstances of his passion, correspond with each branch. The work thus comprises forty-eight meditations.

thou wouldst be harder than the stones, if thou wert not shaken with fear, moved by compassion, broken by repentance and softened by love at the memory of the sacrifice of such a Victim !"[1]

St Bonaventure employs, very happily, the allegory of the vine in order to describe the sufferings of Christ, the mystical Vine.[2]

The vine, he says, is pruned, it is subjected to wounds. Jesus, who, according to his own words, is the *true Vine* (John xv, 1), has himself also been cruelly wounded by the Jews. When the vine shoots, it is bound. Jesus was bound during his passion. The leaves of the vine form a shade beneath which we may take rest; Christ, uplifted on the cross, is the mystical Vine which protects us by his overshadowing. Each of the seven words which were uttered by Jesus on the Cross is an evergreen and bountiful leaf of our true Vine. The flowers, filled with perfume, of this divine Vine, are the most high virtues of which Christ has set us an example.[3]

The writer also pictures the flowers which grow at the foot of the cross, chiefly the violet which symbolizes the humble heart that loves to be hidden, the red rose which represents charity and the shedding of the blood of Christ, and the lily which is the emblem of chastity.[4]

III—MEDITATIONS ON THE LIFE OF CHRIST OF THE PSEUDO-BONAVENTURE — THE FRAN-CISCAN PREACHERS OF THE XIV AND XV CENTURIES

THE *Meditations on the Life of Christ* is an original work inspired by St Bernard, which had a very great influence in the fourteenth and fifteenth centuries.

It was for a long time attributed to St Bonaventure,[5] because his eminently affective methods are to be found therein. Its author is certainly a Franciscan of the thirteenth

---

[1] *Lignum vitae*, n. 29 (vol. viii, 79).

[2] *Vitis mystica* (vol. viii, 159-188). This work, enriched with many interpolations, is also found among the apocryphal works of St Bernard (*P.L.*, CLXXXIV, 635-740).

[3] *id.*, cap. i-xiii (Quaracchi).

[4] *id.*, cap. xiv-xxiii. The Franciscan writers of the school of St Bonaventure may here be noted : Bernard of Bessa (Quaracchi, vol. viii, pp. xcv, ciii); David of Augsburg (1271); Conrad of Saxony (1279), to whom is attributed the *Speculum B. M. Virginis;* James of Milan (end of thirteenth century), who must have written a *Stimulus amoris.*

[5] The edition of Quaracchi places, not without reason, the *Meditations* among the apocryphal works of St Bonaventure. The Venetian edition, 1756, vol. xii, attributes them to the Seraphic Doctor. French translation, Paris, Poussielgue.

century, probably an Italian.[1] It is addressed to the religious of St Clare.

It is a mystical biography of Christ. To compile it the writer borrowed from the Gospel narratives, and also delved into personal revelations in which pious folk had thought to learn unauthenticated details concerning the earthly life of the Saviour. When he is wanting in information, he does not hesitate to provide it from his imagination, and narrates events as they must, according to him, have taken place.[2]

He introduces many pious reflections into his narrative, for his intention is to draw up meditations on the events of the life of the Saviour and not merely to write a narrative with the sole object of satisfying curiosity.[3]

Exegetes disdain works of this kind. It cannot be seen what there is for them to learn in them. But the writer of a history of spirituality may give them due importance on account of the influence they had on the piety of the faithful.

St Bernard, in his *Sermons,* had already composed loving meditations on the principal events in the life of Christ. The pseudo-Bonaventure, by means of his *Meditations,* compiled with instructive method, wishes to accustom his readers to study and contemplate successively, according to chronological order,[4] the facts of the *earthly life* of Jesus, in order to be edified thereby and to draw practical lessons therefrom. Ludolph the Carthusian, at the end of the fourteenth century, had only to follow this model to write his famous *Life of Christ.*

The life of the Saviour, above all his passion, was destined, under the influence of the pseudo-Bonaventure and the Franciscan preachers, to engross the attention of pious souls. St Gertrude declared that to touch the heart there is no religious exercise comparable with meditation on the sufferings of Christ.[5] St Bridget, in her visions, contemplated the scenes of the passion as though they actually occurred before her eyes.[6] Oliver Maillard compiled a

---

[1] According to some MSS. he must have been named Joannes de Caulibus.

[2] *Meditationes vitae Christi,* cap. ix : *Ego enim in hoc et in aliis vitae Christi actibus intendo, ut in principio tibi dixi, aliquas meditationes tangere, secundum quasdam imaginarias representationes, quas anima diversimodo percipere potest, secundum quod gesta fuerunt per ipsum, vel sicut fuisse credi possunt.*

[3] These pious reflections are chiefly drawn from St Bernard, as the writer himself frequently declares. In the fourteenth and fifteenth centuries, however, some other hand added ascetic developments to the meditations.

[4] The work is divided into six parts, each comprising several meditations : before the Incarnation, the Incarnation, the nativity of Christ, his public life, his passion and death, his resurrection and ascension and Pentecost.

[5] *Revelations of St Gertrude,* Book III, ch. 44 ; Book IV, ch. 22-26.

[6] Birger, *Vita S Birgittae,* n. 6. *Acta Sanct., Oct.,* vol. iv, 486.

History of the Passion.[1] The Rhenish mystics, Tauler
(1361)[2] and Henry Suso (1366),[3] devoted their ardent imagination to all the events of the passion, and lay bare details in it
which are enough to make us shudder. The humble son of
St Francis of Assisi contributed, to a great extent, towards
moving hearts to pity for the sufferings of Christ.

He sets forth, indeed, the scenes of the passion in such a
pathetic manner that he moves his readers to the depths of
their souls. He pictures episodes, which are not mentioned
in the Gospels, but which, such as that of the last meeting
of Jesus with his Mother before his passion, are most
touching.

It took place at Bethania, at the house of Martha and
Mary, on the Wednesday of the last week. Jesus was taking
a farewell meal; his disciples and his Mother were there.
After the meal he approaches his Mother, enters into conversation with her and allows her to enjoy one last time
with him. Mary Magdalen breaks in, and speaking to the
Mother of Jesus, says to her : " I have invited the Master
to eat the Pasch here, but he desires to go to Jerusalem in
order to be taken by his enemies. I implore you not to
allow him to act thus." And Mary says to her Son : " I beg
of you not to go away, but to celebrate the Pasch here.
You are aware of the plots that are being hatched against
you !" " Most dear Mother," answers Jesus, " my Father
wills that I should keep the Pasch at Jerusalem, for the time
of redemption has come. It is now that the prophecies are
about to be accomplished regarding me and that my enemies
will do with me what they will." This answer causes the
two women vivid sorrow, for they understand that Jesus is
going to his death. With voice broken by sobs Mary per-
sists : " I do not wish to be opposed to the designs of the
heavenly Father. . . . But were he to be pleased to redeem
the world in another way, all things are possible to him."
Jesus gently consoles his Mother and Magdalen. " It is
necessary for me to die, but soon I shall rise again and
reappear transfigured in your sight."[4]

The Poor Clare must have wept when she read this meditation. She did not weep alone, for this scene passed into the
mystery plays and made the spectators of the Middle Ages
weep in their turn.

This, moreover, is not the only episode which the dramatic

---

[1] Published in the fifteenth century. Oliver Maillard was a Franciscan.

[2] *Exercitatio super Vita et Passione Salvatoris nostri.*

[3] *The Book of Eternal Wisdom,* ch. i-xx. Bl. Angela of Foligno
(1309). *Visions* (French transl. Hello, p. 49) describes the head of the
suffering Christ from ,which the hairs from the eyebrows and beard
had been torn, as also does the pseudo-Bonaventure (LXXXII, Venice).

[4] *Med. Vit. Christi,* cap. lix (Venetian edition, lxxii).

writers of the period borrowed from the *Meditations*. They knew how to make use of the interview between St John and the Virgin when the Apostle gives an account on the Friday morning of the events of the night : the betrayal by Judas, the judgement of princes and priests, and the evil treatment to which Jesus had been subjected. Nor do they forget the swooning of the Virgin when she meets her Son on the way to Calvary, nor the gesture with which, tearing the veil from her head, she covers the nakedness of her crucified Son before he is lifted up on the cross, nor, above all, her lamentations when the body of Christ, taken down from the cross, is received on her breast.[1]

This passion of the Virgin was described also, with all its painful incidents, towards the end of the thirteenth century, by the Franciscan Jacopone da Todi (1306), the supposed author of the *Stabat Mater*.[2]

It is not only the sufferings of the Mother of Christ which move the reader of the *Meditations*. The scourging of the Saviour, his crowning with thorns, his crucifixion, all the circumstances of his death, are presented as a deeply pathetic drama and with an impressive realism.

Finally, the drama of the redemption ends in the triumphant entry of Jesus into heaven. The whole of the celestial court comes forward to meet the divine Victor, singing hymns of praise. Never has there been such joy in Paradise. Jesus, on reaching heaven, goes towards his Father and, casting himself prostrate before him, says to him : " Father, I give thee thanks that thou hast enabled me to overcome all our enemies. I present to thee our friends who were held captive in Hades. I have promised to send the Holy Spirit to my brethren and disciples whom I have left behind on earth. My Father, I pray thee guard them and keep the promise that I have made them." And then the heavenly Father raises the Son, makes him sit at his right hand, and assures him that all his requests are heard.[3]

The *Meditations* were partly the inauguration of a new development. As affective writings they were addressed but little to the mind and much to the heart. Their aim was to engender the love of Christ less by the uplifting influence of his divine teaching than by the account of his mortal life. Doctrinal reflections give place to coloured descriptions, in which history is supplemented from the imagination, of the earthly existence of the Saviour. It is thus the humanity of

[1] *id.*, ch. lxii, lxiv, lxv, lxix (lxxv, lxxvii, lxxviii, lxxxii). M. E. Male, *L'art religieux de la fin du moyen âge en France*, ch. i, ii, iii, has clearly shown the influence which the *Meditations* of the pseudo-Bonaventure had on the theatre and religious art at the end of the Middle Ages.

[2] *Cf.* Ozanam, *Les poètes franciscains*, ch. iv-v.

[3] *Meditationes*, LXXXIV (XCVIII).

Christ that is brought into high relief. In this way mystics held Christian thought fixed on this humanity which the metaphysical speculations of theologians were inclined to leave forgotten.

Piety—the *Meditations* prove it—may be nourished from sources other than those that are official and canonical. It is enough that a doctrine or narrative be not contrary to the traditional teaching of the Church for it to be legitimately edifying. The pseudo-Bonaventure, and after him the authors of the mystical *Lives of Christ,* introduced into their works accounts and details which would be sought for in vain in the Gospels, but which none the less encouraged numberless souls to greater love and greater generosity. Spirituality and history pursue different ends. They, therefore, adopt different means, although it is most desirable that piety, quite as much as history, should rest on what is true and not simply on what is likely.

The Franciscan Order was famed in the Middle Ages for its preachers.

St Antony of Padua, who was the first of them, was born in Lisbon in 1195. Moved by the preaching of the Friars Minor in Portugal in the year 1217, he joined the Franciscan Order. He preached with great success in Italy and France. The Franciscan Chronicles frequently speak of him. Unfortunately his memory was very soon overshadowed by legend. He died in Padua on June 13, 1231.[1]

To judge from the rare sermons of his which remain to us his style of preaching had a literary turn which calls to mind that of St Bernard much more than St Francis of Assisi. Antony was an educated religious who had studied at Lisbon and elsewhere before becoming a Friar Minor. His preaching, popular, no doubt, like that of the Franciscans, possessed, however, in it something that was classical.

But it was in the fifteenth century that the preaching of the Franciscans became specially brilliant through St Bernardine of Siena and St John Capistran. It had a substantial effect on the piety of the faithful.

The Franciscan preachers addressed themselves to the emotions of their audiences. It was, as it were, a tradition left them by their founder, whose soul was so full of religious poetry. They also excelled in the dramatic element. In Italy pulpits were erected in the open air in public places capable of holding many thousands of people.[2] The sermons,

---

[1] *Cf.* A. Lepitre, *St Antoine de Padoue,* Paris 1901 (there is an English translation). In this book will be found mentioned the sources of the history of St Anthony. Cf. *Fioretti,* XXXIX-XL.

[2] In France, on account of certain abuses, preaching in the open air was forbidden in the fifteenth century.

delivered in popular language, lasted for several hours, and the preachers passed easily from one subject to another according to the needs of their hearers.[1]

These needs were indeed great in the Italy of the Renaissance. Meditation on great Christian ideas, which had fully occupied the Middle Ages, had given way to the emancipation of the mind and of the flesh. A rediscovered cultus of antiquity, ill understood, encouraged the people to abandon practices of penance and to substitute for them the shameful liberties of the Epicureans. If the Renaissance period was an age of arts and letters, it is, on the other hand, marked by a most pronounced decay in piety and morals. The chief mission of the preachers, as formerly of St Francis of Assisi, was to exhort to concord and peace. They had, above all, to recall to mind the great duties of Christian morality and to purify souls overtaken by the universal corruption.

St Bernardine of Siena was the promoter of this apostolate of purification. The Franciscans who preached after him, such as St John Capistran (1456) and St James of the Marches (1476), the Blessed Albert of Sarteano, Bernardine of Feltre, Bernardine of Fossa, followed him as their chief and their model. Born at Siena in 1380, St Bernardine joined the Friars Minor in 1402. In 1438 he was given the charge of ruling the convents of the Strict Observance in Italy, with the title of vicar-general.

This movement, known as the Observance, came into being at the end of the fourteenth century in that part of Greccio, where the last of the Spirituals had survived, rendered, however, wise and entirely freed from Joachitism. It had as its object the bringing back of the Friars Minor to the austerity of the Franciscan Rule. The Observants were assisted in their task, in Italy, by the Great Schism of the West, in which the Friars Minor, divided between the two obediences, enjoyed a greater autonomy and were more easily able to bring changes into their convents. About the same time, in France, St Colette, a woman of unusual energy (1447),[2] brought about a double reform, that of the Poor Clares and of the Friars Minor, which took the name of Colettines. The Observants became so numerous that it was no longer possible for them to remain subservient to the Conventuals. In 1517 Pope Leo X separated them, and con-

---

[1] Cf. P. Thureau-Dangin, *Un prédicateur populaire dans l'Italie de la Renaissance, St Bernardin de Sienne,* Paris 1897 (Eng. trans., *St Bernardine of Siena*).

[2] She was born at Corbie in Picardy in 1380. She died at Ghent in 1446. Her ecstasies were frequent and prolonged. She also possessed the gift of prophecy. Her life was written by Peter de Vaux, her confessor. *Acta Sanc.,* 6ᵃ *Martii,* pp. 538 ff., Paris 1865. *Cf.* A. Pidoux, *Sainte Colette,* Paris; E. Sainte-Marie-Perrin, *La Belle Vie de Ste Colette de Corbie,* Paris 1920.

stituted the Conventuals and the Observants as two distinct
and independent Orders.[1]

The administration of the Italian Observants prevented St
Bernardine from yielding himself to the ministry of preaching
—a work which he had begun about 1417.[2]

His great subject was devotion to the name of Jesus.
Faithful to the tradition of St Bernard and of Henry Suso
(1365), he nobly celebrated, in his sermons, the beauties and
virtues of the name of Jesus, as also the sweet consolations
which it brought to the Christian soul. He called upon his
hearers to inscribe this name, or at least abbreviations of it,
on both public and private monuments.[3] He himself caused
it to be painted on tablets which he distributed to the people
during his preaching in order to make them reverence it. It
even came to these tablets being carried in procession.[4]
The novelty of this devotion produced criticism. Bernardine
was even accused of heresy, and had to betake himself to
Rome in order to justify himself. The lawfulness of the new
devotion was admitted, and from this time onwards the
name of Jesus was more and more venerated in the Church,
to the great benefit of the piety of the faithful.

In their sermons St Bernardine and the Franciscan
preachers loved also frequently to speak of the passion of
Christ. It is they, in company with the sons of St Dominic,
who made the suffering Christ worshipped and beloved by the
people. In this connection the work of the preachers was
even greater than that of the authors of mystery plays.

The faithful of the Renaissance epoch not only needed to be
moved by the description of the sorrows of Christ; it was
also necessary to make them tremble at the thought of their
last end. The Franciscans and Dominicans were not found
lacking in this, and their words were so fruitful that medita-

---

[1] The Franciscans then formed two Orders, independent of one
another, differing in name, habit and manner of life : the *Friars
Minor Conventual,* availing themselves of dispensations and having
possessions in common, and the *Friars Minor of the Regular Observance,* who carried out fully the Franciscan Rule. Although each of the
Orders had its own superior, the Pope decreed that the Observants
alone should use the title of *Minister-General of the whole Order of
Friars Minor, Successor of St Francis.* The Observants later formed
new branches, the *Discalced* in Spain, the *Reformed* in Italy, the
Recollets in France. In the sixteenth century appeared the *Capuchins.*

[2] Thureau-Dangin, *op. cit.,* ch. ii.

[3] The abbreviation adopted by St Bernardine was the trigram I H S,
the first letters of the Greek word 'ΙΗΣΟΤΣ. Later on they were looked
upon as forming the initial letters of *Iesus Hominum Salvator.* St
Ignatius of Loyola adopted the same trigram as St Bernardine of
Siena.

[4] Barnabaeus Senensis, *Vita prima antiquior S Bernard. Sen.,* 9, 14,
in *Acta Sanct., ibid.,* pp. 109, 111. Luciano Banchi, *Le Prediche
volgari,* vol. ii. With regard to tablets bearing the name of Jesus, cf.
Acta Sanct., ibid., p. 139.

tion on death became a spiritual exercise adopted by all who endeavoured to follow the way of Christian perfection.[1] It was also at that time that were composed treatises on the *Art of Dying.*[2]

IV—BL. ANGELA OF FOLIGNO AND ST CATHERINE OF BOLOGNA

THE Franciscan Order furthermore produced, in the Middle Ages, two great Italian mystics, who remind us of St Gertrude and St Catherine of Siena, and who have left us their writings: Angela of Foligno and Catherine of Bologna.[3]

Angela lived at Foligno, in Umbria, where she died in 1309. She was previously married and the mother of a family.

If we are to believe her statements, she must have passed part of her life in sin. She was converted and received great enlightenments from God, who showed her all the ugliness of her state and inspired her with a keen sorrow for it. She stripped herself of her possessions and gave herself up to prayer and meditation on the Christian mysteries, above all on the passion of Christ. When she had lost all the members of her family—her mother, her husband and her children—she consecrated herself entirely to God and put herself "under the rule of Blessed Francis."[4] She gave encourage-

---

[1] "The Franciscans and the Dominicans, by addressing themselves unceasingly to the emotions, ended by transforming the Christian temperament; they made Europe weep over the wounds of Jesus Christ, and brought fear into the hearts of the crowds by speaking to them of death." E. Male, *L'art religieux de la fin du moyen âge en France,* p. 383, Paris 1908. It was towards the end of the fourteenth century that death is often represented either in sculpture or in painting. From this period also dates the dance of death so often represented. *Cf.* E. Male, *op. cit.*

[2] See the *Ars moriendi* of Gerson, *Works,* Antwerp 1706, vol. i, 447. See also the impressive chapters of the Dominican Henry Suso "On how to die well" and "On Sudden Death," *Book of Eternal Wisdom,* part II, chap. 21-24. *Œuvres mystiques* du B. Henri Suso, trad. Thiriot, Paris 1899, vol. ii, pp. 139 ff.

[3] Mention must also be made of B. Raymond Lull (1315) surnamed the *Illuminated Doctor,* and author of the *Ars generalis sive magna,* which was a method of converting infidels. His life was exciting. He made several journeys among the infidels and was ill-treated by them. His mystical exaltation has its faithful expression in the *Book of the Lover and the Beloved,* attributed to him. It is a colloquy between the Friend (the Lover) and God (the Beloved) on divine love.

[4] *Life and Revelations,* chap. xx. What we know of the Saint was gathered together by her confessor, the Friar Minor Arnaud de Corbie, who wrote under her dictation. Bollandus published the work of Arnaud in 1643 in the first volume of the *Acta Sanctorum,* January 4, with chapters differently numbered from those of Arnaud, which are referred to in the margin. In 1714 another edition of the *Life and Revelations* was printed at Foligno. The *Miscellana Francescana,*

ment to that section of the Friars Minor who desired to remain faithful to the primitive Rule of the Order.

After having been purified in the crucible of sufferings and temptations, God raisèd Angela to the most perfect mystical states. She was not, to the same degree as St Gertrude, "the saint of the humanity of Christ," although she had many visions, famous on account of their realistic character, of the scenes in the passion of the Saviour.[1] Rather is she the saint of the transcendency of God. Her visions and her ecstasies put her in direct relationship with the Divinity whose immensity, incomprehensibility and ineffability she experienced most vividly. In her *Revelations* Angela unceasingly complains of her inability to express what she saw and heard.

"All that I have just uttered," she often said to Friar Arnaud, her secretary, "is nothing. There is no sense in it. Our poor human language . . . can do no more. When it has to do with things divine and their effect language becomes absolutely dead."[2] The unfortunate secretary was all bewildered. "He was there like an idiot listening without understanding . . ." he says. "Sometimes," he adds, "she made use of words which to me were absolutely unknown and strange. It was immense, powerful, dazzling . . . I seemed to see something unheard of; not knowing what, I remained there without writing."[3]

The visions which Angela had of God were intellectual. Her soul perceived God within her without corporeal shape.

"One day," she says, "I was in prayer, uplifted in mind; God spoke to me in peace and in love. I looked and I saw. You will ask me what it was that I saw? It was himself, and I can say nothing more. It was a fulness, it was an inward and overflowing light for which neither word nor comparison is worth anything. I saw nothing corporeal. That day it was like heaven on earth : a beauty which closes the lips, the supreme beauty that contains the supreme Good. The assembly of the saints stood round, singing praises before that majesty so fully beautiful. All appeared to me in a second."[4]

---

from 1889, have interesting studies on Bl. Angela. The works of Bl. Angela were occasionally edited under the title of *Theologia crucis*, Pavia 1538. They have been translated into French; *La Théologie de la croix ou les œuvres et la vie de la B. Angèle de Foligne*, Cologne 1696, Paris 1601. E. Hello did a well-known, though not very literal, translation : *Le Livre des Visions et Instructions de la B. Angèle de Foligno*, Paris 1868.

[1] *Life and Revelations*, chap. x, xxx, xxxi, xxxii, xlvi (Arnaud).
[2] Second prologue of Friar Arnaud (Hello, 5th edit. 1914, pp. 27-28).
[3] *ibid.*, pp. 28, 29.
[4] *Life and Revelations*, chap. xxi (Hello, p. 88). Angela had also imaginative visions concerning the scenes of the passion of Christ.

Angela also perceived intellectually the divine attributes : power, wisdom, justice, love, ineffability.[1]

But the blessed one of Foligno not only wrote in order to astonish us and to fill us with the sense of the greatness of God. She wished also to instruct us. In particular she teaches us the nature of mystical union such as she experienced it. Mystical union is characterized, according to her, by the sense of the presence of God in the soul. God comes suddenly, without being called or prayed to, and places in the heart a fire, a love and an unknown sweetness emanating from himself. Again, the soul perceives the coming of God within it when it hears his most sweet word which crowns it with joy, and when it feels the divinity with an impression of delight (*sentit eum sentimento valde delectabili*).

Nevertheless, doubt may still exist. The soul may still not know with certainty if it is God or another intelligence that produces the feelings which it experiences. It acquires the certainty that God is present within when it feels him in a way entirely unusual, with an intensity that surprises it. At the same time, divine love, ardent as a flame, removes all self-love from the soul and instils into the mind thoughts which cannot come from any creature. The soul most clearly understands these thoughts, and is kindled with the desire to express them outwardly. There is received also another gift : that of desiring wholly all that God wills. The human will becomes totally identified with that of God.

Blessed Angela mentions again two more signs which confirm the others and increase this certainty as to the presence of God. The first is an unction which suddenly renews the soul and which renders all the members of the body docile and submissive to it. No trouble can then approach it, and there is certainty that God is there and that he speaks. The other sign that fully reveals to the soul the presence of God within is an embrace.[2] God embraces the rational soul as no father or mother has ever embraced child, nor creature embraced creature. The embrace in which Jesus presses the soul to himself (*stringit ad se animam rationalem*) is ineffable. No one in the world can tell, or even believe, unless experienced, the sweetness of this kiss.

Blessed Angela had many ecstasies; she ever found in them something new. " Each ecstasy," she said, " is a new ecstasy, and all the ecstasies are one indescribable thing." Furthermore, the revelations and visions succeed each other

---

[1] *Life and Revelations*, chap. **xx ff.**

[2] *Amplexatio quam facit Deus animae rationali. Acta Sanct.*, cap. xi (chap. 52, Arnaud). The doctrine of mystical union is mostly in this chapter, which I summarize from the text of the *Acta Sanctorum*.

"without resemblance."[1] What wonderful variety in the mysteries of the mystical world!

Not less wonderful is the variety of the ways by which God leads to them. God, it seems, took Angela from sin into which she had fallen. He quickly purified her in order to admit her among the number of privileged souls freely crowned with most wonderful graces and enjoying the divine embrace.

It was by a very different road, that of the spiritual combat, that St Catherine, Abbess of the Poor Clares of Bologna, arrived at the mystical state. She had to put forth all her energy in order to overcome violent temptations to which she was previously subjected. Her mysticism, moreover, is wholly directed towards the struggle.

Born at Bologna in 1413 Catherine lived for some years at the Court of Ferrara as maid of honour to Margaret of Este.[2] Catherine, whose soul was pure and fashioned to dwell in intimacy with Christ, left the world and placed herself under the direction of a pious virgin at Ferrara named Lucy, who directed a community of young maidens.

It was while there that she began to suffer those temptations which were to render her "a very experienced master of the spiritual combat, *peritissima militiae interioris magistra.*[3] God prepared her for the struggle by granting several spiritual favours, intended to sustain her courage. She had it revealed to her that all her sins were fully forgiven her. And that she might have a great horror of the least fault, the Lord made her suffer, in a vision, the terrors of the Last Judgement.[4]

It was above all through diabolical illusions that she was put to the test. The devil appeared to her occasionally in the form of the Virgin Mary or of Christ crucified, and commanded her, under the pretext of perfection, to perform things that were impossible in order to cast her into despair.[5] The Saint thus went through violent temptations to disobedience, which put her soul into a kind of agony and just missed making her abandon the religious life.[6] It is one of the wiles of the devil, she said, to suggest at certain times good and holy thoughts as to virtue, and then to tempt the soul to the contrary vice in order to discourage it.[7]

---

[1] *Life and Revelations*, chap. lvi.

[2] We have two *Lives* of St Catherine in Italian. The first by the Friar Minor Observant, Dionysius Paleotti, the other, fuller, *Vita altera,* by Christopher Mansueti of Monte-Carlo, published in 1595. A Latin translation of the two *Lives* will be found in the *Acta Sanct.,* March 9, pp. 36-89, Paris 1865.

[3] *Vita altera,* cap. i, 6.

[4] *id.,* cap. i, 7.

[5] *id.,* cap. ii, 10-13.

[6] *id.,* cap. ii, 14.

[7] *id.,* cap. ii, 10.

These temptations did not cease when Catherine became a Poor Clare at the monastery of Corpus Christi at Ferrara. The devil then suggested thoughts of blasphemy.[1] But most painful of all to her were doubts as to the real presence which assailed her when she was before the Holy Eucharist. When she had to communicate she was obsessed by them to the point of losing her senses.[2]

God consoled his faithful servant with extraordinary mystical graces. One Christmas night the Virgin Mary appeared to the Saint. She held the divine Child in her arms and passed him for a few moments to the holy Poor Clare.[3] Ecstasies alternated with visions. In one of them Catherine, then Abbess of the Poor Clares of Bologna, had the revelation of the day of her death,[4] which took place on March 9, 1463.

The biography of St Catherine explains the character of her book : *The Seven Spiritual Weapons Against the Enemies of the Soul*.[5] It is an autobiography as much as a treatise on spirituality. The holy nun, under the pseudonym of Catella, narrates the struggles which she had to sustain and the means she employed in order to overcome them.[6] She also speaks there of the spiritual favours with which God rewarded her faithfulness. A short time after her death this book, under the title of *The Revelation of St Catherine*,[7] became much circulated in Italy for the very great help of those souls who had to fight the good fight of the Lord.[8]

---

[1] *id.*, cap. iii, 27.

[2] *id.*, cap. iii, 29. *Die quadam . . . crevit adeo tentatio et pugna illa . . . ut quasi ebria nimio dolore pene defecerit. . . .*

[3] *id.*, cap. v, 47-48. These temptations ceased some years before the death of the Saint.

[4] *id.*, cap. ix.

[5] *id.*, cap. vi. This work was written in Italian in 1438 at the monastery of the Poor Clares at Ferrara. It only became known shortly after the death of Catherine, who spoke of it to her sisters at Bologna (*ibid.*, cap. vi, 58). The work was translated into Latin by the first biographer of the Saint, the Friar Minor Dionysius Paleotti.

[6] Cf. *id.*, cap. iv, 36.

[7] *id.*, cap. vi, 57.

[8] We also note here certain Franciscans of the fifteenth century who have written on the subject of mysticism : Peter Saupin, Bishop of Bazas (1417); John Canales of Ferrara, who died at Bologna in 1462, author of a *Liber . . . de coelesti vita*, Venice 1494; and, above all, Henry Harphius (1477), who wrote the famous *Theologia mystica* of which we shall say more further on in connection with the German mystics.

CHAPTER VII

ST DOMINIC AND
THE DOMINICAN SCHOOL

THE WORK OF ST DOMINIC—DOMINI-
CAN PREACHING : ST VINCENT
FERRER — HAGIOGRAPHY : JAMES
DE VORAGINE—DOMINICAN MYSTI-
CISM IN ITALY : FRA ANGELICO
OF FIESOLE, ST CATHERINE OF
SIENA—THE GERMAN DOMINICAN
MYSTICS : ECKHART, JOHN TAULER,
HENRY SUSO

I—THE WORK OF ST DOMINIC

ST DOMINIC[1] met St Francis of Assisi several times
in Rome. They once found themselves together at
the house of Cardinal Ugolino. The latter wished to
select bishops from among the Friars Preachers and
the Friars Minor. He asked the two founders what
they thought of his project. Out of modesty, neither of them
would be the first to reply. At last Dominic began to speak
and begged the Cardinal to leave his religious alone in the
humility of their vocation. Francis upheld this answer with
all his energy.

Dominic had the highest regard for the founder of the
Friars Minor. He greatly admired his eminent sanctity and
wished to collaborate with him : " I wish, Brother Francis,"
he said to him, " that your Order and mine were one, and
that we had, in the Church, but one manner of life."[2]
Before separating the two Saints gave each other a fraternal
kiss.

In spite of the difference in the Rules—the Dominicans

---

[1] See the documents respecting the history of St Dominic in the *Acta
Sanctorum,* August, vol. i, pp. 341 ff., Paris 1867, and in Jean Guiraud,
Saint Dominique, Paris 1899 (this book has been translated into
English), in which will be found on pp. 207-211 a complete bibliography.
Cf. Mandonnet, *Frères Prêcheurs (La théologie dans l'orde des),* in the
Dict. de Theol. cath.

[2] Thomas of Celano, *Leg.* XXXIII, *B. Francisci,* 148-150 (E. d'Al.,
280).

followed the Rule of St Augustine[1]—the two Orders had resemblances which explain the wish of St Dominic.

In the thirteenth century there had been a great revolution in the religious life.

Hitherto monastic institutions had in view, above all, the personal sanctification of the monks. They did not, as a rule, consist of apostolic workers whose end was to evangelize the people. It was by way of exception, and at the formal request of the Popes, or bishops, that the monks became missionaries, like those who converted the Anglo-Saxons, in the sixth century, under the leadership of St Augustine, and those who, later on, evangelized Germany under St Boniface. The religious Orders founded in the twelfth century were either military Orders—such as the Knights of St John of Jerusalem, the Knights Templars and the Teutonic Knights—or Orders having as their object the ransoming of Christians reduced to slavery by the Saracens—like the Trinitarians of St John of Matha and St Felix of Valois or the Order of our Lady of Mercy of St Peter Nolasco and St Raymond of Pennafort. But there was no congregation devoted by vocation to the exercise of apostolic zeal.[2] The Dominicans and Franciscans, on the contrary, are preachers whose mission is to evangelize Christian people and even infidels.

About 1215 Dominic formed, at Toulouse, a company of preachers with a view to the conversion of the Albigenses.[3] His religious were called Friars Preachers. Dominicans and Franciscans, then, were not, like the sons of St Benedict and the other more ancient Orders, cloistered. They extended their activities abroad and preached. " God wishes us to go into the world," said the Penitent of Assisi. Dominic, in turn, raised his Canons Regular to the dignity and the functions of the apostolate : *Virum canonicum auget in apostolicum*, as expressed in a liturgical text in his Office.

[1] Cf. *Regula S Augustini et Constitutiones F. F. Ordinis Praedicatorum, jussu* Antonii Cloche, Rome 1690.

[2] At the beginning of the fifteenth century also the author of the *Imitation* never suggests that his monks have to exercise any kind of ministry outside their convent.

[3] St Dominic was born in Spain, at Calaruega in the Kingdom of Leon, about 1170. When about twenty-four years of age he was a Canon of the Cathedral of Osma. He lived a most regular life in accordance with the reform of Gregory VII and according to the Rule of St Augustine. Towards 1206 he, together with his Bishop Diego, became auxiliary to the Cistercians, who had received from Pope Innocent III the mission to work for the conversion of the heretics in the South of France. He gathered some missionaries around him who became the nucleus of the Order of " Holy Preaching." The Order was canonically erected in July, 1215, by Fulk, Bishop of Toulouse. It was approved in 1217 by Pope Honorius III as an Order extending its influence throughout the Church. St Dominic also founded convents of Dominican nuns. He died on August 6, 1221.

Although less vigorously than St Francis, Dominic desired his religious to live on alms. He founded a mendicant Order, which had to look to providence for everything. Dominican convents were not allowed to possess landed property. Such regulations, similar to those of the Poor Man of Assisi, seemed, at a period when all monasteries were rich, so novel that the conception formed by the populace of the religious life was altogether changed.[1]

St Dominic himself was particularly attached to the virtue of poverty. He was not completely able to realize his ideal in this regard on account of opposition encountered among his Friars. He was not able, any more than St Francis, to make his houses live on alms from day to day. It must be recognized that such a degree of perfection was hardly possible in so extended an Order with so large a number of religious. As far, however, as each individual was concerned they all had to practise rigorous poverty as to clothing and dwelling.[2]

In addition to being a mendicant Friar, the Dominican is also a Canon Regular, bound to the choir Office and the community life, when not prevented by preaching. The Rule obliges him to combine, in a great measure, the contemplative life with the active. In the convent he must keep silence; he has to fast from the Feast of the Exaltation of the Holy Cross (September 14) to Easter, and also every Friday; he must never eat meat. Dominic gave himself up also to other austerities; he wore a rough hair-shirt next to his flesh and an iron chain round his loins. He often submitted himself to the discipline. He was engaged in constant prayer and desired his Friars to be the same. The Dominican Rule understood so well how to fashion the religious as a man of prayer as well as of action that we find mystics of the highest order, such as Tauler and Henry Suso, among the Friars Preachers.[3]

But it was above all apostolic zeal that shone forth in the Dominican, whose mission it was to preach Christian truth. This zeal is nourished by knowledge, indispensable to the preacher. St Dominic was, according to the expression of Dante, "a learned and holy religious." He advised his brethren to study science, letters, and chiefly theology and

---

[1] " Dominic did not ask of the Holy See the power of grasping six and giving but two or three [benefices] to pious uses; not the first vacant benefice, nor the tithes that belonged to God's poor, but the right to defend the faith " (Dante, *Paradiso*, XII). In order to express that likeness between the two Franciscan and Dominican Orders, as well as the pious and hereditary love which united them from the beginning, Dante made the praises of St Francis to be sung by a Dominican, St Thomas Aquinas, and the eulogy of St Dominic by a Franciscan, St Bonaventure (*Paradiso*, XII).

[2] *Cf.* J. Guiraud, *Saint Dominique*, pp. 164-168, 189.

[3] The Dominican nuns, as founded by St Dominic, are exclusively devoted to contemplation.

Holy Scripture. He allowed his young religious to follow the courses at the great Universities of Paris, Bologna, Padua, Palencia, Oxford. In this regard Dominic had views entirely different from the Seraphic Saint of Assisi; he wished his Order to be learned. In this he succeeded, for, from the thirteenth century, the most prominent professors of law and theology were Dominicans : St Raymond of Pennafort, Humbert de Romans, Albert the Great, Cardinal Hugh of St Cher, Peter of Tarentaise, and, above all, St Thomas Aquinas. The great encyclopædist of the thirteenth century, Vincent of Beauvais, was also a Dominican.

The Dominican Order, comprising the Friars Preachers and the Dominican nuns, seem to have been completely organized by their founder.[1] It demonstrates the practical mind of Dominic even more than his mystical tendencies. A little later the faithful living in the world were reached by a third Order—this offered them a fruitful means of attaining perfection.[2]

Dominican spirituality is already known to us through St Thomas Aquinas. It is usually learned and almost entirely built on scholastic theology.

Dominican spiritual writers specially insist on renunciation of our own will and on the mortification of our selfish desires. The man who strips himself of his will attains to humility, to the destruction of self-love; and as a necessary consequence he gives himself up entirely to God's will, and identifies himself therewith in such a manner that his own will is but one with the divine, which constitutes Christian perfection.

In the work of sanctification, the will, above all, has as its object the avoidance of obstacles that are opposed to the action of God within us. It must hold itself entirely dependent on the divine decrees. As in the teaching of St Augustine, so in the Dominican school there was a marked tendency to consider the position of divine action in the acquisition of goodness. Does not this follow from the Thomist and Dominican teaching concerning physical predetermination? Albert the Great founds his exhortations on

[1] There appears to be some doubt respecting the Third Order which does not seem to have been created by St Dominic himself. See the Bollandists, *Acta Sanctorum,* August 4.

[2] The Dominican Order did not, however, escape the general laxity which invaded everything during the Great Schism and at the beginning of the Renaissance. But the reaction was not long in coming. Towards the end of the fourteenth century Blessed Raymund of Capua, Lawrence of Ripafratta, and, above all, John Dominici, began a reform in the convents of the Friars Preachers, which St Antoninus, the famous Archbishop of Florence, was to continue in the fifteenth century. Those that wished to return to the original Rule were called Dominicans of the Observance. *Cf.* Augustine Rossler, *Cardinal J. Dominici, ein Reformatorenbild aus der zeit des grossen Schisma,* Freiburg im B. 1893.

blind obedience to divine providence on the principle that
" No being is able to subsist or act by its own power, but acts
by virtue of God himself who is the first mover, the first
principle, and cause of all action, working in all that acts."[1]
Nothing then can escape God's will. Moreover, it must be
trusted without reserve and be submitted to beforehand in all
its intentions.

The Dominican school—and this is another of its special
marks—connects asceticism and mysticism with the gifts of
the Holy Spirit. Its theologians, following in this their
master St Thomas Aquinas, set forth their spiritual teaching
when they treat of Christian virtues and gifts. It is the gift
of wisdom which produces, according to their explanation,
supernatural states, such as those of rapture and ecstasy.[2]

With regard to Dominican mysticism, it consists, with the
exception of that of St Catherine of Siena, in abstract
theories, chiefly borrowed from Dionysius the Areopagite.[3]

II—DOMINICAN PREACHING : ST VINCENT FERRER, JEROME SAVONAROLA—HAGIOGRAPHY : VINCENT OF BEAUVAIS AND JAMES DE VORAGINE

DOMINICAN preaching is generally more learned and less
popular than that of the Franciscans. We can judge from
the sermons of John Tauler and of Henry Suso, which contain very exalted mystical teaching. Nevertheless, at the
beginning of the fifteenth century the Dominican Order was
rendered famous by a Spanish preacher, St Vincent Ferrer,
who had the gift of inspiring the multitudes with enthusiasm.[4]

Vincent began his apostolate in 1397 during the Great
Schism, preaching throughout the country which owned
obedience to Avignon. He was quite an itinerant preacher.
He evangelized Spain, Provence, Liguria, Piedmont, Savoy,
Switzerland, Flanders, and, above all, France. He was
accompanied by a group of penitents of both sexes, who were
a species of flagellants under severe discipline and of blame-
less conduct. He also took with him priests and singers for
the Offices. When he arrived at any place all work ceased
and everyone came to listen to the preacher, who occasionally

---

[1] Albert the Great, *De adhaerendo Deo,* cap. xvi. See, amongst others,
respecting the renunciation of our own will, St Vincent Ferrer,
Tractatus de vita spirituali, cap. iv-vi; St Catherine of Siena,
Dialogue, i, 40.

[2] *Cf.* St Antoninus, *Summa Theologica,* pars IV, tit. X, cap. iii ff.
Verona, 1740, vol. iv, pp. 504 ff.

[3] St Vincent Ferrer, who explains practical spiritual teaching, speaks
of union with God in accordance with the Dionysian theory. *Tract.
de Vita spirit.,* cap. iv.

[4] Cf. *Acta Sanct.,* April 5. St. Vincent Ferrer was born in 1357 at
Valencia in Spain. He died at Vannes in Brittany in 1419. Bayle,
Vie de S Vincent Ferrier, Paris 1855.

spoke for as much as six hours a day. He often gave his sermons in some public place so that he could secure a larger audience. His aim was to soften the hearts of sinners by the account of the passion and to inspire them with fear by the description of the Last Judgement. Like the Franciscans, St Vincent Ferrer made crowds weep over the sufferings of Christ and familiar with the thought of death.

He did not publish his sermons. We have several small works of his, in particular a *Treatise on the Spiritual Life,*[1] which is a kind of spiritual directory drawn up for the religious of a convent of his Order. It contains the principles of asceticism, applied in a practical manner, and with remarkable common sense, to the government and ministry of the Friar Preacher.

It is only right to include among the Dominican preachers " the truly pious Brother Jerome Savonarola " of St Mark's, Florence. A mystical champion, he raised up the populace against vice in high places, and was put to death in 1498. Many, however, looked upon him as a saint, and his writings deeply edified successive generations of the faithful.

The most famous, the *Triumphus crucis,*[2] represents Christ, according to the taste of the period, as a victorious hero. Jesus is seated in a chariot. Before him march the holy men and women of the Old Testament. The Apostles and preachers are near the chariot to send it forward. Then, following after, come the Martyrs and Doctors of the Church. This triumphal theme has inspired artists and ascetic writers. The latter also delved into the other works of the famous Dominican, especially into the *Rules of Spiritual Life,*[3] which were inspired by St Vincent Ferrer. Savonarola drew up therein austere principles that have inspired writers of modern times. In order to attain to peace of heart, he says, we must not only strip ourselves of the love of all creatures and of self, but also despise and hate our own life.

The chief hagiographers of the Middle Ages belong to the Order of St Dominic. Vincent of Beauvais and James de Voragine are the best known. The fourth part of the *Universal Mirror* of St Vincent of Beauvais, the *Historical Mirror,* is much more of a hagiography than a history of the world. It prefers to confine itself to narrating the lives of holy people who have lived since the creation of man. The miracles worked through the relics of the blessed, the extraordinary occurrences that filled their lives, have, in the eyes

---

[1] *Tractatus de vita spirituali,* published for the first time at Magdeburg in 1493. Père Rousset, O.P., has given the Latin text with a translation : *Les Traités de la Vie et Perfection spirituelles de S Vincent Ferrier et du B. Albert le Grand,* vol. i, Paris 1899.

[2] Often re-edited and translated into Italian and French. The complete works of Savonarola were published at Leyden, 1633-1640.

[3] Rousset, *op. cit.,* 231-236.

of Vincent, a far greater importance than the succession of emperors and kings and the battles they fought. The true heroes of the world are the Saints.

This conception of history was very general in the thirteenth century; preachers popularized it in their sermons. Moreover, the people themselves greatly desired to have, in convenient book form and as attractive reading, the lives of the Saints which were only to be found in learned works or in the liturgical books like the *Martyrologies* or the *Lectionaries*. James de Voragine[1] satisfied this desire by composing his famous *Golden Legend*.[2] He gives an account of the lives of the Saints in the order of the calendar, beginning with the time of Advent.

The Bollandists have severely criticized the work of James de Voragine. And, looking at it from their critical point of view, it can hardly be approved,[3] for the Golden Legend abounds in fabulous stories and fabrications. But could the author have done otherwise at a period when the marvellous was sought after much more than historic truth? His work, as has been said of it, " was not the work of one man but rather of all Christendom."[4] Neither the writer who composed it nor the readers who were edified by it could conceive it otherwise. It exercised an enormous influence on popular piety. It is by means of it that we must explain many of the bas-reliefs and stained-glass windows of our cathedrals. Like the work of Simeon Metaphrastes, of which it has all the failings, it has sanctified many Christian generations. It behoves the history of spirituality, therefore, to treat it with clemency.[5]

III—DOMINICAN MYSTICISM IN ITALY: FRA ANGELICO OF FIESOLE, ST CATHERINE OF SIENA

It was not only by means of preachers and hagiographers among the Dominicans that Christian piety was developed. There are divers ways of making known the divine word; painters and sculptors are also in their way preachers. Now,

---

[1] Born near Genoa about 1230; died about 1298. He joined the Order of St Dominic and became Bishop of Genoa.

[2] *Legenda aurea,* see the edition of Graesse, Wratislaviae 1890. Translated into French by Batallier, Lyons 1476, by Brunet, Paris 1843, and by Th. de Wyzewa.

[3] *Acta Sanctorum, Praefatio generalis,* § iv, vol. i.

[4] E. Male, *L'art religieux du XIIIᵉ siècle en France,* p. 320.

[5] Other Friars Preachers have also left collections of lives of the Saints. Bartholomew of Trent drew up in 1240 his *Liber epilogorum in gesta sanctorum.* Roderick of Cerrata made, about the same time, a collection of the *Vitae Sanctorum.* The *Speculum sanctorale* of Bernard Guidonis was composed from 1324-1329. Finally Peter Calo (1348) made his immense compilation of the *Legendae sanctorum. Cf.* Mandonnet, art. *Frères prêcheurs,* p. 904.

by a rare privilege, in the fifteenth century a school of artists of genius arose within the bosom of the Dominican Order. Fra Guglielmo made himself famous by his collaboration in the magnificent tomb of St Dominic at Bologna. But the greatest Dominican artist is the painter Fra Giovanni Angelico of Fiesole.[1] St Dominic, at the first general Chapter of the Order in 1220, enacted that holy pictures should be placed in the convents. It was in order to obey this direction that Fra Angelico beautified the walls of St Mark's, Florence.

The saintly artist prepared himself for his works by meditation and prayer. Each of them is a mystical uplifting, reflecting the soul of the blissful brother, nurtured in theological study, austerity and intimate union with God. The Dominican expression *contemplata aliis tradere* is perfectly followed. Fra Angelico never took up his tools without first having recourse to prayer, and it was on his knees that he painted the face of Christ or that of the Virgin. Is there any sermon on the passion which inspires more faith, love and sorrow than the symbolical presentment of Calvary in the chapter-hall of the convent of St Mark? The sorrowful and gentle head of the dying Saviour, bent forward to the sinner with a movement of inexpressible love, makes us think of such a vision of the Crucified as was granted to Angela of Foligno and to other mystics.

Those whom Fra Angelico paints are idealized beyond description. They must be seen, and when we have seen them we are spellbound, and our eyes fill with tears. Mystics, when they come out of their raptures, tell us that they have seen or heard things which language is radically unable to express. May we not believe that the mystical soul of Fra Angelico had caught a glimpse, in his prayer, of the face of the suffering Christ, or of that of the Virgin at the foot of the cross, or saluted by the angel at the moment of the Annunciation, and that he has outlined certain of their traits in his frescoes? No doubt a knowledge of the history of painting is necessary to understand his work. He has borrowed from the art of the Renaissance what he found good in it. But if we would truly know this exclusively religious work, and would grasp the soul of it, it is in the

---

[1] *Cf.* Henri Cochin, *Le bienheureux Fra Giovanni Angelico de Fiesole,* 4th edit., Paris 1908. Fra Angelico was born at Mugello, near Florence, in 1387. In 1407 he entered the Dominican convent of Fiesole, a convent of the Observance which had accepted the reform of the famous Dominici. He left there in 1436. He afterwards stayed at the convent of St Mark's, Florence, which he decorated so wonderfully. He also lived at Rome at the convent of the Minerva, where he died in 1455. Among his works may be mentioned the *Annunciation* and the *Dormition of the Virgin,* the *Madonna della Stella,* the *Coronation of the Virgin,* the *Madonna de San Marco,* the *Calvary,* and the *Adoration of the Magi.* Fra Angelico painted only religious subjects.

light of the mystical visions of Bl. Angela of Foligno, of St Gertrude, of St Bridget and St Catherine of Siena that it must be studied. Fra Angelico was himself a mystic.

St Catherine of Siena, the great Italian mystic, had a social mission similar to that of St Hildegarde and of St Bridget of Sweden. This explains her life and her writings. Her biography, like that of St Bridget, her contemporary, is a chapter in the history of spirituality in which is shown the political and religious activity of the mystics of the fourteenth century.

Mysticism, at this period, acted as a support to the ecclesiastical hierarchy in the grip of most serious difficulties. The Church had to struggle against disorders among both clergy and monks. The continuous wars, the sojourn of the Popes at Avignon, the Great Schism which it brought about, inflicted most serious harm on her. The mystics, like the ancient seers of the people of Israel, denounced, on behalf of God, the faults of sacred ministers and suggested to the heads of the Church the means of remedy they should bring to bear. They also strove to restore peace between the peoples and the cities.

It was in view of such a mission that God prepared St Catherine of Siena. He chose in her a humble and feeble instrument, according to the world, as he was to choose, somewhat later, a poor country girl, Joan of Arc, to save France.

Catherine was born of honest commercial parents at Siena on March 25, 1347.[1] She received no instruction. She never knew how to write, and had to have recourse to secretaries to transcribe her works. But God communicated to her the infused knowledge of divine truths, so that in her *Letters* and her *Dialogues* she spoke like the most learned doctors concerning them.

Her life was one long series of extraordinary mystical occurrences. At the age of six, her historians tell us, she had a vision of Christ extending his hand over her to bless

---

[1] The most important historian of the Saint is Blessed Raymund of Capua, her confessor : *Vita S Catharine Senensis,* or *Legenda Major.* The original text is in Latin. *Acta Sanctorum,* April, vol. iii, pp. 862-967, Paris 1866. French translation by E. Cartier, and a better one by Père Hugueny, O.P., Paris 1903. Raymund of Capua was born in 1330. He was Master-General of the Order of Preachers and died at Nuremberg in 1399. His biography of St Catherine is as much a work on mystical theology from life as a history. For complete bibliographic information see Comtesse de Flavigny, *Sainte Catherine de Sienne,* Paris 1895, 2nd edit., pp. 603 ff. ; Johannes Jörgensen, *Sainte Catherine de Sienne,* Paris 1919, pp. 603-614 ; *History of St Catherine of Siena and her Companions,* by A. T. Drane, Prioress-General of the Dominican Nuns in England ; Edmund Gardner, *St Catherine of Siena,* London 1907, pp. 423-428.

her.[1] Persecuted by her family because of the vow of virginity which she had taken and the fearful austerities which she practised, she finally obtained permission from her father to follow her desire. She took the habit of the Third Order of Penance of St Dominic and lived in retreat for some years.[2]

Our Lord himself guided her in the ways of perfection. He taught her things concerning the spiritual life, often appeared to her, and contracted with her a mystical marriage, the sign of which was a mysterious ring placed on her finger and visible to herself alone.[3] Her raptures were frequent. One of them was so violent and so prolonged that it was called the mystical death of Catherine. It lasted four hours, during which she had a glimpse of the happiness of the elect, the torments of hell and those of purgatory. She derived from this vision an intense love for souls and an ardent desire to work for their salvation.[4] The Saint also received the Stigmata of the Passion. But her members did not bear, like those of St Francis of Assisi, the visible marks of them. Nevertheless, she felt them acutely.[5]

Mystical phenomena, according to her biographers, succeeded each other almost without interruption during her whole life. Are they all authentic? Blessed Raymund of Capua, who had familiar intercourse with the celebrated tertiary, admits that he was "often and in many ways tempted to incredulity."[6] It is easy, in fact, even for a true mystic to mistake some of her imaginings for divine facts. The prudent Dominican required evidence of veracity; that which appeared to him to be most convincing was the efficacy of the prayers of Catherine to obtain for others the grace of sanctification.

The mission of the Sienese virgin, from this point of view, may also serve as a test. What may be called the public life of St Catherine began about 1370. What she accomplished in it is so important and extraordinary that the hand of providence seems obvious therein.

Surrounded by her spiritual family, composed of women who, like herself, were members of the Third Order of St Dominic and of the Friars Preachers, she undertook several journeys beneficial to the salvation of souls and to the interests of the Church. She went to Pisa, to Florence, to Avignon, where she persuaded Pope Gregory XI to leave that town and to return to Rome, and finally proceeded her-

---

[1] Raymund of Capua, *Legenda Maj.*, pars I, cap. ii.
[2] *id.*, cap. iii, viii.   [3] *id.*, cap. ix-xii.
[4] *id.*, pars II, cap. vi.   [5] *ibid.*
[6] *id.*, pars II, cap. ix. It is well known that the canonization of a saint does not authenticate all the mystical facts related of that saint.

self to Rome, whither she was summoned by Urban VI in 1378, at the beginning of the Great Schism, and where she died on April 29, 1380. Very often in ecstasy, in constant communication with God, animated by the spirit of prophecy, this great seer seemed to descend from a sort of Sina to lash the faults of both clergy and monks, to dictate their duty to princes, to read a lesson to cardinals and to counsel popes.

She carried on her work above all by her holiness and by her writings. The latter comprise principally the *Letters* and the celebrated *Dialogue*.[1]

The collection of *Letters* comprise business letters connected with the different missions with which she was entrusted and letters of guidance addressed to her women companions and her disciples. Catherine was, in a manner, the *spiritual director* of a circle of friends, her *bella brigada,* as she called it, which had formed itself around her. Her letters of guidance expound the doctrine of perfection in a beautiful way; they remind us of those of St Francis de Sales.

The *Dialogue* is so called because it is drawn up in the form of a colloquy between the Eternal Father and the Saint. She addresses four prayers to God. The first for herself, because before sanctifying others it is necessary to sanctify oneself. God replies by teaching spiritual discretion, which by the knowledge of self and of God makes us render to each—to God, to our neighbour and to ourselves—that which is due. The second prayer concerns the salvation of the world and peace between Christians. The Lord assures Catherine that he desires the salvation of the world, as is shown by the gift which he made to it of the Word Incarnate, and of all the other means of sanctification. The third re-

---

[1] The *Letters* of St Catherine were written in Italian. Published by Gigli, *Opere di Santa Caterina,* Siena 1713, vols. ii and iii, and by Tommaseo, *Epistolario di Santa Caterina,* Firenze 1860, 4 vols., re-edited by Pietro Misciatelli, Siena 1912. A French translation of the *Letters* of St Catherine has been made by E. Cartier, Dominican Tertiary. The *Dialogue* was written in Italian, published at Bologna 1472, Naples 1478, Venice 1494; by Gigli, *Opere di Santa Caterina,* 1727, Siena, vol. iv; by Mathilda Fiorilli in the series *Scrittori d'Italia,* Bari 1912. Latin translation by Raymund of Capua, Brescia 1496. French translations under these titles : *La Doctrine spirituelle,* Paris 1580; *La Doctrine de Dieu,* by L. Chardon, O.P., Paris 1648; *Dialogue de Ste Catherine de Sienne,* by E. Cartier, Paris 1855. The best translation is that of P. Hurtaud, O.P., 2 vols., Paris 1913. The *Dialogue* was written in 1378, two years before the death of the Saint. Another work of St Catherine comprises twenty-six *Prayers* uttered by the Saint in her ecstasies and set down by her secretaries. They were published by Gigli, and translated into French by Chardon in 1648, after the *Dialogue*. A new translation was published by the Librairie de l'Art Catholique, Paris 1919. There were added to them the prayers of the Saint on her deathbed, and the words she spoke at her last moments, the famous *Il Transito.*

quest deals with the reformation of the clergy; the Eternal Father converses with the prophetess on the dignity of the priesthood, on the holiness of good pastors and on the vices of the bad. Finally, the answer to the fourth prayer deals with divine providence ordering events with a view to the salvation of souls.

This treatise is a kind of apocalypse in which God is deemed to speak by the mouth of Catherine in ecstasy,[1] in order to reproach worldlings on account of their vices and ecclesiastical pastors for their disorders. All are invited to do penance. The most biting strictures on the morals of the fourteenth century alternate with outbursts of passionate love for the Church and for the salvation of souls. There is also to be found in the *Dialogue* an abundant theology respecting virtue, sin and its punishment, penance and the Word Incarnate.[2] The *Summa* of St Thomas Aquinas is to be clearly seen in certain chapters, and in them is felt the influence of those theological conversations which the Saint must have had with her Dominican companions and confessors.

The spiritual teaching of St Catherine is, like that of many other writers of the Middle Ages, founded on the knowledge of God and of ourselves.

The knowledge of oneself inspires humility, destroys self-love and makes one realize one's nothingness. It teaches us that we are nothing of ourselves and that we derive our being from God. Thus, the knowledge of self leads to the knowledge of God who is all; it also produces in us divine love, for with the knowledge of God comes love.[3] The Saint received such lights in self-knowledge that she saw her own nothingness. This sight might have discouraged her if God had not sustained her. It was thus that she escaped temptations to pride. Our Lord once said to her : "Thou art that which is not, I am that I am. If thou preserve this truth in thy soul never shall the enemy deceive thee, thou wilt escape all his shares."[4] There were times when she felt her unworthiness so keenly that she attributed all the evil

---

[1] Raymund of Capua, *Leg. major*, Prologue, and part III, chap. i, affirms that Catherine dictated the *Dialogue* during her ecstasies. This is very extraordinary because an ecstatic is able neither to speak nor to move when in ecstasy. Père Chardon, in the *Avertissement*, at the beginning of his translation, does not accept the statement of Raymund.

[2] The question might be asked as to the nature of the collaboration of Catherine's secretaries in the composition of the *Dialogue*. Did they limit themselves simply to writing under the dictation of the Saint, or did they provide the theological language for the doctrines she taught?

[3] *Dialogue*, 1st Answer, chap. ii; French translation, Hurtaud, vol. i, pp. 12-13; 2nd Answer, chap. xlii, pp. 244-245.

[4] Raymund of Capua, *Leg. major*, I, cap. x.

that was committed in the world and all the misfortunes that had befallen the Church and that threatened it to her faults.

The knowledge of self may thus lead to the highest sanctity, and she recommended it, above all, in her letters of guidance.

"Thou askest me," she wrote to one of her companions, "how to make perfect that love which is imperfect? This is the way : to correct and chastise the motions of thy heart by the knowledge of thyself, by the hatred and contempt of thy imperfection. . . . Make for thyself two dwellings, my daughter : one in thy cell, so as not to go gossiping everywhere, and thou must not leave it save of necessity, from obedience to the prioress or from charity; then make thee another spiritual cell which thou wilt always carry with thee, the cell of true self-knowledge; there thou wilt find the knowledge of the goodness of God toward thee. To speak truly these two cells are but one, and if thou construct one of them thou must perforce make the other also, without which thou couldst not fail to be led into trouble or presumption. If thou knewest but thyself, thou wouldst fall into discouragement; if thou knewest but the divine goodness, thou wouldst be tempted to become presumptuous. These two forms of knowledge then must needs be united one with the other and make but one. Acting thus, thou shalt arrive at perfection, for through knowledge of thyself thou shalt acquire the hatred of thy sensual nature. . . . In the knowledge of God thou shalt find the fire of divine charity. . . ."[1]

St Catherine describes the various stages to be passed through in order to arrive at the knowledge of God and to reach perfection.

After depicting the unhappy state of the sinful soul she portrays it passing through servile fear, then rising to interested love, followed by faithful and perfect love in which it is fully united to God. The role of the three powers of the soul : the memory, the understanding and the will, in this mounting towards perfection, is expounded according to the principles of Thomist philosophy.[2] In this state of perfect love the Christian is entirely stripped of self-will, which is dead in him.[3] Mystical union is precisely defined.[4] It requires the sense, the experimental knowledge of God in the soul. It is by this that mystical union is distinguished from ordinary union through grace.

"To those" [that have reached the perfection of love],

---

[1] *Letter* 49, Tommaseo's ed.; French translation, Jörgensen, *Ste Catherine de Sienne,* pp. 190-191.

[2] *Dialogue,* 2nd Answer, i-xlvi, Hurtaud, i, 105-261.

[3] *id.,* Hurtaud, i, 250.

[4] St Catherine does not make use of Dionysius the Areopagite to expound her mystical teaching.

says the Lord in the *Dialogue,* " I give the grace to feel that
I am never separated from them, whilst in others I go away
and I come again, not that I withdraw from them my grace,
but the sense of my presence. With those very perfect ones
that have reached great perfection and who are entirely dead
to their own will I act in a different way. I remain with
them uninterruptedly by my grace and by the experience
which I give them of my presence. As soon as they are
willing to unite the mind to me by a sense of love they may
do so, because their desire has reached to so great a union
with me through the sense of love that nothing in the world
can part it. . . . These most perfect souls never lose the
sense of my presence within them.''[1]

This idea of transforming mystical union is one of the best
that has been given. We have already met with it in the
writings of St Gertrude. This union from time to time becomes more intimate and is transformed for the moment into
ecstasy.[2] The soul then enjoys " the happiness of those that
are immortal and, in spite of the weight of the body, the
soul is endowed with the alacrity of the mind.''

" Also the body is many a time uplifted from the earth by
reason of this perfect union which the soul effects with me
[its God], as though the body had lost its weight and had
become light. Nevertheless, its heaviness has been in no
way reduced; but as the union of the soul with me is more
perfect than the union between the soul and the body the
power of the mind fixed on me raises the weight of the
body from the earth; the body remains motionless, all ex-
hausted through the love of the soul, to such an extent that,
as thou hast heard some of my creatures say, it could no
longer live if my bounty did not encompass it with its
strength.''[3]

Thus, in ecstasy, the mystic has no longer consciousness
of the body; the powers of the soul are brought together

[1] *Dialogue,* 2nd Answer, xlviii, xlix, Hurtaud, i, 268, 273.
[2] Raymund of Capua thus describes the ecstasy of St Catherine and
the phenomenon of levitation (*Life,* Part II, chap. ii) : " The ex-
tremities of the body—that is to say, the hands and feet—became
shrunken. This contraction affected first of all the fingers, then the
whole of the members, which adhered so tenaciously where they touched
that they would have been crushed and broken before they could have
been torn assunder. The eyes became completely closed, the neck
assumed the rigidity of death, so that it would have been dangerous
to the health of the Saint to touch her at that moment. . . . Whilst
Catherine was carried heavenwards by this rapture of the mind, . . .
her body was also raised from the earth with the soul, so that the force
which attracted the mind was easily seen.'' *Cf.* Saudreaux, *Les faits
extraordinaires de la vie spirituelle,* Paris 1908.
[3] *Dialogue,* 2nd Answer, xlix, Hurtaud, i, 273-274. Certain visions
occasionally took place during ecstasy. The Saint indicates the means
of ascertaining if they come from God or from the devil, Hurtaud, i,
242, 385-390.

and united to God, immersed in him. They are entirely bound, and the exercise of them suspended.

Faithful to the teaching of St Thomas, the virgin of Siena declares that the soul, in the mystical state, cannot directly see the divine essence. God is apprehended only through the effect of his charity, which is made manifest in divers ways according to his goodness and pleasure in making himself known. The vision which the soul receives remains obscure; it is as it were in darkness compared with the vision enjoyed by the elect in heaven.[1] The mysticism of St Catherine inclines to learning. It possesses a philosophical aspect that is not to be found in the Benedictine school. The thought of the virgin of Siena is usually prompted, in its beginnings, by abstract conceptions of the divine realities.

"O Deity, Deity, ineffable Deity," she cries in one of her *Prayers,* "O Supreme Goodness, who hast made us in thy image and likeness, and wholly through love! In producing other creatures thou wast content with a *Fiat.* But in creating man thou didst say : Let us make man in our image and likeness. Thou hast willed, O ineffable love, that all the Trinity should consent to his creation in order to communicate the form itself of thy Trinity, O Deity eternal, to the powers of the soul.

"Thou, O Eternal Father, who containest and upholdest all things in thyself, in order to impress thy image on man, hast given him memory in order to retain and preserve all that the understanding hears, sees and knows of thee, O infinite Goodness. The understanding shares through this knowledge in the wisdom of thine only Son. The gentle clemency of the Holy Spirit is communicated to it by the will, that will which raises itself to thee, wholly filled with thy love and clasping as with the hand all that the understanding perceives of thy ineffable goodness. . . ."[2]

IV—THE GERMAN MYSTICS OF THE DOMINICAN ORDER : ALBERT THE GREAT IN THE XIII CENTURY; JOHN TAULER, HENRY SUSO IN THE XIV

THE German mystical school of the Middle Ages was found chiefly among the Friars Preachers.

It made itself noteworthy on account of its exalted theories and its irresistible tendency to speculation. In spite of its merits this school became somewhat discredited, for those who founded it put forward errors which have laid a heavy

[1] *Dialogue,* 2nd Answer, xlix, xxxii, Hurt. i, 276, 206.
[2] *Première oraison,* French translation, Librairie de l'Art Catholique, Paris 1919, pp. 11-12.

charge on their fame. These errors were a local product, and the Dominican Order could not be held responsible for them.

Albert the Great,[1] the master of St Thomas Aquinas, must be placed among the German mystics of the Middle Ages if the treatise *De adhaerendo Deo*[2] was his, which has not been fully proved. In any case the author belongs to the same family.

It was in the fourteenth century that the great Rhenish mystics of the Dominican Order appeared. They were somewhat abandoned after the seventeenth century because of an apparent likeness between some points in their teaching and the dreams of the Quietists.[3] But towards the middle of the nineteenth century Père Heinrich Suso Denifle, Dominican, restored them to a place of honour through his learned study of them, and above all by the publication of an anthology drawn from their writings.[4]

It will be useful for us to understand a little the Rhenish environment in which they lived and the influence to which they were subjected.

In the fourteenth century there existed in the Rhenish provinces several free religious associations, amongst others that of the *Beghards* and *Beguines,* that of the Brethren of the Free Spirit, and that of the Friends of God. The first of these seems to have begun in the Low Countries. Towards the end of the twelfth century associations of women were formed there. Their members lived, either dispersed in the towns and villages, or gathered together in vast Beguinages, where usually each Beguine had her little house. The little town was governed by a superior and by an ecclesiastic. They took the three usual vows, but only for a time. The Beguines were free to leave the Beguinage on the day that they decided to return to the world. Whilst they remained there they gave themselves up to prayer, to nursing the sick

[1] Blessed Albert the Great was born at Lauingen in Suabia, according to some in 1193, to others, 1206. He studied at Padua and in Paris. Having entered the Dominican Order, he taught theology in the Dominican convents of Paris and Cologne. From 1260 to 1262, he was Bishop of Ratisbon; he then re-entered the Convent of Cologne, where he died in 1280. He was one of the first to make use of the writings of Aristotle. He had great influence both as philosopher and as theologian. *Cf.* Mandonnet, *Dict. de Théol. cath.,* art. *Albert le Grand.*

[2] *Alberti M. Opera Omnia,* edition P. Jammy, 21 vols, Lyons 1651, vol. xxi; edition Borgnet, 38 vols., Paris 1890, vol. xxxvii. Père Rousset, O.P., has translated them into French : *Les traités de la Vie et Perfection spirituelles de S Vincent Ferrer et du B. Albert le Grand,* Paris 1899, vol. ii. The *Paradisus Animae, libellus de virtutibus* (a collection of dissertations on the virtues) is also attributed to Albert the Great, Lyons, vol. xxi.

[3] Bossuet, *Instruction sur les états d'oraison,* Book I, i-viii.

[4] *Das geistliche Leben, Blumenlese aus den deutschen Mystikern und Gottesfreunden des* 14 *Jahrhunderts,* Graz 1873.

and to needlework. Similar associations of men were also created, but they were not so numerous. Those who belonged to them were known as *Beghards*.

These associations spread over France, Italy and, above all, Germany. But they had not the protection of a firm monastic discipline. Grave disorders slipped in and many of their members fell into heresy. In the fourteenth century a distinction was made among the Beghards and Beguines between those that were orthodox and those that were heretical. The latter were somewhat numerous in the Rhenish towns. At the Council of Vienne, moreover, in 1311, the German bishops petitioned for the solemn condemnation of the heterodox Beghards.[1] The spirituality of these heretics resembled Quietism, and led to most immoral consequences.[2]

The Beguinages, excellent at first, were vitiated little by little by the sect of the *Brethren of the Free Spirit*.[3] This sect, it is thought, is connected with Amaury de Bène, who died in Paris about 1208, and with Ortlieb of Strasbourg. It represented the freethought and moral independence of the Middle Ages, and its tendency towards Pantheism was very marked. Averroism, and above all the theories of John Scotus Eriugena, appear to have found acceptance among them. The *Brethren of the Free Spirit* were fairly numerous in Germany, especially at Cologne, in the fourteenth century, in spite of the efforts of the Inquisition to suppress them. Organized under the form of a secret society, they spread their errors, often with great success. Even Catholic theologians were not wholly free from them and lapsed into a false mysticism.[4]

This anxious period of the fourteenth century gave birth to other associations. The faithful were vividly impressed by the Great Schism. Many, with the desire to maintain among themselves and others the religious life, grouped themselves together outside the compass of ecclesiastical authority. In

---

[1] *Errores Beguardorum et Beguinarum de statu perfectionis in concilio Viennensi* (1311-1312) *damnati a Clemente V.* There were eight condemned propositions. *Cf.* Denzinger-Bannwart, *Enchiridion symbolorum et definitionum*, 1908, n. 399-406. (The name *Beghard* or *Beguine* was derived from Lambert le Bègue, priest of Liége, who founded a hospital and church for the widows and children of Crusaders about 1170. [Translator's note]).

[2] *Cf.* F. Vernet, *Dict. de Théol. cath.*, art. *Beghards, Beguines heterodoxes*.

[3] F. Vernet, *Dict. de Théol. cath.*, art. *Frères du libre esprit*.

[4] For details concerning the false mysticism of this period, see Tauler, *Sermon for the First Sunday of Lent*, French translation Sainte-Foi, Paris 1855, vol. i, pp. 273 ff.; and Ruysbroeck, *The Mirror of Eternal Salvation*, chap. xvi (*Works of Ruysbroeck the Admirable*, translated into French by the Benedictines of St Paul de Wisques, vol. i, pp. 115 ff.); *Le livre des sept clôtures*, chap. xv, p. 181; *L'ornement des noces spirituelles*, Book II, chaps. 74-77 (Benedictine translation, vol. iii, pp. 194-202).

the Valley of the Rhine an association of ecclesiastics and laity was formed under the name of Friends of God, whose object was to foster speculative mysticism and to live according to it themselves. The *Friends of God* practised absolute detachment from all things, and gave themselves up to the rigours of asceticism. It was also their intention to combat the disorders of the clergy; nor do we always find that they were animated by a kindly attitude towards their ecclesiastical leaders. But there were among them lofty souls, although somewhat sentimental and a little exposed to illuminism. John Tauler and Henry Suso had frequent dealings with the *Friends of God,* and the latter strove to render their writings popular.

The Rhenish atmosphere was then, in the fourteenth century, a centre of religious and mystical excitement. The trials which the Church passed through at that time could not but over-excite minds and encourage them to seek in a closer union with God to make amends for evils here below. This was doubtless one of the motives for the marked preference shown by the German mystics for a deep study of the contemplative state.

Meister Eckhart may be considered as the founder of this school of mystics.[1] He was born at Hochheim, in Thuringia, about 1260.[2] He entered, when still young, the Dominican convent of Erfurt. In 1300 he went to study in Paris. He returned there in 1311 to teach, after having been Provincial in Saxony twice running. He afterwards went to Strasbourg to take up preaching. The heterodox Beghards were then numerous in that town. Eckhart was accused, no doubt wrongly,[3] of having had a tenderness towards them. In 1326 he was professor of theology at Cologne, at the convent of general studies for the Dominicans.

It was then that he was summoned, on suspicion of heresy, before the tribunal of the Archbishop of Cologne, Henry de Virneburg. Eckhart appealed from there to the Pope. He died whilst this appeal was in progress, revoking[4] all that

[1] The Canon Regular, Jan van Ruysbroeck, native of the Low Countries, also had a great influence on the German school, as we shall see.

[2] Quétif and Echard, *Scriptores ordinis praedicatorum*, Paris 1719. vol. i, 507; Denifle, *Archiv für Litteratur und Kirchengeschichte des Mittelalters*, vol. v, 349-364. See an excellent article on Eckhart by F. Vernet, *Dict. de Théol. catholique,* art. *Eckart,* Paris 1910.

[3] *Cf.* Denifle, *Archiv für Litt.*, vol. ii, 619 ff. Fr. Denifle tends to justify Eckhart as much as possible. Others accuse him too much, perhaps. *Cf.* Ch. Schmidt, *Études sur le mysticisme allemand au XIVe siècle,* Paris 1847, p. 113.

[4] Denifle, *Archiv für Litt.*, 1886, vol. ii, 631 ff. According to H. Delacroix, *Essai sur le mysticisme spéculatif en Allemagne au XIVe siècle,* Paris 1899, pp. 228, 238, Eckhart's retractation must only have been " implicit, conditional."

might be found, either in his writings or discourse, erroneous in matters of faith or capable of being wrongly interpreted. Two years after his death, on March 27, 1329, twenty-eight propositions, drawn from his works, were condemned by Pope John XXII : seventeen—the first fifteen and the last two—as heretical, and the others as ill-sounding, rash and doubtful.[1]

Few of the works of Eckhart, thoroughly authenticated, have come down to us; no doubt after his death those the orthodoxy of which might have been contested were removed. The edition of sermons in the German language, published by Pfeiffer,[2] is very wanting. The same must be said of the collections of Latin writings.[3] It will thus be understood how difficult it is to draw the exact thought of Eckhart from those scraps of works which have escaped destruction. Doubtless it is on that account that impassioned controversies, not yet ended, have arisen around the name of the famous mystic.

According to some, Eckhart taught the most absolute idealistic Pantheism. In philosophy he would be the forerunner of Hegel. His mysticism must clearly end in the complete identification of the soul with the divinity, and must have as its object the leading of man to the knowledge of his unity with God.[4] Eckhart must have been inspired by the Pantheism of the *Brethren of the Free Spirit,* which sect, spread over Germany, had given birth to the heretical Beghards and Beguines. In fact, we shall find a resemblance between the doctrines of the Beghards condemned by the Church and certain propositions of Eckhart censured by Pope John XXII. Hence the German mysticism of the fourteenth century must have sprung from an heretical sect. But its chief representatives, whilst continuing to follow the early tendencies of its founder, had modified their teaching in order to approach more closely to orthodoxy.[5]

Lively protests have been raised against these serious accusations. Pantheism is characteristic neither of the philosophy nor of the mysticism of the school of Eckhart.[6]

---

[1] Bull *In Agro dominico*, of March 27, 1329, of John XXII, re-edited by Denifle, *Archiv für Litt.*, vol. ii, 636-659, and by Denzinger-Bannwart, *Enchiridion symbolorum*, 1908, n. 501-529, which reproduces the text of Denifle.

[2] *Deutsche Mystiker der vierzehnten Jahrhunderts,* Leipzig 1857, vol. ii. See also certain sermons : Haupt, *Journal*, T. xv; A. Jundt, *Histoire du Panthéisme populaire au moyen age,* Paris 1875, pp. 231-280; Birlinger, *Alemannia*, 1875-1876, vols. iii-iv.

[3] *Cf.* F. Vernet, *op. cit.*, pp. 2060-2061, 2079.

[4] Schmidt, *Etudes sur le mysticisme allemand au XIVe siècle*, pp. 31, 100, 256 ff.

[5] Schmidt, *ibid. Cf.* Puyol, *L'auteur du livre De Imitatione Christi,* Paris, 1899, pp. 378 ff.; De Wulf, *Histoire de la philosophie médiévale,* Louvain 1905, p. 482.

[6] W. Preger, *Geschichte der deutschen Mystik im Mittelalter,* Leipzig 1874, vol. i, pp. 394, 402; 1881, vol. ii, pp. 111-116.

F. Denifle,[1] above all, strove, by laying stress on the Latin works of Eckhart, to show that the chief of the German mystics was a scholastic, and not, properly speaking, a pantheist, and that those texts have often been considered as erroneous which were merely obscure. The learned Dominican admits, however, that Eckhart erred, though less than is often stated.

The propositions of Eckhart condemned by John XXII are manifestly impregnated with Pantheism. The mystical union of the soul with God, as it is taught there, strongly resembles a complete identification. " We are wholly transformed into God," taught Eckhart, " and we are changed into him in the same way that, in the Sacrament of the Eucharist, the bread is changed into the body of Christ; I am thus changed into him because he makes me one with his being and not merely like to it; by the living God it is true, that therein there is no distinction."[2] " The consequence is that the operation of the just man becomes absolutely blended with the divine; man does all that God himself does. All that belongs to the divine nature belongs also entirely to the just and divine man; that is why this just man performs that which God performs and that he created, conjointly with God, heaven and earth, and is the begetter of the divine word, and without this man God cannot do anything."[3]

It is towards idealistic Pantheism that the mysticism of Eckhart would seem to incline : that which is divine in us can only be the intelligence, which is not a creature but an uncreated being. "There is something in the soul," says Eckhart, "that is uncreated and not creatable; that is the intelligence, and if it were the whole soul, that would be uncreated and not creatable."[4]

The Averroistic school taught that the intellective soul is not multiplied as often as the human body, but that it was only one for all men : *Quod anima intellectiva non multiplicatur multiplicatione corporum, sed est una numero.* The intellect is something single for the whole and entire human

---

[1] *Archiv für Litt.*, vol. ii, pp. 417-687.

[2] Prop. 10 : *Nos transformamur totaliter in Deum et convertimur in eum; simili modo sicut in sacramento panis convertitur in corpus Christi: sic ergo convertor in eum, quod ipse me operatur suum esse unum, non simile; per viventem Deum verum est, quod ibi nulla est distinctio.* Denziger-Bannwart, n. 510.

[3] Prop. 13 : *Quidquid proprium est divinae naturae, hoc totum proprium est homini justo et divino; propter hoc iste homo operatur quidquid Deus operatur, et creavit una cum Deo coelum et terram, et est generator Verbi aeterni, et Deus sine tali homine nesciret quidquam facere.* Denziger-Bannwart, n. 513. *Cf.* Prop. 20-21 : *Quod bonus homo est unigenitus Filius Dei. Homo nobilis est ille unigenitus Dei, quem Pater aeternaliter genuit.*

[4] Prop. 27 : *Aliquid est in anima, quod est increatum et increabile, si tota anima esset talis, esset increata et increabilis, et hoc est intellectus.* Denziger-Bannwart, n. 527.

race, and is united to each member of mankind only in an accidental manner. It is the sensible soul that constitutes man according to his species.[1] Eckhart, like Averroes, seems to make the intellect a being in a manner divine. The Beghards, too, were not far from this most suspicious doctrine. According to them "all intellectual nature is naturally blessed in itself;" it "has no need of the light of glory in order to be raised to the vision and the beatific enjoyment of God."[2]

The identification of the will of the pious man with the divine will, such as it is understood by Eckhart, also reminds us of the Quietism of the Beghards. The latter taught that "man, in this present life, is able to attain to so great and high a state of perfection that he may become entirely free from sin, and can no longer grow in grace."[3] Consequently, the one who reaches this degree of perfection need neither fast nor pray, because "in this state his senses are brought under subjection to the mind and to reason so completely that he may grant to the body all that it pleases." He is not obliged to obey the Church any longer, nor to "perform acts of virtue," which belong to imperfect man.[4] We can guess the immoral consequences that the Beghards were able to deduce from such principles.[5]

Eckhart condemned these consequences with all his strength. But certain points in his teaching approached them somewhat closely, and perhaps too much; they inclined the Christian soul to undue indifference under the pretext of submission to God. "The good man," said Eckhart, "ought to conform his will to the will of God so well that he should will all that God wills : because, in a certain manner, God wills that I have sinned, I should not wish not to have committed sins; such is true penitence : The man who might have committed a thousand mortal sins, if well-disposed, ought not to desire not to have committed them."[6]

[1] Mandonnet, *Siger de Brabant et l'averroisme*, pp. 9 ff.

[2] *Errores Beguardorum et Beguinarum de statu perfectionis in concilio Viennensi* (1311-1312) *damnati a Clemente V* . Prop. 5 : *Quod quaelibet intellectualis natura in se ipsa naturaliter est beata, quodque anima non indiget lumine gloriae ipsam elevante ad Deum videndum et eo beate fruendum.* Denziger-Bannwart, *Echiridion symb.*, n. 475.

[3] *Errores Beguardorum,* prop. 1 : *Quod homo in vita praesenti tantum et talem perfectionis gradum potest acquirere, quod reddetur penitus impeccabilis et amplius in gratia proficere non valebit.* Denz-Bann., 47.

[4] Prop. 2, 3, 6. Denz.-Bann., 472, 473, 476.

[5] Prop. 7. Denz.-Bann., 477. In fact, immorality was great among the heretical Beghards and Beguines.

[6] *Errores Ekardi,* prop. 14-15 : *Bonus homo debet sic conformare voluntatem suam voluntati divinae, quod ipse velit quidquid Deus vult: quia Deus vult aliquo modo me peccasse, nollem ego, quod ego peccata non commisissem et haec est vera paenitentia. Si homo commisisset mille peccata mortalia, si talis homo esset recte dispositus, non deberet velle se ea non commisisse.* Denz.-Bann., 514-515.

An equally blameworthy indifference is counselled with regard to interior holiness and to the kingdom of heaven.[1] If we ought not to desire even spiritual joys and the glory of heaven, prayer becomes unnecessary. Moreover, it is little recommended.[2]

Eckhart had famous disciples, Dominicans like himself. The convent of Erfürt sheltered several, among others Eckhart the Younger (1337),[3] who had a kind of devotion to his master, but whose errors he knew how to avoid. A treatise *On Reason Active and Potential* is attributed to him,[4] in which mysticism is expounded in conformity with the German school and according to the most arduous scholastic theories. But the best known of his disciples are John Tauler and Blessed Henry Suso.[5]

John Tauler was born at Strasbourg about 1290, and probably studied at Cologne. He joined the Dominicans not later than 1308, and became one of the most appreciated preachers of his time. He was called *the Sublime Doctor, the Illuminated Doctor.* His instructions were usually given in the orthodox Beguinages. He loved to preach resignation, renunciation of personal interest, love of retreat and high mysticism.

For a long time it was thought that Tauler had been converted to the perfect life by a layman. Fr. Denifle has shown that the inventor of this legend[6] was a bourgeois named Fulman Merswin (1382)[7] of Strasbourg, a member of the association of the *Friends of God.* Tauler preached at

[1] Prop. 8 : *Qui non intendunt res, nec utilitatem nec devotionem internam, nec sanctitatem, nec praemium, nec regnum caelorum, sed omnibus his renunciaverunt, etiam quod suum est, in illis hominibus honoratur Deus.* Denz., 508.
[2] Prop. 7, 9. Denz., 507, 509.
[3] F. Vernet, *Dict. de Théol. cath.*, art. *Eckart le Jeune.*
[4] *Von der wirkenden und möglichen Vernunft,* edited by W. Preger, in the *Sitzungsberichten der Philos. Hist. Klasse der Akademie,* Munich 1871, pp. 176 ff., and again in the edition of Tauler's sermons, Frankfort 1826. See two *Sermons* and one letter of Eckhart the Younger in *J. Tauleri opera omnia,* edit. L. Surius, Cologne 1603, pp. 11-13, 46-48.
[5] Tauler calls Eckhart " the remarkable theologian," " the venerable father." See *J. Tauleri opera.*, Surius, p. 831, 832. Suso often speaks of the " very holy master Eckhart." He sees him in his mystical visions, *Vie de Suso*, chaps. viii, xxiii, *Œuvres mystiques du B. Henri Suso,* French translation, Thiriot, Paris 1899, vol. i, pp. 36, 97.
[6] This legend is related in the *Meisters-Buch* (ed. Ch. Schmidt, Strasbourg 1875) a writing emanating from the *Friends of God* circles. Denifle, *Taulers Bekehrung kritisch untersucht,* Strasbourg 1879.
[7] The author of the *Livre des neuf rochers* (ed. Ch. Schmidt, Strasbourg 1859). This work, long attributed to Suso, censures the disorders which desolated the Church. It is written in the form of visions. Each of the nine rocks shelters a category of souls more or less advanced in perfection.

Cologne for several years, and died at Strasbourg in 1361.
He has left his *Sermons,* of which only a part was published,
in the Rhenish dialect.[1] There are also his didactic essays,
especially the *Considerations (Exercitatio) on the Life and
Passion of the Saviour.*[2] The *Institutions* is an apocryphal
work in which another hand has summed up the teaching of
Tauler.[3]

Tauler is more speculative than affective. His works show
a preference for reasoning. But how delicate and penetrating
is the analysis with which he dissects the soul in order to
lay bare its most hidden tendencies ! He was a great director
of consciences and much esteemed by Bossuet. In the last
century the English Oratorian, Faber, evinced something of
Tauler's style.

The learned Dominican is one of the most powerful
theorists of German mysticism, one of its most profound
intellectualists. His sermons set forth an abstract teaching,
lofty and scholastic. He knew, however, how to make his
hearers listen, by awakening their attention and whetting
their curiosity by means of picturesque comparisons in order
to convey a lesson and engrave it on the mind for all time.
When, for instance, he deals with temptations which beset
the beginnings of the Christian life, he thus describes the
pursuit of the stag by hounds :

" It sometimes happens," he says, " that when the hounds
approach the stag and hang on to him to tear him, if he
sees that he is unable to free himself from their teeth he
drags them with him to a tree, against which he crushes
their heads and thus escapes from them. We ought to do
the same. When we cannot overcome our temptations and
free ourselves from them, we should throw ourselves towards
that tree of the cross and the passion of our Lord Jesus
Christ, and strike against this tree the head of the dog which
attacks us : so shall we escape its bites."[4]

If in spite of our efforts the temptation continues we must
bear with resignation this trial which will render us more
pleasing to God.

" In the same way that we are nourished by God in the

---

[1] Leipzig 1498; Frankfort edition, 1826. A French translation of the
Frankfort edition was done by Charles Sainte-Foi, 2 vols., Paris 1855.
See the Latin translation in Surius, *Joannis Tauleri opera omnia,*
Cologne 1603. A French translation from this Latin version of Surius
has been recently made by E. P. Noel, O.P., in eight volumes, Paris
1911-1913, with a good Introduction and notes.
[2] See this work in Surius.
[3] The *Institutions* have been translated into French and published
separately, Paris 1668, 12mo, without the name of their author. There
was a new edition, Paris 1909.
[4] *Sermon pour le 2ª dimanche de l'Epiphanie,* French translation,
Sainte-Foi, vol. i, 193. The Sainte-Foi translation is cited because
it is made from the German.

Eucharist," he says again, "so also do we make him our food when he chastises us and smites our conscience. He is not content to chastise us himself, but wishes us also to be troubled by all creatures. The pious man is chased and pursued like the wild deer to be presented to the emperor—it is pursued without relaxation, the hounds bite and tear it. But when it is in this state it is more pleasing to the emperor than if it had been taken without effort. The eternal God is this glorious Emperor who wishes game thus taken to be placed on his table.[1]

Tauler also knew how to make use, with great art, of biblical images in order to render accessible as far as possible his knowledge of souls and his learned theological speculations.

"The fisherman throws his fish-hook in order to take the fish," he explains, with reference to our correspondence with grace, "but he does not succeed unless the fish seize the hook. If the fish seize the bait, the fisherman is certain to take it and to draw it towards him. Thus God has thrown into the whole universe and over all creatures, beneath our feet, before our eyes and before our soul, his fish-hook, his bait, his net to draw us to him by means of all the things of this world. He draws us by things pleasing, he leads us on by things which afflict us. He who is not drawn has himself only to blame, for he has not bitten the bait which God has thrown him; he has refused to allow himself to be taken by his hook and in his net. Otherwise God would have certainly taken and drawn him to himself. We must then not blame God if we are not drawn."[2]

Blessed Henry Suso, colleague and contemporary of Tauler, possessed somewhat different qualities. He was, above all, affective, almost emotional. Henry Suso had a loving nature, full of poetry and tenderness; he was surnamed *Amandus*. He was a Suabian,[3] from the country of the love-singers, the Minnesänger. But it was not of human love that he sang.

When he was thirteen years old he entered the Dominican convent of Constance; after several years of little fervour in the religious life, according to his own account, he was converted, submitted himself to frightful austerities and tasted the joys of divine love.[4]

---

[1] *Sermon II pour la Fête du Corps de N.S.*, Sainte-Foi, i, 102.

[2] *Sermon II pour le vendredi-saint*, i, 371-372.

[3] Henry Suso was born at Ueberlingen, on the borders of Lake Constance, about 1295. He died at Ulm, January 25, 1365. He was beatified by Pope Gregory XVI on April 16, 1831.

[4] *Life of Suso*, chap. i. Edition Denifle, *Die Schriften des heiligen Heinrich Suso*, i, Munchen 1880. French translation, G. Thiriot, O.P., *Œuvres mystiques du B. Henri Suso*, vol. i, Paris 1899, p. 13.

It is love for the eternal Wisdom, for which he had a special devotion, which consumes him.

The German school of mysticism extolled the intelligence; Meister Eckhart, as we have seen, was inclined to identify all intelligence with God. Suso devoted himself to the eternal Wisdom, the divine Intelligence, of which he was the apostle, the knight, the lover. It is this intelligence that he contemplates in his ecstasies, and that he lauds in his writings.[1] It is therewith that he contracts a spiritual marriage; the sign of this mystical alliance was the name of Jesus, the name of the eternal Wisdom incarnate, which Suso engraved on his breast, on his heart, with a stylet.[2]

It was at this time, in the early days of his conversion, that in a rapture he had a kind of intellectual vision of the eternal Wisdom. He relates that "His soul was enraptured, either within or without the body. He then saw and heard what no tongue can tell. What the servant [Suso] saw had no shape nor any other manner of being, and nevertheless he felt a pleasure equal to that which the sight of all the forms of all things might have afforded him. His heart was filled with desires, yet these desires were fulfilled, his soul was joyful and content. . . . The Friar Preacher did nothing but contemplate this resplendent light, and forgot himself entirely, and not himself only but all other things. Was it day or was it night? He did not know. It was like the sweetness of eternal life in a sensation of silence and repose. Then he said : ' If what I see and what I feel is not the kingdom of heaven, truly I know not what it can be.' . . . This ecstasy lasted fully half an hour or an hour. He was unable to say whether his soul remained in the body or was separated from it. . . . His body suffered so much during this short rapture that it seemed to him that nobody, except in death, could suffer so much in so short a space of time."[3]

The eternal Wisdom was indeed for Suso a well-beloved companion. When he sat down to table he begged it to come there with him and share his meal. In Suabia, at the beginning of the year, the young men were accustomed to go out in the night to sing songs in order to receive crowns from their sweethearts. Blessed Suso, too, was wont to sing songs on that night to express his love for the eternal Wisdom, in the hope of winning a spiritual crown. In the

[1] The chief work of Suso is his *Book of Eternal Wisdom*, of which he gave a Latin translation entitled *Horologium Sapientiae.*

[2] With regard to this, see the *Life* of Suso, chap. i-v, Thiriot, i, 13-28. It was the three letters I H S which Suso engraved on his breast. See also chap. xlix of the *Life* of Suso. Suso greatly recommended devotion to the name of Jesus. See also his *Letter* XI.

[3] *Life,* chap. iii, Thiriot, i, 17-18.

spring, in accordance with a Suabian usage, it was his custom to plant a mystical maypole of prayer and praise in honour of this holy Wisdom.[1]

But love was filled with suffering and austerities. From his conversion until the age of forty years Suso wore, day and night, a hair-shirt interwoven with sharp steel. He was racked by a cross of wood studded with nails, which he wore next to the skin between his shoulders. He slept fully dressed on an old plank. Such mortifications affected his health, and he was obliged to stop them.[2]

Nor was he spared moral tortures. When his studies were ended at Cologne he returned about 1336 to Constance where he became Prior. There he wrote the *Book of Wisdom* and the *Book of Truth*. The orthodoxy of the latter work was questioned, and in 1336, at a general Chapter of Friars Preachers held at Bruges, the Prior of Constance was deposed. Suso was attacked as to his honour, abandoned by his friends, and inwardly forsaken by God.[3]

We know one by one his sorrows. He gave an account of them, as well as of his mystical favours, to one of his spiritual daughters, Elizabeth Staglin, a Dominican religious of the convent of Toss. She took them down, and thus drew up the *Life* of her director.

The ardent soul of Suso also showed itself in the works that he wrote. There are, it is true, some treatises on speculative mysticism in which use is made of the writings of Dionysius the Areopagite and St Thomas Aquinas. But speculation quickly becomes transformed into exaltation. The heart of Suso is too full of love to allow him to speak for long on reasoning only.

"O Wisdom altogether beautiful," he cries in the *Morning Salutation*, "O Wisdom enlightening and eternal, my soul sighed after thee this night and this morning; I awoke thinking of thee in the depth of my heart, O my love. I beseech thee, my loving Saviour, that thy presence which is so desirable, ward off all danger from both my body and soul. Do thou fill with thy different graces the most secret recesses of my heart and kindle it with the fire of thy divine love. Oh! most sweet Jesus Christ, turn thy loving countenance towards me, for this morning my soul throws itself towards thee with all its strength, and I salute thee from the inmost depths of my heart. I desire that the thousand angels that serve thee should bless thee a thousand times for me this day, and that the hundred thousand heavenly spirits who dwell near thee should worthily glorify thee for me ten thousand times. I desire that all that is beautiful and

---

[1] Cf. *Life*, chap. xi, x, xiv.   [2] *Life*, chap. v-xx.
[3] *Life*, chap. xxi ff.

lovable in thy creatures should praise thee to-day in my place. Let all creatures bless thy glorious name which is our consoling protection now and for all eternity. Amen."[1]

The four principal German works of Suso were revised by him towards the end of his life and combined in one whole with the title *The Pattern*. They are : his *Life, The Book of Eternal Wisdom, The Book of Truth*, and *The Little Book of Letters*.[2] This collection of letters is far from being complete. Suso also left us some *Sermons*.[3]

The *Book of Eternal Wisdom* was highly esteemed in Germany in the Middle Ages, almost as much as the *Imitation of Christ*. Suso wrote it in order to rekindle the fire of divine love which seemed to be almost extinguished, in this fourteenth century, so disturbed in every way. With this end in view he first of all gives a description, with frightful realism, of the sufferings endured by Christ during his passion. Then he speaks of sin, of the rigour of the judgements of God. The second part of the book treats of death, and the third contains one hundred short meditations on the passion.[4]

As to the *Book of Truth*, it was written in order to refute the errors of the Beghards and of the *Brethren of the Free Spirit*, which compromised the mystical German school, and particularly Meister Eckhart. Suso deals therein with most difficult questions of mysticism, and is inspired by Dionysius the Areopagite. His explanations are often obscure, at times somewhat doubtful. It is easy to understand that they might have brought the orthodoxy of the writer under suspicion.

Nicholas of Strasbourg, who lived in the fourteenth century, also belongs to the German Dominican school. His *Sermons*[5] deal with mysticism. According to certain

---

[1] Thiriot's translation, *op. cit.*, p. 328.

[2] The works were edited in 1482 by the Dominican Felix Fabri, at Augsburg. They were re-edited in 1512. Surius the Carthusian translated this last edition into Latin at the request of Blosius, *Henrici Susonis opera*, Cologne 1555. In the nineteenth century, Cardinal Diepenbrock brought out a better edition of the works of Suso, *Heinrich Suso's Genannt Amandus, Leben und Schriften*, Regensburg 1828. Père Denifle published *The Pattern* according to the best MSS., *Die schriften des heiligen Henrich Seuse*, München 1876-1880.

[3] No single edition contains all the letters of Suso. His *Sermons* are to be found in Diepenbrock, 3rd edition, corrected by Denifle, and in Surius. The works of Suso were translated into French by Cartier, *Œuvres du B. Henri Suso*, Paris 1856, but not from the German. Père G. Thiriot made a much better translation from recent German editions, *Œuvres mystiques du B. Henri Suso*, Paris 1899, 2 vols.

[4] The Latin translation of the *Book of Wisdom*, done by Suso with the title *Horologium Sapientiae*, was edited in a critical form by Strange, Coloniae 1861.

[5] F. Pfeiffer's edition, *Deutsche mystiker des vierzehnten Jahrhunderts*, vol. i, Leipzig 1857.

writers,[1] Hermann of Fritzlar, who narrated the *Lives of the Saints* from a practical standpoint, was a Dominican.

In the convents of Dominican nuns in Germany, under the influence of the Friars Preachers, and above all of Henry Suso, a brilliant group of mystical religious blossomed forth, the names of some of whom have been preserved to us. The monasteries of Toss, of Unterlinden at Colmar, of Adelhausen at Freiburg in Breisgau, of Oltenbach near Zurich, of Val St Catherine near Dissenhofen on the Rhine, and of Engelthal were filled with holy enthusiasm.[2] Several of these religious wrote their *Visions* and their *Revelations,* such as Christine Ebnerin (1356)[3] and Adelaide Langmann (1375)[4] of the convent of Engelthal, Margaret Ebnerin (1351)[5] of that of Medingen.

The Dominican mystical school of the fourteenth century then had an exceptionally important influence in Germany.

[1] Pfeiffer, *ibid.* Denifle, *Das geistliche Leben,* p. xiii, thinks that he was a layman. Others think he was a Franciscan.

[2] Cf. *Life of the Dominican nuns* of Unterlingen at Colmar and of Adelhausen at Freiburg in Breisgau, edited by Pez, 8 vols. of the *Bibliotheca ascetica,* Ratisbon 1725. *Fleurs dominicaines, ou les mystiques d'Unterlinden,* 1230-1330, by the Vte de Bussières, Paris 1864.

[3] *Life and Visions,* edited by Lochner, Nuremburg 1872. Denifle, *Das geist. Leben,* p. xii.

[4] *Revelations,* published by Strauch, Strasbourg 1872. Denifle, p. xiii.

[5] *Revelations,* MS. of the convent of Medingen. Denifle, p. xiii.

CHAPTER VIII
THE TEACHING OF
THE GERMAN MYSTICS OF THE
FOURTEENTH CENTURY

BEFORE explaining this teaching it is necessary to mention some other writers not belonging to the Dominican Order but who are of the German school. The most famous is the Canon Regular Jan van Ruysbroeck.

Blessed Jan van Ruysbroeck should be added to the German mystics of the fourteenth century. He was born, it is true, in the Low Countries, and it was there that his life was spent. He wrote his works in the Flemish language. In spite of this he exercised a deep influence on the German school;[1] his teaching greatly resembles that of Tauler and Suso, who were both inspired by him.

He was born in 1293 in the village whose name he has retained. Ruusbroec, now Ruysbroeck, is situated on the Senne, between Brussels and Hal.[2] From the age of eleven years he lived under the direction of Master John Hinckaert, Canon of St Gudule, in Brussels. Ordained priest at twenty-four, he became chaplain to that church. It was at this time that he began to write against the sect of the *Brethren of the Free Spirit,* which in those parts had at its head a famous plotter named Bloemardinne.

With the desire to lead a more perfect life Ruysbroeck withdrew with several companions, in 1343, to a hermitage in the forest of Soignies known as Groenendael (*Viridis Vallis,* or *Vauvert*). There, in the year 1350, they took the habit and Rule of the Canons Regular of St Augustine. Such were the beginnings of the famous Abbey of Groenendael.

It was in this retreat that Ruysbroeck wrote his works. He was stimulated in this labour by Gerard, the prior of a neighbouring Carthusian monastery at Groenendael, and by

---

[1] Denifle cites Ruysbroeck, in his *Das geistliche Leben,* almost as much as the German writers.

[2] The *Life of Ruysbroeck* was written by Henry Pomerius, Canon Regular of the monastery of Groenendael, where Ruysbroeck lived and died. The text of this *Life* has been edited in the *Analecta Bollandiana,* vol. iv, 1885, pp. 263 ff. The devotion paid to Blessed Ruysbroeck in the Low Countries was approved by the S.C. of Rites on December 1, 1908.

numerous visitors greatly versed in mystical theology, such as the Dominican Tauler and Gerard Groot, the founder of the famous association of the *Clerks and Brothers of the Common Life,* at Deventer, in Holland. Ruysbroeck died at Groenendael in 1381.

For a long time the works of Ruysbroeck were only known in translations. The best known is the Latin translation by Surius.[1] The original text, written in Flemish, or more correctly in the Brabançon dialect, was published from MSS by J. David, professor at the University of Louvain.[2] The Benedictines of the Abbey of St Paul de Wisques, at Oosterhout, in Holland, have undertaken a French translation from the Flemish text.[3]

Ruysbroeck was a prolific writer. Twelve of his treatises have come down to us. The more important, those that contain a complete exposition of his teaching, are : *The Mirror of Eternal Salvation* or *The Blessed Sacrament,* which explains mystical union by the theory of the image and resemblance with God; *The Book of the Seven Enclosures,* or greater and greater renunciations of the soul in order to attain to union with the divine Persons : *The Seven Degrees of the Ladder of Spiritual Love,* which expresses a similar doctrine; *The Kingdom of the Lovers of God,* in which is taught the efficacy of the gifts of the Holy Ghost to lead to contemplation; *The Book of the Highest Truth,* written at the request of Gerard the Carthusian to explain the obscurities of the preceding work; *The Adornment of the Spiritual Marriage,* the most famous work of Ruysbroeck, in which are described the three forms of the spiritual life : the active life, the interior life, the contemplative life. The title is explained by the text : *Ecce sponsus venit, exite obviam ei,* understood in a mystical sense.[4]

Ruysbroeck is one of the greatest of mystical theorists. He made himself remarkable by depth and abundance of

[1] *D. Joannis Rusbrochii Opera omnia,* Cologne 1552. The best edition is that of 1609.

[2] *Werken van Jan van Ruusbroec,* Ghent, Annoot-Braeckman, 6 vols., 1858-1868. Published under the ægis of the *Société des Bibliophiles flamands.*

[3] *Œuvres de Ruysbroeck l'Admirable,* translation from the Flemish, Brussels, vol. i, 3rd edition, 1919; vol. ii, 1917; vol. iii, 1920. Three volumes have appeared with excellent Introductions.

[4] The other works are—*The Twelve Virtues* by which we approach contemplation. Resignation and renunciation of one's own will is insisted on. *The Twelve Points of the True Faith* is a paraphrase of the Nicene Creed. *The Four Temptations* was chiefly directed against the false liberty of the Brethren of the Free Spirit. *The Tabernacle,* a mystical application of the various parts of the Old Testament tabernacle to the seven spiritual mansions of the soul. *The Shining Stone,* a mystical application of verse 17 of chap ii of the Apocalypse. *The Book of the Twelve Beguines,* a book of piety for the Beguines.

expression and thought, and by his wide knowledge united with his outbursts of love.[1]

In his works he expounded a very abstract doctrine, at times most difficult to understand. He prefers to deal with the most obscure points of mystical theology, and treats them in a very personal way. He also at times bewilders his readers and has placed his orthodoxy in doubt.[2]

A comparative study, however, of the treatises of Ruysbroeck soon shows, beneath somewhat different expressions, a similar teaching to that of the German mystics. To Ruysbroeck, as to Tauler and Suso, mystical union is explained by the Dionysian theory of the return of the soul to divine unity.

The Franciscan family did not remain altogether aloof from the German mystical movement. Mark of Lindau,[3] Provincial of the Province of Strasbourg, and Otto of Passau,[4] lecturer at the Franciscan convent of Bâle, have left us interesting treatises. But the best known German Franciscan writer of the period is Henry Harphius, also known as Henry of Herp. Bossuet[5] speaks of him on several occasions as a mystic rather inclined to exaggerations and as one abused by the Quietists. He was Provincial of the Observants of Cologne and then Guardian of the convent at Malines. He lived in the fifteenth century,[6] but his teaching is similar to that of the German writers of the century before. He copied Jan van Ruysbroeck, especially in the last two books of his *Mystical Theology,*[7] his chief work.

It is also necessary to mention Rudolph of Bibrach, a Suabian Friar Minor of the fourteenth century, to whom is attributed the treatise *Of the Seven Ways of Eternity.*[8]

---

[1] *Cf.* G. J. Waffelaert, S.T.D., Bishop of Bruges, *The Union of the Loving Soul with God* or *Guide to Perfection,* according to the teaching of Blessed Ruysbroeck. Translated from Flemish by R. Hoornaert, Paris, Lille, Bruges, 1916.

[2] The Chancellor Gerson violently attacked the *Adornment of the Spiritual Marriage* of Ruysbroeck in his *Letter to Bro. Bartholomew,* Carthusian, *Gersonii Opera,* vol. i, pp. 59 ff., Antwerp 1706. He accuses him of not sufficiently avoiding Averroist errors. *Sermo in Coena Domini de humilitate,* vol. iii, pp. 1124-1125.

[3] He wrote a *Treatise on the Ten Commandments.* Denifle, *Das geist. Leben,* p. xiii.

[4] He wrote the *Throne of Gold for Loving Souls* (Denifle, p. xiv). Selected sentences drawn from the Fathers and mystics with the author's comments.

[5] *Instruction on the States of Prayer,* Bk. I, ii, vi; *Schola in tuto, quaestio* IV, n. 90.

[6] Harphius died in 1478.

[7] *Theologia mystica,* divided into three books, edited at Cologne in 1538, then re-edited at Rome with corrections in 1586. A French translation was published by Machault, Paris, in 1617.

[8] Attributed to St Bonaventure and wrongly placed among his works; published in Venice 1756, vol. xii, pp. 99-203. The ways of eternity are : desire of eternal things, meditation, contemplation, charity, supernatural revelations, etc.

This mystic, however, was inspired much more by St Bonaventure than by the German writers. St Augustine, Hugh
and Richard of St Victor and St Bernard are his favourite
writers.

We know from what has already been said[1] some of the
general characteristics of German spirituality in the fourteenth century.[2]

It is usually speculative and intellectual; it yields the
first place to the intelligence. When it treats of the union of
the soul with God theories are never, as with the affective
writers, excluded. In this it is inspired by St Thomas
Aquinas, whose mysticism is wholly saturated with intellectualism. Questions, therefore, most high, such as the
divine Being and his relations with the Christian soul, the
Blessed Trinity, the contemplative union of man with the
divinity, are those on which it dwells most often.

Another characteristic of German mysticism is that it is
abstract; in that it resembles Dionysian theology. St
Bernard dealt with mystical facts that he had either experienced himself or that had been experienced by others
around him. He was careful not to form theories respecting
them. The German process is quite otherwise : it consists in
starting with theological principles, and, by means of strict
logic, deducing from them final consequences, no matter
through what obscurities it be necessary to pass, and no
matter, as in the case of Eckhart, to what conclusions they
might lead. Such mysticism is somewhat lacking in the
control derived from experience and justification from facts.
Is it not one of the tendencies of the German mind to start
from an *a priori?*

Moreover, the mysticism from beyond the Rhine is wholly

[1] Denifle, *Das geistliche Leben,* Graz 1908, summarized the practical
parts of this teaching under three heads : purgative way, illuminative
way, unitive way. But he has not given references. The Comtesse de
Flavigny and Mlle. de Pitteurs, *La vie spirituelle d'après les mystiques
allemands du XIVe siècle,* a translation and adaptation, Paris 1903,
have only given summary references.

[2] Other than the mystics mentioned in the previous chapter, Denifle
(*Das geist. Leben,* pp. xii-xiv) again cites these anonymous treatises :
Treatise of the Three Questions, edited by Denifle, Strasbourg 1879.
The Friend of God in the Oberland, sometimes confused with Nicholas
of Bâle (Schmidt, *Nikolaus von Basel, Leben und Schriften,* Vienna
1866). *Book of Spiritual Poverty,* ed. Denifle, Munich 1877. *The Book
of Love,* attributed to Suso, MSS. Zurich library. *Theologia Ger-
manica,* book of a Friend of God of the fourteenth century, ed.
Pfeiffer, Stuttgart 1855. *Sermons and Prayers in Old German,* ed. W.
Wackernagel, Bâle 1876. *Sentences and Poems of German Mystics,*
published by *Germania,* vols. iii and xviii.

A synthesis of German mysticism will be chiefly drawn from Tauler,
Suso and Ruysbroeck. I leave Meister Eckhart aside on account of the
uncertain condition in which his works have come down to us.

shut up in the soul; it does not go outside itself. St Francis of Assisi associated all created beings with his outbursts of divine love, which he used as so many ladders to raise himself towards God. Hugh of St Victor and many others with him arrived at the contemplation of God through the contemplation of creatures. German mysticism of the fourteenth century is little influenced by the sense of nature. It is thus thrown back on itself, on its *ego*, without opening the window to things outside. It analyzes the soul in order to make it take knowledge that God is within, and that it should become more and more closely united to him.[1] Outward beings are not ordinarily looked upon as helps towards this union. German piety is concentrated in the interior of the soul; it goes out only to lift itself up to God.

"The spiritual life," says Tauler, "consists in two movements : the one of concentration, which is brought about by the gathering up of all the sensible powers in the higher powers—that is to say, in the very depth of the soul; the other of expansion, by which we go out of ourselves and raise ourselves above ourselves by the renunciation of all personal right in our own will, our desires and our activity."[2]

Finally, German mysticism is universal in its application; it is not reserved as elsewhere for restricted categories of the faithful. It is addressed to all without distinction; so much so that we find it set forth, in its most lofty form, to quite ordinary people. What is perhaps unique in the history of spirituality is that Tauler, a German mystic, delivered his teaching in sermons for the liturgical year. And his sermons were intended as much for the ordinary faithful as for religious and orthodox Beghards or Beguines. There exists in the German soul a mystical tendency which explains how it was that the Rhenish Christians of the fourteenth century became enthusiastic for high spirituality.

German mysticism may be summed up under these three heads : the total renunciation of ourselves, of our own will, and absolute submission to the divine will which prepares for union with God; the nakedness of the intelligence or its being completely stripped of every sensible and intellectual image, conditional to this union; finally, mystical union itself, which takes place by means of a kind of return of the

---

[1] *Cf.* Tauler, *Second Sermon for the Feast of Christmas; Sermon for the Sunday within the Octave of Christmas.*

[2] *First Sermon for the Feast of Christmas,* French translation, Sainte-Foi, i, p. 99. This tendency to make everything centre round the ego explains how German protestant philosophers of the eighteenth and nineteenth centuries fell into idealistic Pantheism which deifies the human mind. They obeyed a kind of mystical inspiration that belongs to their race.

soul to the divine unity. This doctrine is not confined to the Germans; nevertheless, they had their own way of understanding it.

I—THE RENUNCIATION OF SELF

WHEN man is truly converted, has done penance for his sins, acquired Christian virtues and mortified his passions to such a degree that he does not yield in any way to his sensuous nature, he should without relaxation practise entire renunciation of himself, without which there can be no perfection.[1]

The Rhenish mystics placed the efficacy of the gifts of the Holy Ghost in high relief as a means of raising the soul to a state of holiness. "Three of these gifts," says Tauler, "prepare man for a sublime and true perfection : the four other gifts finish it inwardly and outwardly and prepare it for the highest end, that state of most pure, most glorious and true perfection,"[2] which is mystical union.

The first three gifts are : divine fear, which makes us avoid sin; piety, which inspires us with patience and enables us "to endure all things both within and without"; knowledge, which "teaches us to learn inwardly the warnings and exhortations of the Holy Ghost. Of the other four gifts, two, strength and divine counsel, have as their end the guidance of man in this complete renunciation of himself, and total abandonment to God which precedes mystical union. Finally, the sixth and seventh, which are intelligence and wisdom, "lead man in a superhuman way into the deep and divine mystery, where God knows and understands himself, where he tastes with joy his own wisdom and his own essence."[3]

Renunciation of ourselves and resignation to the divine will, inspired by the gifts of strength and counsel, should extend to everything that concerns us : in the first place, to the position which God has given to us here below, to the vocation and profession in which we find ourselves. The Lord calls men in different ways and the roads by which we go to him vary. We must then trust to divine providence, and occupy the place allotted to us in peace. Everyone

---

[1] *Cf.* the *Institutions* of Tauler, chap. xxvi. In almost all the Sermons, Tauler preaches repentance and mortification of the passions. *Cf.* Ruysbroeck, *The Mirror of Eternal Salvation.* The asceticism of the German writers is austere.

[2] Tauler, *Sermon III for Pentecost*, French trans., Sainte-Foi, ii, 35-36. *Cf.* Ruysbroeck, *Book of the Kingdom of the Lovers of God,* chaps. xiv-xxxvi.

[3] Tauler, *id.,* Sainte-Foi, ii, 37, 42. Cf. *Sermon II for the Feast of the Holy Trinity; Sermon II for the Twelfth Sunday after Trinity.*

should be content with his vocation, for God is the Master to do what he wills.[1]

We must also accept the happenings of life with great resignation, whatever they be. Are they not directed by God with a view to his glory and to our sanctification? " There is no trouble that happens to thee," said Tauler, "that has not been counted and prepared by him who numbers the least hair that falls from thy head. He has foreseen this trouble from all eternity, he has thought, loved and willed it. Thou hast a pain in thy finger or a headache, thou hast cold feet, thou art hungry or thirsty, thou sufferest from the words or actions of thy neighbour, or thou art subjected to some other trial more or less painful; well, the object of all that is to prepare thee for that supernatural life, the source of so many delights; all has been foreseen and ordained by God, has been measured, weighed and counted; all must needs happen thus and not otherwise. If my eye remains in my head it is because God has willed it and foreseen it from all eternity; if this eye should fall and I should become blind the heavenly Father has in the same way foreseen and decreed it from all eternity. He has given to this event, apparently so unimportant, an eternal counsel and deliberation. . . . If we accept these trials as coming from him they will lead us to true peace. . . . Whether or no you have deserved them remember that they come from God, return thanks to him, give yourself up to him and suffer in patience."[2]

" True abnegation," says Henry Suso in turn,[3] " is the root of all virtues and all beatitude. It is the source of a sweet tranquillity in a thorough resignation in small things as well as in great."

The beggar with whom, according to certain writers,[4] Tauler conversed had never been unfortunate in spite of his sufferings and destitution, because he had resolved to be attached to the divine will alone and to desire only that which God willed. Perfect resignation renders us happy. We must also bear with resignation and patience the loss of our honour, of our reputation and of all to which we are attached to the end that we may be stripped of all.

During an ecstasy Henry Suso heard these words : " Until now it is thou that has smitten thyself with thy own hands

---

[1] Tauler, *Sermon I for the Sixteenth Sunday after Trinity*, ii, 395 ff. Cf. *Sermon I for the Tenth Sunday after Trinity; Sermon for the Sixteenth Sunday after Trinity; Sermon II for the Twentieth Sunday after Trinity.*

[2] Tauler, *Sermon I for Epiphany*, i, 161, 162. *Cf.* Albert the Great, *De adhaerendo Deo*, cap. xvi.

[3] *The Little Book of Letters*, Letter II, Fr. trans., Thiriot, ii, 275.

[4] *Cf.* Sainte-Foi, i, 65-67. This conversation of Tauler with the beggar is not in the German edition of his sermons.

[with the discipline], thou didst stop when thou wouldst, and thou hadst compassion on thyself; I desire now to tear thee from thyself and to cast thee defenceless in the hands of strangers who will smite thee. Thou shalt be present at the ruin of thy reputation, thou shalt be exposed to the contempt of certain blinded men, and thou shalt suffer more from that than from the wounds inflicted by the sharp nails of thy cross. When thou didst give thyself up to acts of mortification thou wast great, thou wast admired; now thou shalt be humbled, annihilated."[1] This spiritual mortification is much more difficult than that of the body. But it is indispensable to him who would raise himself to a high degree of holiness.[2] He must renounce his self-love entirely.

Blessed Henry Suso was one day saddened at the thought of the humiliations to which he had to submit. An inward voice said to him: " Open the window of thy cell, look and learn." He opened it and looked. He saw a dog running in the midst of the cloister carrying in his mouth a piece of carpet. He was playing with this carpet, throwing it in the air, dragging it on the ground; he tore it and made holes in it. An inward voice then said to him: " Thus shalt thou be tossed and torn by the mouths of thy brethren." He thought to himself: " Since it cannot be otherwise resign thyself; see how this carpet lets itself be ill-treated in silence; do thou the same."[3]

The man who desires to become perfect will also renounce all spiritual consolation, for he must know how to endure the most crucifying inward sorrows when the Lord sends them. The Lord may will that we be abandoned by him and by men, that we be in doubt and in sadness, that we even be tempted to despair. We must accept all with patience since he wills it.[4]

Nothing is more distressing than this state of abandonment in which God occasionally allows us to be cast.

" Man," says Tauler, " is then left entirely to his own strength, so that he no longer knows anything either of the graces and consolations of God, or of all that he had formerly acquired. All that is taken from him, removed or hidden, so that he no longer knows which way to turn or where to go. . . . Man is here deprived of himself, left in complete abandonment. He is swallowed up in the depth of the divine will; and there, alone, in this destitution and need of all things, he consents to remain not only for a week or a

[1] *Life of Suso,* chap. xxii, Thiriot, i, 88. *Cf.* Tauler's *Institutions,* chap. i.

[2] Tauler's *Institutions,* chap. xxvi. *Cf.* Ruysbroeck, *The Adornment of the Spiritual Marriage,* Part I, *The Active Life.*

[3] *Life of Henry Suso,* chap. xxii.

[4] *id.,* chaps. xxii-xxiii. *Cf.* Tauler, *Sermon II for the Second Sunday in Lent,* etc.; Suso, *Book of Eternal Wisdom,* chap. ix.

month, but for a thousand years or for all eternity if it be God's will.

" To be ready to suffer the pains of hell eternally (if, which is impossible, God should wish to cast us there whilst still leaving us his love), to abandon oneself to the judgement and will of God, that, my children, is an act of resignation higher than all others. . . . By way of additional bitterness, man in this state sees tendered to him all the miseries, all the temptations and vices which he had formerly overcome, which engaged him in fresh struggles much more terrible than those which he had to sustain in the state of sin. Man then should suffer humbly and abandon himself to the divine will as long as it may please God."[1] The sufferings inherent in this painful trial will be accepted after the example of Christ, who was quite willing to feel himself abandoned by his Father during his passion.

The German mystics are perhaps the first to speak of that sorrow which the abandonment whereto God appeared to leave it inflicted on the soul of Christ. The Saviour, in fact, must have felt all the sufferings which can overtake humanity. Now, one of the most painful is certainly that of the loving soul that God seems to have abandoned. It is easily understood that the mystics were those who brought out this aspect of the passion, that forlornness which drew from the dying Christ the heartrending cry : *My God, my God, why hast thou forsaken me?* (Ps. xxi, 1).[2] When we have renounced all outward and inward joys, our fortune, our reputation, for the intimate joy brought about by the friendship of God, there is left still something in us to be sacrificed; it is self-will, the last that remains to us.

"A man has to die in each one of us," says Tauler, "if we desire to be well with God. What name should we give to this man? His name is self-will, or attachment to ourselves. . . . So long as this self-will remains alive within us it forces its offshoots through all the inner and outer powers of man where the spirit of Christ should take root until it is all laid waste and destroyed."[3]

Self-will dies when our deeds are done for the love of God without asking why—*i.e.*, without regard to our self-love, but solely in order to glorify the Lord, and God it is who works in us these things. " Every time that man seeks or

[1] Tauler, *Sermon III for Pentecost*, ii, 39-40.
[2] These thoughts are found in Suso, *Book of Eternal Wisdom*, chap. xviii; Ruysbroeck, *Mirror of Eternal Salvation*, ii; Tauler, *Exercitatio super vita et passione Christi*, cap. vii, xlvi. Devotion to the passion of Christ is an excellent means of union with God. Tauler, *Sermon for the Ninth Sunday after Trinity*, ii, 294; Suso, *Book of Truth*, chap. v.
[3] *Sermon I for Palm Sunday*, i, 348, 350. *Cf.* Ruysbroeck, *Mirror of Eternal Salvation*, chap. ii-iii.

desires in his works something which God can or is willing to give him, he is like the merchants [whom Jesus drove from the temple]. If thou wouldst be wholly free from this traffic, do thy works solely for God, and think no more of thyself than as though it were another that did them; in acting thus thy works will become spiritual and divine. The merchants are driven from the temple, and God alone remains there when man has nothing else but God in sight."[1]

The will must empty itself, so to speak, of itself; it must renounce willing for itself, to the end that it only wills what God wills. It should reduce itself to nothingness, plunge itself in emptiness, free itself from all spirit of possession. When it has renounced all self-seeking it can be united to the divine will.[2] It is thus that the soul produces silence within and renders itself able to receive the visit of God and to hear his voice.

"Understand for certain, my dear children," continues Tauler, "that if some other than Jesus come to speak in the temple, Jesus immediately is silent, as though he were not there; and indeed he is not when the soul receives within it strange guests to hold converse with them. For Jesus to speak in the depths of the soul it must be alone and silent; it is then that he enters in and begins to speak."[3]

Having reached this supreme degree of renunciation, "we resign, through love, our will and all that belongs to us to the free will of God, in such a way that we are unable, nor do we desire, to will otherwise than God wills. Thus is our will freely taken and cloistered by love in the will of God without return."[4]

This beautiful teaching as to renunciation is pushed too far by Tauler. Doubtless the famous mystic is not formally a Quietist; to accuse him of it would be an injustice. But truth obliges us to recognize that, in certain of his *Sermons*, his prepossession for reducing our own will to nothingness has caused him to disregard, at least in word, the rights of the virtue of hope.[5]

[1] *Sermon II for Palm Sunday*, i, 355, 356. Cf. *Sermon II for Pentecost*, ii, 24: "Thou shouldst go out from and empty thyself entirely of thy self-will, of thy love and of thy own thoughts. Even more, if heaven were to lie open before thee, thou shouldst, before entering there, ask if it be the will of God."

[2] Tauler. Cf. *Sermon of Sexagesima*, i, 244 ff.

[3] Tauler, *Sermon II for Palm Sunday*, i, 358. Cf. *Sermon for the Eighth Sunday after Trinity*.

[4] Ruysbroeck, *Book of the Seven Cloisters*, chap. xiii, French Benedictine translation, i, 178.

[5] The teaching of Tauler was also criticized in the sixteenth century by Ekkius. It fell to Blosius to defend the famous Dominican. Henry Harphius also puts forward exaggerated teaching on renunciation of our own will, pushed to the extent of indifference. *Theologica mystica*, lib. I, viii-xii, Rome ed., p. 132 ff.

It is true that we must not be too attached to the sensible joys which are to be found in the service of God, but ought we wholly to renounce the *thought* of heavenly joy as he advises?

"Yes, my son," he says, "thou shouldst go out of thyself in such a way that thou love him alone and that thou seek neither pleasure nor profit nor the advantages that he is able to provide, but only his glory, even though he might never reward thee for it, although thou knowest well to the contrary; but the thought of the reward should be as though veiled and never occur to thy mind. Thou shouldst only consider his glory; thy heart should as it were melt in its love for him; so that thou forget thyself entirely and that thou never seek in God anything of thine own, otherwise thou wouldst perform thy good works not for him but for thyself."[1]

II—THE GERMAN THEORY OF THE NAKEDNESS OF THE INTELLIGENCE

IN mystical union the will of man is identical with the will of God; also it should prepare for this identification by prolonged exercises of more and more perfect submission to the divine will.

An intellectual preparation is thus needful, for intimate union with God implies a transcendent knowledge of the divinity. This preparation is only achieved when man reaches the "nakedness of the intelligence." This "nakedness of the intelligence" corresponds with intellectual purification, the groundwork of contemplation in the pseudo-Dionysius. Its functions are explained in the scholastic theory of knowledge.

According to the Thomist philosophy the things we know are first of all sensible. "The senses gather from the objects which surround them images which represent them to us."[2] These images or phantoms (*phantasmata*), kinds of portraits of outward things, are preserved in the memory.[3] "Then comes the intellect which takes away, by a kind of abstraction, all that yet remains of the material and sensible, thus rendering them intelligible. They assume, so to speak,

---

[1] Tauler, *Sermon for Sexagesima*, i, 245-246. Père Noël, in his Introduction and notes to his translation of the Latin version of Surius of the *Œuvres complètes* of Tauler, tries to justify Tauler.

[2] Tauler, *Sermon II for the Vigil of Epiphany*, i, 158.

[3] The German mystics, like the scholastics, divided the faculties of the soul into memory, understanding and will. Tauler, *Sermon I for Christmas*, i, 98; Albert the Great, *De adhaer. Deo*, cap. ii. We have seen what must be done with the will towards mystical union. It remains to see the ·treatment to which memory and understanding should be subjected.

the nature of reason."[1] It is the active intellect which thus strips sensible images to make of them intelligible species which it commits to the passive intellect. The latter transforms them into intellectual representations or ideas.[2]

We must bear in mind that the school calls *image* the sensible imaginative representation of an object, and intelligible *species* the abstract form of this object, suggested to the passive intellect in order to become an idea. Now in order to reach contemplation the mind must be completely freed from both images and species, for it should be raised above the sensible and intellectual to be closely united to God.

" Happy he," we read in the treatise *De adhaerendo Deo,* " who continually expunges from his mind sensible representations and images; who retires within himself and there raises himself to God; who finally ends by, in a manner, forgetting sensible forms, and thus attains inwardly, with naked, simple and pure intelligence and a like will, to the object of the most complete simplicity to God. Cast away then from thy mind all phantoms (*phantasmata*), species, images and forms, created and unconcerned with God, in order to be occupied inwardly with the Lord with the intelligence, heart and will entirely naked. For the end of all spiritual exercises is this : to be carried towards the Lord God and to repose inwardly in him through fully purified intelligence and most fervent love, without sensible images and without fetters."[3]

We may remark that in Tauler's *Institutions*[4] the soul must have arrived at a certain state of perfection in order to banish every image from the mind. It would be harmful to wish too soon to become attached to God by an act of pure understanding freed from all imagination. For images connected with repentance and with past faults, with the life and passion of the Saviour, are useful and sanctifying. He who has not long dwelt on these would not be able to raise himself to holiness. But there comes a moment when these images make little impression, and the soul feels within itself an ardent thirst for the Sovereign Good; it has a lively desire to be united to the divine nature. When anyone feels himself affected in this way he not only may, but even rightly should, strip himself of all images, although holy, of which he may have previously made use. He will then dwell on the divine essence and on the Holy Trinity.

[1] Tauler, *Sermon II for the Vigil of Epiphany,* i, 158.
[2] *Cf.* Tauler, *Sermon for the Sunday before Epiphany.*
[3] *De adhaer. Deo,* cap. iv. *Cf.* cap. vi, viii. *Cf.* Ruysbroeck, *Mirror of Eternal Salvation,* chap. xix; *Seven Degrees of Spiritual Love,* chap. xiii; *Adornment of the Spiritual Marriage,* lib. II, chaps. ii-iv; Suso, *Life,* chap. lv; *Book of Truth,* chap. v.
[4] *Institutions,* chap. xxxv.

" And if we would know," the *Institutions* go on to say,
" why the soul that has reached a certain state should
renounce every kind of image, it is because these are only a
means to lead us to the full naked truth. If, then, I wish
to reach this truth, I must leave behind me, little by little,
the road which leads to it; I must follow in order all the
thoughts which guide me to it, beginning by the lowest, then
passing to those that are halfway, and raising myself at last
to the most lofty in order not to lose a single point of the
truth which I seek. For one of the most noble occupations
of man during this life is to be transported by reason into the
ideas that represent the divinity."[1]

The German mystics, in accordance with a very general
tradition, teach that mystical union takes place with the
divine essence and not with the humanity of Christ, although
it is through this humanity that we reach the divinity.[2]

Now there is no image capable of enabling us to know God
and of uniting us to him, for he surpasses infinitely all our
conceptions. The incomprehensibility of God, following the
example set by Dionysius, is pushed very far by our mystics.
We know God in a purely negative manner. Suso also, with
a reminiscence of Eriugena, calls God a *nothing,* an *eternal
nothingness ;*[3] for none of the names which we give him are
applicable to him.

" We are unable to speak of him," he declares; " I mean
as of something that can be signified by speech. After all
said and done nothingness cannot be signified, it cannot be
said what it is, however great a teacher one may be or however many books one may write. But so far as words can
tell this nothingness may be reason, being, joy; which is true,
but far from the truth, and much further from it than an
ignorant rustic's talk about a real pearl."[4]

The intelligence, acting according to the natural order
which makes use of forms and images, will then never truly
know God. This is why, if it would attain to contemplation
in which God is truly known, it should cease to act. God will
then act within it. " Theologians teach us," says Tauler,

[1] The *Institutions* of Tauler, chap. xxxv, Fr. trans., Paris 1899,
p. 340. Cf. *Sermon I for Christmas; Sermon VI for Pentecost.*
[2] Tauler, *Sermon for the Twenty-third Sunday after Trinity;* Suso,
Book of Truth, chap. iv; Ruysbroeck, *Mirror of Eternal Salvation,*
xviii.
[3] Suso, *id.,* chap. i : " God might be called an eternal nothingness;"
chap. v : " This nothingness according to unanimous consent called
God;" Thiriot, ii, 219, 239. *Cf.* Albert the Great, *De adhaer. Deo,*
cap. ix. John Scotus Eriugena makes use of the word nothing to
express the ineffability of God. *De divisione naturae,* lib. II, cap.
xxviii-xxx.
[4] *Book of Truth,* chap. v; Thiriot, ii, 240. *Cf.* Tauler, *Sermon for
the Sunday before Epiphany.*

"that there is in us an active intelligence, and another that is passive. The former contemplates images and outward things, or extracts from them forms which it strips of all that is material and accidental, and these it afterwards deposits in the passive intellect which transforms them into spiritual images. The passive intellect, after having been, as it were, fertilized by the active intellect, preserves the images thus received and knows by means of them the things which the active intellect conveys to it. It cannot, however, know them unless the active intellect renews its enlightenment. Now that which the intellect performs in the natural man, God does in the same way in the man detached from all things. He removes, so to speak, the active intellect, puts himself in its place and effects what it would do; for this man, by freeing himself from all personal activity, in a manner, reduces the intellect to silence. God then must needs act in its place and himself provide the passive intellect with its object and its light."[1]

If the intellect be stripped of itself it becomes raised to the simple and pure mind, it receives the brightness of the splendour of the divine light which takes the place of the light of reason.[2] " In contemplation," says Ruysbroeck, " man passes beyond all his powers and their activity and arrives at a state of void in simple nature and at purity of mind. Now this state of void is the disappearance of all images. Simple nature is the regard turned towards eternal truth. Purity of mind is union with the mind of God.[3] . . . Thereby is shown the eternal truth which floods our naked sight— that is, the eye of our soul, the essence, the life and the work of which consists in contemplating, flying, running, and in ever passing beyond our created being. . . ."[4] Having reached " the divine darkness, to that delightful state in which all forms and all images are silent," to that supernatural and divine silence in which all is calm and peaceful,[5] the soul shares in the very knowledge of God. It then learns far more than would be possible with its natural reason.[6]

[1] Tauler, *Sermon for the Sunday before Epiphany*, i, 136-137. Cf. *Sermon III for the Fifth Sunday after Trinity*.
[2] *id.*, *Sermon II for the Vigil of Epiphany*.
[3] Ruysbroeck, *Mirror of Eternal Salvation*, chap. xix. Benedictine translation, i, 132.
[4] *ibid.*, chap. xviii. Cf. *Kingdom of the Lovers of God*, chaps. xxxi-xxxiv.
[5] Tauler, *Sermon II for the Twentieth Sunday after Trinity*, ii, 453.
[6] *id.*, *Sermon for the Sunday before Epiphany*, i, 187 : " The active intellect can never [of itself] have two images at the same time. . . . Now, when God himself fertilizes the passive intellect, he engenders there several images at a time. . . . But these images are not of ourselves . . . they are the work of the Master of nature." Cf. *Sermon II for Epiphany*, etc.

This teaching is quite correct. Nevertheless, has not German mysticism a tendency to reduce mystical union to a purely passive state?[1]

Doubtless it acknowledges that Christian perfection, speaking generally, implies the necessity of works. Tauler is very positive on this point when he speaks of the false mystics of his time. " No one," he says, " ought to be free with the liberty of the children of God without keeping his commandments and practising virtue. No one is able to be united to God in the complete void if he have neither charity nor divine desire in the heart. No one can become holy without good works."[2] It is, however, to be regretted that, in several of his *Sermons*,[3] he makes use of expressions which tend greatly to restrict the usefulness of works in the spiritual life.

In any case, according to Tauler, mystical contemplation is a state of almost complete passiveness. At the moment that it takes place the intellectual faculties are stripped not only of every image or species, but also of all activity. " In order that God may act properly within thee," he says, " thou must be in an absolute void, so that all thy powers are stripped of their activity and of their possessions that they be in a state of pure negation of themselves, deprived of all their energy and leaning only on their pure and simple nothingness. The deeper the nothingness the more true and intimate union with God is essential. . . . If thou will that God speak to thy soul impose silence on all thy powers. There is no question here of action, but far rather of complete cessation of every act."[4]

Now the greater number of writers assert that the soul is not totally passive in the mystical state. We have heard ecstatics such as St Bridget, St Catherine of Siena, Bl. Angela of Foligno, tell us that if, during ecstasy, the body were asleep and unable to give an account of what was happening around it, their souls were awake to the extent of seeing supernatural things. The activity of the mind is then supernaturally raised in the mystical state; there is no complete cessation of every act, but rather superactivity.

[1] This tendency is not found in Ruysbroeck. Cf. *Adornment of the Spiritual Marriage*, Bk. II, chaps. lxxiv-lxxvi.
[2] *Sermon for the First Sunday in Lent*, i, 292, 293. Cf. *Sermon for the Sunday before Epiphany*.
[3] Tauler, *Sermon for Sexagesima; Sermon II for Epiphany; Sermons I and II for the Fifth Sunday after Trinity*.
[4] Tauler, *Sermon II for the Feast of Corpus Christi*, ii, 107. Cf. *Sermon II for the Seventeenth Sunday after Trinity*. Man has no longer any activity that belongs to him : it is God who effects that which takes place within him, and man is limited to receiving his action. *Sermon II for the Eighteenth Sunday after Trinity*.

III—MYSTICAL UNION ACCORDING TO THE GERMAN WRITERS

ACCORDING to Tauler[1] we are all called and invited to this intimate and tender union of the soul with God. He also teaches all the faithful without distinction what they must do to prepare for it.

Like all mystics he declares that it is inexpressible, and that it cannot be reached by knowledge alone. " The greatest doctors of Paris," he says, not without a certain slyness, " with all their science could not attain to it, and if they wished to speak of it they would be reduced to silence; the more they wished the less they would be able and the less would they understand. Neither an abundance of natural gifts nor the richness of supernatural gifts is able to bestow the understanding of them either on the saints or on the angels. And, nevertheless, a simple man, humble and given up to God, feels something of them inwardly, although he can neither understand it nor express it, so far is this union beyond the thought of every creature."[2]

The mystical union fills the heart of man with a lively joy. " When the true divine light, which is none other than God," says Tauler, " has arisen . . . it procures in an instant, for the man whom it enlightens, greater joy, contentment and delight than all those which the whole world can give us."[3] The beatitude which the contemplative state procures is a participation, passing and suited to our present condition, in the heavenly beatitude.[4]

It is divine love which brings about union of the soul with God. " There is, indeed, in love a uniting and transforming virtue. Love transforms him that loves into him that is loved, and *vice versa,* so that the two lovers become as nearly as possible one and the same."[5]

These general characteristics of mystical union are already

[1] *Sermon I for the Twentieth Sunday after Trinity,* ii, 441. Such also appears to have been the thought of Ruysbroeck, *Book of the Highest Truth,* chap. vii, and of Henry Suso. We know that many mystics reserve this union for those who are specially called to it by God.

[2] Tauler, *Sermon I for the Twentieth Sunday after Trinity,* ii, 441.

[3] *id., Sermon III for the Fifth Sunday after Trinity,* ii, 242, etc.

[4] Suso, *Book of Truth,* chap. iv : " The beatitude spoken of may be obtained in two ways. One is the more perfect, it is beyond all possibility here below. . . . But beatitude taken as being a participated communion is possible. . . ." Thiriot, ii, 232. *Cf.* Ruysbroeck, *Book of the Highest Truth,* chap. xii.

[5] Albert the Great, *De adhaerendo Deo,* cap. xii. *Cf.* Tauler, *Sermon for the First Sunday after Epiphany.* Ruysbroeck, *Adornment of the Spiritual Marriage,* Bk. III, chaps. iv-vi.

known to us. What is important to know is the philosophical explanation of this union as put forward by the German writers.

This explanation is based on the Neoplatonic theory, christianized by Dionysius the Areopagite, of the return of the soul to divine unity. We must briefly see, therefore, how our mystics understood this theory before showing how they utilized it.

According to the pantheistic teaching of Neoplatonism the multiple proceeds from divine unity, and it afterwards returns to that unity. The whole world is summed up in these two movements of beings : the one descending, by which the many go out from the one; the other ascending, which consists in the return of the many to the one.

The German mystics, following the Areopagite, stripped this theory of its pantheistic elements, and retained these two general ideas : we come from God and we return to him; we come from him by creation, and we return by contemplation.

All created beings, in fact, have existed eternally in the divine essence as in their exemplar. They have always been present in the thought of God as the prototype and model on which they have been created. So far as they conform to the divine idea all beings were, before their creation, one same thing with the essence of God, in the same way as ideas are one and the same with the intelligence which conceives them.

All creatures were then with God. From this unity the many have sprung. God has, in fact, created, in time, different beings conformably with the image that was in him. They then come from him, not as emanating from his substance, as say the Neoplatonists, but created according to the eternal concept.

" Eternally," says Suso, " all creatures are God in God, and have there no fundamental difference other than has been stated. So far as they are in God they are the same life, the same essence, the same power, they are the same One and nothing less. But when they go out from God by creation, when they take their own being, then each has its own particular being with the form proper to it, which gives it its natural essence." [1]

Man has then been created according to the eternal image which God has in himself. The German mystics teach that this image has been deposited in the higher part of our soul, and thus we have a resemblance with God, with the Blessed Trinity.

[1] Suso, *Book of Truth*, chap. iii; Thiriot, ii, 223. *Cf.* Tauler, *Sermon* II *for Palm Sunday*; Ruysbroeck, *Mirror of Eternal Salvation*, viii; *Adornment of the Spiritual Marriage*, Bk. III, chap. v; Albert the Great, *De adhaerendo Deo*, vii.

"God, the heavenly Father," says Ruysbroeck, "has created all men in his image and likeness. His image is his Son, his own eternal wisdom. . . . Thus, then, is this image, which is the Son of God, eternal before all creation. It is in relation with this eternal image that we have all been created. For in the most noble part of our soul, where dwell our higher powers, we are established in the state of an eternal and living mirror of God; we carry his eternal image engraved there, and no other image can ever enter. This mirror remains beneath the eye of God unceasingly, and thus has part with the image of God, engraved there to all eternity. It is in this image that God has known us in himself, before we were created, and that he knows us now, in time, created as we are for himself. This image is found essentially and personally in all mankind; each possesses it whole, entire and undivided, and all together not more than one alone. In this way we are all one, intimately united in our eternal image, which is the image of God and the source in us all of our life, and of our call into existence. Our created essence and our life are attached to it without mediation as to their eternal cause. Nevertheless, our created being does not become God any more than the image of God becomes a creature."[1]

This image which is thus in us appears to be a natural gift, for it is placed in us by God at the moment of the creation of the soul. On the other hand, its effects rather incline us to think that it is a supernatural grace. The German mystics are not clear as to this point in their system. Certainly they distinguish between the natural and the supernatural orders. Nevertheless, this distinction, to their minds, is not as sharply defined as among later theologians of the sixteenth century.

The image set in us is something divine. It is the divine image according to which we have been created. We are not, however, transformed thereby into the divine Being, for the soul which possesses it in its depths always remains distinct from God.

[1] Ruysbroeck, *Mirror of Eternal Salvation*, chap. viii, Benedictine French translation, i, 87-88. Tauler says the same thing : " Let us consider how we have been formed to the image of the Blessed Trinity. The divine image exists truly within us in a simple and natural manner, although less noble than that which it represents. . . . All the [doctors] . . . agree that it properly dwells in the higher powers— the memory, the understanding, the will. It is by means of these, in fact, that we are capable of receiving the Blessed Trinity and enjoying it. Other [doctors] place this image in the most intimate and most secret depths of the soul, where the soul possesses God really and essentially ; where God works, exists, rejoices in himself, and is united so firmly to the soul that it would be as impossible to tear him from it as to separate him from himself "—*Sermon* II *for Trinity Sunday*, ii, 81-82. *Cf.* Harphius, *Theologia mystica*, Rome 1586, 153, 396, 409.

This divine likeness exists, then, in all mankind, but very often it is hidden by sin and imperfections. The end of all the labour of the spiritual life is to free it, to make it appear and to unite us by it to God. By the practice of virtue, above all of renunciation, we arrive at the nakedness of the intelligence, and at that which is required in order to give ourselves up to contemplation.[1]

But the most important part of the theology of our mystics is that which deals with the return of man to God. This return will be accomplished in heaven. Here it can only be begun by mystical union.

The mystical union which constitutes this return to divine unity has three characters : it takes place in the essence of the soul and not in its faculties ; it admits of no mediation between the soul and God ; finally, it suppresses, in a way, the difference that exists between God and itself ; it is union without difference, and from that fact it is unity.

1. *Union in the Essence of the Soul.*

First of all, it is in the essence itself of the soul and not in its faculties, " in the most intimate and most secret depths of the soul "[2] that the union takes place. " The essence of the soul," says Suso, " is united to the essence of the nothingness [God], and the powers of the soul to the acts of the nothingness, to the acts which he performs within himself."[3]

In contemplation, man is then not united to God through the intelligence, the will or the memory, but through the very substance of the soul.

Bossuet declares this to be impossible and contrary to theology.[4] St Bernard and St Thomas Aquinas also both hold that the soul cannot perceive God except by means of an infused image and with the co-operation of its faculties.

Correct or not, this teaching is the logical outcome of the German system. In fact, mystical union can only take place where God has placed his image in us—that is, in the depth of the soul, in that depth which from its nature is incapable of receiving anything other than the divine being. For creatures cannot penetrate there ; they remain without, in the

---

[1] *Cf.* Ruysbroeck, *Mirror of Eternal Salvation*, chaps. x-xvi ; *Book of the Seven Cloisters*, chaps. x-xvi ; *Adornment of the Spiritual Marriage*, Bk. II.

[2] Tauler, *Sermon II for Trinity Sunday*, ii, 82 etc.

[3] Suso, *Book of Truth*, chap. v. *Cf.* Ruysbroeck, *Book of the Highest Truth*, chap. viii ; *Adornment of the Spiritual Marriage*, Bk. III, chaps, i, ii.

[4] *Instruction on States of Prayer*, Bk. I, viii. *Cf.* Gerson, *Epistola ad fratrem Bartholom. Carthus.* (*Gersonii opera*, vol. i, p. 61).

powers of the soul, where are gathered the images which created objects have imprinted in us. The depth of the soul, then, is the place where God dwells, where he is united to us, where " God the Father utters to us his Word."[1]

Moreover, the man who desires to arrive at mystical union should " withdraw himself from all his senses," collect all the lower powers, concentrate them in the higher, and shut himself up in the depth of his soul in order to unite himself to God.[2] It is in this way that he will go from the multiple to the one, according to the mystical progress so recommended by Dionysius the Areopagite.

2. Union without Mediation.

Since it takes place between the divine essence and the essence of the soul, mystical union does not admit of an intermediary ; the soul is united directly and immediately to God.[3] In the same way as the air is united without intermediary to the brightness and heat of the sun, and as the fire enters the red-hot iron directly, so is the inward man plunged in God.[4] Besides, there is no image that can intervene between the soul and the divinity which is higher than every image. This doctrine, since the time of Dionysius the Areopagite, is, as we know, admitted by many mystics.

It is because it takes place in the essence of the soul that mystical union is something obscure and full of darkness ; for we can only have knowledge through our powers, and these are only able to lay hold of and know objects through their images. Now, in the depth where God's action takes place, created images cannot enter.

" It is precisely," says Tauler, " because all images reach the soul from without that this mystery of union is hidden from it, and this is a great advantage for it. Lack of knowledge steeps it in admiration. It seeks to account to itself for that which takes place within it; it certainly feels that there is something, but knows not what it is. . . . It is this knowledge, full of ignorance and darkness, which causes us to be attached to the divine action within us and makes us seek to know it the more."[5]

[1] *Cf.* Tauler, *Sermon for the Sunday within the Octave of Christmas,* i, 111-112.

[2] *ibid.,* i, 116-117.

[3] Tauler, *Sermon for the Fifth Sunday after Epiphany,* i, 226.

[4] Ruysbroeck, *Book of the Highest Truth,* chap. viii. Ruysbroeck acknowledges a union by mediation, that which is obtained with God by grace (*id.,* chap. iii). With regard to mystical union it excludes all intermediary between God and the soul. *Adornment of the Spiritual Marriage,* Bk. III, chap. i, 2.

[5] Tauler, *Sermon for the Sunday within the Octave of Christmas,* i, 118.

It may also be pointed out that mystical union takes place directly with the divine essence, with the divine unity, and not immediately with the divine persons.

St Augustine has given us a description of the mystical union of his mind with the eternal wisdom. St Bernard has extolled the spiritual marriage of the soul with the divine Word. Dionysius the Areopagite had a conception of this union as of the return of man to the divine unity, and, since he inspires the German writers, the latter teach, like him, that the perfect man is united to the very essence of God, " in which the Trinity of the divine Persons possesses his nature in essential unity."[1] The soul is doubtless united to the divine Persons, to the Trinity eternally acting through the Persons, for wherever God is he acts : God the Father begets his Son, and, conjointly with him, produces the Holy Spirit. The soul is then united to the Trinity in his eternal activity, to God eternally acting according to the Persons. But mystical union implies repose, joy, beatitude; and it is in his essence, his unity, that God is eternally in repose, in beatitude. It follows that mystical union is finally achieved in the divine essence.[2]

United to the divine essence, the soul is then, through that essence, united to the three Persons of the Blessed Trinity. For God works in the soul. The production of the divine Persons, the generation of the Word and the procession of the Holy Spirit take place in the soul raised to mystical union.

" [God] acts in the soul by direct operation ; he acts in that depth where no image ever penetrates, which is only accessible to him ; this is what no creature is able to do. God the Father begets his Son in the soul, not like creatures by means of an image, but after the manner in which he engenders him in eternity. Would you know how the divine generation is accomplished? God the Father knows himself and enters perfectly into himself. He sees down into the uttermost depths of his being, and sees himself not by the help of an image but with his own essence. Thus it is that he begets his Son in the unity of the divine nature. It is also in this manner that he begets him in the depth and essence of the soul, and that he unites himself to it."[3]

In this ineffable union the heavenly Father speaks his eternal Word in the depth of the soul, and the same act which begets this Word engenders also the soul thus united.

[1] Ruysbroeck, *Book of the Highest Truth,* chap. xii. See *Book of Truth,* Suso.

[2] Ruysbroeck, *Mirror of Eternal Salvation,* chaps. xxiii-xxv ; *Seven Degrees of Spiritual Love,* xiii-xiv ; *Book of the Seven Cloisters,* chap. xv.

[3] Tauler, *Sermon for the Sunday within the Octave of Christmas,* vol. i, p. 114. See in Noel, *op. cit.,* an explanation of what Tauler means by the depth of the soul.

The eternal Father may then say of the Christian thus transformed into God : Thou art my beloved Son.

" Let him who desires to feel these things," continues Tauler, " enter into himself; let him be uplifted high above all images and all operations of the inward and outward powers, above all that has come to him from without; and let him afterwards become wholly lost and melted in his own innermost depths.   Then it is that the power of the Father comes to him and calls him, both by itself and by his only Son.   And in the same way that the Son is begotten of the Father and flows back into the Father whence he came, thus is this man engendered by the Father into the Son, and flows back into the Father with the Son and becomes only one with him.   It is of such a man that God said : *Thou shalt call me Father,* and thou shalt not cease to enter in after me; this day have I begotten thee through my Son and in my Son.   Then also does the Holy Spirit pervade those depths with ineffable love and joy, and flood them wholly with his gifts."[1]

This teaching can quite well be reconciled with the theology concerning the adoptive divine filiation of the Christian. But with the mystic this filiation is, at certain moments, conscious.   The soul feels, in some way, the divine contact, and receives therefrom an immeasurable joy.

Ruysbroeck compares this direct contact to the divine essence with the essence of the soul to touch.   It is a divine touch which inebriates the soul with happiness.   " [Man] feels within himself," he says, " this divine touch of God, which is a renewal of grace and of all divine virtue.   And you must know that this grace of God penetrates to the lower powers, that it touches the heart of man, evoking in it a tender love and a sensible attraction towards God.   This love and this attraction penetrate the heart and the senses, the flesh and the blood and all corporal nature, giving to the whole man such an impulsion and impatience that often he does not know what to do.   He is in a condition like that of a drunken man who has lost command of himself."[2]

3. *Union without Difference.*

But immediate union between the essence of the soul and the divine essence is not yet unity.   It is then necessary to

[1] Tauler, *Sermon* II *for Trinity Sunday*, ii, p. 84.
[2] Ruysbroeck, *Book of the Highest Truth*, chap. ix.   Cf. *Book of the Seven Cloisters,* chap. xv.   Henry Suso also makes use of the comparison of an inebriated man to express the joy experienced by the mystic.   *Book of Truth*, chap. iv.   Harphius teaches that this union, this spiritual marriage of the soul with God, brings about inseparability (*inseparabilis conjunctio*).   This expression is obviously exaggerated.   *Theol. myst.* lib. I, cap. ci, pp. 422 ff.   No mystical state carries with it the assurance of never being separated from God by sin.

go still further and to arrive at a form of union in which the soul is no longer conscious of being distinct from God, although in reality it is so. It must no longer perceive any difference between itself and God. This is *union without difference,* the highest mystical union, as pictured by the German school.

This union consists in a sort of return of the soul to the divine type, according to which we were created, and God has deposited it in our souls. The inward man, at the zenith of perfection, thus comes back to the point of departure, to his uncreated being, existing in the divine essence. In this way he realizes as fully as possible his return to divine Unity.

How is this possible? Tauler often speaks of this *union without difference,* but without much effort to explain it. " In this state," he says, " [the soul] is as though lost, it can no longer either know itself or find itself; it no longer knows anything but the infinitely simple being of God.[1] . . . These two gifts of the Holy Spirit [understanding and wisdom] lead man in a supernatural manner into the depth and into the divine abyss, where God knows himself and understands himself, where he tastes with delight his own wisdom and his own essence. The mind becomes lost so deeply in this abyss that it no longer knows anything of itself, distinguishing no longer either its words, its actions, its ways, its tastes, the things it knows or its life; for all is a single wellbeing, simple, pure, one; an ineffable abyss, an essential unity.[2] . . . The soul and the body are lost in a manner in this profound sea [God], and man loses, so to speak, the natural activity of his powers. . . . It is thus that the abyss created draws to itself the abyss uncreated, and that these two form, in a manner, one single divine being; for the mind of man is lost in the mind of God."[3]

Such expressions would be disturbing were it not that in one of his sermons Tauler protests strongly against false mystics who thought themselves to be, " in a manner, God himself, in the lofty contemplations to which they were uplifted to the divinity."[4]

Henry Suso also makes use of very strong expressions to characterize the union without difference. " [In this union] man forgets himself," he says, " and has no longer know-

---

[1] Tauler, *Sermon III for the Fifth Sunday after Trinity,* ii, 226.

[2] *id., Sermon III for Pentecost,* ii, 42.

[3] Tauler, *Sermon II for the Fifth Sunday after Trinity,* ii, 234. Cf. *Sermon I for New Year's Day,* i, 127 : " Man has passed from creatures into God, from the natural being to the divine." Cf. *Sermon I for the Thirteenth and the Seventeenth Sundays after Trinity.*

[4] *Sermon for the Twenty-first Sunday after Trinity,* ii, 466. Tauler often insists, in his sermons, on the distinction between the mystic and God.

ledge of himself, he disappears, loses himself in God, and
becomes one mind with him, just as a little drop of water is
drowned in a quantity of wine."[1] Everything takes place in
mystical union as though the soul were wholly identified
with God. It cannot perceive any difference between God
and itself. In its eyes the divine Being must not be other
than that which it itself is. Nevertheless, in the depth of its
being it remains distinct from God, nor does it confuse itself
with him.

"Dost thou not understand," Suso declares, "that this
powerful and annihilating return to nothingness causes, on
the whole, all difference to disappear, not as regards being,
but as regards our way of understanding. . . . The soul
always remains a creature; but when it is lost in nothingness
it does not know whether it is a creature or nothing; if it be
united or no."[2]

It is thus that the soul returns to God to become lost in
him, to see every difference disappear, whilst still remaining
a creature. It is not easy to reconcile these two apparent
contradictions.[3]

Meister Eckhart solved the difficulty, as we know, by an
explanation which appeared to identify the mystical soul with
God. Henry Suso sought for an orthodox solution in his
Book of Truth, and involved himself in incomprehensible
ambiguities which frightened his superiors.[4]

As far as his idea can be understood, the unity of the
mystical soul with God is not a unity of nature—which would
be Pantheism—but a unity brought about by the entrance of
the soul into the very knowledge of God and into his beatitude. In this state the soul knows nothing else but God, it
no longer knows itself; it also rejoices in the very joy of
God in unspeakable repose.[5]

Ruysbroeck explains this more fully. Union without

[1] Suso, Book of Truth, chap. iv; Thiriot, ii, 230.
[2] Suso, Book of Truth, chap. v; Thiriot, ii, 241, 244.
[3] In this connection, Henry Suso said: "If man is unable to understand two contraries—that is, two contrary things in one—then truly
and undoubtedly it is difficult to explain this to him. If at last he
understand it, then indeed he has already travelled halfway along the
road which leads to the life of which I wish to speak." Book of Truth,
chap. v; Thiriot, ii, 237.
[4] It was after these explanations in his Book of Truth that Suso was
accused of teaching false doctrine by the chapters of Bois-le-Duc and
Bruges (1335-1336).
[5] Suso, Book of Truth, chap. v: "The soul, once it has reached the
pure contemplation of God, takes all its life and all its being into the
depths of this nothingness, and draws thence all that it is, so that it
is full of happiness. Speaking according to the method of being that
belongs to this contemplation, it knows nothing either of knowledge or
of love or anything else. It reposes solely and entirely in nothingness,
it knows nothing unless it be that Being which is God and nothingness."
Thiriot, ii, 245.

difference consists in a species of annihilation of the soul through enjoyment of the essence of God.[1]

The love which brings about mystical union is essentially one of joy; the distinction between itself and God is suppressed in the sense that the soul is made to enter into the same joy and beatitude as the divine essence. Ruysbroeck always places joy, repose, beatitude in God, in the divine unity, in the divine essence, as distinct from divine activity. It is in the divine essence that the three Persons enjoy essential beatitude.[2] This is why, through union without difference, the soul enters into the divine beatitude, is united to the divine essence and becomes one with it.

"Then," he says, "comes unity without difference; for the love of God ought not only to be considered as overflowing with all joys and inwardly conducing to unity, but, freed from all distinction : it is an essential rejoicing, according to the naked essence of the divinity. Enlightened men have discovered within themselves a deep and essential contemplation, unreasoning and above reason, and an inclination to rejoice which surpasses every mode and every essence, plunging them into the abyss of unfathomable beatitude where the Trinity of divine Persons possesses its nature in essential unity. Here beatitude is so simple and without plan that all essential contemplation fades away, as does all inclination and distinction of creatures. For all uplifted minds become melted and annihilated by the joy they find in the essence of God, who is the superessence of all essence. There they escape from themselves and are lost in a fathomless lack of knowledge. All brightness is brought back to darkness, where the three Persons enter again into unity and rejoice without distinction in essential unity. This beatitude is essential to God alone : to all spirits it is superessential. In fact, no created essence is able to become one with the essence of God and itself perish, for then the creature would become God, which is impossible."[3]

Ruysbroeck, in his treatise on *The Adornment of Spiritual Marriage,* seems to explain more clearly this return to the divine unity.

The soul, through mystical union, must lose, in some measure, its own likeness in order to return to the likeness, to the divine idea, according to which it was created. This divine likeness, placed in the depth of the soul at its creation, must be entirely freed by contemplation. By means of this likeness the soul must be, so to speak, absorbed. In the divine essence it would thus find the ideal existence which it had in God before it was created. It would then see God

---

[1] Ruysbroeck, *Book of the Highest Truth,* chap. xii.
[2] *ibid.*
[3] *ibid., Œuvres de Ruysbroeck l'Admirable,* ii, 220-221.

with a brightness which is the divine essence; it would even be this divine brightness. Therefore, as in the divine essence are found the ideas according to which God created souls, the mystic returns to the divine essence and unity, without, however, being confused with God or losing his personality.

It is thus that John Gerson[1] understood Ruysbroeck, although, without accusing him of Pantheism, he keenly reproaches him for making use of expressions which seemed to suppress all distinction between God and the contemplative soul. I do not pretend to state whether Gerson's interpretation of Ruysbroeck's theory be correct. It is difficult to grasp the exact sense of certain formulas employed by the mystics.[2] It must be admitted, however, that several of those which Ruysbroeck makes use of are somewhat confusing.

" All that lives in the Father, in the secret unity," he says, " lives in the Son in the full light of the outward flow; and the simple depth of our eternal likeness ever dwells in darkness without form, whilst the immeasurable brightness which shines in the bosom of this darkness makes manifest and reveals the secret of God; and all those who are uplifted above their created being to the contemplative life are one with this divine brightness. They are the brightness itself, and they see, feel and discover beneath this divine light that, according to their ideal or uncreated being, they are themselves this abyss of simplicity, whence the brightness shines forth

[1] *Epistola ad Bartholomaeum Carthus. super tertia parte libri Joannis Ruysbroeck. De ornatu spiritualium nuptiarum: ponit autem tertia pars libri praefati quod anima perfecte contemplans Deum, non solum videt eum per claritatem quae est divina essentia, sed est ipsamet claritas divina. Imaginatur enim sicut scriptura sonat quod anima tunc desinit esse in illa existentia quam prius habuit in proprio genere et convertitur seu transformatur et absorbetur in esse divinum, et illud esse ideale defluit quod habuit ab aeterno in essentia divina, de quo esse dicit Joannes in Evangelio: Quod factum est in ipso vita erat* (John i, 3, 4). *Gersonii opera,* vol. i, p. 60. *Cf.* p. 61: *Tanquam videlicet anima desineret existere in esse proprio et transformaretur in illud esse divinum ideale quale habuit in Deo ab aeterno. Sermo in Coena Domini, de humilitate: ut dicit Averroes: Tu sola videns videntem insequeris. Tu sola sognitive ad principium tuum regrederis, ut fias unum ens cum divina essentia. Tertia parte libelli, De ornatu spiritualium nuptiarum. Anima, inquit, contemplantis, ita conjungitur Deo, ut fiat ipsum illud esse vitale et ideale quod aeternaliter in Deo praehabuit.* Vol. iii, pp. 1121-1125. Several of Ruysbroeck's contemporaries thought they could discover inexactitudes also in the treatise *Adornment of the Spiritual Marriage.* Cf. *Ruysbroeck l'Admirable,* Benedictine translation, vol. iii, Introduction, pp. 15-17. See also Bossuet, *Instruction sur les états d'oraison,* Bk. I, I, i-v.

[2] See John de Schoonhoven's defence of Ruysbroeck against Gerson, *Gersonii opera,* i, pp. 63 ff. Gerson, however, admitted that the writings of Ruysbroeck were free from error. But he declared that the obscurity of the formulas used by the famous mystic rendered them dangerous. Gerson's answer to the letter of Schoonhoven will be found in *Gersonii opera,* vol. i, pp. 80 ff.

without limit in divine modes, and, according to the simplicity
of being, remains within wholly and eternally simple, without
modes. . . . Thus do contemplatives attain to their eternal
type, in the likeness of which they were created, and they
contemplate God and all things with a simple regard and
without distinction in the divine brightness. . . . God wills
that we go out from ourselves to the divine light, and that
we strive to attain supernaturally to this likeness, which is
our own proper life, in order to possess it with him in an
active and fruitful way in eternal beatitude. . . ."[1]

" He who is united to God by contemplation, and is enlightened by the truth, can understand it through itself. For
to grasp and understand God, as, beyond all comparison he
is in himself, is to be God with God, without any obstacle or
mediation being possible between him and us.[2] . . . [The
mind] receives the brightness which is God himself, above
every gift and every work of the creature, in that free empty-
ing of the mind, in which, through the love of joy, it loses
itself and receives the divine brightness without mediation,
all transformed at once into this very brightness which it
receives.[3] . . . The mind becomes so freely opened in order
to clasp the bridegroom when he presents himself that it is
transformed into the very immensity which it grasps. This
is to embrace and to see God through God himself, in which
consists all our beatitude."[4]

If we did not know from other sources how strongly Ruysbroeck insists on the permanent distinction between God and
the soul in mystical union, might we not be justified in understanding these expressions in a heterodox sense? But the
writings of mystics, even more than those of others, must
be interpreted in their obscure passages by those which are
clear. Nor must we forget, moreover, that Henry Suso and
Ruysbroeck have been beatified by the Church, and that she
has thus, in a measure, upheld the orthodoxy of their
teaching.

This being said, it is permissible to express regret that the
German mystical writers in certain passages employ an am-
biguous and obscure terminology capable of being understood in an erroneous sense. The contemporaries of Ruysbroeck were dissatisfied with his use of " expressions which
had to be qualified " because, " if taken literally, they would
be faulty."[5] Nor do we find this judgement too severe. We
may also be allowed to think that the German writers were

---

[1] *Adornment of the Spiritual Marriage*, Bk. III, chap. v; Fr. trans.,
iii, p. 215-216.
[2] *id.*, chap. i, p. 208.
[3] *id.*, chap. ii, p. 210.
[4] *id.*, chap. iii, p. 212.
[5] Henry of Langenstein, in a letter to Gerard Groot, written in 1383.
Cf. *Œuvres de Ruysbroeck;* Benedictine translation, vol. iii, p. 16.

too strict in their application to contemplation of the Dionysian principle of the return of the soul to divine unity.

From these points of view the German mystics of the fourteenth century, in spite of their great merits, cannot unreservedly be praised.

CHAPTER IX

PRACTICAL MYSTICISM AT THE END OF THE FOURTEENTH AND IN THE FIFTEENTH CENTURIES IN THE LOW COUNTRIES

MODERN DEVOTION : THE BRETHREN OF THE COMMON LIFE : GERARD GROOT, THE CANONS REGULAR OF WINDESHEIM, THOMAS À KEMPIS —THE PROBLEM OF THE ORIGIN OF THE " IMITATION OF CHRIST "[1]

TOWARDS the end of the fourteenth century we find a reaction from speculative spirituality. The theories which we have just been studying seem to have produced a feeling of lassitude. They might satisfy the mind, but what was their practical utility? Some of them even led to error. Hence we find a very pronounced return to affective spirituality, tentative and without system or art, reduced to simple practice, without linking together or reasoning, which had in view solely counsel for souls suitable to their needs rather than inquiry into the mysteries of mystical union.

Next, what was the use of these abstract studies when there was so much to be done that was better? In the fourteenth and fifteenth centuries the much-needed reform of the Church was spoken of on every side. The yearning of the *Imitation of Christ,* probably familiar at that time, must very often have been expressed. " If men would only use as

---

[1] Chief sources : Thomas À Kempis, *Vitae Gerardi Magni et Florentii; Chronicon montis Sanctae Agnetis (Opera omnia Thomae À K.,* ed. Amort, Cologne 1759, vol. iii). Gerardi Groot, *Epistolae,* ed. Acquoy, Amsterdam 1857. John Busch, Canon Regular of Windesheim, *Chronicon canonic. reg. Capituli Windesemensis,* ed. Rosweyd, Antwerp 1621. *De viris illustribus de Windesem; De origine modernae devotionis.* Dr. Pohl, *Thomae Hemerken À Kempis opera'omnia,* now being published at Freiburg im B., vols. i-vi published, 1902-1918. *Cf.* Acquoy, *Het Klooster te Windesheim en sijn invloed,* Utrecht 1875-80, 3 vols. Auger, *Etude sur les mystiques du Pays-Bas du moyen âge,* in the *Mémoires* crowned by the Belgian Academy, Brussels 1892. See also further on, the bibliography on the *Imitation.*

much diligence in rooting out vices and planting virtues as they do in proposing questions there would not be such great evils committed, nor scandals among the people, nor such relaxation in the monasteries."[1]

Disillusionment as regards knowledge, formerly felt by St Bernard, and expressed with such force at the beginning of the *Imitation,* is again met with in men's minds at the end of the fourteenth century. This was doubtless one of the reasons that made the *Imitation* so much beloved in this Low Countries environment.

" What doth it avail thee to discourse profoundly of the Trinity if thou be void of humility and, consequently, displeasing to the Trinity? In truth lofty words make not a man holy and just; but a virtuous life maketh him dear to God. I had rather feel compunction than know its definition.[2] . . . Leave off that excessive desire of knowing, because there is found therein much distraction and deceit. Men of learning are very glad to appear and to be called wise. There are many things the knowledge of which is of little or no profit to the soul. And he is most unwise who attendeth to such things as serve not his salvation. . . . If thou wouldst know and learn anything to the purpose, love to be unknown and esteemed as nothing.[3] . . . Truly learned is he who doeth the will of God and renounceth his own will."[4]

Theories, then, must be let go in order to strive to live with fervour. Thus shall we bring about reform within ourselves and endeavour to reform others. With this end in view simple spiritual maxims, directly practical, without scientific pretensions, are suggested to pious souls for meditation.

I—THE " BRETHREN OF THE COMMON LIFE " AND THE CANONS REGULAR OF WINDESHEIM

THESE tendencies produced, towards the end of the fourteenth century, a very important mystical movement in Holland which was known as the *New Devotion.* It had as its pioneer a holy man, Gerard Groot,[5] and it produced

---

[1] *De Imit. Christi,* lib. I, cap. iii.
[2] *id.,* lib. I, cap. i.
[3] *ibid.,* cap. ii.
[4] *ibid.,* cap. iii. *Cf.* lib. III, cap. xliii. These thoughts doubtless were also found suitable in the time of St Bernard, when the scholastic method arose and Abelard startled the mystics by the boldness of his reasonings. This is why, if the *Imitation,* as we have it to-day, was obviously written in the Low Countries at the beginning of the fifteenth century, the elements it contains may have been much older.
[5] Busch, *Chronicon can. reg. cap. Windesemensis,* lib. II, cap. xvii : *Magister Gerardus Magnus primus fuit nostrae reformationis pater et totius Modernae Devotionis origo Cf.* Thomas A Kempis, *Vita Gerardi Magni.*

writers who have had the honour of being credited with the composition of the *Imitation of Christ.*

Gerard was born at Deventer, in Holland, in 1340. He first studied in the town of his birth, then at Aix-la-Chapelle, at Cologne and at the University of Paris, where he graduated as Master of Arts.[1] He afterwards returned to his own country and led a somewhat mundane life. He was converted in 1374, and retired to his paternal home with the first members of the association known as that of " The Common Life."

It was not, however, until 1381 that the confraternity of the *Brethren of the Common Life* was organized by the care of one of Gerard's disciples, Florentius Radewijns of Leerdam, a Master of Arts of the University of Prague. Gerard had gathered round him certain young clerks of Deventer capitular school in order to make copies of books of which he was a great lover. Florentius conceived the idea of forming a community of copyists; funding their resources in common to enable them to live. Such was the beginning of the *Brethren of the Common Life.*[2]

Its members did not take vows. They lived under the authority of Florentius and of Gerard Groot, dividing their time between the work of copying and pious exercises. Gerard, who was in touch with Ruysbroeck, would have liked to have given his disciples the Rule of the Canons Regular of St Augustine; but he died in 1384, before having realized his project. He left behind him a reputation for great virtue.[3] It was Florentius Radewijns[4] who finally organized the association.

The school at Deventer with its pious copyists remained as it was. But at Windesheim, between Deventer and Zwolle, a monastery was built, where the Rule of the Canons Regular of St Augustine was followed. Deventer became, in a sense, the noviciate of Windesheim.

Thus was the famous Congregation of Windesheim founded, which combined both the *Brethren of the Common Life* and Canons Regular.[5] It was approved by Pope Boniface IX in 1395. In 1464 it comprised eighty-two monasteries all attached to Windesheim. Among them was Groenendael and its foundations.

---

[1] E. du Boulay, *Hist. de l'Université de Paris,* vol. iv, 956.
[2] Busch, *Chronic. Wind.,* lib. I, cap. i; Thomas A Kempis, *Vita Florentii.*
[3] He was a deacon. None of his writings have come down to us.
[4] Florentius Radewijns died in 1400, at the age of fifty.
[5] There were also *Sisters of the Common Life.* The chronicle of their head house at Deventer has just been published by Dr. de Man, *Hier beginnen sommige stichtige punten van onsen oelden zusteren,* The Hague, 1919.

The *Brethren of the Common Life* and the Canons of
Windesheim excelled as copyists and possessed some famous
caligraphers. Their work was known to and praised by John
Gerson.[1] Printing at this period had not been discovered,
and works were multiplied through the copyists.

Gerard's foundation also brought about a genuine reform
in religious life. Its influence made itself felt in both Germany and France. But in the sixteenth century there came
a change. One part went over to the Protestant reformation,
and the remainder died out in the seventeenth century.

Many spiritual writers worthy of mention were nurtured in
the Congregation of Windesheim.[2] Their doctrine was at
first put forward without intent to teach in the form of
simple, practical, disconnected phrases. They were like a
series of maxims after the manner of Rochefoucauld or
Vauvenargues, except that they were maxims of piety.
Certain precepts of moral life, gathered together by his disciples, have come down to us from Florentius Radewijns.[3]
The organizer of the *Brethren of the Common Life*, in spite
of the close relations which existed between Groenendael and
Windesheim, seems to have inspired those around him with a
dislike of speculative spirituality. None of his disciples cultivated it; all, however, studied the writings of Ruysbroeck.

In the early days the Canons Regular of Windesheim did
not write books. They simply delivered conferences to their
brethren with the sole object of edifying them. These conferences were kept and compiled. Those who had the gift
added to them from their own knowledge. Thence we have
the *rapiaria* or collections of anonymous phrases. John Vos
de Huesden,[4] one of the first priors of Windesheim, was
famous for this kind of conference, so much so that some
writers have expressed the view that Thomas À Kempis
owed the teaching of the *Imitation of Christ* to him.[5]

The writers among the disciples of Florentius Radewijns
are : Gerard of Zutphen, Gerlac Peterson, Henry de Mande
and, above all, Thomas À Kempis.

---

[1] *De laude scriptorum. Gersonii opera,* vol. ii, p. 694, Antwerp
1706.

[2] *Cf.* Thomas À Kempis, *Vitae discipulorum Florentii,* ed. Amort,
vol. iii. Busch, *op. cit.*

[3] Thomas À Kempis placed them at the end of his *Vita Florentii. A
Tractatulus devotus de extirpatione vitiorum et passionum et de acquisi-
tione verarum virtutum.*

[4] He took the religious habit in 1388. An *Epistola de vita et passione
D.N.J.C., et aliis devotis exercitiis,* is attributed to him which might
have been only one of his conferences. But it is now admitted that he
was not the author of this *Epistola.*

[5] See Puyol, *L'auteur du livre " De Imitatione Christi,"* Paris 1899,
pp. 467-471, for unmistakable resemblances between the conference of
John Vos de Huesden and the *Imitation.*

The first of these has left us two books : the *Spiritual Ascents* and the *Exercises*. These are the oldest works on spirituality belonging to the " New Devotion."

After Thomas À Kempis, Gerlac Petersen (Gerlacus Petri)[1] is the most famous writer of his school. His reputation is due to his *Soliloquium cujusdam regularis*.[2] It is an inward monologue in which the soul addresses itself. Sometimes it changes to conversations and colloquies with God. It is a work similar both in gist and form to the *Imitation*. This suggests the question whether the *Imitation* was known to Gerlac or whether its author was inspired by him.

Light is thrown on one side of this problem by the writings of Henry de Mande, in which the *Imitation* is frequently and literally quoted.[3] Many of these writings are earlier than 1415. The *Imitation*, then, must either have been known to the Canons of Windesheim before this date or else the author of it must have copied from Mande.

Henry de Mande lived at the Court of William Count of Holland in his youth. Converted by the preaching of Gerard Groot, he entered Windesheim in 1392. He wrote several spiritual works in German, in which he treats of renunciation of the old man, of union with Christ, of the interior life, of the spiritual life and of the contemplative life. Like Gerlac Petersen he has left a colloquy of the devout soul with its well-beloved (*cum dilecto*); but his work is not so well known. He suffered from severe bodily infirmities which he bore with piety and thankfulness to God.[4]

John de Schoonhoven, Subprior of the convent of Groenendael, which was incorporated with the Congregation of Windesheim in 1413, wrote an epistle to his nephew Simon, from which the author of the *Imitation* must have copied several passages.[5] John de Schoonhoven was a disciple of Ruysbroeck; it was he who defended him against the attacks of Gerson. The letter to his nephew was written about 1383; it would seem that it was several years earlier than the *Imitation*.

[1] Born at Deventer in 1378; took the religious habit at Windesheim in 1403, and died there in 1411.

[2] Entitled also *Ignitum cum Deo soliloquium*, Cologne 1616. Gerlac also wrote a *Breviloquium de accidentiis exterioribus*, and another book, *De libertate spiritus*.

[3] *Cf.* Augustine de Backer, S.J., *Essai bibliographique sur le livre* " *De Imitatione Christi*," Liége 1864. V. Becker, *L'auteur de* " *l'Imitation* " *et les documents néerlandais*, The Hague 1882, pp. 170 ff.

[4] Busch, *Chronic. Windes.*, lib. II, cap. xliii.

[5] These passages are found in Bk I, chaps. ii, xiii, xx. Becker, *L'auteur de* " *l'Imitation*," pp. 177-180.

II—THOMAS À KEMPIS

THOMAS À KEMPIS, or Thomas Hemerken À Kempis, was born in 1379 or 1380 at Kempen, in the neighbourhood of Dusseldorf in the Rhine Province.[1] When thirteen years old he went to Deventer for his education, and in 1398 was admitted by Florentius Radewijns into his community of copyists.

The next year he went to the monastery of Mount Saint Agnes near Zwolle, where his brother, John À Kempis, was Prior of a community of Canons Regular of St Augustine. After eight years of probation he made his profession there, and some years after, in 1413 or 1414, he was raised to the priesthood. He died in 1471, Subprior of his convent.

Thomas lived in calm and peace, surrounded with books. His life is summed up in his Flemish device : *In Haeckens und Braeckens,* " In little corners and little books." He copied books—his reputation as a caligrapher was widely extended—he also composed them. He is looked upon as the most noteworthy ascetical writer of his school; the *Imitation,* the literary style of which is wonderfully like his own, was attributed to him.

His work is divided into two parts : an ascetic part, which comprises a considerable number of tracts and sermons; and an historical part, containing the biographies of Gerard and his disciples.[2] He also wrote the history of St Lydwine of Schiedam (1380-1433), that Dutch virgin who lived a life of sickness and suffering, the mystical role of which she made so apparent.[3]

In his tracts and in his sermons Thomas À Kempis deals with monastic life and virtues,[4] the interior life,[5] the life and

---

[1] *Cf.* Dr. Pohl, article on *Thomas Hemerken À Kempis,* in the *Kirchenlexicon.* No biography of Thomas À Kempis was left by his contemporaries. German writers call him Thomas Hemerken À Kempis, as he calls himself in the *Chronicle of Mount St Agnes,* in which he writes the history of his convent.

[2] The tracts and sermons are contained in the first six volumes of Dr. Pohl's *Thomae Hemerken À Kempis opera omnia,* Freiburg im Breisgau, 1902-1918. The historical part will be in vols. vii and viii, which have not yet appeared.

[3] *Vita Lidewigis virginis,* Pohl, vi, 315 ff. *Cf.* Huysmans, *Sainte Lydwine de Schiedam,* Paris 1901.

[4] *Liber de tribus tabernaculis; De fideli dispensatore; De disciplina claustralium; Epistola devota ad quemdam regularem; Libellus spiritualis exercitii; Brevis admonitio spiritualis exercitii; Alphabetum monachi; Epitaphium monachorum; Vita boni monachi; Sermones ad novicios.*

[5] *De vera compunctione; De recognitione propriae fragilitatis; Recommendatio humilitatis; De mortificata vita; De bona pacifica vita; Manuale parvulorum; Doctrinale juvenum; De solitudine et silentio; Hospitale pauperum.*

passion of Christ,[1] the Virgin Mary, and lastly, with mystical union.[2] No theory is to be found there. The teaching is always set forth in a simple unvaried style in the form of counsels or sentences.

This is how he recommends the religious to keep to his cell :

" Be careful to keep thy cell that it may keep thee. There is no safer place here below for the servant of God ; there are we hidden, and there we pray freely to the heavenly Father behind closed doors. It is ever dangerous to leave one's cell ; to remain there is to find rest and true devotion. He who accustoms himself to his cell quickly finds peace of heart and is sheltered from many and very great dangers. Solitude is the mother of devotion, whereas the soul is troubled by a throng. Christ, who could not escape the crowd, nevertheless often removed himself far away. The solitary life is pleasing to God and to the angels ; it is ever the friend of peace."[3]

In the monastery the religious should observe his Rule everywhere : in the choir where he sings, in his cell where he reads and writes, in the frater where he eats with soberness whilst hearkening to the Word of God. For : " When monastic discipline is thoroughly accepted it leads to great perfection. It saves from eternal damnation and enables us to reach a high place in heaven. It consists above all in keeping silence, in celebrating the divine office with devotion and applying ourselves without idleness to manual labour. If discipline be vigorous in the monastery great peace and sanctification are found there. If discipline be threatened disorder is introduced, vice is nurtured and virtue perishes. When discipline is respected heavenly grace abounds, devotion flourishes, study is pleasant, meditation sweet, prayer fervent. . . . The soul is filled with joy, the mind receives heavenly light, the flesh is mortified. . . ."[4]

The monk must practise every virtue, especially those of poverty, humility and patience, which are his three tabernacles.[5] " Love to be unknown and counted as nothing," says Thomas À Kempis. " That is more useful and healthful to thee than to be praised by men. Humble thyself in all and towards all and thou shalt compel all the world.

---

[1] *Meditatio de incarnatio Christi; Sermones de vita et passione Christi; Orationes de passione Domini et beata Virgine et aliis sanctis; Orationes et meditationes de vita Christi.*

[2] *Soliloquium animae; Hortulus rosarum; Vallis liliorum; Cantica; De elevatione mentis.*

[3] *Libellus spiritualis exercitii,* cap. iv. Cf. *De Imitatione,* lib. I, cap. xx.

[4] *Libellus de disciplina claustralium,* cap. i.

[5] *De tribus tabernaculis* is the tract which deals with poverty, humility and patience.

Thou shalt also be pleasing to God and esteemed by men; the devil will quickly fly from thee because of the virtue of humility which he greatly loathes. . . .

"Choose poverty and simplicity; be contented with little, and thou shalt not be tempted to murmur. To be poor in this world for Christ's sake and to take the lowest place is a great gift of God. . . .

"Do good to all men, both good and bad, and be not burdensome to others. Despise no man, nor do harm to another. Have compassion on the sorrowful, help him who is in need, and thou shalt never be puffed up. Look upon those that offend thee and despise thee as thy best friends and protectors. For if thou understand things well thou shalt draw great profit from them. . . .

"Keep thy heart from all wandering. Let not thy mouth utter idle words, and guard strictly thy senses. . . ."[1]

The precepts of Thomas À Kempis on the interior life are very like those of the *Imitation.* The Christian soul addresses itself either to show its own wretchedness or to encourage it to practise inward mortification.

"I know, O Lord, that thy judgements are equity; and in thy truth thou hast humbled me (Ps. cxviii, 75). These are the words of the holy prophet and the humble king David. What sayest thou, O vile man, thou that art but earth and dust? Why hast thou high thoughts of thyself, and why art thou puffed up with pride? Darest thou liken thyself to an honest man when thou art in very truth a sinner, wholly born in sin and full of vice and passion? Verily, if thou look into thyself honestly thou wilt rightly think of thyself as the worst of all. . . ."[2]

"To die to sin and to do violence to nature is in truth a heavenly saying. We cannot find true inward peace as long as we are not dead to ourselves and not disposed to die afresh each day. I must, moreover, determine to die for Christ every day and to begin again to reform my life and overcome myself. Furthermore, I must strive every hour and every moment to go out of myself, to quit myself completely because of Christ, and to destroy the love of self in his love. . . ."[3]

"If thou desire to live truly for God, thou must trust thyself to him and renounce thyself. Put thy heart in thy duty, and thou shalt always have peace. Set thyself to do more, and thou shalt do what is required of thee with less difficulty. Learn to overcome thyself in all things, and thou shalt enjoy inward peace. To have the will to do our duty is the way to

---

[1] *Alphabetum monachi*, Pohl, iii, 317-321.
[2] *De recognitione propriae fragilitatis*, cap. i.
[3] *De mortificata vita*, Pohl, ii, 386.

go to heaven. Great peace is acquired by means of patience and silence. He who is patient is truly wise. . . ."[1]

The author of the *Imitation* sometimes complains of dryness and inward barrenness. We find the same in Thomas À Kempis :

" To feel the want of sensible graces is more painful than to lack the good things of nature whatever they may be. Spiritual dearth is a hard affliction for the soul. The just man is often tried by the secret privation of inward consolation. The soul is chastened for its good, so that in prosperity it presume not too greatly of itself. For the Lord knoweth what is needful to thee. It is often a hindrance to thy salvation to desire so eagerly to attain to it. . . ."[2]

As constantly in the *Imitation* the monologue often gives place to a dialogue with Christ, or a prayer :

" Now, O blessed Saviour, grant me participation in thy grace; do not desert me in my need, for I have still many faults that must be destroyed within me. I have not yet wholly renounced myself, nor am I yet wholly dead to the old man. I am not freed from the love of creatures and from perverse affections. Nature is still deeply rooted within me, and constantly asserts itself. . . . Be merciful to me, O well-beloved Lord, for in thy strength all my enemies shall fall. . . ."[3]

The spirituality of Thomas À Kempis is wholly inward. It reduces sanctity to renunciation of self as conditional to perfection and union with God. All, even meditation on the last end, it directed towards this renunciation.[4] The *Imitation*, as we shall see later, has the same teaching.

Thomas À Kempis sings wonderfully of mystical love. He sings of it in his *Cantica*,[5] in his *Soliloquium animae,* and a little in all his works. His style reminds us of that of the *Imitation* and of the mystics of the twelfth century.

Theory respecting mystical union must not be sought in his writings. When he speaks of it, however, we can see that he has read the German writers. He is acquainted with their theories as to the nakedness of the intelligence, and on the divine image in the depth of the soul through which union is brought about. He even makes use of some of their philosophical formulas in his mystical elevations, which formulas appear to be unknown to the author of the *Imitation*.

" Behold now I seek thee, O my God," he cries, " not with my bodily senses nor by means of sensible images. I seek thee within me and beyond my reason, there where thou

---

[1] *De bona pacifica vita, id.,* ii, 395.
[2] *De Spirituali inopia, id.,* ii, p. 367.
[3] *De mortificata vita pro Christo,* Pohl, ii, 390.
[4] Cf. *Soliloquium animae,* cap. ii, vii, xxi.
[5] Pohl has published one hundred and ten of them, vol. iv.

makest thyself manifest to my mind, O eternal truth, immeasurable goodness, incomprehensible brightness . . . I beseech thee, O my God, and I implore thee from the depth of my heart to deliver me and to free my soul from all worldly passion and from every corporeal image, so that by the aid of thy light I may find thee within me, who was created in thy precious and incorruptible likeness. . . . Lift, then, my soul above what is earthly, and purify the affections of my heart. Do thou renew me according to the inward man and reform, by the sevenfold grace of thy Holy Spirit, thy likeness within me. . . . O God, my truth and my mercy, grant that I may see thee without bodily shape, without imaginative species and without created light. Grant that I may see thee with the knowledge that belongs to a pure soul, thou who didst promise to show thyself to the pure of heart. . . . Grant me, Lord, to see in thy light true light, not the light either of heaven or earth, nor the light of angels, nor that of man, but the light eternal, uncreate, immeasurable, ineffable, incomprehensible. . . ."[1]

This light which alone is able to enlighten the soul so ardently desiring it is the Word of God. It is with it that the soul becomes united as with its well-beloved and its only Spouse.[2] The soul expresses its desire to be united to its heavenly lover in burning words : " All that I see on earth produces a heavy weariness within me. All human consolation is to me burdensome, and I can only find relief from my sorrow in the perfect union of my heart with thee, O Word divine. It is thou, O Lord my God, who art the cause of my sorrow, the author of my weakness; so burning is thy love that I am unable to endure it. Thou dost wound me in the depth of the soul with fiery darts, thou dost consume me, thou dost wholly pierce me, and my strength gives way. Why dost thou leave me to languish? Why make me groan and not satisfy the yearning which oppresses me? Why so quickly fly away afar off into inaccessible darkness? Do not forsake me, O holy friend, who desire to see thee ! Do thou no longer hide thyself but give grace to him that seeks thee, and come quickly, for without thee I cannot live. . . ."[3]

The New Devotion was the beginning of an aspect of piety which ended in the regulation of spiritual exercises.

This tendency to reduce prayer to precise method is to be observed in the *Rosetum exercitiorum spiritualium*—published in 1494—by Jean Mombaer or Mauburne, Canon Regular of Mount St Agnes, and a disciple of Thomas À Kempis. The

---

[1] *De elevatione mentis ad inquirendum summum bonum,* Pohl, ii, 399-402.
[2] *id.,* Pohl, ii, 403-408.
[3] *De elevatione mentis ad inquirendum summum bonum,* Pohl, 408-409. Cf. *Soliloquium animae,* cap. i.

writer therein treats at length of meditation and of the methods to be followed as an aid to it.

The Benedictine school, under the influence of the mystics of Windesheim, also turned their attention towards this "prescribed piety." It thus abandoned that "freedom of the mind" which the Oratorian Faber so admired in the ancient Benedictine school. In the first half of the fifteenth century the Venerable Louis Barbo (1443), founder of the Benedictine Congregation of St Justina of Padua, had already drawn up a method of prayer : *Modus meditandi et orandi.* He gives a type of meditation for every day of the week.

But it is the Spanish Benedictine, Dom Garcia de Cisneros (1510), Abbot of Montserrat, who really regulated spiritual life in his famous *Ejercitatorio de la Vida espiritual.* He is inspired by the *Rosetum* of Jean Mombaer and by the writings of Gerard of Zutphen. But as Garcia de Cisneros' work should be studied in connection with the *Spiritual Exercises* of St Ignatius, it must not be dealt with in this volume.

III—THE PROBLEM AS TO THE ORIGIN OF THE "IMITATION OF CHRIST"

As we have seen, the spirituality of the Congregation of Windesheim is very simple. It insists on inward renunciation, humility, patience, mutual support, which virtues, combined with due observance of the monastic rule, bring peace to the heart, make the true religious the perfect follower of Christ, and raise his soul to the dignity of the mystical Spouse of the Word. And this is the spirituality of the *Imitation.*

Must we conclude that this wonderful book belongs to the school of Windesheim, and that its author was Thomas À Kempis? This is a serious problem which led to impassioned discussion, especially in the seventeenth century.[1]

All critics[2] agree that the *Imitation* was known and pon-

---

[1] The present title, *The Imitation of Christ,* is hardly correct. It is derived from the first words of the heading to the first chapter : *Of the Imitation of Christ and of Contempt of all Worldly Vanities.* It was the custom in the Middle Ages to use the first words at the beginning of a book as its title rather than its subject-matter. Strictly speaking, each book, as in the MSS. and older editions, has a separate title : (lib. I) *Admonitiones ad interna trahentes ad spiritualem vitam utiles;* (lib. II) *Admonitiones ad interna trahentes;* (lib. III) *Liber internae consolationis;* (lib. IV) *Devota exhortatio ad sacram communionem.* These different titles enable us to see that there is no fixed order for the four books of the *Imitation.* Many MSS. and editions put the fourth book before the third. There is no more necessary bond between the books of which it consists than between the different chapters of each book. The famous work must have been formed by combining together the four treatises, which at first were independent of one another.

[2] The bibliography on this question will be found in A. de Backer, *Essai bibliographique sur le livre " De Imitatione Christi,"* Liége 1864. E. Puyol, *L'auteur du livre " De Imitatione Christi,"* 2nd section,

dered at the beginning of the fifteenth century by the *Brethren of the Common Life* and the Canons of the Windesheim Congregation; it is they who speak of the famous work for the first time.

The oldest MSS. contain only the first book; they date from 1421 to 1424. The complete MSS. date only from 1427. Now, it is about 1400 that certain sentences from the first book are to be found among the writings of the religious of Windesheim.

The copyists of Deventer, of Windesheim and of the other monasteries belonging to the Canons Regular of the Low Countries largely contributed by their work to the rapid spread of the *Imitation*.[1] From the second half of the fifteenth century it was read throughout the whole of Christendom. The Low Countries, then, were a sort of second birthplace of the famous chef-d'œuvre. Might they not have been its actual birthplace?

Opinions on this point differ. Some[2] think that the *Imitation* was written in Italy, in the thirteenth century, between 1220 and 1245, by John Gersen, an Abbot of the Benedictine Monastery of St Stephen at Vercelli. But this theory seems untenable, for no writer quotes the *Imitation* before the beginning of the fourteenth century, and no MSS. before 1421 contain it. How can we possibly imagine that such a great work could have thus remained unknown for more than a century?

Others,[3] relying on certain MSS., are of opinion that the *Imitation* should be attributed to Jean Gerson, Chancellor of the University of Paris. This is unlikely, for we have a list of the authenticated works of Gerson drawn up by his contemporaries. The *Imitation* does not appear among them. Moreover, the style of the Chancellor is too different from that of the *Imitation* to suggest that he was its author.

The greater number of critics[4] think they can show that

---

bibliographie, Paris 1900. Dr. Pohl, *Thomae Hem. À Kempis opera omnia*, vol. ii, pp. 433 ff., Freiburg im B. 1904. Vacandard, *Revue du clergé français*, vol. xxv (No. 149), pp. 499-500. Becker, *Les derniers travaux sur l'auteur de l'Imitation* (*Précis historiques* 1889).

[1] Thomas À Kempis himself wrote a famous MS. (the Antwerp MS.) of the *Imitation* in 1441.

[2] Chiefly the Benedictines, especially Mabillon (Puyol, *op. cit.*, p. 92), Mgr. Puyol has recently supported the Gersen theory of the *Imitation*: *L'auteur du livre " De Imitat. Christi"; Descriptions des Manuscrits et des principales éditions du livre " De Imit. Christi,"* Paris 1898. He has also published four other volumes on the variants, teaching and text of the *Imitation*.

[3] See the essay at the beginning of Gerson's *Opera omnia*, edition Ellies du Pin, vol. i, pp. lix f., Paris 1706.

[4] One of the most famous is Eusèbe Amort († 1775), Canon Regular of St Augustine of the convent of Pollingen (Puyol, *L'auteur*, pp. 4-8; Pohl, *op. cit.*, pp. 433-434). Among modern writers, Funk, Spitzen, Pohl, Vacandard, *L'auteur de l'Imitation* (*Revue du clergé français*. vol. lvi, 633 ff.), etc.

the *Imitation* was written by Thomas À Kempis. This is the most solid theory, based as it is on the striking resemblances which are to be found between the tracts of the Subprior of Mount St Agnes and the celebrated chef-d'œuvre. Moreover, the chronicler of Windesheim, John Busch († 1479), in the second edition of his *De viris illustribus de Windesem* (cap. xxi) written in 1464, attributes the *Imitation* to Thomas À Kempis.

However important they may seem, these reasons do not succeed in convincing those who are antagonistic to the À Kempis theory respecting the *Imitation*.[1] For should the famous work be earlier than the Subprior of St Agnes he might have been inspired by it and have copied its style in his works. Moreover, the witness of Busch is rather late, since it was wanting in the first edition of *De viris*. It is further weakened by the statement of a contemporary copyist, who attributes the *Imitation* to a Carthusian.[2] In the lifetime of Thomas À Kempis it would appear that the authorship of the famous work was not fully settled.

The *Imitation*, then, remains an anonymous writing. The unknown author held literary glory in too great contempt to sign his work. " Let not the authority of the writer offend thee," he says to the reader, " whether he was of little or great learning, but let the love of pure truth lead thee to read. Inquire not who said this, but attend to what is said."[3] No doubt we shall never know his name.

It is almost certain that he belonged to the Congregation of Windesheim. He drew up a collection of maxims, prayers, upliftings and colloquies drawn from different writers or from the depths of his own soul for the use of the religious of his Order. This collection first consisted of one small work, to which three others were added afterwards. Thus combined, they formed *The Imitation of Christ*.[4]

---

[1] *Cf.* Puyol, *L'auteur*, 1st section, pp. 491 ff. ; Tamissey et Larraque, *Preuves que Thomas À Kempis n'a pas composé l'Imitation* (*Annales de Philosophie chrétienne,* vols. iii and iv, 1861, 5th series).

[2] *Cf.* Becker, *Les derniers travaux*, p. 26. The copyists, with one exception, arrange the books of the *Imitation* in their MSS. in a different order from that of Thomas himself in 1441 (Becker, *id.*, 243), which would not have been the case had they considered Thomas the author of the work.

[3] *De Imitatione Christi*, lib I, cap. v. The author of the *Imitation* adopts the impersonal. He occasionally quotes sentences from the poets or from Seneca (lib. I, cap. xiii, xx), introducing the quotation with the words *Quidam dixit.*

[4] M. Mourret thinks that the four books of the *Imitation* are " only the *rapiarium* of a man of genius " (*Histoire générale de l'Eglise,* vol. v, p. 130).

CHAPTER X

THE REACTION FROM EXCES-
SIVE SPECULATION AND FALSE
MYSTICISM IN FRANCE AT THE
BEGINNING OF THE FIFTEENTH
CENTURY

PIERRE D'AILLY AND JEAN GERSON —NICHOLAS DE CUSA IN THE RHINELAND

THE reaction from speculative mysticism among the spiritual writers in the Low Countries was one of peace. It was content to pass high theories over in silence, to censure the excesses of scholasticism reservedly, and to reduce spirituality to simple disconnected maxims in a form that disdained all scientific pretence.

In France the movement against new speculation was different. Theology rose up, at times violently, against dangerous mystical theories, and especially against the false mysticism which was spreading a little everywhere and disturbing souls. It was the University of Paris, the most famous school at that time, which, at the hands of two of its Chancellors, recalled to mind the rules of true mysticism.

I—PIERRE D'AILLY

PIERRE D'AILLY (Petrus de Alliaco),[1] the famous Cardinal Archbishop of Cambrai, a rigid Gallican, who had a considerable influence at the Council of Constance, was one of the first to react against the false mysticism which had spread so widely towards the end of the fourteenth century.

[1] He was born at Compiègne in 1350. When thirteen years old he entered the college of Navarre, in Paris, where Nominalism was in the ascendant. In 1381, he became doctor of theology, and shortly afterwards Rector of the college of Navarre. In 1389 he was elected Chancellor of the University. In 1395 he was made Bishop of Puy, then in 1397 Archbishop of Cambrai, and was created Cardinal in 1411. He died on August 9, 1420. His life may be summed up in the efforts which he made to bring the Great Schism to an end; in this he was even assisted by his errors as to the papacy and the constitution of the Church, which were, however, serious. *Cf.* L. Salembier, *Petrus de Alliaco*, Lille 1886; *Dict. de théol. cath.*, art. *d'Ailly*.

He wrote two treatises *De falsis prophetis*.[1] In the first he denounced the wiles and intrigues of heretics and other evil teachers who, under the veil of hypocrisy, laid waste the Church. Pierre d'Ailly recognized in them those false prophets of whom Christ speaks, who, although in sheep's clothing, are in reality ravening wolves. The second treatise attacks the widely spread evil of astrology, against which Gerson also wrote.[2] But whilst reproving superstitions due to star-gazing, both Pierre d'Ailly and Gerson admitted that, within proper bounds, stars had a certain influence on terrestrial beings. Moreover, the study of the stars in itself is perfectly lawful.[3] The chief superstition connected with astrology was the claim to foretell the future by reading the stars. Pierre d'Ailly took this occasion to deal with false prophecies and to lay down rules to enable us to distinguish the true. True prophecy comes from God, whereas the devil is the author of the false. Their distinction, therefore, is simply the application to particular cases of the discernment of spirits.

At every epoch in the history of the Church spiritual writers have striven to throw light on the wiles of the devil and to discover the different ways in which he imitates the action of God. The Fathers of the desert knew how to give advice, fraught with great experience,[4] on this subject, and that advice has been faithfully followed since.

At the end of the Middle Ages diabolical interference had greatly increased, and many were deceived by it. It became necessary to show with fulness and precision the characteristics of the prophet inspired by the spirit of evil, and to compare them with those of the prophet who speaks in the name of the Lord.

I do not propose to enlarge on the theories of Pierre d'Ailly on this subject, as they will be met with more completely in the writings of Gerson. Moreover, the Archbishop of Cambrai did not acknowledge the evidential value of rules for the discernment of spirits. According to him they were only able to afford probabilities as to the nature of the causes of prophecies. For it sometimes happens that the devil foretells what is true, and God sometimes makes use of evil instruments in order to predict the future. How then can the moral status of the prophet teach us with certainty the

---

[1] Edited together with the *Opera omnia* of Gerson, édition Ellies du Pin, Antwerp 1706, vol. i, pp. 499-603.

[2] Gerson, *Trilogium astrologiae theologizatae; De respectu caelestium siderum*, vol. i, pp. 189 ff. See also the treatise of Pierre d'Ailly, *Contra astronomos*, vol. i, pp. 778 ff.

[3] See the letter of Pierre d'Ailly to Gerson in defence of astronomy, vol. i, p. 226, *Opera omnia*.

[4] Cf. *Christian Spirituality*, vol. i, pp. 111 ff., 129 ff.

origin of that which he announces? But Pierre d'Ailly's criteriology is here defective. It is seemingly suggested by the Nominalism of William of Ockham († 1347).[1] If, in certain cases, it is not possible to discover the nature of the mind which has inspired the prophet, it is not always so unless we must declare that God has rendered it impossible for us to find the truth.

This is not the only error which Pierre d'Ailly has borrowed from William of Ockham. He also owes to him his great moral principle that nothing is right or wrong in itself; it is the divine will which renders our actions good by allowing them, or evil by forbidding them. It is divine will which absolutely determines what is good or evil : that which God wills is good and that which he does not will is evil. Nothing is evil in itself, an act is sinful solely because God has forbidden it, and not because it is opposed to the eternal law which is in God. There is, therefore, nothing positive in duty; it is relative, since it might have been otherwise if God had so willed.[2] From this Ockham concluded that it was possible for man to perform an act of merit whilst hating God, since God might, had he so willed, have commanded it; and perfection consists in willing all that God wills or might will. The more the will becomes identified with God the more it is perfect.

The Church has condemned these mystical consequences arising from a false theological principle.[3] The great danger of them may be foreseen. How was it that Pierre d'Ailly, the enemy of false mysticism, did not see it? He himself thus paid a tribute to this period of theological decadence in which he lived, a decadence against which he, nevertheless, so reacted.

It would be unjust to regard the spiritual teaching of the Archbishop of Cambrai only from this unfavourable light. These few blemishes ought not to cause us to disregard the merits of his mystical work. It is contained in the *Treatises*

[1] An English theologian of the Franciscan Order, born towards the end of the thirteenth century. He became the head of the Nominalists, who admitted only the reality of the individual. The expressions genus and species, as representing what is universal, correspond with nothing real. On the contrary, the Realists claimed that universals, or what are generally known as abstractions, really exist as the mind conceives them. This controversy is known as the quarrel concerning universals.

[2] *Cf.* L. Salembier, *Petrus de Alliaco*, p. 224. Gerson also admits this doctrine, and expounds it in his *Liber de vita spirituali animae, Opera omnia*, vol. iii, pp. 13, 26, and in the *Centilogium de impulsibus*, p. 147. But Gerson does not grant the mystical consequences which were deduced from this teaching by Ockham.

[3] John of Mercuria had taught them. *Cf.* d'Argentre, *Collectio judiciorum de novis erroribus*, vol. i, Part I, p. 344.

and Sermons (*Tractatus et sermones*), so often reprinted and translated.[1] The small works which are comprised in this collection describe the different degrees of spiritual life and the theory of meditation and contemplation. We shall find Gerson dealing with these questions of spirituality and treating them with a more masterly hand. But if in this the pupil is superior to the master he does not wholly eclipse him. Moreover, he has in several points followed him, especially on that of devotion to St Joseph. Towards the end of the fourteenth century the cult of the holy patriarch became considerably developed in the Church. Pierre d'Ailly and Gerson[2] were the great pioneers of this development. St Bernardine of Siena only came after them.

Finally Pierre d'Ailly, as is shown by his commentary on the *Canticle of Canticles,* tasted the charms of divine love. He, therefore, rightly occupies a place in the history of mysticism.

II—JEAN GERSON—HIS STRUGGLES AGAINST FALSE MYSTICISM—HIS MYSTICAL THEOLOGY

JEAN LE CHARLIER DE GERSON was born on December 14, 1363, in the village of Gerson, a hamlet of Barby near Rethel, in the Diocese of Rheims. When he was fourteen years of age he entered the famous college of Navarre in Paris, where, after falling an innocent victim to a mutiny among the students, he changed his name from Charlier to that of Gerson, which in Hebrew signifies an exile or outcast. Indeed, Gerson was destined one day to become an exile and a fugitive.

While at Paris he had as his master Pierre d'Ailly, whom he succeeded in the exalted posts of Chancellor of Notre Dame and of the University. It was then that he began, in a spirit of moderation, to labour for the extinction of the Great Schism which had troubled the Church for seventeen years. The role of peacemaker which he adopted towards the Avignon Pope displeased the members of the Universities and the King of France, and drew their anger upon him. But Gerson's position was entirely compromised after the death of the Duke of Orleans (1407), who was assassinated by order of the Duke of Burgundy. The Chancellor resolutely embraced the side of the Armagnacs against the Burgundians,

---

[1] Published at Strasbourg in 1490, at Mainz in 1574, at Douai in 1634. A French translation at Lyons, 1542 and 1544. The *Tractatus et sermones* are a collection of several small tracts published at different dates: *De quatuor gradibus scalae spiritualis; Speculum considerationis; Compendium contemplationis; De duodecim honoribus sancti Joseph; Commentary on the Canticle of Canticles.*

[2] Gerson, *Considérations sur St Joseph* (in French), vol. iii, 842-868; *Josephina,* Twelve canticles in Latin verse on St Joseph, vol. iv, 743-783.

and brought about the condemnation of the immoral theory of tyrannicide, as upheld by Jean Petit, by the doctors of the Sorbonne, and then by the Council of Constance, in 1415 and 1416.

The Duke of Burgundy, Jean sans Peur, refused to forgive Gerson for this opposition. He swore he would bring about his downfall. After the Council of Constance, where his influence won the day, the Chancellor was unable to return to France. He withdrew to the Benedictine Abbey of Mölk in Germany, where, like Boëthius, he wrote his treatise on *Theological Consolations (De consolatione theologiae)*, an apology in the form of a dialogue, in which he justified his attack on the teaching of Jean Petit.

When Jean sans Peur had been assassinated in 1419 on the bridge at Montereau, Gerson left Germany. He did not return to Paris, where the Burgundians held sway, but, travelling in disguise as a pilgrim, he retired to Lyons, whither he had been sent for by his brother the Prior of the Celestines and Archbishop Amadeus of Talaru.

He lived at the convent of the Celestines for about four years. The Celestines were founded by Peter, surnamed Morrone,[1] who was Pope for five months under the name of Celestine V in 1294. In 1300 Philippe le Bel brought them to France, and in 1312, after the Knights Templars had been suppressed, the Temple at Lyons was given to them. Gerson's brother became the first Prior of the new monastery.

The Chancellor, doubtless with the desire to combine missionary work with contemplation, wrote while at Lyons several works of instruction for the faithful to warn them against the errors of the period.

He was also engaged in a touching work of charity as regards young children whom he found neglected. It was with a view to giving himself up entirely to this that he left the convent of Celestines and established himself in the cloister which connected the collegiate Church of St Paul with the Church of St Lawrence. The children belonging to that quarter of the town were attracted by his kindness. He taught them to read, instructed them in the elements of Christian doctrine and heard their confessions. He set forth the feelings which prompted his heart with regard to children in the beautiful treatise : *De parvulis trahendis ad Christum,* which was written at Lyons and is an enchanting commentary on the words of the divine Master : *Suffer little children to come unto me.*

Gerson brought his well-beloved children together every

---

[1] The Celestines followed the Rule of St Benedict in its primitive austerity. Pierre d'Ailly wrote the life of their founder : *Vita beatissimi patris D. Petri Celestini V pontificis maximi (Acta Sanct.. May 19).*

day. It is related that when he was near to death, after making them assist at Mass in the Church of St Paul, before sending them away he made them recite aloud this touching prayer : *My God, my Creator, have pity on thy poor servant Gerson!* The children looked upon these gatherings as a great treat. But one day when they were all assembled as usual in the cloister awaiting the beloved master he did not come. Being anxious, some of the children went up to his cell. They found him there at the point of death. Filled with tears, they ran out into the streets crying out : *O God, our Creator, have pity on thy servant and our father Jean Gerson!* This was on July 12, 1429.[1]

Gerson was a famous theologian, a powerful orator and a great mystic.[2] We shall deal here with his mysticism only.

The soul of Gerson is specially attractive. In it the heart and mind are equally balanced. It is never allowed to become hardened by speculation, whilst feeling is always under the control of reason. Both affective and speculative spirituality are thus united, but in such a way that they react on one another : the affections inspire speculation with life, and these, ever regulated by the most accurate theology, guide the affections and prevent them from straying into false mysticism. Gerson delighted in St Bonaventure, whom he greatly resembled. He lived at a period, towards the decline. of the Middle Ages, when good mystical and ascetic counsel was necessary. He endowed it with masterly common sense.

Gerson's spirituality may be divided into two parts :[3] the

---

[1] Cf. *Vita Joannis Gersonii*, in the *Works* of Gerson, Antwerp 1706, vol. i, pp. xxxiv-xxxvii. J. B. Schab, *Joannes Gerson, Professor der Theologie und Kanzler der Universität Paris, eine Monographie*, Wurzburg 1858. A. L. Masson, *Jean Gerson, sa vie, son temps, ses œuvres*, Lyons 1894. L. Salembier, *Dict. de Théol. cath.*, art. *Gerson*.

[2] He was also a great defender of the religious life against Matthew Grabon, who denied the right to the faithful to practise, as far as possible, poverty in the world. He also forbade to take religious vows outside the existing Orders, or to form religious communities such as that of the Brethren of the Common Life, without taking vows. These errors were denounced by Gerson at the Council of Constance (*Opera*, vol. i, pp. 467 ff. ; vol. ii, pp. 669 ff.). Gerson also deplored the excessive wealth of convents and chapters, which was only too truly a cause of corruption. The chapters were almost always closed to commoners. *De nobilitate ecclesiastica* (vol. iii, 213 ff.).

[3] The works of Gerson on mystical theology are chiefly to be found in vol. iii of Ellies du Pin's edition of the *Opera omnia* of Gerson, Antwerp 1766. The principal ones are : *La Montagne de la contemplation; La Théologie mystique spéculative et pratique; L'éclaircissement scolastique de la théologie mystique.* Several small treatises : *La Méditation (tractatulus consolatorius); La perfection du cœur; L'illumination du cœur; La simplicité du cœur; La droiture du cœur; Le traité de la pauvreté et de la mendicité spirituelle; L'alphabet du divin amour.* In vol. i are found treatises on : *De l'examen des doctrines, de la probation des esprits,* and *De la distinction des vraies*

one negative, a clearance of the ground, in which the errors of false mysticism so prevalent at the beginning of the fifteenth century are pointed out and subjected to criticism; and the other, positive, constructive, containing full and sure spiritual teaching.

1. *Gerson and False Mysticism—The Discernment of Spirits—True and False Visions.*

First of all Gerson condemns agnostic mysticism.

Doubtless it must be admitted, with Dionysius the Areopagite, that God is known in contemplation by negation: *Theologica mystica procedit per abnegationes.* But, asks the Chancellor, do not those writers exaggerate who push this negation so far as to suppress in the mystic all true knowledge of God, to the extent that God would not even be known as being, as truth, or as goodness? The soul would thus not know God in any positive way, as though he were nothingness.[1] Those who force this Dionysian theory too far must arrive at this false conclusion. For, whatever be the nature of contemplation, God and his attributes remain known by faith.

It is also necessary for contemplatives to meditate at times on the life and passion of Christ, on Christian virtues, and on the last ends.[2]

All the faithful, moreover, are not called to the contemplative life, as opposed to the teachings of certain mystics who wished to make all Christians contemplatives; which, says the Chancellor, is a dangerous error. There are some among the faithful who are only suited to the active life. Their ardent and passionate temperament could only be tamed by hard work and engrossing business. The calm needed for contemplation would expose them to very great temptations; it would be a crime to persuade them to it. Also they would be incapable of contemplating divine truths, and their failure would discourage them. Those who from their position are compelled to live an active life, such as prelates, pastors or

---

visions des fausses. Gerson also wrote ascetic treatises (vol. iii): *Le livre de la vie spirituelle de l'âme; Des passions de l'âme; Sur la prière; Sur les tentations; Sur la conscience scrupuleuse; Les exercises appropriés aux dévots peu instruits; Sur la communion; La préparation à la messe; La préparation à la mort.* And, finally, written in French: *Dialogue spirituel de Gerson avec ses sœurs; Discours sur la virginité; Considérations sur S Joseph* and *Conférences spirituelles.*

[1] *De theologica mystica speculativa, Consideratio* ii, *Gersonii opera,* vol. iii, p. 365; *De consolatione theologiae,* lib. IV, *Prosa* 3, vol. i, p. 174. It will be remembered that Suso called God a nothingness.

[2] *De simplicitate cordis,* notula 15, vol. iii, p. 463.

mothers of a family, would sin if they left those dependent on them in order to lose themselves in contemplation.

Finally, for those who would contemplate God some preparation is needed; we must not hurry on and throw ourselves into mysticism too soon. Moreover, it is not wise to teach this theology to all without distinction. With these reserves, however, there is nothing better than to encourage folk, even those most occupied, to retire often within themselves to think of God and to bemoan their faults. Thus understood, some approach to contemplation ought to be performed in all active life. In the same way, contemplatives should give themselves to some extent to manual work or to other like occupations, for unceasing contemplation belongs to heaven and not to this world.[1]

Gerson recommends those who feel themselves truly drawn to mystical contemplation to place themselves under the direction of prudent counsellors, and not to try to follow their own inspirations. Let them beware of their imagination, let them ever rely on the principles of faith, let them meditate on the law of Christ. Then shall they acquire humility and despise not the advice of others. Otherwise they will fall into error. Mystics are apt to gain esteem by holding fast to false and absurd doctrines, and are thus much more exposed to fall into them than are those people who are void of devotion.[2]

The Beghards and Turlupins, who took their own ideas as a rule of truth, reached to such a height of foolishness as to consider that man, once he had attained to calm and tranquillity of mind, was freed from all divine law. We may imagine what their moral code must have been.[3] Others have come to immoral conclusions by another route, that of sentimentality. They have mistaken the inordinate motions of the heart for supernatural marks of grace, looking on their passions as something divine. In this case the illusion is all the more easy in that mystical theology often speaks of the spiritual marriage of the soul with God. There is always the fear that, unless we be wholly dead to the senses, which is not the state of the newly converted, thought can scarcely avoid confusing spiritual with carnal marriage. This is why among false mystics immorality is pretty often found to occur.[4]

Others again, more refined, seek intellectual enjoyment in mysticism. They mistake their speculations or imaginations

---

[1] *De monte contemplationis*, cap. xviii, xxiii, xxvi, vol. iii, pp. 555-562; *De exercitiis discretis devotorum simplicium*, vol. iii, 614-615.
[2] *Epist. contra praed. resp.*, vol. i, pp. 81-82.
[3] *De triplici theologia, consid.* viii, vol. iii, 369; *De consol. theol.*, lib. IV, 3.
[4] *De consolat. theol., ibid.*, vol. i, 174; *De monte contempl.*, cap. xxxvii, vol. iii, 571-572. *Cf.* vol. i, 80.

for spiritual life, and think that the pleasure they find in them is true devotion. In order to emphasize this mystical dilettantism they affect far-fetched methods in speaking of spiritual matters and conjure up most daring metaphors. They say that in high contemplation one is submerged in the profoundest depths, that divine love is annihilation or the return to nothingness. This false devotion is most pernicious for religious, rendering them proud, infatuated with themselves, irregular and insubordinate towards superiors, even if it do not bring them to apostasy.[1]

Finally there is a tendency, which we have already met with, towards Quietism, which inclines the mystic to be oblivious to his salvation and to neglect prayer and good works.[2]

The pious Chancellor is not content with a passing reference to these errors : he returns to them again and again. His mind seems to be haunted by them, so anxious is he to protect from them both his readers and those whom he directs. In reading his works we can grasp the extent to which false mysticism was ravaging the Church.

In order to combat it the more effectively Gerson drew up precise rules to enable us to gauge the value of the doctrines taught by mystics, to test the spirit by which they are animated, and to distinguish true visions which they may have from false.[3]

All doctrines must be accepted, he says, that are taught by the General Councils—Gerson's Gallicanism sets them above the Pope—by the Pope, the bishops, learned doctors of theology, and by those on whom heaven has bestowed the gift of the discernment of spirits.[4]

When it is an individual who teaches we must ascertain whether his doctrine agrees with Scripture and tradition. Special care must be taken to inquire as to the state of him or her whose ideas are put forward either by word or writings. Gerson is particularly severe on women who meddle by word or writing with mysticism. He retained a bitter memory of those—with whom he appears to have confused St Catherine of Siena—who had advised Gregory XI

---

[1] *Epist. contra praed. defens.*, vol. i, 80. Several of these criticisms are directed against the German mystical school.

[2] *De directione cordis, Consid.* ix, vol. iii, 470.

[3] These rules are to be found in the treatises : *De examinatione doctrinarum; De probatione spirituum; De distinctione verarum visionum a falsis*, vol. i, pp. 7-59.

[4] *De examin. doct.*, i, 1-6. Rules for the examination of doctrine are summed up in these four lines : *Concilium, Papa, Præsul Doctor bene doctus—Discretor quoque spirituum de dogmate consent.—Qualis sit doctrina, docens quis, quique sodales—Si finis sit fastus, quæstusque, sive libido.* This treatise was written at Lyons about 1123.

to return to Rome and whose return brought about the Great Schism.[1]

The moral attitude of hearers or readers of mystics may also help us to gauge their teaching. When a writer is flattered by his adepts there is every likelihood that it is not from a pure love of truth. We should call to mind that Gerard, the brother of St Bernard, never congratulated the Abbot of Clairvaux on his success lest he should incite him to pride.[2] Finally, any teaching calculated to excite the passions, the triple concupiscence spoken of by St John, would obviously be detestable.[3]

These rules, which were drawn up in 1423 at Lyons for the Carthusians and Celestines, have as their complement the treatise *De probatione spirituum* which Gerson had written in 1415 at Constance, when the Council was dealing with the writings of St Bridget.

The discernment of spirits, he says, is a gift of God. Happy are those who possess it. But if we are unable fully to acquire it, it can at least be encouraged by study and experience. For it is not only from books that the discernment of the spirit which animates the mystic must be ascertained. We must have felt within ourselves the struggle between the conflicting spirits. Moreover, the man, learned yet without experience, is like a doctor with diplomas who has never practised his art.[4] The following are some of the Chancellor's suggestions, the fruit of his experience, which may be useful for the discernment of the spirit which animates those who believe themselves raised to extraordinary supernatural states.

First of all we should examine the state of health of the mystical claimant. Folk with weak heads easily see visions and revelations, as do those also who lack common sense. We should also distrust novices in the service of God, with whom uncontrolled fervour sometimes causes illusion, especially in the case of women. Finally, we should study the character of the mystic in order to be able to appreciate his moral worth and degree of knowledge.

Having got to know the mystic, we should examine into the smallest details of his visions. For when the vision comes from God, everything connected therewith must conform to truth and seemliness. A lying spirit, on the contrary, is unable wholly to feign the true. This examination should be strict, like that which theologians make in connection with the canonization of saints.

[1] *De examinatione doct.*, ii, 2-3. St Catherine of Siena was not canonized in Gerson's time.
[2] *De examinatione doct.*, ii, 3.   [3] *ibid.*, 4-6.
[4] *De probatione spirituum, Consid.* 1-6. See the rules given by St Catherine of Siena as to the discernment of true visions. Raymund of Capua, *Vie de Ste Catherine de Sienne*, chap. ix.

He who receives the confidences of mystics and listens to the account of their visions or their revelations should be at first most reserved. He should be careful not to accept what is told him at a first interview. Still less should be compliment them. Rather should he treat the new mystic with severity to discourage pride. In order to inculcate feelings of lowliness he should speak humiliatingly. Acts of humility are an excellent means of arresting diabolical visions, and one often employed by the saints. If the vision be from God it will, on the contrary, become more evident.

At the first disclosure from one who claims to have had visions the motive which prompts him to speak must be sought. Is it vanity, in order to make himself important? Or is it simply a need that is felt of consulting and taking counsel? Intentions should be deeply probed. Often enough the apparent reason that has made the mystic speak is good. But there may be secrets or remote intentions which are bad. Thus Jean de Varenne, priest of the Diocese of Rheims, and John Huss began by edifying their followers, but with the view later on of drawing them into heresy. If he who speaks of visions desire to consult and take counsel he ought to show a disposition to allow himself to be guided and not feel obliged to believe what he has seen as true on the pretext that he has an inward conviction that it comes from God.

Account should also be taken of the life of the visionary. Is it contemplative or filled with numerous occupations? Does he live alone or in community? If a woman, is it her custom to come frequently to confession and to weary her confessor with endless stories and useless talk?

Finally, discernment of spirits requires the knowledge from whence they came and whither they go. This is the most difficult. St Bernard admits that he never knew with certainty whence the spirit which actuated him came, although several times he knew that the Holy Spirit was within him. In fact, there are divers spirits which may inspire us : the spirit of God, the spirit of evil, our good angel, our own spirit, our reason or imagination. Visions which these produce resemble each other in many ways, and usually only differ in details which practised theologians know how to discern. Also we are very often mistaken in thinking that thoughts and feelings come from God, when they have a purely human source. We have trouble enough in our temptations to distinguish between feeling, reason and will. We are often in doubt as to whether we have given consent or not. How much more, then, should we not hesitate when it concerns extraordinary phenomena, such as visions and revelations.[1]

---

[1] *De prob. spirit., Consid.* 7-12. Cf. *Judicium Gersonii de vita Stae. Erminae,* vol. i, pp. 83 ff.

During the Great Schism false visions and revelations were so prevalent that Gerson was untiring in his efforts to warn his correspondents against them. It was not enough just to let them know. He desired to point out clearly the signs of true revelation and divine vision, so that minds might be fully enlightened on this difficult question.

The true coin of divine revelation, says Gerson, is distinguished from the false one of diabolical illusion by its weight, which is humility in the mystic and not pride; by its flexibility, which is discretion and not excess in austerity; by its solidity, which is patience under scorn and vexation; by its shape, which is truth; and by its colour, which is the golden tint of charity.[1]

We should then be inclined to accept the statements of those who have never evinced a desire through vanity to have visions or revelations; who are not lacking in moderation or discretion in practices of penance; who suffer with patience—humble patience and not obstinate pride—the annoyances and mockery which are usually the lot of visionaries; who foretell events which become realized; finally, those who are actuated by true love for God and not its counterfeits, such as a sensual love, by which women with an indiscreet zeal for pious practices are often deceived.

The Chancellor frequently had occasion to make use of these tests in order to discard false visionaries.[2] He had come across some who claimed to have been taught by God that they were to become Popes and would end the Great Schism. He had known pious women who pretended to fast to excess in order to pass for saints. Others had gone mad as a result of their untimely privations. Occurrences of this kind are no doubt to be found at every period. They were much more numerous towards the end of the Middle Ages, when a wave of false mysticism threatened to overwhelm true piety. The evils which then oppressed the Church were the concern of all thoughtful men.

The rules laid down by Gerson were not only of use to him as a means of unmasking false mystics. They enabled him to be one of the first to recognize and proclaim the divine mission of Joan of Arc.

In his retreat at Lyons the Chancellor heard of the exploits of the maid of Domrémy. In France this girl was the sole topic of conversation. She, a poor country girl, who had tended her flocks and claimed to have been sent by God to

---

[1] *De distinctione verarum visionum a falsis*, vol. i, pp. 43-45. This treatise is addressed to a Celestine monk, and was written after 1401. The same is found in the *Imitation* (lib. III, cap. vii): *Merita non sunt ex hoc aestimanda, si quis plures visiones aut consolationes habeat . . . sed si vera fuerit humilitate fundatus et divina charitate repletus.*

[2] See also his *Tractatus adversus artem magicam*, vol. i, 210-219.

free the kingdom from the power of the English and to give it back to its lawful king, gave proof of her mission by supernatural signs, such as revealing the secret thoughts of those around her and foretelling the future. Clothed and armed like a man, mounted on horseback and bearing her standard, she led her soldiers to victory. She had just delivered the town of Orleans. After the battle she returned to woman's clothing. Her virtues were proclaimed, and wonder was expressed at the way she had repressed disorders among the soldiers whom she commanded.

Many questions regarding her were suggested to the learned. Was she a human personality or was it a phantom in the form of a young girl? Was what she had accomplished explicable on human grounds? If it was to be attributed to supernatural causes were they divine or diabolical? Ought faith to be put in the statements of this girl, and ought her acts to be approved?[1]

The University of Paris, wholly devoted to the Anglo-Burgundian cause, was, if it had any bias, unfavourable to the maid of Domrémy. It must even have approved her condemnation, which took place afterwards. But two of its doctors, Jacques Gelu, Archbishop of Embrun, and Jean Gerson, did not hesitate to proclaim that Joan had indeed been sent by God. The Chancellor declared that the pious heroine was most certainly a young girl, a true human personality. Why should she not have the spirit of prophecy and of miracles since, according to the doctors of the Church, God from time to time, in the course of ages, sends prophets and wonder-workers to carry out his great designs? And let it not be said that it was unseemly for a woman to command men, since of old time the Lord had entrusted such missions to Debbora, to Esther and to Judith. Moreover, Joan was pious and very holy; there was nothing in her that was against her being an instrument in the hands of God. Her mission therefore was divine; it must be acknowledged.[2]

The Church, by her canonization of Joan of Arc, has endorsed Gerson's judgement and has also emphasized the supernatural character of the mystical experiences with which she was favoured.[3]

[1] *De puella aut virgine aurelianensi, Opusculum* i, vol. iv, pp. 859-860. The authenticity of these two tracts on Joan of Arc have been disputed. Ellies du Pin attributes them to Henry of Gorkum, a Dutch theologian who was on the side of Joan of Arc. But he was wrong. *Cf.* Quicherat, *Procès de Jeanne d'Arc,* vol. v, p. 462.

[2] *id.,* pp. 860-861. In the second tract, pp. 861-868, Gerson justifies Joan of Arc for wearing men's clothing.

[3] See Mgr. Touchet, Bishop of Orleans, *Vie de Sainte Jeanne d'Arc,* Paris 1920, and *La Sainte de la Patrie,* Paris 1920, 2 vols., respecting these facts and the sanctity of Joan of Arc. Other biographies, such as those of Wallon, d'Ayrolles, Dunand, Sepet, Debout, Gabriel Hanotaux, Petit de Julleville, do not deal with the sanctity of Joan of Arc at any length.

2. *The Mystical Theology of Gerson.*

The battle which the famous Chancellor waged against false mysticism would have been only partially successful if he had not presented us with an exact idea of true mysticism. Error can only be efficiently refuted by replacing it by truth.

Mystical theology, Gerson explains, comprises extra-ordinary happenings which occur to holy souls. It consists in the intimate experiences of the heart closely united to God, in the affections and sentiments with which some faithful souls are inspired by the Holy Ghost. The knowledge of God by experience, of which mysticism consists, distinguishes it from scientific theology, which deals with abstract ideas. It is known by different names : contemplation, ecstasy, rapture, liquefaction of the soul, mystical union, inward joy.

In fact, only those who have had experience of these phenomena are able rightly to speak about them. But it does not depend on ourselves to be favoured with them ; the Holy Ghost produces them in whomsoever he will. It would thus seem that mystical theology is not a knowledge attainable by all, but is reserved for those who are raised by God to extraordinary states.

Nevertheless, theologians who have never had personal experience of these special graces are able to write about them from what has been said about them by the saints. They have had it in their power to study the testimony of many mystics, to compare them and to deduce certain laws which appear to govern these supernatural phenomena. Thus scholastic theologians, even though lacking in great piety, are sometimes better acquainted with the science of mysticism than persons who have been in ecstasy. The latter have experienced practical mysticism, the former know it in a speculative way.[1] Gerson desires practical mysticism to be regulated by speculative, which latter he then goes on to expound.

Speculative mysticism is the theory regarding the affections and feelings of the soul raised to the supernatural state. Gerson builds it up on the principles laid down by scholastic theology, to which he faithfully adheres. St Bonaventure and the school of St Victor are his chief guides.[2]

He begins by describing the faculties of the soul so as to determine the role of each in contemplation. The soul has six faculties. Three faculties of knowledge, or three eyes,

[1] *De theologia mystica speculativa,* pars prima, 1-8, vol. iii, pp. 365-370.

[2] Gerson made a special study of St Augustine, St Bernard, the St Victor school, St Thomas Aquinas, St Bonaventure and William of Paris. Cf. *Gersonii opera omnia,* vol. iii, 369, 434, 545, 571.

which are : imagination or the carnal eye, reason or the reasoning eye, and simple, higher intelligence (*intelligentia simplex*) or the spiritual eye. The other three are affective : the sensible or animal appetite, the rational appetite or the will, and a supernatural appetite called *synteresis*.

The acts proper to the faculties of knowledge are : reflection (*cogitatio*), which is brought into operation by sensible images; meditation (*meditatio*), which by effort seeks truth beyond sensible realities; and contemplation (*contemplatio*), or the spirit with the aid of grace, of spiritual and divine truths. This contemplation cannot be brought about by the imagination alone, or by reason alone; it belongs to the higher intelligence : *per sublimem intelligentiam habetur.* But meditation, properly understood, leads to contemplation in the same way that reflection becomes, in the normal way, meditation.

Motions belonging to the faculties or appetite are : passion or concupiscence, which proceeds from the animal appetite; devotion which springs from the will; and finally love—not any love, but ecstatic and beatifying love, which belongs to the higher appetite of the soul and of *synteresis*.[1]

Gerson then examines the properties and effects of this love proper to contemplation and to mystical theology. It has three properties : it transports with delight in God, it unites with God, it satiates the soul with joy and happiness.

In rapture the lower faculties, the imagination and the reason, cease to act. They are in darkness. They are absorbed by the higher part of the soul which is uplifted. When ecstasy takes place they become bound so that they cannot act; the soul is arrested in contemplation.[2] It is what Gerson calls the *simplification* of the heart.[3] This *simplification* is both intellectual and moral. The mind is deprived of sensible images, as required by the Areopagite, in order to be raised, first by abstraction, to the universal Good. This idea has its basis in the particular good of each created being, but it is formed by an abstractive process of the intelligence. Gerson thus repudiated the Nominalism of William of Ockham without falling into the exaggerations of Realism. The mind ascends from the idea of goodness in general to that of God, the heavenly Father, the Benefactor, the Saviour, the Friend and Spouse of the soul. While the mind becomes *simplified* by abstraction, the heart tears itself from sensible things in order to become wholly spiritual.

Love—the second virtue—unites us to God and makes our

---

[1] *Theologia mystica speculativa*, pars 11ᵃ, IIIᵃ. Cf. *De meditatione*, vol. iii, p. 449; *De simplificatione cordis*, p. 457; *De oculo*, p. 484.

[2] *De theol. myst. speculativa*, pars VII, vol. iii, p. 390-393.

[3] *De simplificatione, stabilitione seu mundificatione cordis*, vol. iii, pp. 457-467.

mind one with him. It renders our will conformable to his. In a word it transforms us. How is this transformation to be understood?

Gerson sets forth several explanations which have been given, but which he does not accept.[1] Some have seen in this transformation a return of the soul to the eternal and divine idea according to which it was created. The soul would thus lose its own being, and would become in a way God. This absurdity (*insania*) was taught by some mystics. Now, in no case can the soul lose its own being. Its transformation into God must not be understood in the strict sense of the word. Others think that the love of God in the soul is not distinct from the Holy Ghost. This opinion, attributed to Peter Lombard, is thrust aside, for charity is a divine gift distinct from the third person of the Trinity. Certain others have drawn comparisons from creatures capable of giving some idea of this spiritual transformation of the mystic into God. In the same way, they say, that a drop of water thrown into a cask of wine ceases to be water, and is wholly changed into wine, and that food which we take loses its own being to become our flesh, so the soul is transformed into the divine being. Gerson recalls, in this connection, that some pious woman, on hearing these exaggerated comparisons, was so moved that she immediately expired in convulsions.

This transformation again is explained by the words of St Bernard : *The soul is much more in that which it loves than in the body to which it gives life* (*De praecepto et disp.,* cap. xx), as though the soul of the mystic left the body to pass totally into God. The connection which several have wished to establish between mystical union and eucharistic transubstantiation is equally without justification. For in no case can the soul lose its own personal being. Which remark also applies to the substantial union of matter and form to which certain writers would compare mystical union. This union might be more rightly compared to red-hot iron, which has the properties of fire without losing the nature of iron. Thus the mystical soul is rendered wholly divine without ceasing to remain itself. All these explanations are rejected by Gerson.

They are not, however, all to be condemned, and several are approved by very learned writers. Once again we see the Chancellor's distrust of theories which seemed to modify the distinction between the soul and God in mystical union.

According to him, mystical love produces a double effect. It strips the soul of all that is sensible and earthly. It brings about this suppression, by, as it were, the separation of the soul from the mind; then it unites the wholly spiritual part

[1] *De theol. myst. speculativa,* pars VIII.

of the soul to God. It renders it like to the Holy Trinity.
The soul is not only united to God, but made like to him;
making but one with him by conforming its will to his. But,
however close we suppose this union, the personality of the
mystic remains intact.

Mystics explain this conformity of the soul with the divine
goodwill in various ways.[1] Some restrict it to the complete
acceptance of the will of God made manifest by the divine
precepts. It would thus suffice to cleave to the preceptive
will of the Lord. Others require more. The higher will of
man, the sensitive part of his will, should also adhere to the
permissive will of God to the extent of not complaining,
either of the damnation of some or of the sins which God
allows, nor of his own damnation, if, through the just judgement of the Lord, it should happen. Doubtless man may not
desire that there should be sin, nor wish for his damnation in
an absolute way, but only in the case of God's permissive
will. This teaching, though perhaps permissible, seemed to
Gerson dangerous. He thought it inadvisable to suggest it
to everyone. In fact, it might very easily lead to Quietism.

The third property of this love is finally the procuring of
peace, joy, satiety. The soul rejoices fully, and its joy is
reflected in the body.[2]

Love, then, has the chief role in mystical union. But it
does not consist of love alone, as some would hold. Mystical
union is both contemplation and ecstatic delight in one. The
higher part of the mind remains active; it is sensible to
spiritual realities. For it is impossible for the soul to attain
to God, to feel him within, to possess him by love, without
having a knowledge of him corresponding to this love.
When our senses touch an object it is brought to our knowledge. Thus the spiritual contact of our soul with God is a
knowledge of God.[3]

During mystical union a most perfect prayer escapes the
soul : it does not consist in words, nor is it produced by the
imagination : it is found in the higher part of the soul, and in
the heart united with God by an outburst of intense love.
This is the only prayer that truly gives honour to the Lord.
It is indistinct from mystical union, of which in fact it is one
aspect.[4]

Thus mystical union is effected by love. It takes place in
the higher part of the soul—the lower part being bound—
by a contemplative and affective act, which unites the soul to

---

[1] Gerson deals with this in the *De directione seu rectitudine cordis,*
vol. iii, pp. 468-479.

[2] *Theol. myst. specul.,* pars VIII, *consid.* 42.

[3] Gerson studies this question in the tract *De elucidatione mysticae
theologiae,* vol. iii, pp. 422 ff.

[4] *Theol. myst. specul.,* pars VIII, *consid.* 43-44.

God so as, morally speaking, to become one with him, and
crowns it and satiates it with joy.
Such is speculative mysticism.

In the practical part of his treatise on mystical theology[1]
Gerson expounds the necessary conditions and the means to
be taken to become a contemplative.

First, we must await the call of God: *Dei voluntatem
attendere seu vocationem.* Then temperament must be
studied. Is it anxious, restless, unfitted for contemplation?
Or are the conditions of life unsuited to it?

He who is destined to be raised to the contemplative state
should strive towards perfection, eschew absorbing pursuits,
mortify curiosity, be courageous in difficulties; he should
seek the causes of the passions and motions of the soul,
should choose the time and place most favourable to contemplation, and allow himself but moderate food and sleep.
He should be given to pious meditation capable of developing
divine love within; finally, he should free his mind from every
sensible image.[2]

These practical suggestions are taken by Gerson from the
older mystical writers, chiefly from Dionysius the Areopagite,
and they comprise what may be called the negative preparation for the mystical state.

The positive means for its attainment are : meditation and
contemplation.

Gerson wrote a treatise *On Meditation.*[3] It is an intense
application of the mind to the discovery of truth for edifica-
tion. Mystical meditation ought always to have as its object
the development of divine love and devotion. It is by this
distinguished from purely scientific meditation, and ap-
proximates to our modern form of prayer which combines
prayer with reflections.

Gerson fixes no rules for meditation, for each one must
seek the method most congenial to his temperament and ask
advice of his director. Novices may find meditation difficult.
It is also possible to be given to it to excess. The devil
constantly troubles with useless and obscene thoughts those
who make their first endeavour in meditation. For all these
reasons the counsel of a wise director cannot be dispensed
with.

Meditation leads to contemplation; it is the necessary
means without which, except by miracle, we cannot attain to
it. The Chancellor has summed up his teaching on contemplation in the book *On the Mountain of Contemplation.*[4]

[1] *Theol. myst. practica,* vol. iii, pp. 399 ff.
[2] *id., consid.* 1-12, vol. iii, pp. 401-422.
[3] *Tractatus consolatorius de meditatione,* vol. iii, 449, 455.
[4] *De monte contemplationis,* vol. iii, pp. 545-579.

He distinguishes two ways of contemplating supernatural realities : with the mind, and with the heart.

The first consists in an act of the mind, enlightened by faith, which considers God in his essence, his nature and his works. It is that of the learned; it occasionally tends to pride. The other way inclines rather to love than to knowledge. It enables us to taste God, to relish his love, his goodness. The faithful who are without learning may attain to this contemplation, which is the better. For intellectual contemplation, which cannot be transformed into loving contemplation, is of little use to the soul.

Contemplation with the heart then is the summit of this mountain which we have to climb. The faithful soul approaches it by degrees. First of all by humble confession of faults, by tears of penitence, and by mortification of the flesh. In the beginning he experiences great inward desolation at tearing himself from the joys of this world without as yet feeling those of piety. If he overcome this trial he rises to the second degree, that of secrecy and silence : the soul drives from the breast all care and thought of the world. Then comes the third degree of contemplation, that of perseverance. The soul is then in a state of perfection in which it lives in the love of God. It experiences such consolations of divine love that it becomes indifferent to tribulation and to all that happens in the world around it. One thing only concerns it : to love God. It is still able to increase in divine love, for it is only at death that the soul is finally fixed in a state of perfection.

This ascent of the holy mountain is painful. The soul meets with many obstacles which it has to overcome. Gerson describes these at the end of his treatise, and suggests the best means to master them, means which many generous souls employ with success. Why, then, should we not imitate them? Gerson, who constantly cultivated divine charity within him, was himself a great imitator of these faithful souls.

The year before he died he desired once more to sing of that mystical love, the flames of which devoured his soul. This song is a commentary on the *Canticle of Canticles,*[1] dedicated to a Carthusian, in which the highest note of Christian mysticism resounds; that note which was struck by St Bernard, Hugh of St Victor and the author of the *Imitation.* It may be said that this song was written in a

---

[1] *Opera omnia,* vol. iv, pp. 27 ff. This commentary comprises two parts. In the first, the shorter, Gerson treats of the nature of love and of its kinds. In the second, he explains the fifty (mystical number) properties of divine love. St Francis de Sales praised this commentary in his *Treatise on the Love of God.* Cf. *Alphabetum divini amoris,* vol. iii, p. 773.

sort of ecstasy, a prelude to the joy of the elect. On July 9, 1429, three days before his death, Gerson wrote the last note of his song; then he departed to sing in heaven. St Francis de Sales rightly said that he died of love in a transport of love.[1]

III—NICHOLAS OF CUSA AND LEARNED IGNORANCE

THE anti-intellectual controversy known as the *Learned Ignorance* is also connected with the reaction which took place in the fifteenth century against excessive mystical speculations.[2]

It was asked if the soul was not able to attain to God by its own affective power, by its summit (*per mentis apicem*), by its most noble part known as synteresis. Are not the thoughts, the intellectual part of the soul, an obstacle to devotion? In other words, ought piety to be intellectual or agnostic?

Certain writers inclined towards mystical agnosticism, and found themselves in conflict with Gerson, who held that reason and feeling should obtain equally in devotion. Others, among them Nicholas of Cusa,[3] whilst rejecting with energy an excess of scholasticism, seemed to claim for intelligence its proper part in contemplation. The discussions which took place on *Learned Ignorance* are one more proof of the difficulties into which an excess of intellectualism had plunged the minds of the fourteenth century.[4]

[1] Gerson also nobly eulogized the Virgin Mary, especially in his twelve treatises on the *Magnificat*, vol. iv, 235 ff. We should note once again the most wise counsel which he gives to the scrupulous. He recommends them first of all to give their bodies that care which is needful. Scruples often arise through excessive fatigue. Then, faults of past life must not be dwelt on, except to ask pardon of God for them in a general way. They must obey their confessor when he forbids them to make past confessions again. They should perform the duties of the active life with earnestness. Nor should they dwell too much on themselves or their actions. Their minds must not be too greatly filled with the dread of offending God, but they should yield themselves with confidence to his mercy. They must not allow themselves to be affected by evil thoughts, however frequently they occur, but must reject them without worry. It is often better to despise and turn the mind from them rather than resist; they are not sins even though they should cause physical disorder. They thus become occasions for acts of virtue. *Contra scrupulosam conscientiam,* vol. iii, pp. 241-243.

[2] E. Vansteenberghe, *Autour de la Docte Ignorance. Une controverse sur la théologie mystique au XVe siècle,* Münster i. W. 1915.

[3] In a treatise in three books, *De docta ignorantia.* The works of the famous cardinal were published in Paris in 1514 and at Bâle in 1565, in 3 folio volumes.

[4] It was in the monasteries of Upper Bavaria and Lower Austria that the controversy raged from 1451 to 1460 between Vincent, the Carthusian of Aggsbach, a rigid anti-intellectualist, Bernard de Waging, Benedictine of Legernsee, Maitre Marquard Sprenger of Munich, John of Weilhaim, Prior of Melk, and Nicholas de Cusa, moderate anti-intellectualists.

CHAPTER XI

THE ENGLISH MYSTICS—PRAC-
TICAL MYSTICISM IN ITALY
IN THE FIFTEENTH CENTURY

ST FRANCES OF ROME, ST LAWRENCE JUSTINIAN AND ST CATHERINE OF GENOA

TOWARDS the end of the Middle Ages two English writers wrote important treatises which have
recently been republished.

Walter Hilton († 1396), a Canon Regular of
St Augustine, who lived at Thurgarton, is well
known from his *Scale of Perfection*.[1] Juliana of Norwich, a
recluse who passed her life near the Church of St Julian at
Norwich, wrote her *Revelations*.[2]

In Italy during the Great Schism mysticism held sway.

In Rome St Frances was favoured with extraordinary
lights and mystical graces which are recorded by her
biographers. She wrote nothing herself.

St Frances was born in 1384.[3] Married at the age of
twelve years to Lorenzo Ponziani, she was a model wife and
mother. Her great piety inspired her with the idea of
founding, in 1425, a monastery in Rome, which was the
cradle of the *Oblates della Torre Specchi*.

The intention of Frances was to sanctify those living in the

---

[1] *Scala perfectionis,* London 1494, 1507, 1659. English translation
by Fr. Guy, O.S.B., London 1869, republished by Fr. Dalgairns.
From the sixteenth century onwards he was thought by mistake to have
been a Carthusian of Sheen. The *Imitation* also was wrongly attributed
to him. Possibly the oldest English translation of this work was by
him. *Cf.* Puyol, *L'auteur du livre De Imitatione Christi,* 1st section,
pp. 339 ff.; *Descriptions bibliographiques des manuscrits . . . du livre
De Imitatione Christi,* Paris 1898, pp. 327 ff. The reason that W. Hilton
was thought to be the author of the *Imitation* is that one of
his works, *De Musica ecclesiastica,* begins, like the *Imitation,* with
these words from the Gospel, *Qui sequitur me.* Hence the confusion.
MS. copies of the *Imitation* made in England by the Carthusians
were called *Musica ecclesiastica.* W. Hilton wrote other spiritual works
which still remain in MS. *Cf.* Autore, *Dict. de theol. cath.,* art.
Hilton.

[2] *Revelations of Divine Love,* edited by Serenus Cressy, O.S.B., in
1670. Republished in London, 1907.

[3] *Acta Sanct.,* March 9. Cf. *Vie de Sainte Françoise Romaine,* by
Dom Rabory, O.S.B., Paris 1884.

world who were somewhat neglected. The object that the
Order of Oblates had in view was the gathering together of
the ladies and young girls of the Roman nobles who, without
taking formal vows, followed the exercises of the religious
life, and thus set an example of Christian renunciation.
Their Rule was that of St Benedict as observed by the
Olivetans.[1] The holy foundress herself joined them after the
death of her husband in 1436. She died there in 1440,
universally reverenced by the Roman people for her piety
and charity.

St Lawrence Justinian (Lorenzo Giustiniani)[2] was a man
of the same stamp as his contemporary Gerson. He had a
practical mind. His writings, disregarding all vain speculation, had as their chief object the sanctification of religious
and of the secular clergy. They are noticeable also for their
affective style.

In the fourteenth and fifteenth centuries the great wealth
of the monasteries was a cause of corruption only too real.
Lawrence Justinian strove, like St Antoninus, Archbishop of
Florence, St Vincent Ferrer, Dionysius the Carthusian (1471)
and so many others, to bring back the religious to the spirit
of their vocation. He laid down excellent regulations for his
Canons Regular of St George, whose first General he was.
When he became Archbishop of Venice he laboured for the
sanctification of his clergy, whose moral state was far from
satisfactory.

These undertakings largely explain the practical style of
the distinguished prelate's spirituality. His apostolic and
mystical soul is fully revealed in his sermons and spiritual
letters. He exercised a real influence through his ascetic
treatises, and he was often cited in the sixteenth and seventeenth centuries.[3]

Italy, the land of mysticism, again gave us, at the beginning of modern times, St Catherine of Genoa, that great
mystic who may be compared to St Catherine of Siena and
Bl. Angela of Foligno.

---

[1] The Olivetans were founded in 1313 on Monte Oliveto by Bernard
Tolomei. *Cf.* Dom Marechaux, *Vie du B. Tolomei,* Paris 1893.

[2] He was born in Venice in 1380, of an ancient family. In 1424 he
became the first General of the Order of Canons Regular of St George
in Alga, then Bishop of Venice in 1433. Pope Eugene IV bestowed
on him the title of Patriarch of Venice in 1451. He died in 1455.

[3] The best edition of the *Opera omnia* of St Lawrence Justinian is
that of Venice 1751, 2 vols. The ascetic and mystical treatises are in
the second volume : *De compunctione et complanctu christianae perfectionis; De vita solitaria; De contemptu mundi; De obedientia; De
humilitate; De perfectionis gradibus; De incendio divini amoris* (the
passion of Christ); *De regimine praelatorum* (treatise on pastoral
matters).

Mystics, as Gerson has reminded us, have an experimental knowledge of God. Now on account of the wonderful variety of divine works all have not this knowledge in the same way. God shows to each of them a special aspect of his essence. Bl. Angela of Foligno forcibly realized the absolute transcendence of God; St Catherine of Siena, his love and mercy towards men. St Catherine of Genoa was allowed to see and contemplate the incomprehensible purity of the divine essence. The vision and realization of this purity explain her life and works.[1]

She was born at Genoa in 1447 of the illustrious family of the Fieschi, which gave Popes Innocent IV and Adrian V and several cardinals to the Church. She was given a good education, as her writings bear witness. From the age of eight years she began to give herself up to religious exercises and mortification. She never ceased to do penance throughout her life; her biographer tells us that during Lent and Advent she took no other food than Holy Communion. About the age of thirteen, in spite of her desire for the religious life, she married, out of obedience, a young Genoese patrician, Julian Adorno, with whom she lived unhappily for ten years. When she became a widow she consecrated herself to the service of the sick in the great hospital of Genoa. She died in 1510, after a long and painful illness.

One day, while still young, when with her confessor, she had a clear vision of her miseries and failings Her heart received a wound of love which set it wholly on fire.

A vision of purity and the progressive purification of her soul by love; such was her mysticism. " I see without sight," she said, " I understand without intelligence, I feel without feeling, I taste without taste; I know neither shape nor dimension, yet without seeing I see so divine a preparation that all words concerning perfection, cleanness or purity which I uttered before now seem to me to be naught but mockery and fable in comparison with this truth and honesty. The sun which had appeared bright to me before, now seems dark. That which seemed sweet now seems bitter, because all sweetness and beauty becomes spoilt and corrupt by contact with creatures. Afterwards, when the creature is purged, purified and transformed in God, then is seen that

[1] Her *Life* was written by her confessor, Miratoli, and published in 1551. It is quite as much a treatise on mysticism as a biography. Her works are *A Dialogue between the Soul and the Body, Self-Love, the Mind and Humanity of our Lord. Treatise on Purgatory*. The life and the works of St Catherine were written in Italian. A French translation was made by the Carthusians of Bourg Fontaine, published in 1646. *La vie et les œuvres spirituelles de sainte Catherine d'Adorny de Gênes*, 1 vol. 32mo. Père Bouix has translated the *Traité du Purgatoire*, 3rd edition, Paris 1883.

which is pure and true; and this vision, which strictly
speaking is not seen, can neither be thought or spoken of."[1]

The saint saw with a purity of conscience that dreaded the
least fault. "Purity of conscience," she says, "can endure
God alone, who is pure, clean and simple; as for the rest,
no matter what the evil may be, it cannot endure the least
sign of it, nor can this be understood or known except by
one who has felt it."[2]

The words *cleanness* and *purity* were constantly on her lips.
The vision of this purity gave her an extraordinary knowledge of the enormity of sin. "If man were to see the
seriousness of a single sin," she said, "he would rather be
in a fiery furnace, and remain there alive in body and soul,
than endure it within him; and if the sea were a vast fire,
he would rather cast himself into the midst thereof, right to
the bottom, to flee from this sin, nor would he ever go out
thence if he knew that on leaving he would have the sin
within him."[3]

It is love which purifies the soul by transforming it in God,
the infinite purity. St Catherine calls charity pure love,
because of its power to purify that which it inflames. It is
fire that purifies gold. "I clearly understand," she says,
"that when pure love sees the least possible imperfection,
were it not for God's providence it would crush to powder
not only the body but also the soul, were this not immortal.[4]
. . . God enables me to see . . . that his divine essence
is of so great and incomprehensible a purity that the soul,
which has within it the least little imperfection, would rather
cast itself into a thousand hells than present itself before so
holy a majesty in such a state."[5] This purifying love
destroyed in her all pride, all vainglory, by making her feel
how far distant she was from supreme Purity. At the same
time it produced in her an infinite yearning to be wholly
transformed into that Purity. This desire was like an inward
fire which consumed her from her childhood and increased
so greatly that, at the end of her life, she compared it to
the fire of purgatory.

"This world of purification," she said a little while before
her death, "which I see in the souls of purgatory, I feel in
my own soul, especially during the last two years, and I see

---

[1] *Vie de sainte Catherine d'Adorny de Gênes*, chap. ix. The French
is from the edition of 1646 with modified spelling.

[2] *Vie*, chap. xi.

[3] *Vie*, chap. xii. *Cf.* chap. xxiv: "I shall not be astonished to find
purgatory as horrible as hell, seeing that one is intended to purify
and the other to punish, but, as both are made for sin and because
it is so horrible, both punishment and purgation must correspond with
this horror."

[4] *id.*, chap. xv.

[5] *Le Purgatoire*, chap. viii, French translation by Bouix.

and feel it more clearly every day. I see my soul dwelling in my body as in a purgatory such as God has ordained for those souls. It suffers there as much suffering as my body is able to endure without dying."[1] The effects of this purifying love which she felt so intensely within her, Catherine endeavoured to describe in a vivid way in her *Dialogue*.[2] Maybe she here gives the history of an actual soul. Undoubtedly she is inspired by her personal experiences of spiritual realities.

Those represented in the *Dialogue* are the soul, self-love, the mind, humanity and Christ. At the opening, the soul and the body have a conversation on the nature of each and on their respective ends. Self-love is called in to judge, but it combines with the body to draw the soul into sin. Seeing her mistake, the soul becomes converted. God sheds upon her his purifying love. The mind, which is the higher part of the soul, being drawn by God, ranges itself against the body and feeling (human nature), mortifies them and, in spite of their complaint, harshly subdues them. Soon the whole soul is, as it were, submerged and flooded with divine love; the body itself feels the happy effects of it. It is as though lost and beyond its natural being. In the third book, the soul, filled with wonder, asks God why he so loves man who rebels so often against him. Christ steps in to give the answer.

When St Catherine desired to express the violence of the divine love that was within her, she compared it to the torments endured by the souls in purgatory. She was thus led to write her *Treatise on Purgatory*, in which are described from a new point of view the effects of purifying love.

The souls in purgatory are purified from their imperfection through divine love. "Again I see that this God of love," says St Catherine, "this infinitely loving God, throws into the soul in purgatory certain rays and burning lights. These piercing rays and lights, issuing from the infinite love of God, produce two effects—they purify and they annihilate. Consider gold: the longer it remains in the crucible the more it becomes purified; and it may be so purified that all that is impure and foreign to it is destroyed. The love of God does to the soul what fire does to material things; the longer it remains in this divine furnace the purer it becomes. This fire, ever rendering it more pure, ends by annihilating in it all imperfection and all stain, leaving it wholly purified in God."[3]

The torment which the souls in purgatory suffer springs

[1] *Purgatoire*, chap. xvii.
[2] *Vie et Œuvres*, pp. 437-678. The *Dialogue* is divided into three Books.
[3] *Purgatoire*, chap. x.

from an ardent movement imparted to them by love towards
God, and this impulse is checked by the remains of sin not
yet effaced.[1] " For God created the soul pure, simple, clean
from all stain of sin, and with a kind of instinct which draws
it towards him as to its beatific end." Original sin and actual
sin have dispelled this blessed instinct. But " when a soul
returns to its first purity and to the cleanness of its first
creation, this instinct, which impels it towards God as to its
beatific end, is at once awakened within it. Increasing every
moment, this instinct reacts on the soul with terrifying
impetuosity; and the fire of charity which burns it, impresses
it with an irresistible impulse towards its last end, so that
it regards this feeling within it of an obstacle that stops
this impulse towards God as an intolerable suffering; and
the more light it receives, the more intense the torment."[2]

This divine love brings an ineffable joy to the souls in
purgatory, but this joy in no way reduces their torment,
which consists in their inability to be reunited with God.[3]
They are entirely subject to the will of the Lord. They have
no other desire than to remain in this place of torment, fully
conscious that they cannot go to God, purity itself, so long
as their purification remains incomplete.[4]

The *Treatise on Purgatory* was no doubt written by St
Catherine from her revelations, but more particularly from
her mystical states. She attributes to the souls in purgatory
what she herself experienced with regard to purifying divine
love.

Her treatise, moreover, is remarkably accurate in doctrine,
and theologians, not less than mystics, have given it their
attention.

[1] *Purgatoire,* chap. xi.   [2] *id.,* chap. iii.
[3] *id.,* chap. xii. *Cf.* chap. ii.   [4] *id.* chap. i.

CHAPTER XII
THE TEACHING OF THE "IMITATION OF CHRIST" AND THE ANONYMOUS SPIRITUAL WRITERS OF THE MIDDLE AGES
INWARD PIETY BASED ON THE KNOWLEDGE OF GOD AND OURSELVES : GOD AND THE SOUL

DURING the Middle Ages there existed a widely spread form of spirituality which had not been swallowed up by speculative theology, and it reduced all interior life to the knowledge of God and of ourselves.

It is derived directly from St Augustine, who was so greatly studied during the Middle Ages.

In his refutation of the Pelagian heresy, the Bishop of Hippo brought well to light the truth that the heart of fallen man is the most formidable source of incitement to evil. It is much more within than outside ourselves that the battle must be waged. When we are inwardly dead to all that is opposed to our salvation we are safe. Does not one that is dead remain insensible to all outward feeling?

This Augustinian teaching, so psychological and so true, made it more and more understood that the labour of our sanctification is wholly interior, that it is a matter for the soul. Thus the very first condition of spiritual life is the knowledge of ourselves.

St Augustine in his *Soliloquies* makes this prayer to God : "Grant, Lord, that I may know myself and that I may know thee." *Noverim me, noverim te.*[1] He insists over and over again on the necessity for self-knowledge in order to make progress in virtue. To examine the soul, to study its intimate dispositions, and through this knowledge of the soul to come to know and love God; such is the method of that inward piety which the Bishop of Hippo so greatly advocated.

"The humble knowledge of thyself," the *Imitation* again teaches, "is a surer way to God than the deepest search after science.[2] . . . This is the highest and most profitable

[1] *Soliloq.,* lib. II, cap. i.
[2] *De Imit. Ch.,* lib. I, cap. iii.

lesson, truly to know and to despise oneself.[1] . . . Learn to despise outward things and give thyself to things inward, and thou shalt see the kingdom of God will come to thee."[2]

The knowledge of oneself is a sure way of going to God. An anonymous writer says : " Many men are learned yet do not know themselves. They study others and forget themselves. They seek God without and they neglect the interior of their soul where God is present. For my part, I desire to separate myself from outward things ; to retire within myself and be uplifted from my inmost being to that which is highest in order to know whence I come and whither I go, who I am and whence I am, and thus through the knowledge of myself to attain to the knowledge of God. For the more I advance in the knowledge of myself, the nearer I approach to the knowledge of God."[3]

According to the happy expressions of another writer : " To rise towards God is to enter into oneself."[4]

The motto of this spirituality may be expressed in these two words : *God and the soul;* God, our Creator, our Saviour, our end—the greater our knowledge of his goodness, his mercy, his justice, the more we shall love him and avoid offending him ; *the soul*—the disturbing tendencies and mysterious nature of which we must closely examine—studied with such impassioned curiosity during the Middle Ages, as is seen in the famous treatise *De anima,*[5] and the pious analyses of the Christian soul of Hugh of St Victor and St Bonaventure.[6]

" What, then, is this soul," an anonymous writer asks himself, " which has the power of giving life to the flesh, and

---

[1] *De Imit. Ch.*, lib. I, cap. ii.

[2] *id.,* lib. II, cap. i. *Cf.* lib. III, cap. viii. St Bernard, *De Consideratione,* lib. II, cap. iii : " Everything that thou shalt build outside this knowledge of thyself will be like a heap of dust which is at the mercy of the wind.

[3] *Bernardi meditationes seu Meditationes piissimae de cognitione humanae conditionis,* cap. i (*P.L.* CLXXXIV, 485). This writing, which is quoted by St Bonaventure (*Soliloquium,* cap. i), inspired the author of the *Imitation,* who copied from it the passage (cap. v) *quam si te neglecto cognosceres cursum siderum.* Cf. *Imit.,* lib. I, cap. ii. Similar thoughts are found in other anonymous writers : *Liber soliliquiorum animae ad Deum,* cap. xxx-xxxi (*P.L.,* XL, 887-890); *Manuale,* cap. iii (col. 953); *Enchiridion vitae spiritualis ad perfectionem instituens,* cap. vii, republished by Puyol, *L'auteur du livre de Imitat. Ch.,* 1st section, pp. 152-164. See also St Bonaventure, *De perfectione vitae ad sorores,* cap. i, Quaracchi, vol. viii, 108.

[4] *De spiritu et animae* (*P.L.,* XL, 779 ff.), quoted in the *De adhaerendo Deo,* cap. vii, of Albert the Great : *Ascendere ad Deum, hoc est intrare in seipsum.*

[5] See further on, p. 293, note 5.

[6] Hugh of St Victor, *De arrha animae;* St Bonaventure, *Soliloquium.*

yet is powerless to fix itself steadfastly on holy thoughts? What, then, is this soul, at once so strong and so weak, so small and so great, which probes the secrets of God and contemplates heavenly realities, the penetrating genius of which has made so great discoveries in nature and in art? Once more, what is this soul which knows so much of other beings, and is yet completely ignorant of what it is itself and of how it was made?"[1]

The *Imitation of Christ* is itself a most subtle study of the Christian soul. Moreover, although composed by monks and for monks,[2] it will never become obsolete, but remain the book of devotion for the faithful of all generations.

This wholly inward piety is chiefly to be found in anonymous writings.

In the Middle Ages these were spread far and wide. Their authors are hidden, partly, no doubt, from humility, but also occasionally with the object of insuring the success of the works by attributing them to some famous writer. In fact, the greater number of these treatises are grouped round the names of St Augustine, St Anselm, St Bernard, Hugh of St Victor and several others.[3]

Among these anonymous writings Christian piety had long ago discovered edifying works of great value, almost equal to the *Imitation* itself.

In 1498 there appeared at Brescia in Lombardy a small book containing the Latin text of five of these writings: three are attributed to St Augustine, the *Meditations,* the *Soliloquies,* or *Communing of the Soul with God,* and the *Manual;*[4] the fourth is *Meditation* XI of St Anselm on the redemption, one that is certainly authentic; finally, the fifth contains the *Meditations on the Human State,*[5] wrongly put

---

[1] *Augustini meditationes,* xxvii (*P.L.,* XL, 921).

[2] *Cf.* lib. III, cap. lvi.

[3] These writings are found in *P.L.* Those attributed to St Augustine, in vol. xl, 779 ff. ; those to St Anselm, in vol. clviii (see *Dict. de théol. cath.,* i, 1334); those to St Bernard, in vol. clxxxiv; those to Hugh of St Victor, in vol. clxxvii. It is not easy to determine the date of these writings. They were chiefly written in the thirteenth and fourteenth centuries, some of them perhaps in the twelfth.

[4] The *Meditations* (*P.L.,* XL, 901-942) consists of passages taken from St Augustine, St Gregory the Great, St Anselm and Alcuin. Chap. xvi is from St. Peter Damian. According to Mabillon (*P.L.,* XL, 897-902), chaps. xii to xxxvii (excepting chaps. xxvi and xxxi) are by Jean Abbot of Fécamp (1078). I shall quote the *Meditations* under the title *Augustini Meditationes.* The *Soliloquies* (*ibid.,* 863-898) contain numerous passages from St Augustine's *Confessions,* from Hugh of St Victor, St Bernard, St Anselm, Alcuin and Boethius (*De consol. philos.*). The *Manual* is a work of a similar kind.

[5] The *Meditationes piissimae de cognitione humanae conditionis* (*P.L.,* CLXXXIV, 485-508) form the first book of a celebrated anony-

down to St Bernard. These writings have often been republished since, either separately or together.[1] Occasionally also they were included with other small works of special interest.[2] For the above-mentioned anonymous writings are not the only ones that deserve attention.[3]

In all these works certain common features are to be observed.

First, the same system of composition is found in all of them. Their authors delved into the most famous writings of their forerunners, such as St Augustine, St Gregory the Great, St Isidore of Seville, Boethius and Alcuin. The writers of the Middle Ages most frequently quoted are St Anselm, St Bernard and Hugh of St Victor. The greater number of these anonymous writings are like mosaics made up of extracts from several works.[4] That which forms a common bond between them is the intention, the character of the spirituality, which reduces everything to the knowledge of God and ourselves.

Another distinctive characteristic is that we must not ordinarily seek in these works a logical sequence between one chapter and another.

We know that this is the case with the *Imitation,* although written from a much more personal standpoint than the other anonymous treatises. The author places the subjects dealt with together without arranging them in such order as would appeal to the mind. His desire is to teach and not to please. Every chapter of his wonderful work is drafted with care, is helpful to the soul and suggests wholesome thought. Should we wish to form a general synthesis of its teaching and a coherent system of all its parts, showing their connection with each other, we should either be foiled or become entirely

---

mous treatise, *De anima,* which has many resemblances to the *Imitation.* The first book, *Meditationes,* is among the works of St Bernard. I shall refer to it as *Bernardi meditationes;* the second, *De spiritu et anima,* is from St Augustine (*P.L.,* XL, 779-832); the third, *Tractatus de interiori domo,* among those of St Bernard (*P.L.,* CLXXXIV, 507-552 and CLXXVII, 165-170); the fourth, *De anima,* among those of Hugh of St Victor (*P.L.,* CLXXVII, 171-180).

[1] These tracts have often been translated into French, and often republished. The *Soliloquies,* the *Manual* and the *Meditations of St Augustine,* Paris 1691. The five tracts of the Brescia edition were translated by Dom Castel under the title *Dieu et l'âme,* Paris 1913.

[2] The Lyons edition of 1864 adds to the five writings mentioned above the *Contemplationes de divino amore cujusdam idiotae viri docti et sancti.* The author must have been Raymond Jourdan, Abbot of Selles-sur-Cher, who died in 1381.

[3] I shall refer to others in this chapter.

[4] The writer, from whom the greater number of texts was drawn, was chosen to give his name to the whole book. From this point of view, the names under which the anonymous authors have come down to us often offer a clue.

subjective.[1] And would not such an attempt proceed from vanity?

" Never read anything that thou mayest appear more wise or learned. Study rather to mortify thy vices; for this will avail thee more than being able to answer many hard questions."[2]

Finally, in these anonymous writings affective piety predominates. The influence therein of the *Confessions* of St Augustine and the writings of St Bernard is easily recognized. Their authors almost continually address themselves directly to God, and their ardent souls send forth outbursts of divine love which deeply move the reader. Occasionally, as in the *Imitation,* we find a touching dialogue between Christ and the soul. But purely doctrinal considerations are rarely, if ever, to be found. The anonymous writings are collections of pious upliftings of the soul rather than treatises on spirituality.

We shall here consider them as beautiful examples of that inward piety, based on the knowledge of God and of ourselves, which sanctified the souls of so many monks and faithful during the Middle Ages.

I—KNOWLEDGE OF SELF

THIS necessitates above all inward recollection. The soul must strive to turn away from things visible in order, so to speak, to retire within itself to find out what it is and in what state.[3]

The man who thus studies himself first of all acknowledges his great wretchedness when he does not turn to God. The *Imitation* often speaks of this human wretchedness which began with the first fall : the good things of this world only bring us deception; the body, to which is chained the soul, weighs us down and leads us to evil. Temptations give us no peace.[4] In spite of our efforts we cannot wholly avoid sin; sorrow and tribulation often visit us.

" Truly," says in fear the author of the *Imitation*, " it is a misery to live upon earth. The more a man desireth to be spiritual, the more this present life becomes distasteful to him; because he the better understandeth and more clearly

---

[1] Attempts of this kind have often been made. See the synthesis of Heser, in Puyol, *De Imitat. Christi libri quatuor ad fidem codicis Aronensis,* Paris 1898, pp. i-xli. Dumas, *L'Imitation de Jésus-Christ, Introduction à l'union intime avec Dieu,* Paris 1913.

[2] *De Imitat. Christi,* lib. III, cap. xliii.

[3] *De Imit. Chr.,* lib. I, cap. i. *Stude ergo cor tuum ab amore visibilium abstrahere, et ad invisibilia te transferre.* Cf. lib. II, cap. i : *Homo internus cito se recolligit, quia nunquam se totum ad exteriora effundit.* See also *Bernardi meditationes,* cap. xi.

[4] *De Imit. Chr.,* lib. III, cap. lv ; lib. I, cap. xiii.

seeth the defects of human corruption. . . . For the inward
man is very much burdened with the necessities of the body
in this world. . . . Oh, how great is human frailty, which
is always prone to vice! To-day thou confessest thy sins,
and to-morrow thou again committest what thou hast con-
fessed."[1]

The *Soliloquia animae ad Deum* expresses this human
misery in most pessimistic terms which suggest the influence
of St Augustine.

" What then is man that he should commune with God his
creator? Alas! what am I, Lord, who speak to thee? I am
a decaying body, the food of worms, a fetid vessel, fuel for
the fire. What again am I, Lord, who speak to thee? I am
an unfortunate, *born of a woman, living for a short time,
filled with many miseries* (Job xiv, 1). . . . What again,
O Lord? I am a dark abyss, miserable earth, a child of
wrath . . . born in corruption, living in tribulation, and
destined to die in pain. . . . I shall tell thee my misery, O
my God, I do not hesitate to confess to thee my baseness.
Help me, Lord, thou who art my strength by which I shall
arise."[2]

The knowledge of its own misery prompts the Christian
soul to hate itself and to cast away sin, with which it is
stained, by means of pitiless examination of conscience.

" Through the knowledge of thyself," wrote St Catherine
of Siena to one of her companions, " thou shalt acquire the
hatred of thy sensual nature and, armed with the sword of
this hatred, thou shalt preside over the tribunal of thy
conscience to judge thy feelings."[3]

No school has proclaimed the need of this examination
more. Let us hearken to the *Bernardi meditationes:* " As
a severe searcher into the integrity of thy conscience, examine
thy life each day with great care. Take careful notice of
thy progress and failures; what thy morals are and what thy
affections. . . . Discipline thy heart, rule thy actions, correct
thy backslidings. Let there be no irregularity within thee,
and place all thy faults before thine eyes. Set thyself before
thee to judge thyself as before another, *statue te ante te*

---

[1] *De Imit. Chr.*, lib. I, cap. xxii. *Cf.* lib. III, cap. xx. See the
Tractatus de contemplando Deo, cap. ii, 5, of Guillaume de Saint-
Thierry, the friend of St Bernard (*P.L.,* CLXXXIV). Cf. *Augustini
meditationes,* cap. xxi, and, above all, *Bernardi meditationes,* cap. x,
31 : *ex quo peccare coepi, nunquam unum diem sine peccato transire
potui, nec adhuc peccare cesso, sed de die in diem peccata peccatis
addo.* . . . *Levis sum et dissolutus, nec me corrigo, sed ad peccata
quae confessus sum quotidie redeo.* Here are seen the resemblances
with the *Imitation.*

[2] *Soliloq.,* cap. ii. Cf: *Bernardi meditationes,* cap. ii; *Enchiridion,* iv.

[3] *Letter* XLIX, Tommaseo's edition, Florence 1860.

tanquam ante alium, and lament over thyself. Weep for the iniquities and sins by which thou hast offended God."[1]

Pardon for sin will be obtained by confession and " by true contrition and humiliation of heart."[2] Man will thus quiet his troubled conscience and bring peace to his soul. This peace of the soul, this joy of a good conscience, are specially extolled by the author of the *Imitation.* " The glory of a good man is the testimony of a good conscience. Keep a good conscience and thou shalt always have joy. A good conscience can bear very much and is very joyful in the midst of adversity. A bad conscience is always fearful and uneasy. Sweetly wilt thou take thy rest if thy heart reprehend thee not."[3]

The joy of a good conscience must have particularly attracted the attention of a school of spirituality that reduced all piety to the interior life. If man lives in himself he should raise up a beautiful dwelling within him, " the cell of the true knowledge of oneself," as St Catherine of Siena expresses it.[4] This interior dwelling is his conscience. The treatise *De anima,* in its third book, speaks at length of the erection of this interior dwelling of the conscience, which is built by means of reparation for past sins and by wise foresight in order to avoid backslidings in the future.[5]

For once the soul is purified from its faults, the object of examination of conscience is to prevent the soul from falling back into evil. With this in view the Christian should watch himself constantly in order to have a better knowledge of his faults and the divers motions of his heart which might lead him to evil.

The most dangerous of these faults is instability. There is nothing that men of interior life bemoan more than this inconstancy of heart and mind. " The beginning of all temptations," says the *Imitation,* " is inconstancy of mind and small confidence in God. For as a ship without a rudder is tossed to and fro by the waves, so the man who is remiss and who quits his resolution is many ways tempted."[6] " That which is the most fleeting within me," again says the author

---

[1] *Bernardi meditationes,* cap. v. Cf. *De Imit. Chr.,* lib. I, cap. xix : *Mane propone, vespere discute mores tuos; qualis hodie fuisti in verbo, opera et cogitatione, quia in iis saepius forsitan offendisti Deum et proximum. Cf.* lib. IV, cap. vii. Cf. *Soliloquia,* cap. vi; *Augustini medit.,* cap. ii ; *Enchiridion vit. spirit.,* i (Puyol, 153).

[2] *De Imitat. Chr.,* lib. III, cap. lii.

[3] *De Imitat. Chr.,* lib. II, cap. vi, 1-5. *Cf.* lib. I, cap. xi; lib. III, cap. xxiii.

[4] *De Imit. Chr.,* lib. II, cap. vi.

[5] *De anima tractatus de interiori domo seu de conscientia aedificanda* (*P.L.,* CLXXXIV, 507 ff.). It is a kind of treatise on spirituality in which everything is looked at from the point of view of the conscience. The first chapter greatly reminds us of the *Imitation.*

[6] *De Imitat.,* lib. I, cap. xiii.

of the *Bernardi meditationes,* "is my own heart. Every time it escapes me and stretches out to evil thoughts it offends God. O my heart, vain heart, wandering, unstable! When it wanders at the bidding of caprice and is deprived of divine counsel, it cannot rest within itself, and its extreme fickleness carries it away to a multitude of things."[1]

This inconstancy of heart is the more dangerous in that the passions are stirred within us and strive to draw us into evil. Our heart, moreover, will not firmly abide in well-doing unless we mortify our passions and slay them.

This being dead to ourselves to all the evil tendencies that are in man is the end to which this inward piety leads. For "the man that is not yet perfectly dead to himself is soon tempted and overcome with small and trifling things."[2] Is not the flesh, which is our domestic enemy, the most sure help the devil has?[3] The world surrounds us with the snares of covetousness. "Who is able to avoid them? Surely, Lord, it is he whom thou hast freed from pride of the eyes so that he be no longer allured by glances, from whom thou hast taken away the lust of the flesh that he be no longer overcome by it, and whom thou hast healed of arrogance and folly that he be no longer artfully deceived by the pride of life."[4] It is, then, needful that all the labour of sanctification should be directed towards that death to self, of which the *Imitation* makes Christ speak thus:

"But if he [the internal man] will be *spiritual,* indeed, he must renounce as well those that are near him as those that are far off, and beware of none more than of himself. If thou perfectly overcome thyself, thou shalt with more ease subdue all things else. The perfect victory is to triumph over oneself. For he that keeps himself in subjection, so that his sensuality is ever subject to reason, and reason in all things obedient to me, he is, indeed, a conqueror of himself and lord of all the world. If thou desire to mount thus high thou must begin manfully, and set the axe to the root, that thou mayest root out and destroy thy secret inordinate inclination to thyself and to all selfish and earthly goods. This vice by which a man inordinately loves himself, is at the bottom of all that which is to be rooted out and to be overcome in thee; which evil, being conquered and brought under, a great peace and tranquillity will presently ensue. But because there are few that labour to die perfectly to themselves and that fully tend beyond themselves, therefore do they remain entangled in themselves, nor can they be elevated in spirit above themselves. But he who desireth

---

[1] *Bernardi medit.,* cap. ix. Cf. *De Imit. Chr.,* lib. III, cap. xxxiii. *Enchiridion vitae spiritualis,* viii (Puyol, 160).
[2] *De Imit.,* lib. I, cap. vi. [3] *Bernardi medit.,* cap. xii
[4] *Soliloquia,* cap. xii.

to walk freely with me must mortify all his wicked and irregular affections, and must not cleave carnally with selfish love to anything created."[1]

The *Imitation* makes use of a special word to express this absolute renunciation of self—the word *resignatio,* which means a complete sacrifice of oneself and at the same time a trustful abandonment to God.[2] To *resign oneself* is to go out of oneself and to embrace the divine will with all one's strength; it is to be firmly fixed in God by love without having greater desire for either success or reverse until all personal judgement be entirely eradicated from the heart.[3] If we succeed in thus destroying our own will, by that very fact we shall, according to the expression of a contemporary of the *Imitation,* cause the walls of Jericho—that is, our faults—to fall within us.[4]

This total and perpetual renunciation of ourselves is most crucifying. It is the result of a most intense and prolonged effort of the Christian soul assisted by grace.[5] And we must be incited thereto by most powerful motives. These motives must first of all be sought in meditation on the last things. The *Imitation* insists on the safety at the hour of death which is derived from constant self-renunciation.[6]

To know our own misery, to examine the conscience and drive from it sin, to know that our great enemy is within ourselves and that it can only be overcome by interior renunciation, such is the first stage required for this study of the soul in order to reach holiness.

The second consists in " carefully observing in ourselves the divers motions of nature and of grace."[7]

The Christian soul which is freed from sin and has resolutely undertaken the struggle against unruly tendencies feels within it two principles which urge it to action—nature and grace. Although very opposed in themselves, the inspirations which spring from these principles are so subtle

---

[1] *De Imit. Chr.,* lib. III, cap. liii. Cf. *Enchiridion,* cap. ii, iii, vi.

[2] *De Imit. Chr.,* lib. III, cap. xv, xvii, xxxvii; lib. IV, cap. viii.

[3] *Enchiridion vitae spirit.,* vi (Puyol, *op. cit.,* 159).

[4] *ibid.*

[5] *De Imit. Chr.,* lib. I, cap. xxv : *Tantum proficies quantum tibi ipsi vim intuleris.*

[6] *id.,* lib. III, cap. liii : *O quanta fiducia erit morituro quem nullius rei affectus detinet in mundo!* Cf. lib. I, cap. xxiii. The *Bernardi meditationes* also contain meditations on death, judgement and heaven (cap. ii, iv, vii, xiv, xvii). The similarity of thought will be noticed between the *Imitation,* lib. I, cap. xxiii, and this passage (cap. ii) of the *Bernardi meditationes: Cur ergo tantopere vitam istam desideramus, in qua quanto amplius vivimus, tanto plus peccamus?* *Quanto est vita longior, tanto culpa numerosior. Quotidie nempe crescunt mala et subtrahuntur bona.*

[7] *De Imit.,* lib. III, cap. liv.

that it is difficult at times for a man who is not wholly spiritual and interior to distinguish one from the other.[1] Thus the *Imitation* describes them at length with the object of guiding the Christian who desires fully to know himself.

Modern ascetic writers, in conformity with the *Spiritual Exercises* of St Ignatius Loyola, attach considerable importance to the discernment of spirits—that is, to the knowledge of the divers motions produced in the soul by the Spirit of God or the spirit of evil. Nor was the need for this discernment ignored in the Middle Ages. Pierre d'Ailly and Jean Gerson, as we know, pointed out a means of throwing light on the ruses of the devil. The *Imitation*, again, gives rules which help us to distinguish the inspirations of nature from those of grace. They are deduced from a study of the soul itself, all the tendencies of which are closely analyzed.

Here are the sixteen rules (*Imitation*, Bk. III, chap. liv, § 2 ff.) :

" *Nature* is crafty, and draweth away many; ensnareth and deceiveth them, and always intendeth herself for her end : but *grace* walketh with simplicity, turneth away from all appearance of evil, offereth no deceits, and doth all things purely for God, in whom also she resteth as in her last end.

" *Nature* is unwilling to be mortified, or to be restrained, or to be overcome, or to be subject; neither will she of her own accord be brought under : but *grace* studieth the mortification of self, resisteth sensuality, seeketh to be subject, coveteth to be overcome, aimeth not at following her own liberty, loveth to be kept under discipline, and desireth not to have command over anyone; but under God ever to live, stand and be; and for God's sake is ever ready humbly to bow down under all human creatures.

" *Nature* laboureth for her own interest, and thinketh what gain she may reap from others : but *grace* considereth not what may be advantageous and profitable to herself, but rather what may be profitable to many.

" *Nature* willingly receiveth honour and respect : but *grace* faithfully attributeth all honour and glory to God.

" *Nature* is afraid of being put to shame and despised : but *grace* is glad to suffer reproach for the name of Jesus.

" *Nature* loveth idleness and bodily rest : but *grace* cannot be idle, and willingly embraceth labour.

" *Nature* seeketh to have things that are curious and fine, and hateth things that are cheap and coarse : but *grace* is pleased with that which is plain and humble, rejecteth not coarse things, nor refuseth to be clad in old rags.

" *Nature* regardeth temporal things, rejoiceth at earthly gain, is troubled at losses, and is provoked at every slight,

---

[1] *De Imit.*, lib. III, cap. liv.

injurious word : but *grace* attendeth to things eternal, and cleaveth not to those which pass with time; neither is she disturbed at the loss of things, nor exasperated with hard words, for she placeth her treasure and her joy in heaven, where nothing is lost.

"*Nature* is covetous, and is more willing to take than to give and loveth to have things to herself : but *grace* is bountiful and open-hearted, avoideth selfishness, is contented with little, and judgeth it more happy to give than to receive.

"*Nature* inclines to creatures, to her own flesh, to vanities and to gadding abroad : but *grace* draweth to God and to virtues, renounceth creatures, fleeth the world, hateth the desires of the flesh, restraineth wandering about, and is ashamed to appear in public.

"*Nature* willingly receiveth exterior comfort, in which she may be sensibly delighted : but *grace* seeketh to be comforted in God alone, and beyond all things visible to be delighted in the sovereign Good.

"*Nature* doeth all for her own lucre and interest; she can do nothing without reward, but hopeth to gain something equal or better, or praise, or favour for her good deeds; and coveteth to have her actions and gifts much valued : but *grace* seeketh nothing temporal, nor any other recompense but God alone for her reward, nor desireth anything more of the necessities of this life than may be serviceable for obtaining a happy eternity.

"*Nature* rejoiceth in a multitude of friends and kindred; she glorieth in the nobility of her stock and descent; she fawneth on them that are in power, flattereth the rich and applaudeth such as are like herself : but *grace* loveth even her enemies, and is not puffed up with having a great many friends, nor setteth any value on family or birth, unless when joined to greater virtue; she rather favoureth the poor than the rich; she hath more compassion for the innocent than the powerful; she rejoiceth with him that loveth the truth, and not with the deceitful; she ever exhorteth the good to be zealous for better gifts, and to become like the Son of God by the exercise of virtues.

"*Nature* easily complaineth of want and of trouble : but *grace* beareth poverty with constancy.

"*Nature* turneth all things to herself, and for herself she laboureth and disputeth : but *grace* referreth all things to God, from whom all originally proceed; she attributeth no good to herself, nor doth she arrogantly presume of herself : she contendeth not, nor preferreth her own opinion to that of others, but in every sense and understanding she submitteth herself to the eternal wisdom and to the divine examination.

"*Nature* coveteth to know secrets, and to hear news; is willing to appear abroad, and to have experience of many things by the senses; desireth to be taken notice of, and to do such things as may procure praise and admiration : but *grace* careth not for the hearing of news and curious things, because all this ariseth from the old corruption, since nothing is new or lasting upon earth. She teacheth, therefore, to restrain the senses, to avoid vain complacency and ostentation, humbly to hide those things which are worthy of praise and admiration, and from everything, and in every knowledge, to seek the fruit of spiritual profit, and the praise and honour of God. She desireth not to have herself or what belongeth to her extolled; but wisheth that God may be blessed in his gifts, who bestoweth all through mere love."[1]

Grace here is understood to be the sum of all those divine gifts which go to make the spiritual life of the Christian soul. The author of the *Imitation* sings a hymn in honour of this grace.[2] The *Soliloquia* also delight in contrasting the weakness of man with the power of grace. Without it our nature is prone to every evil. There is no crime committed by man which we might not commit ourselves if we were not preserved therefrom by grace.[3]

II—THE KNOWLEDGE OF GOD AND CHRIST

Since we are so weak, should we not turn to God from whom comes all our strength? The soul which knows itself and feels how small a thing it is in itself then attains, through the consciousness of its impotence, its imperfections and its nothingness, to the knowledge of the Highest Good.

"I entered within myself," says the author of the *Soliloquia,* "and spoke to myself thus : Who art thou? and I answered : I am a man, mortal and endowed with reason. And I set myself to reflect on this answer and said : Whence cometh, O God, this creature? Whence, if not from thee? It is thou who hast made me and not I that have made myself. But thou, O Lord, who art thou? Thou, by whom I live and by whom all things live, thou, Lord, art the only true God, omnipotent and eternal, incomprehensible and immense; thou livest for ever, and nothing dies in thee. . . . I give thee thanks, O my Light, who hast enlightened me that I may find thee. When I found myself I knew myself, and when I found thee I knew thee. But I knew thee not

---

[1] *De Imit. Chr.*, lib. III, cap. liv. See in the *Soliloquia* how the snares of Satan (xvi-xvii) and also those of concupiscence (xii) should be discerned.

[2] Lib. III, cap. lv.

[3] *Soliloq.*, cap. xv : *Domine, sic semper gratia et misericordia tua praevenit me, liberans me ab omnibus malis . . . quia nisi tu hoc mihi fecisses, ego omnia peccata mundi fecissem; quoniam scio Domine quod nullum peccatum est quod unquam fecit homo, quod non possit facere alter homo, si desit Creator a quo factus est homo. Cf.* cap. xxiv.

until thou didst enlighten me. . . . But how have I known thee? I have known thee in thyself. I have not known thee as thou art in thine own eyes, but such as thou art for me. I have not known thee without thee, who art the light that has enlightened me."[1]

In the presence of God, the Supreme Being, the soul can only proclaim its nothingness. We know the answer given by Christ to St Catherine of Siena. "Who am I, Lord, who am I? And also tell me who thou art?" she asked of Jesus Christ. "My daughter," he made answer, "thou art that which is not, and I am that which is."[2]

It is the full power of God which is then made manifest to man. This power has made all that exists, and it is as marvellous in the production of small things as of greater, in the creation of the worms of earth as in that of the angels.[3]

Divine Providence takes care of all the beings that are in the world; it applies itself to each one of them as though it were the only one in the universe, as the author of the *Soliloquia* declares with emotion : "It is thou, Lord," he says, "who presidest over all creation, filling every being, ever present everywhere and wholly, having care for all that thou hast created, *for thou didst not appoint or make anything hating it* (Wisd. xi, 24). Thou dost thus consider my footsteps and going; thou watchest over me night and day to protect me, noting with care every movement as an untiring watcher, as if, forgetting all other creatures in heaven and earth, thou hadst to think only of me alone and hadst no longer concern for others."[4]

God's watchfulness follows us unceasingly, not only to watch over us but also to examine our thoughts, our intentions and our actions. The divine eye discovers our most secret motives, it sees what passes in the most intimate parts of our being, whence our designs and actions spring. All is written in the book of life, and one day we shall be judged in accordance with what is written there. God judges with the strictest justice. How fearful then is the need for us to do good and avoid evil, if we would escape eternal punishment.[5]

Thus the knowledge of God leads us to have an exact idea of his justice, and by that means keeps us free from sin. "For," as the author of the *Imitation* says, "he that layeth aside [*postponit*] the fear of God cannot long continue in good, but falleth quickly into the snares of the devil."[6]

---

[1] *Soliloquia animae ad Deum,* cap. xxxi.

[2] Raymund of Capua, *Vie de St Catherine de Sienne,* i, chap. x, French translation, Hugueny, p. 87.

[3] *Soliloquia,* cap. ix : *Omnipotens manus tua, Domine, semper una et eadem, creavit in coelo angelos et in terra vermiculos: non superior in illis, non inferior in istis.*

[4] *Soliloquia,* xiv.   [5] *ibid.*

[6] *De Imit. Ch.,* lib. I, cap. xxiv.

Thus the writings on spirituality which we are examining, while giving the first place to love, are always careful to keep alive in the souls of their readers a sense of the fear of the Sovereign Judge.[1] From this point of view, their teaching is perfectly well balanced and sound.

But love must always have first place. We shall love God so much the more as we better understand his bounties towards us, and these are numberless. But the greatest proof of divine love for us, that which ought to move our gratitude the most, is Christ our Saviour.

There is nothing more touching than the hymns of thanksgiving in the anonymous writings to God the Father, to thank him for the inestimable favour of the redemption. In fact, in what way would the goodness of the Creator have been of use to us if we had not been redeemed by Christ?

"O Lord our God, for how much good are we not beholden to thee, who have been redeemed at so great a price, saved by so excellent a gift, aided by so glorious a boon! How ought not we, wretched ones, to fear thee and love thee, bless thee and praise thee, honour thee and glorify thee; thou who hast thus loved us, saved, sanctified and raised us up! . . . O Lord our God, holy God, good God, God almighty, ineffable, whose nature is limited by nothing, Creator of all things and Father of our Lord Jesus Christ, who hast sent forth from thy bosom this well-beloved Son and our most sweet Lord, that he might make himself manifest to us, take our nature and give his life for us; how can we thank thee sufficiently?"[2]

But Christ is not only our Saviour, he is also the model by which our lives should be ordered. The imitation of Christ, such indeed should be the goal of our efforts; but in order to imitate Jesus we must know him. The study of the divine Master should be the chief duty of the fervent Christian.[3]

"Do not desire," says the author of the *Enchiridion vitae spiritualis,*[4] "to know anything other than *Jesus Christ and him crucified* (1 Cor. ii, 2). If thou knowest Christ well, thy knowledge is sufficient, even though thou knewest nothing of all the rest. Constantly study his life and passion. Contemplate his sufferings in order to suffer with him; how he suffered . . . in order to strive to imitate him; and why he suffered, in order to respond to his charity by loving him in return. Let the continual desire to be able to conform in

---

[1] See especially *Imitation,* lib. I, cap. xxiv; *Augustini medit., iv; Bernardi medit.,* ii-iii; *Manuale,* ii.

[2] *Augustini medit.,* xvii. Cf. *id.,* vi-viii, xiv; *Manuale,* xi, xiii.

[3] Cf. *De Imit. Ch.,* lib. I, cap. i: *Summum igitur studium nostrum sit in vita Jesu meditari.* Lib. I, cap. xxv: *O, si Jesus crucifixus in cor nostrum veniret, quam cito et sufficienter docti essemus!*

[4] vii (Puyol, p. 159). Cf. *Manuale,* xv.

some measure to thy Master grow within thee, by submitting with meekness to every trial, no matter what it may be, which he thinks fit to impose according to his good pleasure."

We know with what a master hand the author of the *Imitation* develops this theme. Christ our Master, *the way, the truth and the life.* (John xiv, 6), invites us to follow him.[1] He teaches us through his doctrine, but still more by his example. That which he teaches us above all is the complete renunciation of self, the perfect *resignatio*. To renounce all things here below, and every desire of the will, in order to be conformed unreservedly to the divine good pleasure—such was the life of Christ.[2] In this renunciation of the Saviour, every virtue is found in a heroic degree—obedience, humility, poverty, contempt of earthly goods, and especially patience in adversity.[3] This perpetual *resignatio* is so crucifying that "Christ's whole life was a cross and a martyrdom."[4] So also should we, if we desire to follow Jesus, enter resolutely into "the royal way of the cross." For we shall seek him elsewhere in vain. By the practice of the *resignatio* he will undoubtedly be found, for "interior renunciation unites with God."[5]

"Lord," asks the author of the *Imitation*, "how often shall I resign myself, *quoties me resignabo,* and in what shall I leave myself?"—"Always," says Jesus, "and at all times; as in little so also in great : I make no exception, but will have thee to be found in all things divested of thyself. Otherwise how canst thou be mine, and I thine, unless thou be, both within and without, freed from all self-will? . . . I have often said to thee, and I repeat it again, forsake and resign thyself, *resigna te*, and thou shalt enjoy great inward peace. Give all for all; seek nothing, ask for nothing back; stand purely and with a full confidence in me and thou shalt possess me."[6]

Jesus is a jealous God. "Thy beloved is of such a nature that he will admit of no other; but will have thy heart to himself, and sit there like a king on his throne."[7]

When the soul has grasped the demands of the divine Master and complies therewith, it becomes the intimate of Jesus and enjoys the sweetness of his love. The vanity of creatures becomes clearly apparent to it. "The love of things created," it cries, "is deceitful and inconstant; the love of

[1] *De Imit. Ch.*, lib. I, cap. i; III, cap. ix, lvi.
[2] *Cf.* lib. III, cap. xv, xvii, xxxvii.
[3] *Cf.* lib. I, cap. xx; III, cap. xxiv; III, xiv, xviii, xix.
[4] *De Imit. Ch.*, lib. II, cap. xii. This twelfth chapter, *De regia via sanctae crucis,* sums up admirably the teaching of the *Imitation* on Christian renunciation as taught by the example of Christ.
[5] *id.*, lib. III, cap. lvi.   [6] *id.*, lib. III, cap. xxxvii.
[7] *id.*, lib. II, cap. vii.

Jesus is faithful and persevering. He that cleaveth to creatures shall fall with them. He that embraceth Jesus shall stand firm for ever."[1]

We must, then, love Jesus. " Love him and keep him for thy friend who, when all go away, will not leave thee nor suffer thee to perish in the end."[2]

And how shall we speak of the joy of that soul which possesses the heavenly Friend and rejoices in his presence?

" When Jesus is present, all goeth well, and nothing seemeth difficult, but when Jesus is absent, everything is hard. When Jesus speaketh not within, our comfort is worth nothing; but if Jesus speak but one word, we feel great consolation. Did not Mary Magdalen arise presently from the place where she wept when Martha said to her, The Master is here, and calleth for thee? Happy hour when Jesus calleth from tears to joy of spirit ! How hard and dry art thou without Jesus ! How foolish and vain if thou desire anything out of Jesus ! Is not this a greater change than if thou wert to lose the whole world? What can the world profit without Jesus? To be without Jesus is a grievous hell; and to be with Jesus a sweet paradise. If Jesus be with thee, no enemy can hurt thee."[3]

The mutual love of Jesus and the Christian soul is expressed in the touching dialogues with which the Third Book of the *Imitation* is filled. We also find outbursts of love for Christ and tender outpourings to the Redeemer of the world worthy of St Bernard in the other anonymous writings, especially in the *Manuale:* " Grant, O Lord my God, thou fairest of the sons of men, that I desire thee and love thee as much as I wish and as I should. Thou art immeasurable and must be loved without measure, above all by us whom thou hast loved without reckoning, whom thou hast saved, and for whom thou hast accomplished such great marvels. O Love who ever burnest without quenching, O Christ Jesus, most good and sweet, O Love, my God, consume me wholly in thy fire, in thy charity, in thy sweetness, thy love, thy tenderness . . . so that being filled with the sweetness of thy love, wholly consumed with the flame of thy charity, I may love thee, my most sweet and fairest Lord, with all my heart, with all my soul and with all my strength !"[4]

---

[1] *id.,* lib. II, cap. vii.

[2] *De Imit Ch.,* lib. II, cap. vii. This passage of the *Imitation* may be compared with chap. xxiv of the *Manuale: Elige illum [Christum] amicum tuum prae omnibus amicis tuis, qui, cum omnia subtracta fuerint solus tibi fidem servabit. In die sepulturae tuae, cum omnes amici tui recedent a te, ille te non derelinquet.*

[3] *De Imit.,* lib. II, cap. viii. Cf. *Manuale,* iv : *Vae miserae animae quae Christum non quaerit nec amat; arida manet et misera.* See also *Augustini meditationes,* xxxix : *Ecce jam morior et Jesus non est mecum. Et certe melius est mihi non esse quam sine Jesu esse, melius est non vivere quam vivere sine vita.*

[4] *Manuale,* x. *Cf.* iv-vi ; xi-xiii.

The loving soul finds an infinite sweetness in meditation on the passion of Christ. When in the throes of tribulation it seeks refuge in the wounds of the Saviour, where, with St Bernard, it desires to fix its abode for ever. " Rest in the passion of Christ," says the *Imitation,* " and willingly dwell in his holy wounds. For if thou fly devoutly to the wounds and precious stigmata of Jesus, thou shalt feel great comfort in tribulation : neither wilt thou much regard being despised by men, but wilt easily bear up against detraction."[1]

The soul must not become too attached to these consolations which are found in the presence of Jesus, otherwise it would seek itself and its own interest. He who loves Jesus for Jesus and not for himself will bless him in tribulation and sorrow of heart as well as in the sweetest of joys. Does not the constant seeking of consolations belong to the hireling? Is it not the love of self rather than that of Jesus? True *resignatio* calls for the renunciation even of the joy to be found in the service of God.[2]

III—MYSTICAL UNION ACCORDING TO THE ANONYMOUS WRITERS OF THE MIDDLE AGES

THESE writings sing the praises of mystical love in language which yields nothing to that of St Bernard and Hugh of St Victor.

" Love," cries the author of the *Imitation,* " is an excellent thing, a great good indeed, which alone maketh light all that is burdensome, and equally beareth all that is unequal. For it carrieth a burden without being burdened, and maketh all that which is bitter sweet and savoury. . . . Nothing is sweeter than love, nothing stronger, nothing higher, nothing more generous, nothing more pleasant, nothing fuller or better in heaven or earth; for love is born of God, and cannot rest but in God, above all things created. The lover flieth, runneth, rejoiceth; he is free and not held. He giveth all for all, and hath all in all; because he resteth in one supreme Good above all, from whom all good floweth and proceedeth. . . . . Love watches, and sleeping slumbers not. When weary, it is not tired; when straitened, is not constrained; when frightened, is not disturbed; but, like a lively flame and a torch all on fire, it mounteth upwards and securely penetrateth all. Whosoever loveth knoweth the cry of this

---

[1] *Imit.,* lib. II, cap. i. Similar thoughts are found in the *Manuale,* xxiii : *Clavi et lancea clamant mihi quod vere reconciliatus sum Christo, si eum amavero. Longinus aperuit mihi latus Christi lancea, et ego intravi, et ibi requiesco securus. Id.,* xxi, xxii : *Copiosa redemptio data est nobis in vulneribus Christi, magna multitudo dulcedinis, plenitudo gratiae, et perfectio virtutum. Cum me pulsat aliqua turpis cogitatio recurro ad vulnera Christi. Cum me premit caro mea recordatione vulnerum Domini mei resurgo.* Cf. *Augustini Medit.* xli.

[2] *De Imit.* lib. II, cap. xi.

voice. A loud cry in the ears of God is the ardent affection of the soul, which saith : O my God, my love, thou art all mine, and I am all thine !"[1]

When the soul is rapt in God and receives the kiss of the Bridegroom, it utters a cry of ineffable sweetness. " I bless thee, O heavenly Father, Father of my Lord Jesus Christ, because thou hast vouchsafed to be mindful of so poor a wretch as I am. O Father of mercies and God of all comfort, I give thanks to thee who sometimes art pleased to cherish with thy consolations me who am unworthy of any comfort. I bless thee and glorify thee for evermore, together with thy only begotten Son, and the Holy Ghost the Comforter, to all eternity. O Lord God, my holy Lover, when thou shalt come into my heart, all that is within me will be filled with joy. Thou art my glory and the joy of my heart. Thou art my hope and my refuge in the day of my tribulation. . . . Give increase to my love that I may learn to taste with the interior mouth of the heart how sweet it is to love, and to swim, and to be dissolved in love. Let me be possessed by love, going above myself through excess of fervour and ecstasy. Let me sing the canticle of love ; let me follow thee, my Beloved, on high ; let my soul lose herself in thy praises, rejoicing exceedingly in thy love. Let me love thee more than myself, and myself only for thee, and all others in thee, who truly love thee, as the law of love commandeth, which shineth forth from thee !"[2]

In mystical union the soul becomes like to God, so that it becomes but one and the same mind with him. But this unity of mind is simply affirmed. Our writers do not attempt to explain it. Theories are held in disregard.

[1] *De Imit.,* lib. III, cap. v.
[2] *ibid.* Cf. *Soliloquia animae ad Deum,* xviii-xix; *Manuale,* iii; *Augustini Medit.,* xxxv. The *Scala claustralium,* cap. v, thus describes mystical union : " During prayer, God suddenly interrupts its course. He unexpectedly fills the soul which so ardently desires his coming, floods it with the dew of heavenly sweetness and fills it with mystical perfumes. He brings rest to its weariness, sates it and refreshes it." (*P.L.* CLXXXIV, 479).

CHAPTER XIII
THE CARTHUSIAN SCHOOL AND ITS SPREAD IN GERMANY FROM THE FOURTEENTH TO THE SIXTEENTH CENTURIES

THE Carthusian school, at the end of the Middle Ages and the beginning of modern times, forms a summary of the teaching as it embodies the mind of the scholastic spirituality. The *Life of Christ* of Ludolph the Carthusian († 1370) is a complement to the pious meditations of St Bernard, of the pseudo-Bonaventure and of many others on the earthly life of the Saviour. Dionysius the Carthusian († 1471), the most prolific writer of his school, continues the tradition of Hugh and Richard of St Victor, of St Bonaventure and of Gerson; he transforms speculative spirituality into affective science. He was, moreover, well acquainted with all the systems and all the ascetic and mystical theories of his forerunners.

The Carthusian Order was, from its beginning, a school of practical mysticism, and it has always remained so. Even when it popularized the speculative mysticism of the German writers of the fourteenth century, it was Lawrence Surius, a Carthusian, who translated them into Latin, his object being to foster the piety of religious and the faithful.

These mystical and practical tendencies are a family legacy handed down from the older Carthusians to their successors. St Bernard had relations with the first monks of St Bruno, and his mystical influence made itself felt in them. He had correspondence with the Grande Chartreuse on monastic perfection—love of God was its most constant theme.[1] The second Prior of the Carthusian monastery of Des Portes, named Bernard, was one of the first to be informed of the appearance of the Abbot of Clairvaux's commentary on the *Canticle of Canticles*. He had earnestly begged this favour.[2]

Cistercians and Carthusians exchanged visits. St Bernard once journeyed to the Grande Chartreuse, happy to find among the sons of St Bruno those traditions of monastic austerity which he so much loved.[3]

Finally, it was to a Carthusian monastery, that of Mont-

---

[1] *S Bernardi epist.*, xi, xii.   [2] *id.*, cliii, cliv.
[3] *Bernardi Vita*, lib. III, cap. ii, 3-4.

Dieu, that the famous *Epistola ad Fratres de Monte Dei* was written, in which the effects of mystical love are somewhat exaggerated.[1]

I—THE ORIGIN OF THE CARTHUSIAN SCHOOL IN THE ELEVENTH CENTURY

THE Carthusian Order was a creation entirely *sui generis*, in which the eremitical life was combined with that of cenobites.

St Bruno,[2] its founder, was irresistibly inclined to the solitary life. He was, nevertheless, perfectly aware that solitude, especially in our climates, has its drawbacks. In order to avoid these as much as possible, he established in his convent of the Grande Chartreuse a semi-community régime. The religious lived singly—at first they were two and two—in their cells where, like the ancient hermits of the eastern deserts, they prayed, worked, ate and slept. Every day they met together in choir in the church for the singing of Matins and Vespers and the celebration of Mass before Terce. The other hours of the Office were recited in their cells. On feast days, meals were served in the refectory; they also heard a sermon. The fast days also were as frequent as at Cîteaux; meat was never allowed. On three days of the week—Monday, Wednesday and Saturday—the food of the monks consisted solely of bread, water and a little salt.

St Bruno did not draw up any Rule, for it was not his intention to found an Order. He left to his disciples traditions and customs which were only codified later. It was Dom Guigues I, the fifth Prior of the Grande Chartreuse, who put in writing the *Customs*[3] of his monastery, at the request of St Hugh, Bishop of Grenoble, and according to the wishes

[1] See p. 130.

[2] St Bruno was born at Cologne about 1032. At the age of fifteen he went to study at Rheims, then at Paris. He was appointed head-master at Rheims, where he taught most brilliantly and had some famous pupils, among them Pope Urban II and St Hugh, Bishop of Grenoble. He became Chancellor of Rheims from 1075 to 1082, but felt the love of the monastic life constantly increasing within him. He entered the monastery of Molesmes, and placed himself under the guidance of St Robert, the future founder of Cîteaux. Wishing for a solitary life, Bruno, with six companions, founded, about 1084, the monastery of the Grande Chartreuse, in the diocese of Grenoble. Bruno lived for some time at Rome under Urban II, then founded, about 1092, the Carthusian Monastery of La Calabra in Southern Italy. He died there on October 6, 1101. *Acta Sanctorum, 6 Octobris.* St Bruno left *Commentaries on the Psalms* and on the *Epistles of St Paul.* (*P.L.,* CLII, 637; CLIII, 1-566). There are also some sermons of his.

[3] *Guigonis, Carthusiae Majoris prioris quinti, Consuetudines* (*P.L.,* CLIII, 635-758). The *Consuetudines* comprised eighty chapters, which formed the first edition of the Carthusian Rule. Later on were added the *Statutes* or regulations of several general chapters which were held after the twelfth century.

of the Prior des Portes, of St Sulpice and of Meyria. This was about 1128.

As stated by Guigues in the preface to his work, the *Customs* are drawn from the older monastic rules, especially the *Letters* of St Jerome, for the eremitical part of the Carthusian life, and from the Benedictine Rule as regards the cenobitic.

At the beginning, the different Carthusian monasteries were subject to episcopal jurisdiction and did not form an Order. It was Anthelm, Prior of the Grande Chartreuse, who, in 1142, held the first general chapter, and united and made subject to the mother-house the greater number of Carthusian monasteries then existing. Thus was the Order constituted.

It has always maintained its primitive fervour, and alone has the privilege of never having needed reform. In 1688, Pope Innocent XI, in the Bull *Injunctum nobis,* was able thus to proclaim the eulogy of the Order : *Cartusia nunquam reformata, quia nunquam deformata.*

II—THE SPREAD OF THE CARTHUSIAN SCHOOL FROM THE FOURTEENTH TO THE SIXTEENTH CENTURIES

THE Carthusian school did not produce any spiritual writer of mark before the end of the thirteenth century.[1] At this period it became famous through Ludolph the Carthusian at Strasbourg; a little later, through Dionysius the Carthusian at Roermond in the Low Countries, and by Lanspergius and Surius at Cologne. Faithful to the primitive spirit of their Order, preference was given by these writers to the study of mystical theology.

Ludolph of Saxony,[2] better known under the name of Ludolph the Carthusian, wrote a *Life of Christ*[3] which had a considerable influence on Christian piety. It was translated into almost every language and had, for more than two centuries, an undisputed vogue.

---

[1] See a full list of Carthusian writers in the *Dict. de théol. cath.,* art. *Chartreux*, by S. Autore.

[2] Ludolph was born in Saxony about the year 1300. He first became a Dominican. Then, about 1330, he entered the Carthusian Monastery of Strasbourg, of which he became Prior. He died in 1370.

[3] *Vita D.N. Jesu Christi e sacris quatuor evangeliorum Sanctorumque Patrum fontibus pie simul ac ample derivata in christianae pietatis educationem et oblectamentum.* Strasbourg 1474; Nuremburg 1478; *Paris* 1592, 1617; Lyons 1530, 1554, 1644. I quote from this last edition. French translations by Menand, Paris 1490, 1500, and by Fresnoy, Paris 1580. Ludolph also wrote a mystical commentary on the Psalms : *Commentaria in psalmos davidicos juxta spiritualem praecipue sensum,* Paris 1506, 1517 and 1528; Lyons 1640.

Whence came this exceptional success? In the first place it was the novelty of the work. So far no complete biography of Christ had been written. The nearest approach to it were the *Meditations* of the pseudo-Bonaventure on the life and passion of the Saviour. But this work, by which, however, Ludolph was inspired, was a mere outline compared with the monumental book of the learned Carthusian. The *Life of Christ* comprises the whole drama of our salvation in all its details, with the eternal generation of the Word and the plan of the Incarnation in the bosom of the Trinity as its prologue, and the Last Judgement, heaven and hell as its epilogue. Thus the lives of Christ and his blessed mother are minutely and consecutively dealt with.[1] So extensive and edifying a subject had never before been suggested to the faithful for meditation.

The writer's object is wholly mystical : to promote the love and imitation of Christ. Let us listen to the dispositions with which he wishes the life of the Saviour to be read.

It must not be read hastily as though pressed for time, but gravely, little by little, in small mouthfuls, so to speak, in order to taste what is read. Before opening the book the tumult of worldly matters must be silenced. And when it has been closed care must be taken to link the thoughts, affections, prayers and the whole work of the day with the things that have been read.[2]

It is a meditation rather than a reading that Ludolph suggests. He himself declares at the end of his work that he wished to draw up a collection of meditations suitable for the development of divine love in the soul.[3] Thus understood the *Life of Christ* is most helpful to sinners who wish to obtain forgiveness of their sins, to beginners who desire to labour for their perfection, to those who have progressed and to the perfect who aspire to contemplation.[4] The method followed by Ludolph may be conjectured. Nowadays we require writers of the *Life of Christ* to proceed faultlessly according to the rules of criticism, and to state nothing that is not supported by well-authenticated documentary evidence. We insist on the historical Palestinian setting in which Christ lived. Mysticism attaches no importance to this historical surface. It is the soul of the Saviour and the souls of those who lived with him that it desires to grasp. Ludolph meant the reading of his work to be a communion of the soul with Christ, a loving meditation, and not a mere study. More-

---

[1] The work is divided into two parts. The first contains ninety-two chapters and the second eighty-nine.

[2] *Vita Christi*, Prologue, Lyons 1644, pp. 2-3.

[3] *id.*, pars II, cap. 89, p. 735: *Habes quippe meditationum spiritualium seminarium ex quibus divini amoris fructus uberior oritur.*

[4] *id.*, Prologue, *ibid.*

over, he paid very little attention to what in these days we call criticism. He bore in mind the saying of St John that all that Christ did or said was not written. He made up for the silence of the Gospel by accounts from apocryphal sources and also inventions of his imagination in keeping with the truths of faith and probability.[1] In this the pseudo-Bonaventure leads the way. In order, moreover, to move hearts the more Ludolph quotes most impressive words on the mysteries of the *Life of Christ* used by St Ambrose, St Augustine, St John Chrysostom, and especially by St Bernard. These quotations are, as it were, the thread of his narrative. The *Life of Christ* thus conceived is a most attractive book of mysticism and we can understand the important influence it had on souls.

Writings, however, equally suited to all epochs are rare. The growth of Protestant heresy brought forth fresh needs. Religious polemics, which had become necessary in order to combat the errors of the Reformation, have made a stricter presentment of Gospel history popular. The work of Ludolph thus became discredited, and soon, for many, possessed but an archæological interest.

Dionysius the Carthusian[2] was a most active writer. His published works comprise forty-five quarto volumes.[3] And yet he was frequently in ecstasy! Some of these lasted as

[1] *Vita Christi,* Prolog., pp. 4-5 : *Nec credas quod omnia quae Christum dixisse vel fecisse meditari possumus scripta sint, sed ad majorem impressionem ea tibi narrabo prout contigerunt vel contigisse pie credi possunt, secundum quasdam imaginarias repraesentationes quas animus diversi modo percipit. Nam circa divinam scripturam meditari, intelligere et exponere mutifarie possumus prout credimus expedire, dummodo non sit contra veritatem vitae, vel justitiae aut doctrinae, id est, non sit contra fidem vel bonos mores. . . . Cum ergo me narrantem invenies: Ita dixit vel fecit Dominus Jesus, seu alii qui introducuntur, si id per scripturam probari non possit, non aliter accipias quam devota meditatio exigit. Hoc est, perinde accipe ac si dicerem: Meditor quod ita dixerit vel fecerit bonus Jesus, et sic de similibus.* It will be noticed that Ludolph here repeats the expressions of the pseudo-Bonaventure.

[2] Dionysius, called the *Ecstatic Doctor,* was born in 1402, at Ryckel, in Belgian Limburg. He belonged to the family of Leeuvis or Van Leeuven. After completing his studies he entered, at the age of twenty-one, the Carthusian Monastery of Roermond, near Liége. His life was divided between prayer and study. He wrote to the princes of Christendom in order to induce them to undertake a new crusade against the Saracens. He died on March 12, 1471, greatly renowned for sanctity. His *Life* was written by a Carthusian of Cologne, Dom Thierry Loher, Cologne 1532, reproduced in *Acta Sanct.,* March 12, pp. 243 ff., Paris 1865. *Cf.* S. Autore, *Dict. de théol. cath.,* art. *Denys le chartreux.*

[3] A complete edition was begun by the Carthusians of Montreuil-sur-Mer (Pas-de-Calais), and was continued at Tournai (Belgium). The first edition was printed at Cologne after 1530 under the care of T. Loher.

long as three hours consecutively.[1] He was surnamed the *Ecstatic Doctor*. He belongs to the number of those mystics, like St Catherine of Siena and St Colette, whose activity was not paralyzed by ecstasy. Dionysius wrote commentaries on Holy Scripture, was a philosopher, theologian, an author of sermons, an ascetic and mystical writer, and had studied every branch of ecclesiastical knowledge.

Dionysius, learned rather than original, summarized the teaching of the writers of the Middle Ages, both the qualities and faults of whom, more particularly their lack of historical criticism, are reflected in his works. He accepts blindly the legends of James de Voragine or Peter Comestor,[2] and, rather than hold their veracity suspect, he adapts, at times unhappily, his theological teaching to them. His treatise *De quatuor hominis novissimis*[3] was keenly criticized, because in virtue of an apocryphal vision[4] he teaches that, through a special permission of God, certain souls in purgatory are in doubt as to their final salvation, and that this torturing doubt is the chief cause of their sufferings. But these defects are primarily due to the notion as to history which prevailed at that time. They did not injure the success of the treatise, which was often republished and translated into different languages, and helped many generations of Christians to prepare for death.[5]

All the ascetic works of Dionysius, and they were many, were equally appreciated. They were addressed to every class of Christian society : clergy, religious and laity, pointing out to all what they should do in order to become reformed.[6] But Dionysius was not content merely to point out duty ; he aimed higher. His readers are instructed in the rules of asceticism. He teaches them to despise the world, to abhor sin, to resist temptations, to pray and to taste the joys of the interior life. These various points of asceticism are dealt with in a series of small treatises,[7] some of which, during the

[1] *Dionysii carth. Vita,* cap. v, *Acta SS.,* p. 249. In his raptures Dionysius had no imaginative visions. God taught him through intellectual images. *ibid.*

[2] Peter Comestor died at the Abbey of St Victor in Paris about 1180. He published a *Historia scholastica* full of legends, Utrecht 1473, Paris 1495.

[3] lib. IV, art. 47.

[4] A vision of a Cistercian monk of Eynsham, *Analecta bollandiana,* vol. xxii, p. 225. We read of visions of purgatory in the *Life* of St Lydwine, *Acta SS.,* April 14, vol. ii, p. 292, Paris 1866; Pohl, *Thomae À Kempis opera,* vol. vi, p. 385, 416, 419.

[5] The *Directoire des Exercises de St Ignace,* approved in 1549, is inspired by them.

[6] *Opuscula insigniora, De omnium ordinum sive statuum institutione, prolaptione ac reformatione,* Cologne 1559, 1 vol.

[7] *De arcta via salutis et contemptu mundi; Speculum amatorum mundi; Liber de gravitate et enormitate peccati; Liber de conversione peccatoris; Ad mundi contemptum exhortatio elegiaca; De oratione; De remediis tentationum; De gaudio spirituali et de pace interna.*

sixteenth century, had a popularity comparable to that of the *Imitation*.[1]

The tracts of Dionysius on mystical theology were gathered together in a collection published at Cologne in 1534.[2] Among them is the treatise, in three books, *On Contemplation*, a work both theoretical and practical, in which the style of the author is well shown. The second part of the work is a summary of the theories of the mystical teachers of the Middle Ages on contemplation. In the two others, Dionysius expounds the conception of it which seems to him the best.

Contemplation, he declares, is an act of the gift of wisdom. This doctrine, belonging to the school of St Dominic, is well-known to us. It was much exploited by Tauler, Suso and Ruysbroeck. Dionysius had made a study of the German mystics.[3] He is also influenced by the writings of Dionysius the Areopagite, which were well known to him and on which he wrote a commentary.[4] Again, he makes the basis of the highest contemplation consist in total, absolute renunciation, " complete abnegation "—the body must be deprived of its comforts, the imagination of its images, the mind of its thoughts; the contemplative must know God by negation. Dionysius, however, understands how to avoid all exaggeration.

Mystical union is characterized, according to him, by a conscious contact of the soul with God, brought about by love which has reached an extraordinary degree of intensity.[5] It will be remembered that Ruysbroeck speaks of the divine touch felt in the soul in mystical union which inebriates with joy. Mystics of the Middle Ages employ analogous terms in order to express the divine action on the soul that God has chosen as a bride. Dionysius continues them and explains them.

He seems to have been the first formally to distinguish two sorts of contemplation : that which by the aid of grace may be acquired by our own effort, called *active* or *ordinary* contemplation;[6] and that which constitutes the mystical state, properly so-called, only reached by those who are called to it.

This distinction came to be accepted little by little in the

[1] Especially the *Speculum conversionis* and the *Speculum amatorum mundi*.

[2] *Opuscula aliquot quae ad theoriam mysticam egregie instituunt*, Cologne. Reprinted separately at Montreuil-sur-Mer, 1894. The ascetic treatises *De fonte lucis et semitis vitae* and *De discretione spirituum*, comprising the mystical conceptions, must be added to them. The last-named tract was long neglected and was only published in 1620 at Aschaffenburg.

[3] Especially Ruysbroeck, whom he described as " a divine teacher," " another Dionysius the Areopagite."

[4] His commentaries on the writings of the Areopagite were published at Cologne in 1536.

[5] See *De discretione spirituum*, xviii.

[6] *De fonte lucis et semitis vitae*, cap. viii.

treatises on spirituality of the future. It put an end to a
regrettable confusion. Writers of the Middle Ages, such as
the school of St Victor and even St Bernard, treat of the
different kinds of contemplation, that of scientific truths and
that of revealed truths and ecstatic contemplation, without
distinction, without telling us precisely what distinguishes
one from the other. Inexperienced readers find a difficulty
in clearly grasping their teaching. In modern times spiritual
writers, guided by Dionysius the Carthusian, will be found to
be more precise.

Dionysius aptly brings the ascetic and mystical Middle
Ages to a conclusion. He sums up this period in an attractive manner, for he is a great affective writer. It is easy to
understand how the writers who came after him, especially
St Ignatius Loyola, St Francis de Sales, Alvarez de Paz, had
so much regard for him and so often quoted him.

It was the Carthusians of Cologne who, in the sixteenth
century, edited the works of Dionysius.

At Cologne, the native town of St Bruno, there was at that
time a Carthusian monastery famous for its intellectual labours
which produced several writers of mark, among them Thierry
Loher, the biographer and editor of Dionysius, Lanspergius,
and Lawrence Surius.

John Lanspergius or Lansberg[1] is chiefly known by his
Colloquies of Jesus Christ with the Faithful Soul,[2] which
reminds us of the *Imitation.* It was he who prepared the
first Latin edition of the *Revelations* of St Gertrude, entitled
Insinuationes divinae pietatis. From these he imbibed a
tender devotion to the Heart of Jesus.[3]

Lawrence Surius[4] is the hagiographer of the Carthusian
school. It is in this role, and also as translator of the
German mystics, that he has interest for the history of
spirituality.

[1] He was born in Bavaria, became a Carthusian at Cologne, where
he died in 1539 when he was about fifty years old. He was surnamed
the *Just* on account of his piety. He laboured for the conversion of the
Lutherans.

[2] *Alloquium Jesu Christi ad animam fidelem,* Louvain 1572, translated into French and several other languages. The works of Lanspergius were published at Cologne in 1693 in two volumes. The
Carthusian fathers of Montreuil-sur-Mer have republished the *Opuscula spiritualia (Opera Joannis Lanspergii Justi).* Lanspergius also
wrote certain spiritual Letters : *Epistolae paraeneticae ac morales*
(Opera, vol. iv, pp. 79-246).

[3] *Cf.* Dom Boutrais, *Un précurseur de la B. Marguerite-Marie
Alacoque au XVIe siècle. Lansperge le chartreux et la dévotion au
Sacré-Cœur,* Grenoble 1878.

[4] He was born at Lübeck in 1522. He went to study at Cologne, where
he formed a friendship with Peter Canisius. In 1542 he became a
Carthusian at Cologne, and died there in 1578.

One of his contemporaries, Aloisio Lippomani, Bishop of Verona (1560), edited eight volumes of *Lives of the Saints*.[1] It chiefly consists of a translation from ancient Greek hagiographers, Palladius, John Moschus, and Metaphrastes. The hagiography of Gregory of Tours is also included. Surius incorporated the work of Lippomani with his own, arranging the Lives of the Saints in martyrological order. But he added many other manuscript biographies, and, in 1570, he published his edition of the *Lives of the Saints*.[2]

The learned Carthusian, in this work, gave greater evidence of piety than of true historical sense. He was particularly careful to allow nothing to pass which could furnish any opportunity for heretical jeers. We must not forget that Protestantism had come into being, and that it attacked with unheard-of savageness the cultus of the saints. This is Surius' excuse. Otherwise we would be justified in treating him with severity on reading in his Preface that he had passed over in silence a great number of accounts in MS. biographies and had retouched the style of the writers whom he quotes.[3] To-day we would describe a proceeding of this kind as tampering with documents. Protestants might with some appearance of truth detract from the value of this work, which, however, in other respects has merit.

Surius brought his work up to the end of June, when he died in 1578. One of the Cologne Carthusians continued it. The work had a great success. Another edition appeared in 1618,[4] continuing the lines followed by Surius.

Doubtless the hagiographic work of Surius is not perfect. It still leaves much to be done by the Bollandists. However, it rendered invaluable service by making the reading of the Lives of the Saints popular. Collections of these pious biographies were drawn up in every language, and it was from the work of Surius that their compilers borrowed. The learned Carthusian thus assisted in maintaining the love of the cultus of the saints among the faithful in spite of the Reform.

It was also his ardent yearning for the sanctification of souls which prompted him to translate the works of the German and Flemish mystics of the fourteenth century into Latin. Surius zealously supported the intentions of the society of the *Friends of God,* which was so flourishing at Cologne, and set itself the task of rendering mysticism

---

[1] *Historiae de vitis Sanctorum,* Rome 1551-1560, 8 vols. Cf. *Acta SS.*, vol. i, *Praefatio generalis,* § v.

[2] *De probatis Sanctorum historiis partis ex tomis Aloysii Lipomani, partis etiam ex egregiis manuscriptis codicibus,* Coloniae Agrippinae, 1570, 6 vols.

[3] Cf. *Acta SS.*, vol. i, *Praef. gen.*, § v.

[4] *Vitae Sanctorum ex probatis auctoribus et manuscriptis codicibus,* Coloniae Agrip., 12 vols. in 6, 1618.

popular. But for him the works of Tauler, Henry Suso and Ruysbroeck would have perhaps remained unknown beyond Germany and the Low Countries. His translations are usually faithful in spite of a tendency to sacrifice thought to elegance of style. Whatever their shortcomings, they had a real influence on the spiritual life of the faithful, and especially on that of religious.

CHAPTER XIV
THE DEVOTIONS OF THE MIDDLE AGES
THE PASSION—THE BLESSED SACRAMENT—OUR BLESSED LADY—THE SAINTS

BEFORE concluding this study it may be useful to refer to the chief devotions which nourished the piety of the faithful of the Middle Ages, and to notice the way they became developed. A more complete idea may thus be obtained of the influence which the mystics of this epoch had on catholic life.

I—DEVOTION TO THE PASSION OF CHRIST AND TO THE SORROWS OF HIS MOTHER

EVER since the twelfth century the writings of St Bernard turned hearts towards the mysteries of the earthly life of Jesus, particularly towards those of his birth and passion. In the thirteenth century scenes from the birth of the Saviour and his death often figured in stained-glass windows, in medallions, and on the façades of cathedrals or in the frontispieces of missals and books of Hours. All the details concerning these great events given by apocryphal gospels, by the *Golden Legend* and by other legendary accounts by ancient and modern ecclesiastical writers, were collected with pious zeal.[1] Do we not love the Saviour the more by a better knowledge of the dogma of the Word made flesh and dying to make reparation for the original fall?

At the beginning of the fourteenth century, under the influence of St Francis of Assisi and the *Mystery Plays,* the faithful were moved to tender feeling at the sight of the Child Jesus in his crib, and especially by Christ dying on the cross. What piety needed at that time was less to be enlightened than to be moved. To this end extremely realistic descriptions of the suffering Christ, capable of exciting piety to its highest pitch, were produced. Mystics, in their visions of the passion, count the number of stripes the Saviour received in the scourging. They note all the outrages

---

[1] *Cf.* E. Male, *L'art religieux du XIIIᵉ siècle en France,* chaps. ii, iii.

inflicted on him by his executioners, and describe the refinement of cruelty with which he was nailed to the cross.

" One day I was rapt in spirit," says Bl. Angela of Foligno.
" The picture of the God-man again appeared to me at the
moment of the descent from the cross. His blood was new,
fresh and red; it flowed from his open wounds or had just
left the body. I then saw such rendings in the joints, nerves
so stretched and bones so dislocated by the force of the
executioners, that a sword passed through me, piercing my
inmost parts; and, when I call to mind the pains to which I
have been subjected during my life, I can find nothing to
equal this."[1]

Religious art has endeavoured to reproduce these pathetic
scenes pictured by mystics.[2] From this emotional devotion
towards the passion sprang the cultus of the wounds of the
Saviour. The wounds of the hands and feet and that of the
side were venerated. St Gertrude often recited the following
prayer : " O Lord of infinite mercy, do thou stamp the image
of thy sacred wounds upon my heart with thy Blood, so that
I may read there both thy sorrow and thy love; and that the
memory of thy bruises may remain there for ever, awaken in
me the pain of thy compassion and enkindle the fire of thy
love."[3] Confraternities were formed in the fifteenth century
under the patronage of the Five Wounds of Christ.

Devotion to the pierced Heart of Jesus naturally followed
from the cultus of the Wounds. It seems to have first
appeared in the monastery of Cistercian nuns of Helfta,
where Gertrude prayed thus before the image of the crucifix :
" Most loving Lord, by the merits of thy pierced heart, pierce
that of Gertrude with the darts of thy love, so that nothing
earthly remains therein, but that it may be wholly filled with
the power of thy Divinity."[4]

Pictures of the pierced Heart surrounded by the two hands
and feet, also pierced, were widely spread among the faithful
in Germany.[5] Devotion to the wounded Heart of Jesus was

---

[1] *Book of Visions* (Hello, 176). *Cf.* St Gertrude, *Revel.*, lib. III, 42;
IV, 36. St Bridget, *Revelations,* Rome 1628, vol. i, p. 22. Tauler,
Exercit. super Vita et Passione Christi, cap. xxi, xxvi, xxxiii. Suso,
Eternal Wisdom, Bk. I, chaps. xiv-xx. Gerson, *Expositio in Passionem
Domini* (*Opera omnia*, Antwerp 1706, vol. iii, 1153-1203), etc.

[2] *Cf.* Male, *L'art religieux de la fin du moyen âge en France,*
pp. 82 ff. Abbé V. Leroquais, *Catalogue descriptif des manuscrits à
peintures de la Bibliothèque de Lyon,* Lyons 1920.

[3] St Gertrude, *Revel.*, ii, chap. iv. With reference to the devotion
to the Wounds of the Lord, see above, pp. 88-9, 306-307.

[4] *ibid.,* chap. v. Bl. Angela of Foligno states in her *Book of Visions*
(Hello, p. 53) : " I was held in a dream in which the Heart of Christ
was shown to me, and I heard these words : ' Here is the spot where
there is no lying, the place where all truth is found.' "

[5] See a reproduction in Male, *id.,* p. 101.

fairly general there towards the end of the Middle Ages.[1] It was destroyed by the Protestant heresy.

The cultus of the wounds of Christ also inspired the devotion to the Precious Blood. The mystics often speak of the Blood of Jesus which flowed like a river during his passion. They desired to plunge themselves into it; they drink of it with love in their visions. " As I stood in prayer," says Bl. Angela of Foligno, " Christ showed himself to me and gave me a deeper knowledge of himself. I was not asleep. He called me, and told me to place my lips on the wound in his side. It seemed to me that I approached my lips and drank the blood, and in this blood still warm I understood that I was washed."[2] From the fourteenth century onwards Offices were drawn up in honour of the Precious Blood.[3]

Piety in the Middle Ages did not forget the sufferings of Mary. It is impossible to meditate on the passion of Christ without thinking of the sorrows of his mother. So great were these sorrows that it is not, say the mystics, in our power to understand them.[4] Just as there is the passion of Christ so also is there the *compassion* of the Virgin.

There were seven prominent occurrences in the passion which were the special cause of the sufferings of Mary.[5] They are known as the Seven Sorrows of our Lady. They were likened, according to the prophecy of the old man Simeon, to so many swords which pierced the maternal heart of Mary. Christian piety, towards the end of the fourteenth century, venerated the Seven Sorrows of our Lady and her anguish. The Virgin was first represented with seven swords through

---

[1] On devotion to the Heart of Jesus in Germany at the end of the Middle Ages, see Karl Richstatter, S.J., *Die Herz-Jesu Verehrung des deutschen Mittelalters,* Paderborn 1919, 2 vols. Many reproductions of pictures of the pierced Heart of Jesus are to be found there, which were venerated by the private piety of the faithful.

[2] *Book of Visions* (Hello, p. 54).

[3] E. Male, pp. 105-106.

[4] Suso, *Book of Eternal Wisdom,* chap. xvii (Thiriot, ii, 119); St Bridget, *Revel.,* vol. i, p. 35; Gerson, *Sermo alius in coena Domini; Expositio in passionem Domini,* vol. iii, 1134, 1193-1196; *Dialogue de la Vierge et de St Anselme sur la Passion (P.L.,* CLIX, 271 ff.); *De Planctu Mariae (P.L.,* CLXXXII, 1133 ff.). The last named belong to the apocryphal works of St Anselm and St Bernard.

[5] There are found two different lists. In the first are : The Prophecy of Simeon, the Flight into Egypt, the Seeking of the Lost Child, the Account of the Betrayal by Judas given by John to Mary, the Crucifixion, the Laying in the Tomb, the Pilgrimages made by the Virgin to the Places where her Son had Suffered. The second list, the best known, includes : The Prediction of Simeon, the Flight into Egypt, Jesus Lost and Found in the Temple, Jesus Smitten, Jesus Crucified, Jesus Dead and placed on the Knees of his Mother, the Laying in the Tomb. E. Male. p. 119-120.

her heart.[1]   Then Christian artists conceived a new idea : the Mother of Jesus, after the descent from the cross, with the body of her Son upon her knees. This scene, the most touching of all, seemed to sum up all the sufferings of the Virgin and to symbolize her anguish in a wonderful way. Thus came the *Pietà,* the representation of the sorrows of Mary which spread throughout the whole of the Western Church.

The sad consolation which Christian piety found in thus meditating on the passion brought about the devotion of the Way of the Cross. From the beginning of Christianity the Holy Places, as witnesses of the sufferings of Christ, were the object of pious veneration. In the fourth century famous persons whose accounts have come down to us, made pilgrimages from the West to the Holy Land. During the Middle Ages, thanks to the Crusades, a large number of Christians were able to visit the Holy Places and to pray at the very spots where, according to tradition, the different scenes in the passion were unfolded. But from the fourteenth to the fifteenth century, on account of the difficulties of the journey, there were scarcely any pilgrimages to Palestine. The idea was then formed of making these pilgrimages in spirit and of venerating, by means of the devotion of the Way of the Cross, the chief stages of the Way of Sorrows. Thus the faithful were able to imitate the blessed Virgin, whose pilgrimages they loved to retrace in the very places where her Son had suffered. The *Stations* of this earlier Way of the Cross were different from our own and varied in different places. The present arrangement of the *Stations* was definitely fixed in the sixteenth century.[2]

II—DEVOTION TO THE BLESSED SACRAMENT

The veneration of the blessed Sacrament acquired great prominence in the Middle Ages. It was made manifest in three special ways—the elevation of the Host and the Chalice in the Mass immediately after the consecration, expositions of the blessed Sacrament in transparent monstrances; and, finally, the institution of the Feast of *Corpus Christi.*

The custom of lifting up the consecrated species in the Mass is very ancient. It is spoken of in the Latin liturgy; an

[1] On the devotion to our Lady of the Seven Sorrows in the Middle Ages, see *Études (de la Compagnie de Jésus),* May 5, 1918, pp. 264 ff. *La transfixion de Notre-Dame,* by J. Dissard.

[2] Thurston, *The Month,* July-September, 1900; Boudinhon, *Revue du clergé français,* 1 Novembre, 1901. Fr. Thurston, S.J., wrote a series of articles on *Popular Devotions* in *The Month,* beginning July, 1900. A summary of these by M. Boudinhon appeared in the *Revue du clergé français,* beginning November 1, 1901.

Ordo Romanus[1] proves its existence in Rome about the year 800. It is preserved in the lesser elevation which is still made at the end of the Canon.

The greater elevation which follows the consecration began in France in the twelfth century. In the century following, it became general throughout the Latin Church. First, the Host only was elevated; later, the Chalice also. The faithful were notified by the ringing of a bell to kneel and adore. They did not, however, bow the head, but gazed at the sacred Host as it was uplifted by the priest. Special virtue was attached to the sight of the Body of Christ.[2]

The piety of the Middle Ages, however, was not satisfied with a sight of the Body of Christ for just a moment at the elevation. In order to yield more completely to this desire, the idea was formed of exposing the blessed Sacrament in a transparent monstrance or ostensory, in which it could be contemplated and adored at leisure. The use of monstrances existed in Germany in the fourteenth century. They had divers forms. In certain countries, especially in England, they took the form of representations of Christ's Body. The consecrated Host was placed in an opening in the breast provided with a glass.

In the fifteenth century, permanent exposition of the blessed Sacrament was forbidden; it was only permitted at certain fixed times, chiefly during the Octave of *Corpus Christi.*

Benediction of the blessed Sacrament is connected with these expositions. In the Middle Ages it was a custom to bless the faithful by making over them the sign of the cross with some sacred object. In the fifteenth century, mention is made in rituals of the practice of giving like blessings with the blessed Sacrament. We know that St Charles Borromeo, who instituted the devotion of the Forty Hours, highly recommended this custom.

The idea of establishing a feast in honour of the Body of Christ is due to the revelations of a nun, St Juliana de Retine (1258), Prioress of the monastery of Mont-Cornillon, near Liége.[3] This feast was first kept in the Diocese of Liége from 1246. Several other dioceses took it up, and in 1264 Pope Urban IV instituted the Feast of *Corpus Christi* for the whole Church, and charged St Thomas Aquinas with the duty of drawing up an Office for it. We know how perfectly the holy doctor carried out this task, and what beautiful

---

[1] For the text, see Duchesne, *Origines du culte chrétien,* 2nd edition, p. 444. Rabanus Maurus in the ninth century also speaks of this elevation, *De institutione clericorum,* lib. I, cap. 33.

[2] Cf. *Revue du clergé français,* June 1 to October 15, 1908. Thurston-Boudinhon, *L'élévation et la génuflexion.* Dom Chardon, *Histoire des Sacrements. L'Eucharistie,* chaps. xi-xiv.

[3] *Acta Sanctorum,* April 5, vol. i, *Aprilis.*

hymns he composed, in which dogmatic precision, piety and poetry are so harmoniously combined.

With a view to adding greater solemnity to the Feast of *Corpus Christi,* they began, early in the fourteenth century, to carry the blessed Sacrament triumphantly in a monstrance through the streets of towns. This was the origin of processions of the blessed Sacrament.

These different forms of eucharistic cultus before they received the official sanction of the Church were the spontaneous outcome of that intense inward piety which was enkindled in souls. The expression of this piety is found among the mystics, almost all of whom have related visions or revelations with which they had been favoured whilst assisting at Mass or receiving communion. St Hildegarde, in a vision of this kind, thus sums up the theology of the eucharistic sacrifice :

"When," she says, "the priest, clothed in sacred vestments, approached the altar to celebrate the divine Sacraments, I saw a dazzling light, filled with a multitude of angels, suddenly descend from heaven, and it spread round the altar and remained there until the sacrifice was finished and the priest had retired. When the gospel of peace had been recited and the oblation that was about to be consecrated placed on the altar, while the priest was singing the praise of Almighty God, which is the *Sanctus,* and was beginning the celebration of the ineffable Sacraments, the heavens were suddenly opened and a globe of fire of inexpressible brightness descended on the oblation and penetrated it as wholly with its light as the sun penetrates a crystal with its sparkling rays. And while it shone upon the oblation, it raised it towards heaven in an invisible way and again let it down on the altar with a motion as of a man breathing air into his breast and then exhaling it. The oblation had become the true Body and Blood of Christ, although in the eyes of the faithful it appeared to be bread and wine.

"While I contemplated these things, there immediately appeared to me, as though reflected in a mirror, the mysteries of the birth, passion and burial as well as the resurrection and ascension of our Saviour, the only Son of God, as they took place when he was on earth. When the priest had sung the canticle of the innocent Lamb, that is to say, the *Agnus Dei,* and was preparing for communion, the globe of fire returned to heaven, and, the heavens being closed, I heard a voice saying, Eat the Body and drink the Blood of my Son to annul the transgression of Eve, and that you may be restored to the divine inheritance. . . . After the communion, when the Sacraments had been entirely consumed, while the priest went away, the heavenly brightness, of which

I spoke at the beginning, that surrounded the altar, disappeared into heaven."[1]

We are not able to form an exact idea of the impression which the story of these visions must have produced in the hearts of their readers. Furthermore, devotion to the blessed Sacrament was the great devotion of the Middle Ages. The wonderful Fourth Book of the *Imitation* is the best proof of this. Its pious author there treats, with piercing eloquence and irresistible words, of the love of Christ in the Eucharist, of the incomparable excellence of this divine Sacrament, of the joys which are prepared for us therein, of its necessity for our souls, of the dispositions needful for its reception. He knows, perhaps better than most of his contemporaries, how to speak of the purity of conscience required to communicate without exposing himself to the danger of driving the faithful from the holy table. Great sanctity must doubtless be desirable to receive communion, for, even if we have the purity of angels or the sanctity of St John the Baptist, we should not be worthy on that account to participate in the divine Sacrament or to celebrate it.[2] But the soul cannot live without the visits of Jesus. This is why the Christian ought often to assist at the sacred banquet if he do not wish to faint in the way of salvation.[3]

The more devotion to the blessed Sacrament increased, the greater also was the respect for the priest. Is it not, indeed, he who consecrates the Eucharist and distributes it to the faithful? We have listened to St Francis of Assisi proclaiming that the priest is higher than the heavenly beings. The author of the *Imitation* likewise exclaims : " High is this mystery, and great the dignity of priests to whom is given what is not granted to angels. For priests alone, rightly ordained by the Church, have power to celebrate and to consecrate the Body of Christ."[4]

So high a dignity is incompatible with an indifferent life. It calls for real sanctity in him who is clothed with it. " Lo ! thou art a priest and consecrated to say Mass : see now that in due time thou faithfully and devoutly offer up sacrifice to God," says the author of the *Imitation*. " Thou hast not

---

[1] St Hildegarde, *Scivias*, lib. II, visio vi (*P.L.*, CXCVII, 590). In this vision, as in those of other mystics, the influence of the famous *Dialogues* of St Gregory the Great, where he speaks so much of the Mass, is felt. Cf. *Dialogue* of St Catherine of Siena (Hurtaud, vol. ii, pp. 10-11).

[2] *De Imitat.*, lib. IV, cap. v.

[3] *ibid.*, cap. iii.

[4] *id.*, lib. IV, cap. v. An apocryphal writing of St Bernard, *Instructio sacerdotis*, cap. viii, expresses itself in similar terms : *Attende igitur, ut praedixi [o sacerdos], et semper in mente habe, jugi memoria retine gratiam tibi singulariter a Deo collatam, quam nec angelis praestitit, nec caeteris hominibus* (*P.L.*, CLXXXIV, 785). Cf. *Dialogue* of St Catherine of Siena (Hurtaud, vol. ii, pp. 1 ff.).

lightened thy burthen, but art now bound with a stricter bond of discipline, and obliged to a greater perfection of sanctity. A priest should be adorned with all virtues and give example of good life to others. His conversation should not be with the vulgar and common ways of men, but with the angels in heaven, or with perfect men upon earth."[1] The mystics, who realized better than others what sacerdotal sanctity ought to be, suffered excruciatingly on account of the imperfect state of the morals of the clergy during the Middle Ages. This explains the severe censures, and even terrible threats, uttered by Peter Damian, Hildegarde, Bridget and Catherine of Siena, to cite these names alone, against the priests and religious who violated their obligations.[2]

Why, then, did the faithful of the Middle Ages, who venerated and loved the Holy Eucharist so greatly, as a general rule, communicate so seldom? In the beginning of the thirteenth century, in 1215, the Fourth Council of the Lateran, in order to prevent entire desertion of the holy table, was forced to enjoin, under severe penalties, annual confession and communion.[3]

An explanation is to be found in the social and political troubles which disturbed the beginning of the Middle Ages. But it also seems to me that the mystics unwittingly contributed to this infrequency of communion by dwelling with extraordinary vehemence on the unworthy reception of the Body of Christ. Alas, they had only too great justification in doing so, for the moral corruption among the faithful and the irregular conduct of many priests and religious caused them to think that the number of sacrileges was relatively high.

St Hildegarde, assisting at Mass, saw the faithful who communicated unworthily. " Whilst the communicants were approaching the priest to receive the Sacrament," she says, " I distinguished five categories among them. Some had bodies bright with purity and souls of fire; others appeared to be sallow of body and with souls darkened. Some were found with hairy bodies and souls stained by great impurity. The bodies of some were wreathed in very sharp thorns and their souls devoured with leprosy. Others, finally, bore stains of blood on their bodies, and their souls gave off a fetid odour like that of a putrefied corpse. All received the

---

[1] *De Imitat. Ch.*, lib. IV, cap. v. Similar thoughts are found in the *Instructio sacerdotis,* cap. viii-ix.

[2] See, for instance, in the *Dialogue* of St Catherine of Siena, the remarks on the *Reform of pastors,* especially in chaps. xii ff. (Hurtaud, vol. ii, pp. 49 ff.).

[3] This is the decree *Omnis utriusque sexus fidelis* regarding the Easter communion.

same Sacrament, but while the first entered into brilliant light the others were plunged into deep darkness."[1]

The horror of sacrilege, which the mystics knew so well how to inspire, prevented Christians, and even religious, from approaching the holy table. Many were divided between the yearning to respond to the invitation of Christ and the fear of profaning the holy mysteries.

" These words," exclaims the author of the *Imitation*, " of so great tenderness, full of sweetness and of love, encourage me; but my sins terrify me, and my unclean conscience driveth me back from receiving such great mysteries. The sweetness of thy words inviteth me, but the multitude of my offences weigheth me down."[2]

In the monastery of Helfta, St Gertrude reckoned a considerable number of nuns who dared not communicate often for fear of doing so badly;[3] but all the mystics did not let themselves be held back by this dread. The fear of communicating unworthily did not succeed in preventing St Gertrude from frequently sharing in the sacred banquet. The sense of her imperfections, on the contrary, drew her with greater ardour towards her Saviour. " At the moment when I approached thy Sacrament which giveth life," she said to Jesus, " as soon as I had collected my mind in order to think of this dread mystery as I should, thou didst once more make me to know, O Lord, how and with what intentions each one ought to enter into sacred union with thy Body and Blood. Even if this Sacrament were to turn to our condemnation, should that be possible, then the love we must have for thy glory and for the love thou hast revealed to us therein [in the Sacrament] should make us deem our condemnation as of small account, provided that it caused thy mercy to shine all the brighter through not being denied to souls unworthy thereof. And when I told thee that those who deprive themselves of communion from a sense of their indignity only do so in order not to profane through presumptuous irreverence the holiness of this Sacrament, thou didst reply in these words : ' Whoever communicates with the intention that I have just expressed—that is to say, with a pure desire for my glory—can never communicate with irreverence.' "[4] Gertrude thus encouraged her companions at Helfta not to deprive themselves of communion by allowing themselves to be hindered " through respectful anxiety of a timid conscience." She invited them to communicate even when,

---

[1] *Scivias,* lib. II, vis. vi. See as to unworthy communion, St Catherine of Siena, *Dialogue* (Hurtaud, vol. ii, pp. 7-8).

[2] *De Imitat. Ch.,* lib. IV, cap. i.

[3] St Gertrude, *Revel.,* lib. IV, cap. vii.

[4] *Revel.,* lib. II, cap. xix.

through the absence of their confessor, they were unable to go to confession immediately before.[1]

The author of the *Imitation* also counsels passing beyond fear, because the Christian has the greatest need of communion in order to avoid sin. "For the senses of man," he says, "are prone to evil from his youth; and if thy divine medicine succour him not, he quickly falleth into worse. The holy communion, therefore, withdraweth him from evil, and strengtheneth him in good. For if I am so often negligent and lukewarm now, when I communicate or celebrate, what would it be if I did not take this remedy, and sought not so great a help?"[2]

This view of communion is also that of Jean Gerson. He speaks of sacrilege in a way to excite the faithful to prepare themselves carefully before communicating, without placing them in danger of deserting the holy table. His desire is that they should come to it often. With this end in view he so guides the consciences of priests and layfolk as to prevent them from depriving themselves for trivial reasons of the celebration of Mass or the reception of communion.[3] Attention to our own needs, even more than respect due to the blessed Sacrament, produced at the end of the Middle Ages a well-pronounced return to the practice of more frequent communion.

III—DEVOTION TO THE BLESSED VIRGIN

THE *Sermons* of St Bernard, as we know, give us an accurate idea of the feelings of tender piety towards the Mother of God in the Middle Ages. Other works might be cited, especially among the writings of mystics, in which the prerogatives and virtues of the Virgin are proclaimed in poetic accents.[4] It pleased Dante, in the *Divine Comedy,* to gather together the titles which were given to Mary in the *Middle Ages.*[5]

Among these titles that of Queen is most often found. Mary is the Queen of heaven and earth. The artists of the twelfth and thirteenth centuries strove to give expression to this royalty. They placed a crown on the Virgin's brow and

---

[1] *id.*, lib. II, cap. xx; lib. IV, cap. vii.

[2] *De Imit. Ch.*, lib. IV, cap. iii.

[3] Gerson, *Incitatio ad digne suscip. corpus Domini; De praeparatione ad missam* (*Opera omnia,* vol. iii, 310-334).

[4] See the *De laudibus beatae Mariae,* attributed without proof to Albert the Great (Alberti Magni, *Opera,* Lugduni 1651, vol. xx), and the *Speculum beatae Mariae,* attributed, also without proof, to St Bonaventure (*Opera,* Mainz, 1609, vol. vi); though it may be by Conrad of Saxony (1279).

[5] *Paradiso,* xxxii-xxxiii.

a budding sceptre in her hand.[1] And thus it was that she
was to be portrayed for the future.

Devotion to the blessed Virgin, as St Bernard has taught
us, chiefly took the form of the celebration of her feasts.
Episodes in the life of Mary which were thus commemorated
were her Nativity, her Purification, her Assumption and the
Annunciation.

To these feasts, which were already ancient, the Middle
Ages added the Immaculate Conception. From the eleventh
century in England and Normandy,[2] and in Ireland[3] since the
ninth century, Christian piety began to venerate the all-pure
conception of the blessed Virgin. In spite of St Bernard, the
Church of Lyons welcomed this feast. In the fourteenth
century belief in the Immaculate Conception, thanks to the
Friars Minor, was accepted in almost all the Universities and
the religious Orders. When the Dominican, Jean de Mon-
tesson, in 1387, endeavoured to oppose it he was condemned
by the University of Paris, which afterwards required of the
new doctors whom it created that they should take an oath
to believe and to teach that Mary was conceived without sin.
Pierre d'Ailly and Gerson were ardent defenders of this great
privilege of the Mother of God.

But, as we might expect, the religious Orders were the
chief contributors to the exaltation of the Virgin and the
development of her cultus. Those thousands of sequences
and hymns in honour of Mary, which the learned among us
publish to-day, were composed by monks.[4] The most beautiful metaphors of the sacred books, especially the *Canticle of
Canticles,* were made use of to celebrate the greatness of the
Virgin. All the ravishing beauties of nature were looked
upon as symbols of her virtues. The flowers of spring,
especially the rose, reflect the splendours of the Queen of
heaven. St Gertrude invoked the Mother of mercy by the
happy title of " the rose without thorns, the white and stain-
less lily, the Virgin, holy and adorned with the flowers of
every virtue."[5]

In the Middle Ages it was the custom for the vassal to
offer his suzerain, as a token of subjection, a head-dress of
roses. The mystics also offered crowns of roses to their

---

[1] E. Male, *L'art religieux du XIIIe siècle,* p. 278. Many cathedrals
were given the title of our Lady.

[2] *Cf.* Vacandard, *Les origines de la fête de la Conception dans le
diocese de Rouen et en Angleterre,* in *Revue des questions historiques,*
January, 1897, p. 166-184. *Études* (of the Jesuits), vol. c, p. 763,
article by A. Noyon.

[3] *Cf.* Thurston, *Revue du clergé français,* vol. xxxix, July 1, 1904.
Brousselle, *Études sur la Sainte Vierge,* Paris 1908.

[4] E. Male, *L'art religieux à la fin du moyen âge,* 214.

[5] *Revel.,* lib. II, cap. xvii.

sovereign Mary. Henry Suso greatly loved this practice.
" Once, at the beginning of the month of May, according to
his custom, he had devoutly offered a crown of roses to the
Queen of heaven whom he loved so much. In the morning
he desired rest and sleep, for he had just returned from the
country and was very tired. . . . But when the hour of
rising came it seemed to him that he was in the midst of a
heavenly choir where the *Magnificat* was being sung. When
it was finished the Virgin advanced towards him and invited
him to sing this verse : *O vernalis rosula:* O young rose of
springtime . . . which he did with joy."[1]

This crown of roses became the symbolic crown of the one
hundred and fifty *Ave Marias,* called the *Psalter of Mary.*[2]
The division into tens and groups of five decades of *Ave
Marias* gradually came about. In 1470 the Dominican,
Alain de la Roche, conceived the idea, from a vision, of
combining the recitation of the Aves with meditation on the
mysteries of the life of Christ and of the Virgin. The
symbolic crown was then formed of three kinds of roses :
white roses, which symbolized the joyful mysteries ; red roses,
the sorrowful mysteries ; and golden roses, the glorious
mysteries. Thus was formed the rosary or the crown of
mystical roses, a devotion which very soon became popular.[3]

The Middle Ages then made use of most graceful metaphors
and delightful emblems wherewith to sing the glories of
Mary. Nor is the liturgy surpassed even by the most affective doctors. From constantly hearing these beautiful titles
in the Offices of the Virgin and in sermons, the idea was
formed of grouping them together and of reciting them as
invocations. This was the origin of the *Litanies* of the blessed
Virgin.[4]

[1] Suso, *Life,* chap. xxxviii. *Cf.* chap. vi, xiv.
[2] A great number of the faithful living in the world wished to imitate
the monks. Instead of the Psalter, which they had no time to recite,
they invented the *Psalter of our Lady,* in which each one of the 150
Psalms is represented by an *Ave Maria.* Neither were they able to
wear the monastic dress, but thanks to a reduced form of this—the
little scapular—they wore in a certain sense the monastic habit, and
thus had a part in the spiritual privileges of the religious life.
[3] The Rosary does not go back to St Dominic. Cf. *Analecta Bollandiana,* 1899, p. 290. Thurston, S.J., *The Rosary,* in *The Month,*
October, 1900 to April, 1901 ; *Le Cosmos,* 1902. Boudinhon, *Revue du
clergé français,* January, 1902. For the contrary theory, see Mezard,
O.P., *Études sur les origines du Rosaire,* 1 vol. Caluaire (Rhone).
[4] The Litanies, in their present form, date from the middle of the
sixteenth century. But they began to be drawn up long before that
date. *Cf.* Angelo de Santi, *Les Litanies de la Vierge,* French translation, Paris 1900.

IV—THE CULTUS OF ST JOSEPH AND THE SAINTS

THERE is no doubt that devotion to St Joseph first began in the Middle Ages.

St Bernard was one of the first to celebrate the grandeur of the vocation and the perfection of the virtue of the glorious patriarch. This he performed in accents which drew attention most strongly to him who had the joy of being so intimately connected with the mysteries of the childhood of Christ. Artists represented Joseph with Mary near the crib on Christmas night, or in the Temple on the day of the Purification. They showed him guiding the Holy Family in the flight into Egypt and working for it in the shop at Nazareth. Monks and religious in their convents could not dwell on the events of the childhood of Jesus without thinking of Joseph. Christian piety was thus brought to render devotion to him who protected Jesus and Mary with such devoted care. By the end of the fourteenth century and the beginning of the fifteenth, this devotion had already become fairly developed. At this epoch Pierre d'Ailly, and especially Gerson and St Bernardine of Siena, were its ardent promoters.

Pierre d'Ailly was, without doubt, the first who wrote a theological treatise on devotion to St Joseph.[1] The work is somewhat dry and speculative; it was, however, the beginning of a doctrinal movement which greatly contributed to the spread of the new devotion.

But the really fruitful initiative was taken by Gerson. The pious Chancellor was not content to proclaim the glorious privileges of St Joseph and to extol his virtues.[2] He demanded that a feast should be kept in his honour. He put forward this first of all in letters which he addressed to individuals, and then in a famous sermon preached at the Council of Constance. In a letter addressed to the Duc de Berry in 1413, he wrote thus:

"Very often, when thinking of the grandeur and dignity of St Joseph, son of David, lawful and virginal spouse of the most pure Virgin St Mary our Lady, according to the witness of the Gospels, and asking myself when and how this holy and sacred marriage might be commemorated, honoured and celebrated by means of a feast, I thought . . . O most noble and Christian prince . . . that your influence might further

---

[1] *De duodecim honoribus sancti Joseph,* d'Ailly's works, Strasbourg 1490.

[2] See his admirable *Considérations sur S Joseph,* in French. They are meditations "on the virginal marriage of our Lady and St Joseph." *Opera,* vol. iii, 842-868. And the *Josephina,* a poem divided into twelve considerations, vol. iv, 743-784.

this religious project. . . . I then beseech you to hear me
in the name of the tender and loving Child Jesus, who willed
to be born in this holy and virginal marriage and to be
nurtured therein. . . . I ask it of you, shall I say in the
name of Joseph, who, virgin himself, was the spouse and
most faithful guardian of the Virgin of virgins, the protector
of the divine Child, whom he carried so often in his arms,
whom he covered with kisses and treated with a familiarity
unknown to any other but himself?"[1]

Gerson's piety was more particularly touched by the most
holy marriage which united Joseph to the Virgin, and,
according to him, was the foundation of all his greatness.
At the Council of Constance, when Gerson asked for the
creation of a feast of St Joseph, he declared that its object
might be either St Joseph's marriage or else his blessed
death.[2]

The Chancellor had great confidence in the protection of
the holy patriarch. He hoped that the spread of his cultus
would dispel the grave perils which threatened public life.
And was not the Great Schism the most serious of all these?
Therefore, in ending his address on St Joseph at Constance,
he begged the Fathers of the Council to place their labours
beneath his patronage in order that " through the intercession
of so great and powerful an advocate, who wields in a measure
a kind of empire over Mary his spouse . . . the Church may
return to one sole pontiff, the true pope, her spouse and the
vicar of Christ."

Whilst Gerson was urging the Teaching Church to do
honour to St Joseph, the great Franciscan preacher of the
fifteenth century, Bernardine of Siena, was causing him to
be invoked by the Italian people. He showed, with captivating eloquence, that devotion to St Joseph, the foster-father
of Jesus, was founded on his eminent sanctity, his greatness,
and the honour given him in heaven.

God, he said, bestows his gifts according to the excellence
of the vocation of his creatures. Now, after Mary, none
received so noble a mission as Joseph. We may then form
for ourselves an idea of the perfection and beauty with which
the Lord was pleased to adorn his soul. For his part, Joseph
fully corresponded with divine grace, and carried out with
wonderful faithfulness the high mission of virginal spouse
of Mary, of protector and foster-father of the Child Jesus.
Thus his sanctity is most high, and enough to render him

---

[1] *Exhortatio ad ducem Bituriae*, vol. iv, 729-730. Two other letters
follow on the same subject. Gerson drew up an Office for the Feast of
St Joseph (*ibid.*, 736-742).
[2] *Sermo de Nativitate gloriosae Virginis Mariae et de commendatione
Virginei Sponsi ejus Joseph*, vol. iii, 1345 ff.

powerful with God. But our confidence will be greatly
enhanced if we remember that Christ has not ceased to show
his filial affection and respect to Joseph in heaven as he did
formerly on earth. How, then, is it possible for the holy
patriarch's petitions to be rejected?

"Remember us then, O blessed Joseph," exclaims St
Bernardine at the end of one of his sermons, "and by thy
powerful prayer intercede for us with him who willed to pass
for thy Son. Do thou also render thy spouse, the blessed
Virgin Mary, favourable towards us, she who is the mother
of him who with the Father and the Holy Ghost liveth and
reigneth for ever and ever."[1]

Devotion to St Joseph continued to increase in the sixteenth
century. Isidore de Insolanis, the Dominican of Milan,[2]
through his writings, and above all St Teresa, through her
wonderful influence, rendered the cultus of St Joseph im-
mensely popular throughout the Church. The famous Car-
melite declared that through the intercession of this great
Saint she obtained all the graces she desired.[3] We may
imagine the effect which such an avowal must have had on
the faithful.

In the Middle Ages, devotion to the Saints chiefly made
itself evident by the celebration of the feasts of patrons.
Saints became the protectors of cities, castles and even
middle-class mansions. Above all, there were patrons of
confraternities and corporations. Every profession vied with
the others in celebrating its saint, and some superstition was
occasionally mixed up in these popular manifestations.

It was in the *Golden Legend* that this devotion to the
saints was usually nurtured. But, as we know, the work
of de Voragine was not the only hagiography of the Middle
Ages. Authentic biographies of holy persons of the period
were composed in the monasteries. Founders of religious
Orders, as well as of the more important monasteries, had
their historians who narrated their lives truthfully. In the
course of this study I have drawn attention to a great number
of such biographies. In surveying the work of Surius and
the immense collection of the *Acta Sanctorum,* we are still
better able to grasp the importance and the value of the
hagiography of the Middle Ages.

[1] S. Bernardini Senensis, O.M., *Sermones eximii, Sermo* I *de S.
Joseph,* vol. iv, pp. 250-255, Lugduni, 1650. This is one of the oldest
prayers addressed to St Joseph which we possess.
[2] *A Summary of the Gifts of St Joseph* is attributed to him.
[3] *Life of St Teresa written by herself,* chap. vi.

CONCLUSION

MYSTICISM, as this study has shown, occupied a great place in the Middle Ages.

It drew its inspiration from the teaching of Dionysius the Areopagite; in which preparation for supernatural union with God consists, as regards the heart, in entire renunciation of earthly goods and of oneself, and, as regards the mind, in stripping it of every intellectual or sensible image.

The Dionysian conception, however, of mystical union was not accepted by all. Some, among whom are the school of St Victor and the Germans of the fourteenth century, thought, with Dionysius, that in mystical union the soul is united to God directly without mediation. They held that the mind perceives the divine essence from time to time, in an instant, with the rapidity of lightning. Others, especially St Bernard and St Thomas Aquinas, thought that this direct vision of God cannot take place here below. The mystic, according to them, perceives divine realities through the mediation of a supernatural image deposited in the soul.

A similar divergence of views is to be found as regards the call of the Christian to mystical union. According to the greater number of spiritual writers, from St Bernard to Gerson, all fervent Christians have not the mystical vocation. This is only bestowed on a small number who are thus privileged. The German writers, on the contrary, claim that God grants it to all without distinction, and that all should be instructed in the means to attain to it. This point of view was somewhat imprudent, and doubtless was not altogether free from blame for the development of false mysticism which so devastated the end of the Middle Ages.

Mystics of the Middle Ages interest us not only on account of their teaching. They exercised an influence in the Church which they never had before and have not had since.

The moral authority which they wielded enabled them to influence even the most exalted members of the ecclesiastical hierarchy, and to notify commands to them as virtually sent from heaven. Especially, with an insistence and force of expression which surprises us, did they demand the reform of the Church. If this reform, so greatly needed, was not brought about while there was still time to avoid the convulsion of Protestantism, it is because ears were closed to their warnings. It is true that all the mystics were not inspired, as were St Bernard, St Hildegarde, St Bridget or St Catherine

of Siena, by a well-tempered zeal. Several, like Joachim of
Flora and Ubertino da Casale, allowed themselves to fall
into a kind of illuminism, well calculated to inspire distrust
of their views as to reform. Nevertheless, the appeals of the
mystics were usually wise and far-seeing. It may be
regretted that they were not more attentively listened to.

The effect which the mystics had on Christian piety in the
Middle Ages was much more far-reaching. Nothing here
intervened to paralyze their influence.

Doubtless the new devotions which were brought into
vogue by the monks and nuns and other religious were not
formally adopted in the Church until they had been approved
by ecclesiastical authority. The initiative, however, was
almost always taken by holy souls who had been favoured by
visions or revelations. It was thus that the numerous
religious Orders of the Middle Ages came into being; their
founders obtained their inspiration from their intimate
relations with God. The newer forms of the cultus of the
humanity of Christ, of special devotion to his passion, his
wounds, his pierced Heart, first saw light in the cloister,
kindled by souls burning with love. From the cloister they
spread among the faithful, and religious art perpetuated
them in touching representations in stained-glass windows
and on the façades of cathedrals. The great development of
devotion to the blessed Sacrament in the Middle Ages had a
like origin, and we may recall to mind how much devotion to
the blessed Virgin Mary owes to the piety of mystics in these
centuries of enthusiastic faith.

The great freedom then left to monastic piety favoured
this wonderful unfolding of holy practices. The monk and
the nun in their convents had to follow their Rule and assist
at the daily exercises of the community. Outside of this
their piety was allowed to develop without hindrance. We
do not find that Suso was interfered with because he crowned
the statue of the blessed Virgin with roses, nor that St
Gertrude was reprimanded for recommending to her companions the new devotion to the pierced Heart of Jesus.
St Margaret Mary, four centuries afterwards, on the contrary, experienced the greatest difficulty in getting her sisters
to accept the devotion to the Sacred Heart. This was
because by that time piety had become subject to regulations,
and any novelty was suspected. This attitude of mind was
unknown in the Middle Ages.

In this way may also be explained the freedom, which we
find almost too great, which was enjoyed by the mystics.
The Middle Ages, as compared with modern times, were a
period of youth and intense vitality; and it is from thence
that we have received the great part of our practices of piety.

It was this epoch also that produced the complete elements which enabled spiritual doctrine, later on, to be formed into a special branch of theology. In spirituality, as in other sciences, practice preceded theory. The Middle Ages, again, were a period in which spiritual doctrine was practised without having been fully synthesized. In the *Summa* of St Thomas Aquinas ascetic and mystical theology are not treated separately from either dogma or morals. The result was that the principles of neither asceticism nor mysticism were placed in that prominence which they assumed later, when they were to control, at least towards modern times, the manifestations of monastic and popular piety.

This freedom had its drawbacks in leaving the way open to illusions. In mysticism self-deception is easy; it may easily cause human or diabolical counterfeits to be mistaken for supernatural and divine states. It also exposes to the danger, as in the case of Meister Eckhart, of interpreting the mystery of the union of the soul with God in a pantheistic sense. It is then scarcely surprising that a false mysticism was produced towards the end of the Middle Ages. According to some historians it was even a preparation for that of Luther. The habit, common to the mystics, of seeking their inspirations and their rules of life in direct communications with God rather than in the hierarchical directions of the Church, favoured the development of the dreams of private revelation. Certain it is that Luther appealed to the mystics of the Middle Ages to justify his own mysticism, entirely emancipated from the authority of the Church.

Dangers such as these, to which false mysticism exposed Christian society, were clearly perceived, especially by Pierre d'Ailly and Gerson. Both of these strove to subject piety to the control of theology, and the mystics to that of the Doctors. Gerson desired spiritual teaching to be based on a sure theological foundation; that which departed from it was to be regarded with uncompromising suspicion. Nor would he allow the seeking of rules for the guidance of pastors or the faithful in private revelations; they must be sought in the official theology of the Church. Theology ought always to take precedence, and exercise the right of supervising mysticism. On these terms only mysticism will not go astray, and will attain its end, which is to raise up a generous enthusiasm in the service of God.

It will be found that these principles have been strictly adhered to in modern times.

INDEX